Library of
Davidson College

MORTUARY VARIABILITY

An Archaeological Investigation

This is a volume in

Studies in Archaeology

A complete list of titles in this series appears at the end of this volume.

MORTUARY VARIABILITY
An Archaeological Investigation

John M. O'Shea
Museum of Anthropology
University of Michigan
Ann Arbor, Michigan

1984

ACADEMIC PRESS, INC.
Harcourt Brace Jovanovich, Publishers

Orlando San Diego San Francisco New York London
Toronto Montreal Sydney Tokyo São Paulo

COPYRIGHT © 1984, BY ACADEMIC PRESS, INC.
ALL RIGHTS RESERVED.
NO PART OF THIS PUBLICATION MAY BE REPRODUCED OR
TRANSMITTED IN ANY FORM OR BY ANY MEANS, ELECTRONIC
OR MECHANICAL, INCLUDING PHOTOCOPY, RECORDING, OR ANY
INFORMATION STORAGE AND RETRIEVAL SYSTEM, WITHOUT
PERMISSION IN WRITING FROM THE PUBLISHER.

ACADEMIC PRESS, INC.
Orlando, Florida 32887

United Kingdom Edition published by
ACADEMIC PRESS, INC. (LONDON) LTD.
24/28 Oval Road, London NW1 7DX

Library of Congress Cataloging in Publication Data

O'Shea, John M.
  Mortuary variability.

  (Studies in archaeology)
  Includes index.
  1. Archaeology--Methodology. 2. Funeral rites and
ceremonies. 3. Tombs. I. Title. II. Series.
CC77.B8083   1984   930.1'028   84-6475
ISBN 0-12-528680-5

PRINTED IN THE UNITED STATES OF AMERICA

84 85 86 87   9 8 7 6 5 4 3 2 1

To Sue

Contents

Preface   xi

1

The Development of an Archaeological Theory of Mortuary Behavior

    GENERAL BACKGROUND   1
    SOCIAL COMPLEXITY AND MORTUARY PRACTICES   3
    SOCIAL DIMENSIONS OF MORTUARY PRACTICES   8
    ARCHAEOLOGICAL STUDIES OF MORTUARY DIFFERENTIATION   13

2

Funerary Remains as Archaeological Phenomena

    ARCHAEOLOGICAL FORMATION PROCESSES   23
    LIMITATIONS IN DETECTION AND RECOGNITION   27

3
Funerary Remains as Archaeological Evidence

    REGULARITIES IN MORTUARY VARIABILITY   32
    CHANNELS OF MORTUARY VARIABILITY AND PRIMARY REFERENTS   39
    INTERPRETATION AND EXPLANATION IN MORTUARY ANALYSIS   44

4
The Analysis of Mortuary Variability: Controlled Experiments

    EXPERIMENTAL DESIGN   50
    SITE DESCRIPTIONS AND SAMPLE DOCUMENTATION   51
    TYPOLOGICAL CONSIDERATIONS   60
    METHODS OF ANALYSIS   64

5
The Ethnographic Background

    THE PAWNEE   71
    THE ARIKARA   75
    THE OMAHA   79
    INTERTRIBAL RELATIONS   82
    SUMMARY   83

6
Mortuary Differentiation and Social Distinction

    THE PAWNEE   87
    THE ARIKARA   161
    THE OMAHA   221
    DISCUSSION   250

7
Temporal Variation in Mortuary Practices

    INTRODUCTION   256
    PAWNEE VARIATION IN SOCIAL DISTINCTION AND
        SYMBOLIC REPRESENTATION   258
    ARIKARA VARIATION IN SOCIAL DISTINCTION AND
        SYMBOLIC REPRESENTATION   270
    CAUSAL FACTORS   279
    CONCLUSIONS   283

8
Ethnic Differentiation in Mortuary Practices

    INTRODUCTION   286
    TESTS   287
    RESULTS   299

9
Concluding Remarks   302

Appendix: Artifact Associations   304

References   317

Index   330

Preface

This study attempts to answer the question, What can funerary remains actually tell us about the organization and workings of past societies?

In recent years the archaeological study of mortuary practices has been revolutionized by the realization that varied treatments accorded individuals in death are related systematically to social differences that existed among the living. By exploiting this relatively simple relationship, archaeologists may study the structure of past societies in unprecedented detail. Yet, despite the expanded interest in mortuary evidence, no coherent archaeological theory of mortuary differentiation has emerged. It is toward the development of such a theory that the present research is ultimately directed.

The present work first consolidates what is known of funerary behavior into a logically consistent archaeological theory of mortuary differentiation, and then considers the reliability of social reconstructions produced by such archaeological analysis. Chapters 1-3 are primarily a consideration of mortuary theory in archaeology, its sources, justifications, and present deficiencies. The remaining chapters present an extended case study, in which archaeological analysis is employed to extract various types of social information from a set of cemetery sites for which independent ethnographic documentation can be used to check the results. The sites used in this testing are of considerable interest in their own right, with four of the six representing previously unpublished site material dating from the late eighteenth and early nineteenth centuries.

The study presented here grew out of doctoral research conducted at Cambridge University under the supervision of Professor A. C. Renfrew and the late Dr. D. L. Clarke. Since that time, additional sites and information have been included in the study; in particular, recent evidence relating to secondary interment among the Pawnee. I acknowledge my debt to Dr. William Bass of the University of Tennessee, Dr. Warren Caldwell of the University of Nebraska, and Mr. Marvin Kivett of the Nebraska State Historical Society for the access they provided to facilities, notes, and collections, and to Mr. John K. Ludwickson and the late Professor John L. Champe, who both contributed greatly to my understanding of historic material culture and Plains ethnohistory in general. In later days, I have particularly benefited from my acquaintance and discussions with Dr. James A. Brown. In addition, I thank Kay Clahassey, who redrew all the maps, and Shirley Ahlgren, Kasha Van Peursem, Jill Lopick, and Camie Moody, who all helped in the final manuscript preparation and typing.

MORTUARY VARIABILITY

An Archaeological Investigation

1

The Development of an Archaeological Theory of Mortuary Behavior

General Background

Although the study of mortuary remains has long been an important area of archaeological inquiry, particularly as a basis for speculation on the nature of ancient societies, the past two decades have witnessed a new interest in funerary analysis. Much of the impetus for this interest has derived from the New World and the New Archaeology. This new interest has stressed the use of mortuary evidence, not as a basis for fanciful speculation on primitive beliefs and religion, but as a means of specifying in detail the nature of extinct social systems.

This renewed interest in mortuary practices can be viewed as part of a more general trend that characterized the early days of the New Archaeology. During this period, there was an attempt to cast off the traditionally imposed limits of archaeological knowledge by showing that even the most remote and ephemeral aspects of past cultures were potentially recoverable to careful and imaginative analysis. These efforts were directed into two types of analysis: (1) the use of variability in ceramic assemblages to infer postmarital residence patterns (cf. Deetz 1965; Hill 1970; Longacre 1970); and (2) the study of mortuary practices to infer social organization and complexity. The ceramic studies received more attention and debate than did the mortuary studies, and although hailed as great breakthroughs at the time, the adequacy of at least some of the ceramic studies has now been called into question (cf. Dumond 1977). The use of funerary remains evoked much less controversy (at least among archaeologists), due in part to the fact that its justification rested largely on ethnographic rather than archaeological data. The ready acceptance may also have been due to a common intuitive feeling among all archaeologists that they are somehow very close to the essence of a past culture when working with burial remains. As a result, social analysis using funerary remains has been incorporated into the mainstream of archaeology on a business-as-usual basis, while the ceramic approach is still viewed with considerable skepticism.

The complete acceptance of mortuary analysis as a useful archaeological technique is perhaps best illustrated by the quantity and breadth of applications that have appeared in recent times. Leaving aside studies whose primary purpose is to test or expand the uses of funerary analysis as a technique, these applications can be divided into two categories: those that attempt direct social reconstructions from funerary evidence; and those that use the funerary context as a constant for analyzing other aspects of past social systems.

The application of funerary analysis to the problem of social reconstruction has been the most common. These studies divide sharply into those concerned with evidence of social differentiation at a single site and those that assess social systems using groups of sites. A representative sample of the single-site studies would include Chapman (1977), Gruber (1971), Hodson (1977), King (1969), Mainfort (1979), Rothschild (1979), Saxe (1971), Shennan (1975), Skinner (1972), Stickel (1968), Tainter (1973), Thomas and Beaton (1968), and van de Velde (1979). These studies cover groups and situations as distant and unrelated as Californian hunter–gatherers, Neolithic farmers in the Netherlands and historic fur traders in Canada. The range and extent of these applications stress the value of funerary data as an archaeological resource, whereas the varied results of these studies evidence the need for a formalized and unified theory of mortuary differentiation for archaeology.

Studies analyzing site systems and more general aspects of the organization and complexity of past societies are also frequent, although not as numerous as the single-site studies. A sample of these includes Braun (1977, 1979), Brown (1971a), Greber (1976, 1979), Hatch (1976), Peebles (1971), Peebles and Kus (1977), Renfrew (1973), and Tainter (1975a, 1977). These studies look beyond the funerary differentiation at a single site and have frequently used evidence from other archaeological contexts in their analyses. These studies have tended to concentrate on relatively complex cultures and have, by and large, provided encouraging results. They are, however, still ultimately concerned with evidence for social differentiation and complexity, in which the funerary remains form the centerpiece.

The use of mortuary occurrences as a context for the study of other processes has been a standard for the study of diachronic change, particularly seriation studies (cf. Doran 1972; Kendall 1971). However, social and economic aspects of past societies may also be analyzed in this way. Such studies, although proportionally less frequent in the literature, herald a mature development in funerary analysis, demonstrating the broad range of questions that can be investigated using mortuary data. Work by Randsborg (1973, 1974) and Kristiansen (1979) was employed to monitor Bronze Age economic systems by assessing the circulation time of bronze artifacts prior to their deposition in graves, and the correlations existing between the amount of imported metal deposited in graves at various locations relative to the economic potential of the region measured in terms of its agricultural potential. In a similar kind of study, Shennan (1977) has used the mortuary context to analyze the Beaker network, by examining the way in which the marked Beaker assemblage was incorporated into the local social systems of various regions. Finally, although not strictly in the realm of archaeological analysis, there is an increasing recognition of the contribution of demographic and biological analysis to the understanding of past societies. Demographic analyses using mortuary data (cf. Acsádi and Nemeskéri 1970; Angel 1969; Ubelaker 1974) are by now quite common. More ambitious studies in the area of human biology are now offering some of the most detailed views of past diet, living conditions and pathology (cf. Angel 1954; Asch 1976; Brothwell 1965; Buikstra 1976, 1977; Cook 1981; Farkas 1970; Lengyel 1972; and Lane and Sublett 1972).

Common to all these applications is the assumption that an individual's treatment in death bears some predictable relationship to the individual's state in life and to the organization of the society to which the individual belonged. It is the justification of this assumption that the developing archaeological theory of mortuary differentiation has attempted to provide. Yet, despite numerous applications, a comprehensive archaeological theory of mortuary variability has not emerged. The theory as it now exists is largely the product of organic development and lacks the central structure necessary to unify its various components and assumptions into a comprehensive system for archaeological analysis. Indeed, the proliferation of ad hoc assumptions that characterize many of these archaeological applications is a clear indication of the inadequacy of the theory in its present form.

One might argue that the developing archaeological study of funerary behavior might have benefited (or perhaps been laid to rest in Leach's view [1977]) from the same kind of detailed scrutiny received by the ceramic studies. Since the theoretical basis for the archaeological analysis of funerary remains lacks an explicit and formal structure, it is all the more important to understand its origins and development.

By documenting this development, we can examine the basis for the theory as it now exists and also gain insight into the deficiencies in its present applications. This body of theory has emerged from three distinct lines of research, each of which has provided a major portion of the justification for this theory, and each of which has brought into the theory its own methodological baggage. In this chapter, these approaches are critically, but briefly, examined as a first step toward the formulation of an archaeological theory of mortuary behavior.

Social Complexity and Mortuary Practices

One source of the recent interest in the analytical study of mortuary behavior in archaeology can be traced to Lewis Binford's study of rural Mississippian mortuary manifestations at the Galley Pond Mound (Binford 1964). Although this study was in many ways no more rigorous than many attempts before it, the approach it suggested was one that did offer potential for archaeological research because it stressed the regularities that exist between an individual's status in life and his treatment in death. Binford, following his work at Galley Pond Mound (1964) and a brief study of cremation burials in Michigan (1963a), attempted to consolidate his views in the essay "Mortuary Practices: Their Study and Potential" (1972). The essay had two basic goals: (1) to attack the traditionalist–diffusionist interpretation of mortuary ritual; and (2) to demonstrate the existence of cross-cultural regularities in the relationship between the organization of living communities, particularly their level of social complexity, and the differentiation that they manifest in their mortuary treatment. It is this second goal that is considered in this section.

Binford's framework was designed to relate the nature of the total social position of the individual at death and his varied interconnections with other members of the society in a regular, patterned way:

> It is proposed that there are two general components of the social situation to be evaluated when attempting to understand the types of social phenomena symbolized in any given burial situation. The first is what we may call, with Goodenough (1965:7) the social persona of the deceased. This is a composite of the social identities maintained in life and recognized as appropriate for consideration at death. The second is the composition and size of the social unit recognizing status responsibilities to the deceased. (1972:225–226)

Binford then argues that one would expect two concomitant correlations or regularities as a logical outgrowth of these two components:

> We would expect direct correlations between the relative rank of the status positions held by the deceased and the number of persons having duty-status relationships vis-a-vis the deceased.

and,

> Also we expect that the facets of the social persona symbolically recognized in the mortuary ritual would shift with the levels of corporate participation in the ritual and hence vary directly with the relative rank of the social position which the deceased occupied in life. (1972:226)

Binford proposes that the position of the individual, and the size and composition of the array of individuals who owe him status duties, constitute the primary vehicle for mortuary differentiation. The systematic link between mortuary differentiation and social position rests on the proposition that the amount of corporate participation, and the aspects of the social persona that are ritually symbolized through differential treatment, vary directly with the relative rank of the individual within the living community. Since ranking and differentiation are often seen as logical concomitants of complexity (cf. Blau 1970), Binford's model fits the standard social dichotomies of simple versus complex and egalitarian versus ranked, and it is not surprising that social considerations at this level should be significant in the testing of his propositions or in the work of other researchers following Binford's lead.

Binford (1972:226) suggests three propositions as a means of testing his formulations against ethnographic data (40 cases of non-state-organized societies from the Human Relations Area Files). Since these test hypotheses form much of the basis for later work in social reconstruction, it will be necessary to examine each briefly to evaluate its validity and implications.

Binford's first hypothesis is by far the most crucial, stating that "there should be a high degree of isomorphism between (a) the complexity of the status structure in a sociocultural system and (b) the complexity of the mortuary ceremonialism as regards differential treatment of persons occupying different status positions" (1972:226). Clearly, if such an isomorphism could be demonstrated, it would sustain the validity of the whole range of social inference based on mortuary evidence. Unfortunately, the nature of the ethnographic data could not support a direct test of this proposition, and it was necessary to restructure the hypotheses to accommodate these shortcomings. Instead of the number of different patterns of mortuary treatment employed, "the number of dimensional distinctions (age, sex, social position, subgroup affiliation, cause of death and location of death) recognized in the performance of formally differentiated mortuary practices" (1972:227), was used. Similarly, in place of a measure of the status structure of the society (an admittedly crude indicator), the form of subsistence production (hunter–gatherer, shifting agriculturalist, settled agriculturalist, and pastoralist) was substituted. With these alterations the hypothesis became: The number of dimensions of the social persona commonly given recognition in mortuary rituals varies significantly with subsistence practice (1972:235). Although this test proposition is still an interesting one, it no longer specifies the nature of the interrelationships between observed differentiation in mortuary ceremonialism and the actual status distinctions that were recognized in the living society. Furthermore, potentially confounding intervening variables, such as degree of sedentism, are introduced into the analysis, weakening the overall design.

Binford was able to demonstrate that in his sample most settled agriculturalists did symbolize a greater number of dimensional distinctions than did the other three subsistence groups (which were virtually indistinguishable).

The second hypothesis is integrally related to the first:

> Given the proposition that distinctions made in mortuary ritual are made in terms of the social persona, the composite of the social identities held in life, there should be a strong correspondence between the nature of the dimensional characteristics serving as the basis for differential mortuary treatment and the expected criteria employed for status differentiation among societies arranged on a scale from simple to complex. (1972:230)

Binford asserts that, among simpler societies, the primary distinction of status differentiation will be based on such general qualities as age, sex, and achievement, whereas in complex societies more "abstract characteristics independent of age, sex, and subgroup affiliation will prevail" (1972:230). To this he compares the frequency of occurrence of six specific dimensions within each of the four previously

TABLE 1.1

Frequency of Mortuary Distinction According to Subsistence Pattern

A. Binford's Observations				
	Hunter–gatherers (H.G.)	Shifting agriculturalist (Sh. Ag.)	Settled agriculturalist (Se. Ag.)	Pastoralist (P.)
Condition of death	1	0	6	1
Location of death	1	1	0	0
Age	2	1	7	1
Sex	12	4	10	3
Social position	6	5	11	0
Social affiliation	4	3	10	1
Total cases	15	8	14	3

B. Significance Evaluation[a]			
	H.G./Se.Ag.	H.G./Sh.Ag.	Sh.Ag./Se.Ag.
Condition of death	+	−	+
Location of death	−	−	−
Age	+	−	−
Sex	−	−	−
Social position	+	−	−
Social affiliation	−	−	−

[a] +, frequencies significant at 0.05 level. −, frequencies not significant at 0.05 level. All significance levels based on a one-tailed test.

mentioned groups based on subsistence practice. Table 1.1A is based on Binford's frequency figures for this test (1972:231), whereas Table 1.1B summarizes the significant differences between groups as determined by using the Fisher Exact Test (Siegel 1956:96). It should be pointed out that the statistical test assigns significance only on the basis of the observed frequencies and is presented as a guide to assess Binford's summary of his own results. Biases inherent in the test, both resulting from sample selection and autocorrelations between the average number of dimensional distinctions per class and the number of specific dimensions observed, are not evaluated by this test. Binford concludes that "the striking differences noted between agriculturalists and hunter–gatherers are taken as confirmatory evidence for the proposition advanced" (1972:231).

Although these test results appear to conform to expectations, Table 1.1B does throw doubt on Binford's assertion that agriculturalists, in general, show a striking difference from hunter–gatherers and suggests rather that sedentary groups differ from the nonsedentary as in the test of his first hypothesis. Further, on each dimension where a statistically significant difference was demonstrated, the dimension occurred with greater frequency in the sedentary agricultural groups. This is largely to be expected because it has already been shown that this group, on the average, symbolized a greater number of mortuary distinctions. Nevertheless, the test provides no real evidence for a shift away from personal qualities among settled agriculturalists, as proposed by Binford. Rather, there appears to be a tendency to symbolize more abstract distinctions as well as the simpler, more personal qualities. Therefore, this test result, although further emphasizing the first hypothesis, must strictly be viewed as unproven. This question will be discussed again in the context of Saxe's Hypothesis 4 (Saxe 1970).

Binford's third hypothesis seeks to interrelate the size of the group of individuals owing duty-status responsibilities to the deceased, the amount of corporate disturbance that the mortuary ritual will create in its performance, and the relative rank of the individual in the society. Given an egalitarian society:

> We can therefore predict that age differences may be discriminated in mortuary ritual by differential placement of burial sites within the life space of the community. The choice of placement would vary with status to the degree that the performance of the ritual involves members of the community at large in the ritual activity and thereby disrupts their daily activities. (1972:232)

For this test, three nominal categories reflecting the various details through which mortuary differentiation can be manifest were defined: treatment of the corpse; preparation of the facility in which the corpse is placed for disposal; and contributions to the burial furniture placed with the body. Each of these three categories was then subdivided into three more specific types of nominal distinction. These nine variables were tabulated against the frequency with which each of the six previously mentioned dimensions of mortuary distinction were symbolized in the ethnographic sample. The results of this test are ambiguous, although the particular assertion concerning the way infant burials tend to be spatially recognized does receive some support. Therefore, at this stage, this relationship must be viewed as unproven although suggesting tantalizing possibilities. This proposition has been further elaborated by Joseph Tainter (1975a; 1977) in a somewhat different form.

Binford's summary of his results gives an adequate review of the position that he has supported:

> These findings permit the generalization that the form and structure which characterizes the mortuary practices of any society are conditioned by the form and complexity of the organizational characteristics of the society itself. Change or variability in either form or structure must take into account the limiting or determining effects exerted on these practices by the nature of the organizational properties of the society. (1972:235)

There is no statement suggesting congruence between the differentiation in the living society and mortuary treatment, nor is a simple one-to-one correspondence between types of mortuary differentiation and social organization suggested. At its most fundamental level, Binford's analysis does establish that, without necessarily specifying the nature of the link, mortuary differentiation does not vary independently of the organization of the society that produced it, but rather that the former is conditioned by the latter. As such, it is the first critical link between the mortuary data and social inference.

Social Dimensions of Mortuary Practices

The term *social persona* has already arisen in the discussion of Binford's study, yet it is in the work of James Brown (1971a,b) and Arthur Saxe (1970) that the impact of formal analysis and role theory is most marked.

Brown's study was based on a formal approach analogous to the formal semantic approaches used in contemporary anthropology (cf. Hammel 1965). The approach attempted to specify the way in which various elements of a culture's funerary treatment served to partition the mortuary population:

> This paper proposes to treat a domain of products of socio-cultural behavior as composed of a structure of products or property space that are defined generally speaking by the juncture of dimensions, which for the archaeologist are physical attributes of cultural significance. (Brown 1971a:93)

This structure of dimensions, partitioning the mortuary population and presented as a key diagram, should then offer a clear indication of the primary structuring of the living society:

> In this presentation, a key type diagram will stand as the map for some of the dimension property spaces derived from a suite of archaeologically based dimensions. It, then, is constructed of the archaeological evidence pertaining to the funerary domain, which by its structure, whether hierarchical or egalitarian, segmented or unified, offers a clear indication of the types of possible behavioral correlates and the social structures to which they pertain. (Brown 1971a:94)

Brown employed this approach to examine the structure of mortuary differentiation at the Spiro site, a Mississippian ceremonial center in eastern Oklahoma. In addition to the archaeological study of the Spiro remains, Brown attempted to use the same procedures to analyze ethnographic accounts of burial among two remnant southeastern chiefdoms, the Natchez-Taensa and the Choctaw. The key diagrams from both archaeological and ethnographic analyses were then compared.

Although this analysis was hampered by poor skeletal preservation at Spiro and by difficulties in the use of ethnographic accounts as comparative data, it represented a major advance in the development of an archaeologically relevant theory of mortuary differentiation and introduced a number of concepts that have not yet received sufficient attention.

First, Brown's approach was directed toward archaeological remains, and by necessity considered postdepositional effects and temporal change as well as cultural behavior as factors affecting his data. This is in contrast to those investigators following Binford's lead, who attempted to understand mortuary phenomena solely through ethnographic data without consideration of the special character of the archaeological context. Brown recognized that both archaeological and ethnographic data had their own properties and biases, and he realized that if such evidence was to be compared it must be at a more abstract level (1971a:94). The use of key diagrams was an attempt at such abstraction.

In fact, Brown's comparison of the structuring of Spiro funerary treatment with the ethnographic examples was not particularly successful because of the inadequacies in the ethnographic accounts of the native funerary practices (1971a:107). This is one of the few criticisms of the ethnographic documentation of mortuary practices to appear in an archaeological literature saturated with their use.

Although Brown's study was directed toward the archaeological context, the formal approach advocated presented serious problems in its application. The approach seems particularly sensitive to sampling error, both in the recovery of the full range of funerary treatments practiced by a society and in the presentation of the relevant elements that actually served to structure the disposal domain (1971a:110). It also seems poorly equipped to cope with temporal change and the variation that it might produce in a cumulative mortuary sample. Although Brown recognizes these difficulties (1971a:107), good archaeological judgment seems to be the only remedy offered.

Brown's study at Spiro represents a necessary complement to Binford's work. It was specifically an archaeological study and operationalized a procedure that was relevant to the kinds of evidence that could be obtained from the archaeological record. Although not developed to a stage where it could cope with the complexities of formation processes in a systematic way, it did offer a potential framework for an archaeological theory of mortuary differentiation. Indeed, a modification of this formal or dimensional approach is advocated in the later chapters of this study.

The second major proponent of the use of formal analysis in mortuary studies and perhaps the individual most closely associated with this approach is Arthur Saxe. Saxe followed Brown's lead in the use of formal analysis, although he based his work much more strictly on a role theory model. His approach differs from Brown's, however, in the fact that archaeological evidence is not considered in his study. Since Saxe's work presents the clearest and most fully developed example of the componential approach, as applied to funerary analysis, it will be considered in detail here.

Saxe attempted to construct a coherent theoretical basis for the study of mortuary ritual and remains by presenting them as an integrated and well-articulated extension of the normal social behavior of a society. He states his basic premise as follows: "When archaeologists excavate a set of burials they are not merely excavating individuals, but a coherent social personality who not only engaged in relationships with other social personalities but did so according to rules and structural slots dictated by the larger social system" (1970:4).

Saxe's framework for mortuary analysis mirrored the componential analysis advocated by Goodenough (1965), which was in turn based largely on Linton's classic essay on status and role (1936). Two of these terms are critical: *social identity*, "a category of persons or what has been called a social position or status" (Saxe 1970:4), including such identities as policeman and mother; and *social persona*, "a composite of several social identities selected as appropriate to a given interaction" (1970:7). Saxe argues that at the time of death a series of choices must be made between the various conflicting social identities of the deceased: "Death thus calls forth a fuller representation of ego's various *social identities* than at any time during life. Therefore there is also the greatest probability of conflicts in compatibility occurring between social identities at death, and the consequent greater demand for choice than in life" (1970:6). And these crucial choices are, of course, made by the living: "In a situation involving disposal of the dead such 'decisions' are made by the living; the determinants of which are to be found in the rights and duties of the identity relationships which adhere between the deceased and the living" (1970:9).

The outcome of these decisions determines the nature and details of the mortuary treatment that the deceased will receive. Therefore, it is reasoned that patterning in the variability of mortuary remains will reflect a consciously selected set of distinctions that will be congruent with the social positions held by the deceased in life.

Saxe proposed the use of componential analysis as a means of identifying the dimensions of the disposal practices underlying the disposal domain and as a means of mapping the individual values on these dimensions into the set of disposal types (1970:38). It is further argued that the graphic representation of such an analysis, the key diagram, has additional useful properties, since the amount of organization implied by a given combination of dimensions can be quantified using a measure of information. Ultimately, the use of this procedure should "enable us to decipher: (1) the way social personae are differentially represented with disposal domains, and (2) the way different social structures are differentially represented among different disposal domains" (1970:63).

To examine this framework, Saxe deduced a set of eight hypotheses that were tested against detailed ethnographic accounts from three groups: the Ashanti, the Kapauku, and the Bontoc Igorot. Table 1.2 summarizes the eight hypotheses and Saxe's conclusions concerning them.

Saxe's work provided a framework that allows the explication of the linkage between the differentiation accorded an individual in death and the positions he occupied in the community in life. Through such a regular linkage, a study of the range of mortuary variability expressed by a society should allow us to infer the nature of the structural organization of the society that produced it. This paradigm, following Binford's lead, has now been largely accepted by archaeologists.

There are, however, some inherent problems in the approach outlined by Saxe. The technique of componential analysis has its own limitations in anthropological analysis (cf. Burling 1964; Schneider 1965), especially regarding problems of multiple unique solutions, equivalency, and indeterminancy.

TABLE 1.2

Saxe's Hypothesized Regularities Underlying Mortuary Behavior[a]

Hypothesis	Results
Intrasocietal regularities	
1. The components of a given disposal domain cooperate in a partitioning of the universe, the resultant combinations representing different social personae.	Components may or may not represent individual social personae; but even if not, they are parts of the information going into such a representation.
2. In a given domain, the principles organizing the set of social personae are congruent with those organizing social relations in the society at large.	The more complex the social system, the greater the number of organizing dimensions that crosscut or obscure more egalitarian principles of age, sex and personal achievement.
3. Within a given domain personae of lesser social significance tend to manifest fewer positive components in their significata relative to others, and conversely.	Holds generally in egalitarian societies; in stratified societies, holds only within each stratum.
4. The greater the social significance of the deceased the greater will be the tendency for the social persona represented at death to contain social identities congruent with that higher position at the expense of other (and less socially significant identities) the deceased may have had in life, and conversely.	Only weakly supported, lesser statuses may or may not be truncated.

(continued)

James Brown, in his formal study of mortuary differentiation at the Spiro site, noted in his conclusions:

> The specific difficulties experienced in handling and interpreting the four paradigms herein devolve principally around the definition of the domain and its boundaries and are, indeed, the same as those experienced by all other attempts (Hymes 1964:17). In archaeological situations, the determination of the relevant sets and component alternatives amount to not only defining appropriate dimensions but also carefully including all of the relevant parts of the domains. (1971a:110)

A second problem involves the distinction made by Goodenough between social identities and personal identities:

> A social identity is an aspect of self that makes a difference in how one's rights and duties distribute to specific others. Any aspect of self whose alteration entails no change in how people's rights and duties are mutually *distributed*, although it affects their emotional orientation to one another and the *way* they choose to exercise their privileges, has to do with personal identity and not with social identity. (Goodenough 1965:3-4; emphases added)

Such an intervening variable, which affects the manner in which a right or duty is exercised, although unpredictable, must be taken into account when the archaeolo-

TABLE 1.2 *Continued*

Hypothesis	Results
Intersocietal regularities	
5. The more paradigmatic the attributes evidenced in the key structure of the domain, the less complex and more egalitarian the social organization. Conversely, the more tree-like the attributes, the more complex and the less egalitarian the social organization.	Hypothesis untestable because of the arbitrary nature of ethnographic observation.
6. The simpler a sociocultural system the greater will be the tendency for there to be a linear relationship between number of components in significata, number of contrast sets necessary to define them, and the social significance of the significata; and conversely.	Some linearity noted, refinement of hypothesis necessary.
7. The simpler the sociocultural system the less divergence will be evident in the treatment of different kinds of deviant social personae, and conversely.	Insufficient data for testing.
8. To the degree that corporate group rights to use and/or control crucial but restricted resources are attained and/or legitimized by means of lineal descent from the dead, such groups will maintain formal disposal areas for the exclusive disposal of their dead, and conversely.	The spatial distribution and density of the dead is plausibly linked to the operation of that society's ecological system.

*a*Hypotheses and results from Saxe 1970.

gist attempts to ascribe meaning to mortuary variability. The failure of Saxe's Hypotheses 1 and 4, in their originally stated form, could well be attributed to variability produced by the operation of personal identities.

Saxe's first four hypotheses, when taken in light of their modifications, form an initially validated basis for explicating the structural interrelationships between the social organization of a society and its mortuary differentiation. They do not, however, consider the relationship between social organization and mortuary differentiation in an archaeological context. The second four hypotheses could not be adequately tested, given the limited nature of Saxe's data and must be treated as unproven. Unfortunately, little attention has been given these premises in terms of further testing using ethnographic data.

The exception to this is the work of Goldstein (1976), who attempted to test hypothesis eight on the basis of 30 ethnographic examples. Her conclusions are significant, especially in the implications they suggest for directional interpretation.

She suggests that hypothesis eight should be restated to reflect the fact that, for a corporate group seeking to legitimize its use or control of scarce resources, *one* manner of ritualizing this relationship is through the maintenance of a permanent, specialized, and bounded disposal area. This should not be construed as being the only way in which such a claim can be legitimized (Goldstein 1976:61). She also states, "If a permanent, specialized, bounded disposal area for the exclusive disposal of a group's dead exists, then it is likely that this represents a corporate group who has rights over the use and/or control of crucial but restricted resources" (1976:61). As Goldstein notes (1976:58), the basic problem is Saxe's attempt to assert the converse; in other words, to weigh the negative evidence as strongly as the positive. This question will intrude on even a larger scale when the inquiry shifts from ethnographic to archaeological data.

Archaeological Studies of Mortuary Differentiation

Since the Society for American Archaeology symposium on mortuary practices, the archaeological literature has been rich in examples of the application of funerary analysis to the problem of past societal organization. The majority of these studies either (1) utilize the premises of Binford and Saxe as an interpretative algorithm to "explain" observed mortuary variability; or (2) have employed funerary analysis as a means of assigning particular societies to one of the evolutionary pigeon holes of Service (1962) or Fried (1967; see also Tainter 1977:330).

These studies have varied widely in their results. Yet, they all share the problem identified by Brown: how to adapt these essentially ethnographic regularities to the study of archaeological phenomena. Investigators have either ignored this distinction or have erected a series of ad hoc rules to bridge the two contexts. Yet, despite the obvious difficulty in applying mortuary analysis to archaeological cases, little effort has been directed toward formalizing the archaeological study of funerary remains. Two exceptions to this trend will be discussed in this section.

Peebles's (1971) analysis of mortuary patterning at Moundville was not strikingly different from many other application papers. What sets the work apart (see also Peebles and Kus 1977) is that the particular ad hoc propositions formulated have a strong generalizing character and were specifically directed at the archaeological representation of mortuary variability.

Peebles first noted that the reason social organization is accessible to archaeologists is that they view a *cumulative* record. Since each individual is assumed to have been buried in accordance with his or her social standing in life, by observing the range and frequency of different disposal treatments, the archaeologist can infer the principles governing that differentiation (1971:69). Simple as this may seem, it represents a major change in perspective from the studies based on ethnographic data and implies the need for distinct analytical procedures that are relevant to the archaeological manifestation of mortuary variability. It also reflects a growing awareness of the need to understand the archaeological record itself, as a necessary first step in understanding past funerary behavior. Finally, although the premise is intuitively obvious, the limitations that it implies may be less obvious.

Since the passage of time is a necessary precondition for meaningful archaeological analysis, the problem of diachronic variation in funerary behavior must be examined. If mortuary remains are to be understood directly, it is necessary to assume that only a single set of cultural directives governing mortuary treatment was in operation during the duration of the cemetery's use. Any temporal effects that alter either the rules governing mortuary differentiation or the manner through which such differentiation was manifest will distort the cumulative picture. Thus, the dilemma: A short use-life minimizes the potential for diachronic change, but may provide an insufficient sample for meaningful analysis, whereas the large cemetery, ideal for social analysis, often has the greatest potential for diachronic distortion. This is strictly an archaeological problem that is neither considered in nor relevant to the ethnographic studies. Peebles also points to incomplete recovery, particularly the recovery of only a portion of the total range of mortuary differentiation employed by a given society, as a serious problem in archaeological studies.

These considerations are indicative of the unique character of the archaeological context and serve to define the problems that an archaeologically relevant theory of mortuary differentiation must satisfy.

In addition to the greater appreciation of the unique character of archaeological phenomena, Peebles introduces analytical concepts that are more appropriate to analysis within an archaeological context. In considering the problem of interpreting the meaning of grave inclusions, Peebles adopts Binford's appealing but nebulous classification of *technomic* and *sociotechnic* (Binford 1962) artifact usage as a means of defining the nature of burial inclusions (1971:69). He refines the definition of sociotechnic artifacts in terms of their ability to symbolize differentiation or ranking. *Supralocal* symbols are defined as symbols that are recognized over a wide area and likely crosscut a number of ethnic boundaries (1971:69). *Local* symbols are those sociotechnic artifacts that serve to rank or differentiate individuals only within a given locality (1971:69). Although Peebles's primary concern is with ranking individuals (and indirectly with ranking the importance of their locality within the Moundville sphere of influence), such distinctions can be made for other cultural processes, such as conquest or trade, that result in a commonality of symbols over a wide region. In addition, the use of data from situations other than the mortuary context itself represents an important step in the use of mortuary information to answer more general questions regarding social process. This lead has been further developed by Peebles and Kus (1977), where independent sources of information, including site catchment potential, have been integrated into the reconstruction of the Moundville social system.

Peebles and Kus (1977) also attempt to define general criteria for the recognition of social ranking within an archaeological context (see also Brown 1981). They posit two independent dimensions in the symbolic representation of an individual's social persona: a *superordinate* dimension, which produces a partial ordering of the graves through energy expenditure or symbols that is not simultaneously based on age and sex; and a second or *subordinate* dimension, which produces a partial ordering of graves that is generally based on age, sex, or achievement during an individual's life history (1977:431). They assert that only in a ranked society will both dimensional effects be observed.

This can be viewed as a step toward resolving the tangled achieved versus ascribed dichotomy borrowed from social anthropology. It fails to distinguish, however, vertical differentiation (i.e., ranking) from the effects of horizontal differentiation, such as corporate group affiliation, which might similarly appear as a superordinate characteristic if it were symbolized in the mortuary ritual. To overcome this problem, two additional criteria were introduced: (1) the amount of energy expended in the mortuary treatment; and (2) the expectation of a pyramid of stratum membership (Peebles and Kus 1977:431). These qualifications would allow for the discrimination of vertical and horizontal differentiation, but they also introduce certain new assumptions, which may not be warranted or desirable.

To summarize, the work of Peebles, and Peebles and Kus, follows Brown's lead in dealing with the problem of mortuary analysis within an archaeological context. Yet, although it highlights the necessity of incorporating the effects of archaeological formation processes into funerary analysis and offers a number of useful analytical concepts for use with archaeological data, it falls short of integrating these concepts into a general framework for the archaeological study of mortuary remains.

Like the Moundville studies, research by Joseph Tainter on the mortuary practices and social organization of Hawaiian chiefdoms and the Middle Woodland period in the central United States is specifically concerned with the understanding and use of funerary remains within an archaeological context. Although directed at rather specific measures of social complexity, these studies represent the most serious attempt to formulate an archaeologically relevant theory for the analysis of social organization through mortuary remains.

Tainter's approach is grounded in systems theory. Of particular importance are the definitions of the terms *structure* and *organization* in this context:

> The structure of a system is meant to indicate the number, nature and arrangement of its articulated components and subsystems (Miller 1965), while the organization is most basically defined as the constraints imposed upon the range of behavior which may possibly be pursued by the elements of the system. (Tainter and Cordy 1977:96)

To integrate this systems model with human mortuary behavior, Tainter turns to the ethnographic studies of Binford and Saxe for two critical relationships. The first is based on Saxe's assertion that the time of death occasions a greater range of the deceased's social identities than in any time in life:

> Since individuals acquire their social identities through membership in the structural components of the social system, the representation in mortuary ritual of the deceased's social identities simultaneously conveys information concerning the structural components in which the individual held memberships. Indeed, to the extent to which a mortuary population contains individuals who held membership in various structural components of a system, one can expect the mortuary population to reflect the structure of the extinct society. (Tainter 1977:329)

The second relationship is based on Binford's assertion (1972:232) that the higher the relative rank of an individual, the greater the amount of disruption in normal community activities the mortuary ritual will cause. This is translated into archaeological terms by Tainter as follows:

> Expanding upon this proposal, we may suggest that both the amount of corporate involvement, and the degree of activity disruption, will positively correspond to the amount of energy expended in the mortuary act. Energy expenditure in turn should be reflected in the size and elaborateness of the burial facility. (Tainter 1973:6)

On the basis of these two links with ethnographic studies, Tainter proceeds to integrate the archaeologically observable mortuary differentiation into his systems model. He begins by defining a set of analytical terms that are appropriate both to the subject of interest, past social complexity, and to the actual materials to be analyzed, mortuary remains. Rather than attempting to describe mortuary patterning directly as specific kinds of social entities, Tainter borrows the sociological concepts of vertical and horizontal dimensions of social differentiation (Blau 1970).

> For the analysis of prehistoric social systems, it is possible to abstract two dimensions of structural differentiation that are of general significance. These might be termed the *vertical* and *horizontal dimensions*. The former clearly refers to the structure of rank grading in a society. The horizontal dimension, on the other hand, encompasses structural components that are equivalent on identical hierarchical levels and between which there are no major, institutionalized differences in rank. Examples of such horizontally differentiated components might include sodalities, individual descent units of segmentary descent systems, task groups, territorial bands, and the like. (Tainter 1977:331)

He then outlines four principal characteristics of a social system for explication: (1) the structural complexity of the system; (2) the nature of the structural differentiation; (3) the amount and degree of organization; and (4) the nature of this organization (Tainter 1977:329). Of these, two aspects—structural complexity and degree of organization—are seen as quantifiable, and as such offer special potential, especially for comparative study. Measures of both of these features assume that the archaeological evidence of energy expenditure in the mortuary treatment will bear a direct and regular relationship to the division of the living society into hierarchical strata.

The first step in making these measurements is to determine the number of distinctive levels of labor expenditure in the mortuary treatment, which are seen as indicating the distinctive levels of rank within the society. The number of such component levels "will mark the degree of structural complexity" (Tainter 1977:333), along the vertical axis.

With these component levels, it is then possible to quantify the amount of organization through the use of the Shannon–Weaver information statistic (Shannon and Weaver 1949). This measure assesses departure from equiprobability of the number of individuals represented in each of the observed strata. The measure of entropy H is defined as $H = p \log 1/p_i$ and is compared with the maximum possible entropy for the classification ($H_{max} = \log N$). This measure takes the form of $D_{(1)}$ (departure from equiprobability), which is defined as $D_{(1)} = H_{max} - H_{obs}$. To measure the degree (as opposed to the amount) of organization, one evaluates the redundancy of the classification, $RD_{(1)} = 1 - (H_{obs}/H_{max})$. The redundancy measure is referred to as the degree of *relative organization* (Tainter 1977:336).

The second measure employed by Tainter is also based on his inferred levels of ranking and reflects the system's degree of rank differentiation. Tainter employs a measure formulated by Harary (1959) that directly reflects the number of subordinates an individual at any given level in a hierarchy will have. By determining the situational position of this highest rank level, one can express numerically the degree of rank differentiation present in the hierarchy (Tainter 1977:337).

These three measurements—the number of levels of energy expenditures, relative organization (redundancy), and rank differentiation—form the relevant variables for Tainter's study of past social complexity. This approach has been applied to Middle and Late Woodland social organization in the Midwest (Tainter 1975a, 1977) and to the Hawaiian chiefdoms (Tainter 1973, 1976; Tainter and Cordy 1977). These latter applications are of particular interest for their complementary use of settlement, spatial and mortuary data in their study of social organization complexity.

Unfortunately, Tainter's procedure rests on several assumptions concerning the behavior of living societies and the nature of archaeological remains that may well be unjustified (see also Braun 1981). As has been previously mentioned, the entire methodology and its results are grounded on the assumption that the observed expenditure of energy in the mortuary ritual will provide a direct and unbiased indication of the rank levels present in the living society. Tainter (1975a) supports this assertion with a test involving 103 ethnographic cases that suggests that increased energy expenditure in the mortuary treatment does tend to covary with the rank standing of the individual (92 cases showed positive increase, 11 no difference). However, it is assumed without further testing that the expenditure of energy that is observed in the archaeological record is congruent with that expended in the ritual as a whole. Although it would seem consistent to assert that, if clear-cut levels of energy expenditure are observed in the mortuary remains, they will reflect conscious rank differences in the living society (Tainter 1977:333), to assume that rank differentiation will always be manifest in terms of gross levels of energy expenditure that can be detected archaeologically must certainly on the basis of the present evidence be rejected. An example of this problem can be seen in Tainter's study of the Anaehoomalu mortuary practices in Hawaii (Tainter and Cordy 1977).

Here, four major modes of interment are defined using the energy expenditure: (1) individuals accorded the construction of a stone wall to mark their place of interment; (2) individuals buried in, or associated with, a canoe or canoe parts; (3) disarticulated bundles of bones; and (4) individuals buried in an articulated state with no associated stone walls or canoe parts (Tainter and Cordy 1977:106). It was further necessary to specify that, if a canoe part was found in association with a cluster of interments, it was considered as having been placed with only one of the burials (1977:107). From an archaeological viewpoint, one must ask, what if only a portion of the canoe parts were preserved, or worse, what if none of the canoe parts had survived for discovery? Clearly, even in the best of cases, one can observe only a subset of the total effort expended in the mortuary ritual, and as such, these levels can hardly provide an unbiased or complete view of the rank levels existing in the living society.

Yet, the quantitative measures of complexity that Tainter (1977:136) advocates as essential must assume that they are complete and unbiased indicators of the system's internal differentiation, or they are meaningless! This same problem intrudes when Tainter asserts that energy expenditure levels will provide a universal or unbiased means of comparing rank differentiation between disparate groups (Tainter 1977:128). At best, levels of energy expenditure inform us as to the minimum level of rank differentiation operating in a given society, and any further claim for the measure cannot be accepted (for a parallel argument see Goldstein 1976:23).

At a methodological level, the model's primary defect lies in the actual determination of distinct energy levels. Tainter offers the following criteria for this determination:

> For the present, degrees of labor expenditure must be evaluated on an ordinal scale by assessment of such factors as (1) the complexity of body treatment (for example, simple inhumation as opposed to cremation or skeletal manipulation), (2) the form and/or location of the interment facility (whether, for example, the body is interred in a simple earthen grave or in an elaborate, labor-consuming tomb), and (3) material contributions to the ritual (evaluated in terms of the effort required to produce or replace an item lost through inclusion in the grave). (Tainter 1977:332)

Clearly, such loose criteria may lead to a variety of unique solutions within the confines of the same data set (see Braun 1981:407). A brief example will suffice to illustrate this point.

In the previously mentioned analysis of mortuary data by Peebles and Kus (1977) at the Moundville site, they present the result of a segment analysis that divides the mortuary occurrence into three basic strata. Table 1.3A summarizes the number of individuals that belong to each segment and the measures of organization and rank differentiation calculated, as outlined by Tainter (1977). It is worth noting, however, that the lowest segment, Segment C, is composed of what might easily be interpreted as two distinct categories: those 341 individuals who were interred with some form of grave offering; and, on the other hand, the 1256 individuals who were

TABLE 1.3

Variation in Measures of Redundancy and Rank Differentiation at Moundville[a]

A. Three-segment solution

Segment	N	P	$P \log_2 1/p$	
A	117	0.0592	0.2414	$H_{max} = 1.5850$
B	261	0.1322	0.3859	$H_{obs} = 0.8751$
C	1597	0.8086	0.2478	$D_{(1)} = 0.7099$
				$R\,D_{(1)} = 0.4479$

Segment	N	N_k/N_1	$S(P_1)$
A	117	1.00	29.53
B	261	2.23	
C	1597	13.65	

B. With the Division of Segment C

Segment	N	P	$P \log_2 1/p$	
A	117	0.0592	0.2414	$H_{max} = 2.000$
B	261	0.1322	0.3859	$H_{obs} = 1.4802$
C_1	341	0.1727	0.4376	$D_{(1)} = 0.5198$
C_2	1256	0.6359	0.4153	$R\,D_{(1)} = 0.2599$

Segment	N	N_k/N_1	$S(P_1)$
A	117	1.00	40.27
B	261	2.23	
C_1	341	2.91	
C_2	1256	10.74	

[a] Based on Peebles and Kus (1977).

buried without accompanying artifacts. Following Tainter's criteria, a second investigator might reasonably separate them into two different classes.

Table 1.3B represents the Moundville data broken into four strata, again with the measures of organization and rank differentiation. This alteration produces marked differences. The redundancy of the classification is decreased by nearly half, while the degree of rank differentiation is significantly increased.

The problem of specifying the relevant domain of variables for mortuary analysis is a problem that is not unique to Tainter's method, and indeed Brown (1971b:1) stresses this as a problem with which any approach must cope. Yet, as Tainter's approach is based so overwhelmingly on this single determination, it seems particularly vulnerable. Until a procedure can be offered to identify these distinctive levels of energy expenditure more objectively and to account for the invisibility of an unknown component of the total energy expenditure in the archaeological context, the assertion of the technique's suitability for comparative study must be viewed skeptically.

A second weakness of the approach is its inability to handle horizontal social differentiation. Tainter sidesteps the problem with the claim that vertical and horizontal differentiation are two aspects of the same phenomenon (Blau 1970) and that by monitoring one, you effectively monitor both (Tainter 1977:333). Yet, such horizontal differentiation or other non-rank-related aspects of the mortuary treatment, if manifest archaeologically, might be misinterpreted as vertical ranking, causing an effect similar to that in the Moundville example. Furthermore, the evidence for the kinds of horizontal differentiation employed by a given society is a question of considerable anthropological interest. This might be expanded to a more general criticism of Tainter's approach. Although the methodology is elegantly designed to extract a rather narrow class of sociometric information from human mortuary remains, it does not address the greater range of information that can be recovered from funerary remains. In fairness, it should be stressed that Tainter makes no claim that it should. But from the perspective of a developing archaeological theory of funerary behavior, the integrative framework must encompass this range of potential information.

In summary, although Tainter's work offers an approach for integrating archaeological data into a systematic framework for the study of social complexity, it is insufficiently general to be useful as a basis for an archaeological theory of mortuary variability. Furthermore, it is based on a set of underlying assumptions that oversimplify the relationship between social differentiation and its archaeological expression in funerary remains to an extent that jeopardizes the technique's validity.

The development of an archaeological theory of mortuary variability has been marked by two distinct approaches: (1) the use of comparative ethnography as a source and testing ground for proposed regularities in social and mortuary behavior; and (2) attempts to apply these ethnographically observed regularities to actual archaeological analyses.

The ethnographic research, as conducted by archaeologists, has tended to overstate the cause-and-effect relationships leading to differential mortuary treatment and to underestimate the actual variability that can be expected in human mortuary behavior (for a similar argument, see Allen and Richardson 1971). Yet, when archaeologists have attempted to test these propositions, the ethnographic data have not conformed to the rigid specifications of theory. Test results rather reflect a more variable, although still regular, relationship between mortuary differentiation and the social structuring of living societies. Saxe's results are particularly illustrative of this tendency. Unfortunately, many archaeological applications of these ethnographic regularities reincorporate the rigid cause-and-effect models, in some cases even counter to the conclusions drawn from ethnographic testing (compare Goldstein 1976:6 with Tainter 1976:93).

There has also been a tendency to be rather uncritical of the ethnographic data used in these comparative studies and of their inherent biases. Ethnographic accounts of native funerary customs are often based on a small number of observations, are often secondhand, and are frequently normative in character. As a result, they do not present the full range of mortuary practices employed by a society, or they may even intentionally exclude variability in such practices in an effort to present a summary description of mortuary custom. The failure to mention a particular attribute of funerary behavior may, as in the archaeological case, be the result of observational error rather than its true absence. For this reason, "proofs" based on massed cases from the Human Relations Area Files or similar collections of ethnographic data may be of questionable value if not adequately and exhaustively screened.

Ethnographic studies have provided a crucial impetus and basis for the archaeological study of mortuary variability. Yet, despite the fact that these studies were performed by archaeologists, little effort has been directed toward the application of these regularities under actual archaeological investigations. As often as not, there is only the implicit assumption that, if an ethnographic relationship can be demonstrated, a corresponding archaeological relation will also be observed.

In summary, extensive research has demonstrated the existence of regularities linking aspects of the living society and its procedure for the disposal of the dead. Most important among these central relationships are:

1. Mortuary differentiation is patterned, and its elements are integrated with other aspects of the sociocultural system.
2. The mortuary differentiation accorded an individual, although not necessarily isomorphic, is consistent with his social position in the living society.
3. The complexity of the system of mortuary differentiation will increase with the complexity of the society at large.

The second approach to the development of an archaeological theory of mortuary differentiation is represented in those studies that have attempted to apply ethnographic regularities to archaeological investigations. The bulk of these efforts can be classified as application studies, which besides general comments on the nature of archaeological remains or supposed limitations placed on archaeological inference, have simply used the ethnographic regularities as interpretive algorithms to "explain" observed mortuary patterning or to categorize a given occurrence into this or that evolutionary slot. Only in the work of Brown, Peebles, and Tainter is there an effort made to approach mortuary variability in a specifically archaeological context. Yet, none of these approaches is sufficiently general in its scope nor sufficiently specific in its recognition of archaeological formation processes to stand as an integrating theory of mortuary variability for archaeology.

The body of general archaeological theory at present, then, contains a number of behavioral correlates linking aspects of social organization with mortuary treatment, and a broad range of hypothesized transformations that attempt to project these correlates into the archaeological context. What is lacking is a fundamental structure that integrates these potential theories into a coherent system for the archaeological study of funerary remains. Such a framework must explicitly address the processes of archaeological context formation and describe the minimum constraints that can be expected to operate in such transformations. The following two chapters offer a possible structure to satisfy these requirements.

2

*Funerary Remains
as Archaeological Phenomena*

The study of mortuary variability has, in common with archaeological research in general, the need to specify the processes that link past cultural behavior and contemporary archaeological phenomena (Binford and Bertram 1977:77). Three basic relationships determine the transformation from past cultural activity to contemporary observation: (1) the amount of structure inherent in a society's mortuary treatment; (2) the archaeological formation processes that mediate funerary behavior and potential observable archaeological phenomena; and (3) the limitations inherent in the detection and recognition of variability among archaeological phenomena. Each of these relationships will have a unique and significant impact on the observation and explanation of funerary remains in an archaeological context.

The regularities linking social organization and funerary treatment have been the most extensively explored (see Chapter 1) and provide a crucial basis for the comprehensive archaeological study of mortuary variability. The latter two relationships have, by and large, been neglected. In this chapter a more in-depth consideration will be given to the processes of formation and detection, in an effort to better understand funerary remains as archaeological phenomena.

Archaeological Formation Processes

To understand mortuary variability one must consider not only the structure and pattern of a culture's mortuary behavior but also the manner through which the behavior has become manifest in the archaeological record. The transformations by which material elements cease to function in the cultural system and eventually become embedded in the archaeological context have been termed *formation processes*

(Schiffer 1976:27). These formation processes might be further specified to distinguish *primary depositional pathways*, by which an object or behavioral trace comes to be incorporated in the archaeological record, and *postdepositional processes*, reflecting the changes that affect these remains after their initial entry into the archaeological context (Clarke 1973:16). To understand funerary remains as archaeological phenomena, the general operation and interaction of these two sets of processes must be identified.

Since the time of Worsaae (Rowe 1962), archaeologists have recognized the uniqueness of the funerary context because of its conscious and purposive elements. The artifact is not in the grave as a result of accident or stochastic processes, in most cases, but rather as a result of conscious and intentional action. The purposive element in funerary deposition eliminates one major source of "noise" with which archaeological analysis must usually deal. Funerary remains are not solely the result of purposive behavior, however, even excluding postdepositional processes.

Depositional pathways can usefully be subdivided into three categories: intentional deposition, coincidental deposition, and accidental deposition. Intentional deposition includes the whole range of mortuary behaviors that are conscious and purposive, such as the construction of a mortuary facility, corpse treatment, and the placement of objects within the grave. Coincidental depositions differ from intentional in that they are not the specific object or focus of the funerary treatment, even though they are a direct result of this behavior. A good example of this kind of deposition is the common practice of burying the dead in their normal daily clothing. As this clothing contains such elements as buttons or beads that would survive the forces of deposition and recovery, the elements would be identified as grave inclusions. Although such objects can be a valuable source of information, the meaning that they carry is different in kind from that of objects specifically placed in the grave for their symbolic content. Clearly, there is a gray area in this defined separation of intentional and coincidental deposition, yet the general distinction is important to a thorough understanding of past mortuary symbolism.

Accidental inclusions also may be highly informative, or they may represent only additional "noise" that must be filtered out of an analysis. Such inclusions might be midden debris in the vicinity of the grave that becomes incorporated; they may be microorganisms or insect larvae that have infiltrated the corpse prior to interment; or they may even be the cause of death, such as a musket ball or arrowhead lodged in the body. Each type of accidental inclusion could reveal useful information, be it the cause of death, exposure practices, season of death or even midden management. However, they are not elements that can be treated as purposive components of funerary behavior.

Despite the problems that may arise when attempting to categorize observed attributes of mortuary behavior with their specific depositional process, the recognition that distinct pathways of funerary deposition exist is essential. This is important, since the potential information content of an attribute will be determined by its depositional pathway. Furthermore, the specific manner in which an attribute came to be incorporated into the archaeological context will be an important consideration in assessing the comparability of attribute observations. Clearly, an analysis of mortuary symbolism would not be justified in giving equal weight to the observation of accidentally included rubbish in a grave and the observation of an intentionally positioned artifact or ornament. Similarly, it might, in some cases, be warranted to analyze intentional and coincidental inclusions separately for their particular information content.

In addition to these primary depositional processes, it is also necessary to consider the range of postdepositional processes that affect a mortuary deposit. Postdepositional processes may be natural or cultural in origin and may serve to obscure or distort patterning present in the archaeological remains. Natural postdepositional processes are well known to archaeologists. For example, organic remains such as soft body parts, leather, and cloth are usually not recovered, although on occasion they can be found (cf. Clark 1965). Similarly, the bones of infants and subadults are less likely to survive than those of adults (Gordon and Buikstra 1981). Natural processes may also remove evidence completely, through erosion or through the deep burial of sites beneath alluvium. Natural forces of this kind generally mask some or all of the organization present in the archaeological remains. Since these effects tend to be regular and relatively predictable in their result, they can, in most cases, be controlled in archaeological research. Other postdepositional processes may pose more serious problems. A wide range of natural processes, including cryoturbation, animal disturbance or water transport, may produce strongly patterned depositions that are noncultural in origin (cf. Wood and Johnson 1978). Clearly, patterning of this sort must be recognized and properly controlled before any meaningful analysis can be carried out. The fact that noncultural processes often produce highly patterned configurations within the archaeological context is often overlooked by archaeologists (see Sullivan 1978:193).

Postdepositional changes resulting from cultural factors may have an even more pronounced effect. Disturbance of a cultural origin may arise from the later activities of the same society or from completely different cultures, and they may be accidental or intentional. A common source of disturbance by the contemporary society occurs when graves are placed in close proximity to one another in a limited area, leading to the occasional destruction of earlier graves. The strictly limited areas of hallowed ground recognized in Medieval England, for example, led to a very rapid and even purposeful destruction of earlier graves, as illustrated in the famed grave digger's scene in *Hamlet* (Shakespeare 1948:647). Among cultures that employ collective mortuary facilities, such as the chambered tombs of Western Europe (Chapman 1981) or the charnel houses of Hopewell in North America (Brown 1979), each new interment may lead to a variety of disturbances of earlier interments. Finally, where a culture practiced multistaged burial programs, as in the Mississippian occurrences at the Spiro site (Brown 1971a), the evidence of original funerary treatment may be all but obliterated by later treatment. Postdepositional processes of this latter kind do more than simply mask aspects of the behavioral patterning, they also may add extraneous elements into the burial context and can cause a breakdown in the individual association of funerary treatments.

A second class of postdepositional processes that is of particular relevance to the study of mortuary variability is the disturbance of the archaeological context by later, unrelated cultures. Archaeological investigations, themselves, would fall into this category. In some cases such disturbance is accidental, as with the reuse of a particular location, which results in the destruction of the earlier remains. In other instances, we may observe the intentional searching out and pillaging of funerary remains for plunder. Such activities, made famous by ancient looting of the Egyptian pyramids (Ceram 1953), is probably more common in prehistory than generally recognized. There is good evidence at the Early Bronze Age cemetery of Mokrin, in Yugoslavia (Girić 1971), that later Sarmatian populations actively plundered the Bronze Age graves in search of buried gold ornaments (1971:195). Similarly, a number of Danish tumuli from the Bronze Age exhibit clear evidence of ancient grave robbery (Glob 1974). Postdepositional disturbances of the first kind, if accidental, usually will only mask patterning. Active grave plundering, however, introduces a strong systematic bias into the funerary sample, which is directed at a particular and important portion of the mortuary population. If unrecognized, the resulting bias could seriously distort the apparent degree of mortuary differentiation practiced by the past society.

This discussion has explored, in a preliminary way, how funerary remains come to reside in the archaeological context and the variety of changes that such remains may experience once in the archaeological context. This progression from human activity to archaeological recovery is summarized in Figure 2.1. To the extent that funerary behavior, which represents the generative source of the archaeological remains, is regular and patterned, the archaeological manifestations of these activities will retain a regular and patterned organization. The amount of this culturally produced organization is at its highest at the moment of deposition and decreases under the effects of postdepositional processes. Postdepositional processes, be they natural or cultural in origin, have the effect of obscuring portions of this organization, or in some cases of introducing additional spurious structure to the remains. The correct understanding and control for these depositional and postdepositional processes form the necessary starting conditions for an archaeological study of mortuary variability.

This discussion has centered on the formation of the archaeological record. In the next section, the structure and limitations inherent in the archaeological observation of funerary remains is considered.

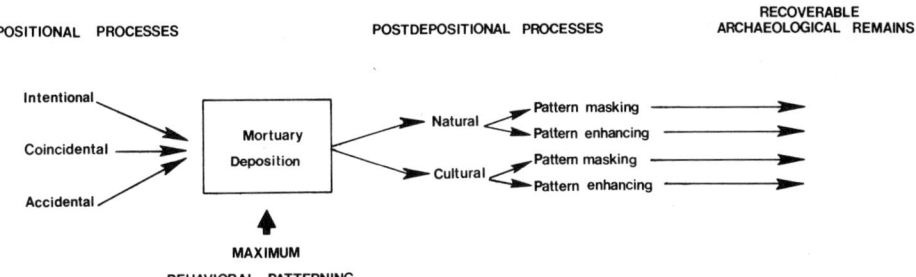

Figure 2.1 A flow diagram representing the processes intermediate between funerary activities and the archaeological recovery of mortuary traces.

Limitations in Detection and Recognition

Although the cultural organization of funerary activities may be highly organized, the archaeologist can observe only: (1) those aspects of the mortuary practice that produced physical changes within the funerary deposits; and (2) that subset of the above that survives the forces of deposition, preservation, and recovery. It has been stated that mortuary remains exist in their most organized state immediately after deposition, and, excluding those postdepositional processes that add spurious structure, it is possible to view the processes of deposition and recovery as a series of filters that progressively mask or eliminate much of the organization present in the original remains (Figure 2.2). The result is an accurate but incomplete representation of past funerary activities. This is the "sample within a sample" property of archaeological remains stressed by Clarke (1973:16). In practice, this means that the archaeologist must first determine what portion of the total funerary system is being observed and then determine the range of conclusions or inferences that can be drawn from the fraction that is observed. These decisions move the investigator from the realm of postdepositional theory and into the areas of retrieval and analytical theory (Clarke 1973:16–17).

At best, an investigator can make only a rough estimate of the completeness or representativeness of the recovered sample of funerary treatments. Inconsistencies between the size of the mortuary occurrence and the associated settlement, or abnormal demographic composition of the mortuary population, may provide an initial base for estimate. Another consideration is the differing probability for both the preservation and the discovery of various types of funerary treatment. Ethnographic accounts of burial in rivers and trees (cf. Ucko 1969) illustrate how varied these probabilities can be. In a similar way, the likelihood that differing disposal types would be correctly recognized as belonging to the same cultural entity must also be considered. This problem is far from trivial, particularly if the disposals are spa-

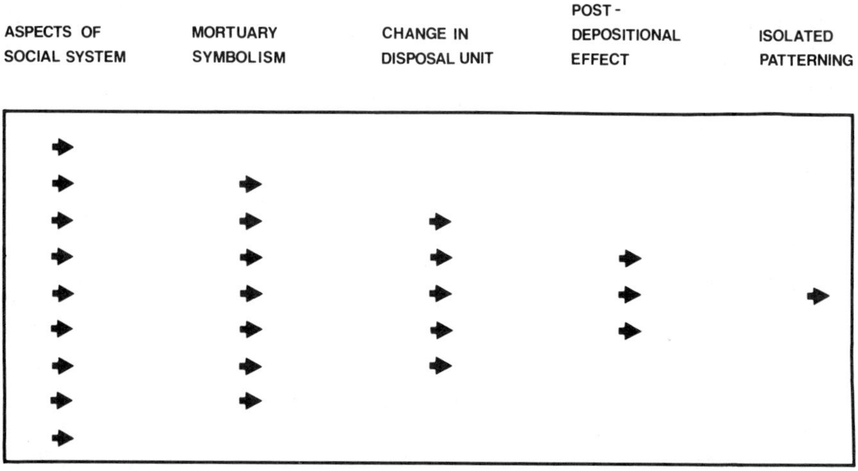

| ASPECTS OF SOCIAL SYSTEM | MORTUARY SYMBOLISM | CHANGE IN DISPOSAL UNIT | POST-DEPOSITIONAL EFFECT | ISOLATED PATTERNING |

Figure 2.2 Schematic representation of the filtering processes that operate to degrade detectable mortuary patterning.

tially discrete or if grave contents are markedly different. This second consideration touches on a more general point: it is not enough that organization be present in the archaeological remains, it must be correctly recognized by the investigator. As often as not, this identification of structure will prove the true limiting factor in a given analysis.

Although determining the fraction of funerary differentiation being observed is a crucial assessment, it is one that must often be open-ended and untestable. Determining the range of statements that can be made from those traces that are recovered, however, is fundamental to any archaeological analysis. Of equal importance to this consideration are the questions: What conclusions can be drawn, or importance assigned, from the observation of a selected attribute? What conclusions can be drawn, or significance assigned, from the absence of a selected attribute?

The use of negative evidence has a long and well-established history in traditional archaeological analysis, where the absence of a particular type of projectile point, or of ceramics, has been sufficient to establish the chronological placement and cultural identity of an archaeological assemblage (Taylor 1969:130). The increased realization of the importance and complexity of archaeological formation processes, however, requires that more attention be focused on the meaning and validity of such observations, and on the conditions or procedures that must accompany their legitimate use.

In a controlled laboratory experiment, the ambiguity associated with a negative result is rarely greater than that associated with a positive outcome. If, for simplicity, we assume a dichotomous variable X that takes either the value 0 or 1, the results $X = 0$ and $X = 1$ should be equally meaningful so far as the acceptance or rejection of a particular hypothesis is concerned. Both outcomes are susceptible to experimental error, spurious variation, or the influence of intervening variables. However, in nonexperimental situations, where less control is possible, the potential ambiguity of a negative outcome ($X = 0$) increases. In such cases, the result of a given measure of X may indicate (1) X is being truly observed and is taking the value of 0; or (2) the true value of X is 1, but for some reason observation of its true value is hindered. This is the problem that confronts the archaeologist, given his limited control over both sample and measurement.

Numerical taxonomists have attempted to control for the increased uncertainty through the use of weighting schemes or through coefficients that completely disregard negative matches. The Gower coefficient and the Jaccard coefficient are examples of these two respective approaches (Sneath and Sokal 1973:129–137). Although these techniques do control for the uncertainty associated with negative occurrences, complete disregard of all negative evidence means that considerable valuable information is being discarded (those cases where the true value of the variable is 0). When one considers that the archaeological record is already a fragmentary residual of the original behavioral manifestations, it seems unwise to further discard a large proportion of the remaining evidence by assuming that all negative evidence is unusable. This is particularly true for mortuary analysis, where one of the main approaches, formal analysis, actively depends on the definition of contrast sets that necessitate the integral use of a nonoccurrence category.

Binford has advocated a more formal approach, suggesting that independent classes of evidence be used as a control on negative evidence (Binford 1968:18). This method takes advantage of the great redundancy that exists within the archaeological record, resulting from the many different manifestations of any given behavior. It is through this redundancy that the archaeologist is able to reconstruct as much of past behavior as he does. Yet, in practice, it is not always possible to specify other classes of evidence to serve as controls that can themselves be observed unambiguously. In many cases, such sources of control for mortuary observation will reside in completely differing contexts. The use of independent classes of observation as control will permit the investigator to assess what portion of the mortuary behavior he is observing; but how does this affect the use of those attributes he does observe?

Although further obscuring the remaining patterning in the archaeological record at the time of recovery, the uncertainty associated with negative occurrences does not distort the pattern further. Although it removes some of the traces, what remains is still a partial and accurate reflection of past behaviors. For the analysis of funerary remains, the impact of this ambiguity, and the uncertainty deriving from the whole range of archaeological transformations, is to impose a kind of directional logic on inference. Since these forces tend to obscure evidence of behavioral patterning, one can infer elements of the behavior that have resulted in a positive representation. One cannot, however, necessarily infer anything from the negative representation of a trait. In practice, this means that a minimum statement can be made, such as "the society was organized into *at least* four distinct rank strata," but such a statement does not preclude the possibility that the society was organized into more than the four strata specified.

Despite these limitations, such statements are valuable. Furthermore, the ability to estimate the significance of negative occurrences may also benefit from other advances in theory. One outgrowth of Saxe's work is the proposition that the more complex and differentiated a society, the more redundant will be its material and symbolic expression of that complexity (compare with Saxe's Hypothesis 6 [1970:112]). If true, this would suggest that the more differentiated a society, the more likely that evidence of its complexity will be available for discovery. In most cases, however, the derivation of more precise statements concerning the societal organization of a past culture will require that other contexts be analyzed. The funerary context, although offering a unique view of past social and economic organization can not realistically be analyzed to the exclusion of other contexts (Sears 1961:229). Only when varied analyses are coupled and focused can an accurate and reasonably precise portrait of past societies be obtained.

In addition to the limitations on pattern identification resulting from depositional and postdepositional processes, further ambiguity can be introduced from two other sources: (1) diachronic variation; and (2) archaeological methodologies for pattern identification.

The effect of temporal processes on funerary manifestations is inescapable, since it is the cumulative nature of mortuary remains that permits social inference.

Despite earlier beliefs regarding special stability (Rivers 1914) or instability (Kroeber 1927) of a culture's funerary practices, it is now recognized that they, like any other aspect of a social system, alter in response to various stimuli and in conjunction with other components of the social system (Binford 1972:238). Temporal change may occur in a directional manner as the result of specific influences (direct or indirect), or it may occur more subtly as drift (Binford 1963b), with gradual stochastic variations in the behavioral norm. Temporal variation presents a serious problem to the analyst interested in a synchronic view of a culture's social organization.

Change in funerary behavior can be of two types. The categories of social differentiation given symbolic expression in the funerary treatment may change, or the categories may remain constant but their symbolic designation might alter. In a situation where fine-grained chronological control is available, the documentation of the dynamics of such change per se can prove of great interest. Where precise temporal control is not available, an additional and potentially dangerous source of systematic bias may be incorporated into the analysis. Incorrectly identified patterns produced by temporal change may result in the appearance of a spuriously large number of categories of funerary differentiation, or even in the appearance of parallel sets of funerary distinctions. In most cases, however, it will simply increase the level of "noise" against which the behavioral patterns must compete for recognition.

Although ambiguity inherent in the archaeological sample is a major factor limiting the recognition of significant patterning or constraint in funerary remains, the very methodologies employed for detecting this patterning may introduce further ambiguity. There seems to be an incongruity between the archaeological problem (the recognition of constraint and patterning from incomplete and fragmentary residues of past behavior) and the statistical methodologies used to recognize such patterning (see parallel argument in Hole 1980). The problem is that the level of discrimination that can be obtained from most statistical tests, given typical sample limitations, is often inadequate to detect the scale of patterning in the funerary remains. Brown noted this inconsistency when he contrasted the advantages of formal and statistical methodologies in mortuary analysis, concluding that, although statistical methodologies were necessary to handle random effects, only formal techniques could be used to analyze unique events or occurrences.

> Each strategy is suited to the discovery of certain types of behavior better than the other. In the statistical strategy, there is an interest in discovering basic relationships that have been obscured by measurement error and random deviation. In the other, there is an interest in discovering property spaces of status or other structural features formed by the intersections of dimensions represented by sets. Uniqueness is discoverable in the latter strategy but not in the former, and conversely, randomness can be systematically excluded in the statistical strategy but not the formal. (Brown 1971b:1-2)

A ready solution does not exist for this operational dilemma. It is possible that research in human perception or artificial intelligence may provide new techniques of pattern recognition with finer levels of discrimination, but their applicability to archaeological problems is not automatic.

To summarize this discussion of pattern detection and recognition in mortuary studies, it seems clear, not only that the archaeological record will manifest less organization than the cultural behavior that generated it, but also that less of this organization that is present will actually come to be detected and recognized. This is not a matter of technique or of the use of one methodology over another, rather it is a statement of the limitations inherent in archaeological pattern recognition. This limit of identification is an inherent result of archaeological formation and recovery processes and in turn requires the use of analytical theory (Clarke 1973:17) appropriate to such data.

The processes of conscious and incidental deposition, and random and systematic loss form the background against which the study of mortuary variability must be viewed. The success of any analysis depends ultimately on its ability to control and balance these basic processes.

3

Funerary Remains as Archaeological Evidence

Thus far, funerary activities have been considered as sociological and archaeological phenomena. From this review it appears that many of the shortcomings in the current body of theory relating to mortuary variability stem from a failure to integrate fully the behavioral regularities inherent to funerary practices with the formation and recovery processes that determine the archaeological manifestation of such behavior.

This chapter presents the outline for an archaeological theory of mortuary variability that attempts to provide this necessary integration. It consists of two basic parts: (1) a statement of the minimum constraints that can be assumed to structure mortuary variability; and (2) a catalog of the primary channels through which mortuary variability can be monitored in an archaeological context.

This framework does not itself constitute a technique for mortuary analysis. Rather, it is an attempt to provide an archaeologically valid basis for funerary investigations that is applicable to a wide range of methodologies. In addition, it provides a procedure by which ethnographic observations can be modeled as archaeological phenomena, and vice versa. The third section of this chapter addresses the problem of explanation and outlines a procedure for the generation and testing of social inferences based on observed mortuary variation. This is not suggested as the only method for such analysis, but it is one deriving from earlier dimensional studies of mortuary variability that seems to offer particular potential for archaeological application.

Regularities in Mortuary Variability

Fundamental to any archaeological analysis is the need for the investigator to know in advance what basic relationships will constrain the variation in the data and the significance that can be attached to this constraint. Typically, each class of archaeological phenomena has its own set of such a priori conventions from which the investigator can begin to understand the observed variability, be it the relative significance of artifacts found on a living surface as opposed to those encountered in midden or the relationship between gradual change in artifact expression and the passage of time. Such conventions serve to ascribe differential significance to particular classes of variability or suggest primary cause-and-effect relationships between human behavior and observed variability. Clarke (1972a:5–6) refers to these principles, in general, as *controlling models*. Most frequently these principles remain implicit, either because they are seen as being intuitively obvious or because their formal testing might be difficult or even impossible. These implicit principles constitute a primitive middle-range theory (Binford 1977:6). Funerary remains, as a distinct class of archaeological phenomenon, also have a set of such conventions, and it is the scope of these conventions that has drastically increased as a result of ethnographic studies of funerary behavior. What has yet to occur is the explicit statement of these implicit conventions such that their validity can be evaluated.

Chapter 1 summarized the major behavioral regularities inherent in practices for the disposal of the dead but noted that they must be transformed to reflect the forces of archaeological deposition and recovery before they could accurately be applied to archaeological research. In this section a series of basic principles that reflect the minimum level of constraint operating on mortuary variability in an archaeological context is offered. Along with each principle, the primary assumptions and circumstantial considerations that impinge on it are discussed. These considerations both circumscribe the situations in which the principle can and cannot be invoked, and highlight those aspects of the funerary record that are most susceptible to distortion from extraneous cultural or postdepositional factors.

The main value of these formulations is that they bring implicit mental models governing mortuary analysis into the open as an explicit and logical foundation upon which analysis can be based.

Principle 1. All societies employ some regular procedure or set of procedures for the disposal of the dead.

Given the assumption that all humans die, a society must confront the eventuality of death, both in terms of the implied social rupture (Malinowski 1955:53), and in terms of the disposal of the physical remains. The universality of this has been asserted by Bendann (1969:45). The kind of disposal practice varies greatly, from simple exposure (cf. the Kamchadal [Czaplicka 1914]) to complex, multistaged procedures (cf. Miles 1965). It has even been argued that the active approach to the disposal of the dead may constitute one marker of truly unique human behavior, as in the Mousterian (S. Binford 1968).

There are, however, several important qualifications to this principle. First, the remains of an individual who is not a member of the social group may receive radically different treatment from that given to a deceased member of the group. This is seen when portions of war victims are retained as trophies (cf. Caribs [Rouse 1948:560]) or when, among tribes practicing forms of cannibalism, the remains may be found with other village refuse.

Second, disposal among certain groups may refer more to the departure of the social individual than to the total elimination of the physical remains. A number of cases are known in which, after appropriate ritual and mourning, portions of the body are preserved in the living space of the community (cf. Papuans [Bendann 1969:54], Yanomamö [Chagnon 1968:50]). Finally, a group may exhibit a temporary lapse in its regular disposal practices as the result of catastrophic or mass death. The plague pits of Europe (Howe 1972) and the extensive massacre burials at Crow Creek (Zimmerman et al. 1980) are good examples of such a drastic, but temporary, shift in mortuary practices.

This principle delimits the basic range of mortuary phenomena as a result of human cultural behavior. Although its own integrative value is relatively low, it provides a necessary basis for the specification of further principles.

Principle 2. A mortuary population will exhibit demographic and physiological characteristics reflecting those of the living population.

That a living population, given known rates of fertility, mortality, and growth, will through time produce remains with a predictable age and sex structure is well established in the field of demography (cf. Coale and Demeny 1966; Petersen 1975). Furthermore, since there are fundamental regularities in the pattern of human mortality, such as the differential force of mortality among age groups (cf. Acsádi and Nemeskéri 1970), it is possible to detect major deviations in a sample population from the expectations for a natural population.

The strict validity of this principle rests on the assumption of complete preservation and recovery. That these assumptions are rarely, if ever, entirely satisfied reflects both stochastic effects operating on recovery and sample composition, and the systematic effects of preservation and differential cultural practices.

Clearly, distortion will be introduced into the sample if, for any reason, all individuals who die in a population are not preserved for archaeological recovery. Often this occurs through the differential loss of subadult versus adult remains (Angel 1969:434) as a result of postdepositional factors. It can also result from a number of culturally based factors, including those directly related to funerary practices, such as the differential treatment of a particular age or sex group, or as the result of other cultural processes not directly related to mortuary practices, such as the more frequent death of men away from the village or the discontinuous use of a particular disposal area. Finally, in the case of mortuary areas that are used for only relatively brief periods, short-term stochastic fluctuations in the level of age- or sex-specific mortality may be artificially emphasized at the expense of the underlying vital parameters of the population.

The importance of this principle is not simply that the archaeologist can estimate the vital parameters of an extinct society from a skeletal series, but that culturally produced anomalies in the skeletal population can be recognized from the demographic parameters. As such, it may be possible to identify types of differential mortuary treatment even if the specific remains of the treatment are not themselves observed.

Principle 3. Within a mortuary occurrence, each interment represents the systematic application of a series of prescriptive and proscriptive directives relevant to that individual.

Just as Principle 1 specifies a regular procedure for the disposal of the dead, Principle 3 asserts that the mortuary treatment accorded any given individual will be related systematically to the treatment received by other members of the society. As a result, the cumulative record formed as a cemetery occurrence will reflect the repetitive application of the culture's normative and differential practices for the disposal of the dead. This principle assumes that only a single set of directives, regardless of their complexity, is operating to produce the observed cumulative sample. The principle does not specify the rationale behind these rules, only that they are regularly applied and that they delimit the mortuary treatment practiced by the society.

Although the regular and repetitive nature of mortuary behavior is the characteristic that permits the archaeologist to infer elements of social differentiation from a funerary occurrence, a number of qualifications must temper such inferences. First, in any given mortuary occurrence the investigator may not observe the total range of the society's mortuary behavior. This frequently will be the case when particular classes of individuals are accorded radically different types of disposal such that they may not be discovered by the archaeologist or, if discovered, may not be recognized as part of the main mortuary manifestation (e.g., cremation versus inhumation, Ucko 1969).

Second, the effects of culture drift (Binford 1963b) may cause a gradual change in the disposal directives or the manner in which they are manifest. Such effects, in the absence of fine-grained chronological control, may produce an artificially enhanced appearance of complexity or even apparently parallel disposal rules. Finally, the degree to which idiosyncratic variation is permitted in the mortuary treatment can vary widely from one society to another. Variation of this kind will produce a background from which regular patterning must be identified and will determine the extent to which the archaeologist may infer the cultural directives structuring the mortuary occurrence. The degree to which such variation is permitted may itself be an interesting indicator of social consensus and control.

In addition to the main assertion of Principle 3, ethnographic studies suggest two further relationships, which can be expressed here as Corollaries 3a and 3b.

> *Corollary 3a.* The nature of the society will pattern and circumscribe the practices for the disposal of the dead.

This premise, formulated by Binford (1972:235), stresses the interdependence of the structure of the society and its mortuary practices. It serves to refine the basic assertion of Principle 3 by noting that the disposal directives do not vary independently of the cultural system in general. It does not presuppose a one-to-one relationship between a specific type of funerary behavior and particular types of societies, although it does not exclude the possibility of limited regularities of this kind.

> *Corollary 3b.* The specific treatment accorded an individual in death will be consistent with that individual's social position in life.

Whereas Corollary 3a added greater resolution to the relationship between the disposal directives and the society as a whole, Corollary 3b, deriving from the work of Saxe (1970), further specifies the constraints affecting the decision process by which individuals are differentiated through the disposal directives. The qualification of this premise rests in the unidirectional utility of the term *consistent*. Although the premise asserts that observed differences will be consistent with actual social differences in life, it does not imply that all differences recognized in life will be given symbolic recognition through mortuary differentiation, nor that any particular living distinction need necessarily be symbolized in an archaeologically observable form. Similarly, the circumstances surrounding the individual's death may be perceived among some groups as an overriding factor in determining the individual's mortuary treatment (e.g., treatment of a man killed in battle among the Cheyenne [Grinnell 1923:163]). In these cases, the particular circumstances of death are seen as completely outweighing other social considerations in determining the treatment that the individual will receive.

To summarize, Principle 3 and its corollaries specify a relationship between (1) archaeological remains and a society's procedure for the disposal of the dead; (2) the general organization of the society and its particular set of mortuary procedures; and (3) the specific mortuary treatment provided an individual and his or her social standing in life. These relationships link the funerary remains as archaeological phenomena and the organizational aspects of the extinct society. They also serve to emphasize the interdependence of the various components within the sociocultural system.

Principle 4. Elements combined within a burial context will have been contemporary in the living society at the time of interment (Worsaae's Law).

This final principle—that elements combined in a single disposal unit will have been contemporary—was first formulated by the Danish prehistorian Jens Jakob Assmussen Worsaae in 1843 (Rowe 1962). It is based on the assumptions (1) that burial is a single, relatively brief event; and (2) that a burial represents a closed context. Within the range of these two assumptions, the principle is a truism, since to have been included with the grave, the elements must have been in existence at the same time. The question of heirlooms becomes a moot point, since, regardless of the actual time or location of manufacture, the item remained available for inclusion until the time of its deposition.

Yet, even given these assumptions, it is not possible to assert the converse of this proposition—that is, that elements not found in combination within a single disposal unit will have existed at different times. This is due to the nonchronological constraints that affect the distribution of elements in a mortuary context following from Principle 3. It is for this reason that studies concerned with the formulation of chronologies based on artifact succession will be more successful in less consciously contrived archaeological settings, such as settlement site refuse, where associations may be less intentionally structured.

There are many situations, however, where the assumptions necessary for the validity of this principle are not met, specifically those where a single disposal unit (or structure), such as a chambered tomb or a charnel house, is employed for the cumulative disposal of the dead or where the burial is not a closed context, due to either natural postdepositional processes or to cultural practices where multistaged funerary treatment result in the exhumation and reburial of the funerary remains. In the latter case, it is not possible to assert this principle. In the former, it may be possible to establish a coarser association by specifying the use-life of the disposal unit as the critical parameter and with the observed artifacts or elements established as co-occurring within the particular span of time. The value of such determinations is limited and in most cases will not provide information that could not be established more reliably from other archaeological sources.

These four principles, along with their concomitants are summarized in Table 3.1. They are viewed as reflecting the minimum statements of the constraints that structure human mortuary behavior as viewed in the archaeological context. As such, they are offered as a foundation for an archaeological theory of mortuary variability that is applicable to a broad range of funerary phenomena. No particular claims of originality or finality are made for these premises. All derive from the current body of archaeological theory or from related fields, and each can be seen lurking, often implicitly, in most archaeological studies of mortuary remains.

The importance of these formulations is that by specifying these statements of

TABLE 3.1

Constraints on Mortuary Variability

Principle 1: All societies employ some regular procedure or set of procedures for the disposal of the dead.
    Assumption: All humans die.
    Considerations: The treatment of foreign dead may differ from that of members of the society.

        Disposal may refer more to symbolic disposal than to the complete elimination of the physical remains from the community's life space.

        Catastrophic death may cause a lapse in the normal disposal practices of a society.

Principle 2: A mortuary population will exhibit demographic and physiological characteristics reflecting those of the living population.
    Assumption: Complete preservation and recovery of mortuary remains.
    Considerations: Specific cultural practices may systematically distort the demographic composition of a mortuary population.

        Discontinuous use of a cemetery will underrepresent the size of the living population.

        Mortuary sites used over a relatively brief period of time may emphasize short-term fluctuations at the expense of the underlying demographic parameters.

Principle 3: Within a mortuary occurrence, each interment represents the systematic application of a series of prescriptive and proscriptive directives relevant to that individual.
    3a: The nature of the society will pattern and circumscribe the practices for the disposal of the dead.
    3b: The specific treatment accorded an individual in death will be consistent with that individual's social position in life.
    Assumption: A single set of cultural directives control the interment characteristics.
    Considerations: The total range of cultural directives relating to the disposal of various classes of individuals in any given mortuary occurrence may not be observed.

        Drift may produce gradual change in disposal directives or in their manifestation.

        The degree of idiosyncratic variation permitted in the disposal practices may vary widely from society to society.

Principle 4: Elements combined within a burial context will have been contemporary in the living society at the time of interment (Worsaae's Law).
    Assumptions: Burial is a single, brief event.

        Burial represents a closed context.
    Consideration: The converse cannot necessarily be asserted because of nonchronological constraints on element occurrence.

constraint they become accessible to scrutiny, challenge, and modification. Furthermore, they provide a basis for the application of formal or statistical methodologies, lessening the need for many of the ad hoc assumptions that hamper many recent applications. Finally, they provide a logical starting point for the search for further regularities in human funerary behavior. Having outlined the constraints structuring mortuary variability in an archaeological context, we next must specify the specific channels through which variability is manifest in the archaeological record.

Channels of Mortuary Variability and Primary Referents

The specification of an archaeological theory of mortuary variability requires, not only that the constraints on variability be identified, but also that the channels through which variability will be expressed in an archaeological context be recognized. Various authors (cf. Binford 1972; Sprague 1968) have classified the primary categories of mortuary observation in different ways. Table 3.2 summarizes these

TABLE 3.2

Classes of Archaeologically Visible Mortuary Variation

General category	Major classes
Biological	Demographic
	Genetic
	Dietary
	Pathologic
Preparation and treatment	Disposal type
	Disposal program
Mortuary facility	Variety of receptacle
	Shape and dimensions
	Raw material(s)
	Orientation
Furnishings	Quantity
	Quality
	Variety
	Source
Locational	Macro—location of disposal area
	Meso—location within disposal area
	Micro—location within the disposal facility
Environmental	Entomological
	Botanical
	Faunal

as six major categories of observation that reflect archaeologically visible evidence of funerary practices.

The first category reflects observations that are based on the physical characteristics of the skeletal remains themselves. The most commonly recognized attributes, after the simple counting of individuals, are age and sex. These characteristics, when compiled for an entire skeletal series, can be employed to estimate the demographic characteristics of the past population (Acsádi and Nemeskéri 1970). Less obvious are those genetically based measures of variation within the skeletal population, such as blood grouping (Farkas 1970; Lengyel 1972) for direct evaluation of genetic affinity or the analysis of the distribution of metric or discrete traits as a similar means of discovering genetically based subdivisions (cf. Jantz 1973; Lane and Sublett 1972). Finally, observations of skeletal pathology can produce crucial information concerning the stress and living conditions experienced by the population as a whole (Angel 1969) or differences in diet and living conditions between subgroups within a single population (cf. Buikstra 1976). Such determinations can provide a valuable and independent means for testing propositions concerning social ranking and descent groupings within a mortuary population.

A related set of variables reflect the preparation and treatment of the corpse for interment. Most notable are disposal type (cremation, inhumation, etc.), posture (if articulated) or pattern of bone association (if disarticulated), and the number of individuals represented in the disposal receptacle. Detailed observation can also reveal the existence of complex or multistaged disposal programs, particularly aspects of preinterment treatment, such as defleshing, ritual mutilation, exposure, partial interment, and exhumation or reburial. Observations of this type can be of particular importance to the determination of the relative expenditure of energy in the burial programs.

The third category summarizes the observations made concerning the mortuary facility employed in disposal, although the range of possible observations will vary with the type of facility used. In the case of simple earthen graves, these observations might include its shape, dimensions, orientation, depth, and the presence of any structural enhancements, such as coverings or linings. In the case of more elaborate structures, observations on design, construction, source of raw materials, and stylistic variations may also be possible. If the disposal receptacle is of a collective type, it may also be possible to assess its use-life. This category of observations, like those reflecting corpse preparation, will be of particular importance in testing for the existence of discrete levels of energy expenditure.

The category of grave furnishings needs little annotation, and typically will include observations on the variety of furnishings, their quantity, quality, and source. As was discussed in Chapter 2, it may also be useful to distinguish intentional grave inclusions, such as implements and furnishings, from incidental inclusions, such as clothing ornamentation.

Locational variability in the occurrence of mortuary attributes is relevant on a number of levels. Spatial attributes may be evaluated on the macrolevel by the location of the disposal area relative to other socially defined spaces or to other disposal areas. On the mesoscale, observed spatial variation within the confines of a single disposal area may be evaluated, while on the microscale, the positional relationships within a single disposal unit can be evaluated. This "Chinese box" property of spatial attributes (see Clarke 1972b:803) makes them an especially powerful analytical tool, particularly when spatial distribution is employed as a dependent variable.

The final category of mortuary observation includes those classes of data that give an indication of the environmental conditions at the time of burial, particularly the season of death or interment. Most of these observations fall into the category of accidental grave inclusions. Although many types of indicators may be recovered through careful excavation, the two most common are the presence of pollen or of insects or insect larvae (cf. Ubelaker and Willey 1978). One could also include observations made on the wood or other materials recovered from the disposal facility. Although observations of this kind are frequently unrelated to the funerary ritual itself, they can provide considerable insight into the details of the society's mortuary behavior.

This classification represents only one way of dividing the archaeologically visible sources of variation associated with mortuary remains. Regardless of the particular summary classification employed, these sets of attributes form the irreducible basis for any archaeological analysis of funerary remains, be it for social reconstruction, seriation, or population studies.

Although this classification has summarized the means through which variation is manifest in the archaeological context, the potential information content of an attribute is not limited to its own unique physical properties; but also includes the total configuration of other attributes relative to it. Taylor has termed these associated characteristics *affinities*, describing them in the following way: "Archaeological data, then, consists of the material result of cultural behavior, and the affinities—quantitative, qualitative, spatial, etc.—which can be found to exist among them, and between them and the natural environment" (Taylor 1969:112). Taylor stresses the general importance of affinities in archaeological research, but they are particularly crucial in the study of mortuary remains, where interest is not so much in the occurrence of a single attribute but rather in the manner in which the occurrence of various attributes is structured to produce grammatical mortuary statements. Unfortunately, even with relatively small samples and with unlimited computer time, the examination of all possible affinities for all observed attributes would pose an overwhelming task. Fortunately, such a global search of affinities is not necessary, since the constraint on mortuary variability described in the section above on regularities in mortuary variability provides a degree of a priori knowledge concerning the overall organization of variables within a mortuary context. It is, therefore, possible to specify a small set of regularly occurring attributes that can be used as referents to monitor potentially significant attribute configurations. These referents to be effective must be primary and generalizable, such that they can be used to describe critical aspects of observed mortuary patterning. In addition, they should be attributes that are relevant to the social differentiation being expressed through the mortuary ritual.

For this purpose the attributes of age and sex are unique in that they (1) are recognized universally as traits by which living societies ascribe statuses (Linton 1936:115); (2) are recognized as primary axes of mortuary differentiation (cf. Goody 1962; Hertz 1960); and (3) are aspects that can accurately and independently be determined from the archaeological remains. Furthermore, because of the constraint on mortuary variability expressed in Principle 3, patterns of differentiation observed relative to these two axes in the funerary sample will be consistent with similar distinctions recognized in the living society. Constraint on an attribute's distribution relative to these two axes can be summarized by means of a contingency table (Figure 3.1). These relationships will provide a view of the most basic level of systematic differentiation recognized in the mortuary ritual.

Although not so integrally linked with the social distinction symbolized as age and sex, the partitioning of space is one of the most fundamental forms of symbolic differentiation employed by human groups. Its frequent and varied use is well established in social anthropology (cf. Lévi-Strauss 1963:132) and archaeology (cf. Goldstein 1976). Like age and sex, it is a primary referent against which the occurrence of other elements can be evaluated and tested. A wide variety of models and techniques are available to aid in the analysis and interpretation of spatial

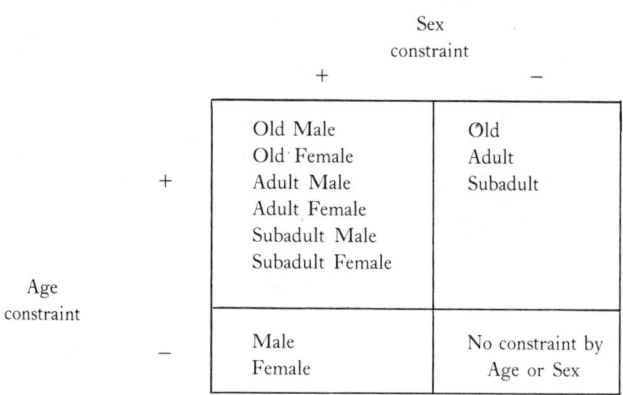

Figure 3.1. Contingency table representing categories of culturally defined age and sex differentiation that potentially can be identified from funerary evidence.

arrangement and patterning (cf. Chorley and Haggett 1967; Clarke 1977; Hodder and Orton 1976; Whallon 1973). Also like the referents of age and sex, spatial location is an attribute that is readily observable and measurable in the archaeological context.

Similar to the patterns of spatial distribution are the formal properties of an attribute's distribution, such as its pervasiveness within the mortuary population and its frequency distribution. The relative pervasiveness of an attribute may suggest critical elements affecting its occurrence. A trait occurring in approximately half of the observed burial units may symbolize a basic, binary division, as would be the case if moiety distinctions were symbolized by a society; whereas an attribute occurring in only a few graves might reflect a more restricted social status, such as the symbol of prominent status or the constrained distribution of an exotic trade commodity. Of course, the measure of simple pervasiveness will not indicate in an unambiguous manner the type of social distinction symbolized through an attribute's occurrence. This must be arrived at through the testing of such observed patterns against expected configurations modeling differing varieties of social and economic structures. Pervasiveness will be consistent with certain types of constraint while tending to be inconsistent with others.

In a similar manner, the frequency distribution of an attribute can provide insight into its use and symbolic meaning. What are the descriptive parameters of the attribute's distribution? Does it approximate a normal or other unimodal curve, or is it discontinuous? As in the case of pervasiveness, the nature of these distributions will be suggestive of certain varieties of constraint. Most important among these are the distinctions between uniform distributions with low variances, unimodal distributions, and discontinuous distributions. These distributions can be tested against those generated from models of particular social processes, as has been done in the archaeological study of exchange systems (cf. Renfrew 1977).

Through the use of these primary referents, the behavior of any attribute in a mortuary occurrence can be monitored and described (Figure 3.2). When observations are then integrated, it is possible to (1) describe the symbolic function of a large proportion of the attributes employed in the funerary treatment; and (2) make inferences concerning the structure and complexity of the system of differentiation acting on the mortuary behavior.

Just as it is possible to describe mortuary variability in the archaeological context with these referents, they can also be used to describe any ethnographically known category of social differentiation. One can specify the age and sex restriction on membership, the relative pervasiveness of membership within the population, and the aspects of funerary treatment that serve to symbolize membership in the social unit. In other words, elements of social organization can be described in terms that are relevant to potential archaeological observation. This translation of ethnographic phenomena into an archaeological form can greatly aid in the process of archaeologi-

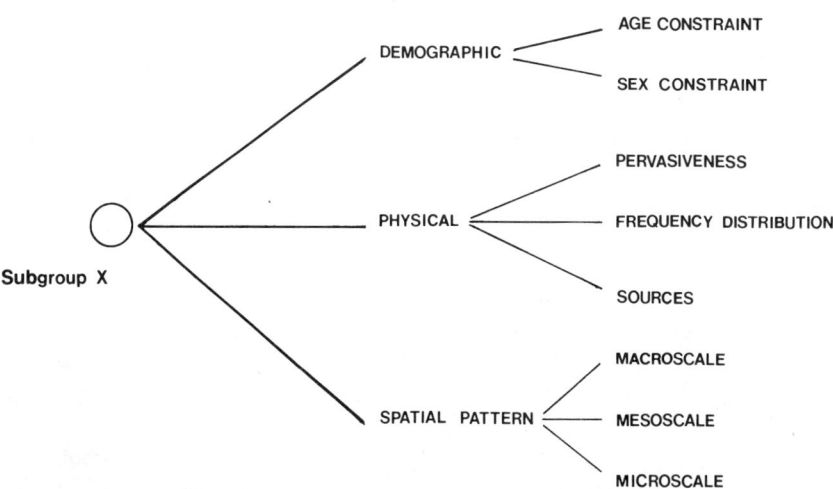

Figure 3.2. A schematic representation of a hypothetical category of mortuary differentiation, broken down into its constituent referent dimensions.

cal explanation of mortuary variability. Since the referent axes are generalizable, it is also possible to work in reverse—that is, to present archaeologically observed patterns of mortuary differentiation as a description of units of social organization. Through this type of converse mapping, moving from an archaeological expression to model its generative social form, archaeology may finally be able to document hereto unknown types of social differentiation or institutions that are not precedented in the ethnographic literature.

Interpretation and Explanation in Mortuary Analysis

The preceding two sections have outlined a formal structure for the archaeological study of mortuary variability that places the behavioral regularities associated with the funerary activities in an archaeological context. Using this framework it is possible to describe variability in a manner that is relevant to the process of explanation, but this new description does not itself constitute an explanation. The process of explanation requires two additional components: (1) correlates (Schiffer 1976), relating particular types of variability to specific varieties of social behavior; and (2) the modeling of social features as archaeological phenomena.

The search for interpretive correlates for mortuary variability has been an active line of archaeological research, although it has proceeded in a hit-or-miss manner without the benefit of a body of integrative theory. The concept of energy expenditure as an indicator of social rank differentiation (Binford 1972; Tainter 1977) is a good example of such a behavioral correlate. From this correlate, which asserts that discrete levels of energy expenditure observed in a mortuary occurrence will reflect the existence of corresponding vertical differentiation in the living society, it is possible to ascribe specific meaning to particular aspects of patterning observed in a funerary occurrence. A second widely used correlate is that of a distribution pyramid of treatments or symbols (cf. Braun 1979; Peebles and Kus 1977) in which positions of successively higher social importance are held by a progressively smaller number of individuals.

Correlates of this kind are essential for the interpretation of mortuary variability. Unlike the formal principles that describe basic constraints affecting mortuary patterning, these correlates permit specific meaning to be attached to particular patterns of variability. Whereas the principles provide a description of the variability, the correlates can be employed to explain variability. As such, they behave more like theorems in an axiomatic system. They can be deduced as hypotheses and tested. Once tested, they can be incorporated into analysis as theorems in a formal sense.

Crucial to the formulation and use of correlates is the process of testing. A hypothesized correlate can be accepted only when it has been adequately tested, and this testing must be carried out in a manner relevant to mortuary phenomena in an archaeological context. If a hypothesized relationship is derived from ethnographic testing, it must be demonstrated that the relationship will still pertain after transformation into the archaeological context. In many cases, as discussed in Chapter 2, this will necessitate a restatement of the correlates to reflect the directional constraints on inference imposed by archaeological formation processes, allowing definitive statements only in instances of positive representation. Goldstein (1976) provides an excellent example of the application of directional logic in her anthropological study of spatial constraint in funerary behavior.

The ability to model categories of social differentiation as archaeological phenomena is important not only for testing correlates but also as a means of interpreting observed mortuary patterning. In the discussion of primary referents of mortuary variability, it was noted that each referent could be generalized; that is, that each was capable of describing patterns of mortuary or social differentiation. Just as one could describe a differential subset of a mortuary population in terms of its demographic, spatial, and distributional properties, one could equally describe any social feature using the same parameters. Such a representation of social differentia amounts to a model of the feature's potential archaeological representation.

This model is, of course, an idealization of the archaeological representation, yet it has two important properties. First, it models social entities in archaeologically relevant terms. Second, the representation is structural in the sense that it produces an expected configuration of variables. This modeling process allows for a best-fit type of matching to be employed, comparing observed configurations of archaeological attributes with the expected configurations for various social distinctions. (For a parallel procedure in historic archaeology, see South 1977.) Such comparisons permit the recognition of many social distinctions that might be symbolically differentiated in the funerary rites of a past society. The comparison of observed with expected configurations can be made more specific by incorporating the behavioral correlates already mentioned into the description of the expected configuration.

The use of the modeling procedure can be illustrated by means of several examples from the archaeological literature. Suppose a society differentiated individuals in death on the basis of moiety membership. Such a distinction if observed in an archaeological context would produce a pattern with a number of predictable characteristics, such as:

1. The mortuary occurrences would be divided into two groups of approximately equal size.
2. The demographic composition of the resulting two groups would be similar to that of the population as a whole.
3. A number of other classes of mortuary distinction would crosscut the group division (i.e., parallel occurrence of other social distinctions in both divisions).

Also, Brown (personal communication, 1980) has suggested as a correlate that horizontal social distinctions will be expressed through attributes of relatively equal energy intensity. Using this correlate, we can predict that the means of symbolically designating these two groups will be through nonvaluable distinctions, such as

TABLE 3.3

Comparison of Mortuary Differentiation at Galley Pond Mound with Expectations for Moiety Representation in a Mortuary Occurrence

Expected funerary attributes	Observed attributes at Galley Pond Mound[a]
1. Division of the population into two groups of equal size.	Funerary population divided into two groups of 17 interments each.
2. No selection by age or sex in group membership.	Males and females in about equal number in two groups (few subadults in total mortuary manifestation).
3. Designation of groups through nonvaluable distinction(s).	Division symbolized through the orientation of interment, either north–south or east–west.
4. Other classes of mortuary distinction crosscutting this division.	Differential interment modes and artifact inclusions crosscut orientation groups.

[a] Detail of observation from Galley Pond Mound from Binford (1964).

TABLE 3.4

Expectations for Superordinate and Subordinate Dimensions of Mortuary Differentiation in a Ranked Society[a]

Superordinate Dimension
1. Some infants, some children, and some adults will be found in every scale category except the paramount category.
2. The apical class will contain only adults, and probably only adult males.
3. Some infants and children will have greater amounts of energy expended in their mortuary ritual than some adults, some women more energy expended in their treatment than some men.
4. The numbers of burials in each scale category will markedly decrease as one goes higher on the scale, thereby reflecting the rank pyramid.

Subordinate Dimension
1. As the chronological age of the individual buried increases, so will the energy expended in that individual's burial.
2. Children and infants will have some items as grave goods that will not be shared by adults; women will have some items as grave goods not shared by men.
3. Energy expended in the lowest level of the superordinate dimension will be greater than that expended in the highest level of the subordinate dimension.
4. The number of individuals in each scale category of the subordinate dimension should reflect the age and sex pyramid of the population through time.

[a] After Peebles and Kus (1977).

varying grave orientation, posture, or spatial separation. In this manner, we have a relatively detailed structural description of the attributes symbolizing moiety membership in a mortuary context.

This description of horizontal differentiation fits well with one class of mortuary differentiation observed by Binford (1964) at Galley Pond Mound. Table 3.3 compares the expected configuration of attributes that would result from the designation of moiety membership in the funerary ritual with the actual configuration of burial attributes observed by Binford.

A second example of this modeling activity can be found in the study of social ranking at Moundville in which Peebles and Kus (1977) specify the expected group size, demographic characteristics, and distribution of other attributes that should indicate the existence of a system of hereditary social ranking. They define two distinct dimensions of mortuary differentiation, a superordinate dimension and a subordinate dimension, which they assert should be observed in the mortuary remains of a rank society, and they specify the expected properties of each in terms of archaeologically observable attributes (Table 3.4). Using these predictions they were able to determine those aspects of Moundville's mortuary variability that were the result of institutionalized social ranking, as opposed to other forms of mortuary differentiation. In this example, as with the first, the success of the analysis is related directly to the specificity of the generated expectations and their suitability for testing with archaeological evidence.

A third example of this dimensional approach is found in Braun's (1979) analysis of hereditary ranking in Illinois Hopewell burial practices. Braun specifies three expectations concerning the symbolic designation of hereditary ranking in a mortuary context:

> (1) There will exist one or more qualitative attributes of burial treatment, including burial location, processing and the presence of specific grave accompaniments, which can be interpreted as symbols of authority and of the activities and prerogatives of positions of authority within a given society. (2) These attributes will be redundant within the mortuary program. That is they will covary or be mutually highly associated within the mortuary program, thereby defining a distinct dimension of variability in burial treatments. (3) This dimension will consist of qualitative distinctions between individual mortuary rites which cross-cut distinctions of individual age, sex, and personal ability, and possibly distinctions of segmentary differentiation as well. (Braun 1979:67)

Although these predictions are more concerned with the configuration of burial attributes than with predicting the size and demographic composition of a hereditarily ranked group, they do illustrate, again, how social differentiation can be modeled so as to provide archaeologically relevant expectations for observation in a funerary context. It also illustrates how the pattern of attributes, and not the presence of any particular attribute, constitutes the crucial test for the existence of any specific type of social distinction.

As can be seen from these examples, the modeling procedure need not be complex, but it should account for two aspects of mortuary patterning:

1. It must predict the values of the referent variables of age, sex, frequency, and, where possible, spatial arrangement.
2. It must predict, using behavioral correlates, the structural configuration of other attributes that will serve to mark the distinction within the mortuary population.

The advantage of working with a predicted structural arrangement of variability is that it is unnecessary to determine in advance which particular attribute or set of attributes will function symbolically in a given mortuary occurrence. Thus, Peebles and Kus (1977:431) can state that they expect a *class* of artifacts exhibiting certain defined characteristics to be distributed in a predicted manner and to isolate a subset of the mortuary population with specific parameters. Through the use of this formal modeling process and behavioral correlates, it is possible to test for potentially any type of social distinction that may be differentiated in a funerary occurrence.

The general approach to social analysis proposed here (and used in the archaeological case studies that follow) is dimensional, in that it focuses on the way in which attributes of funerary treatment partition the mortuary population into identifiable subsets. As such, it represents an outgrowth of the formal approaches advocated by Brown (1971a) and Saxe (1970). Analysis proceeds through four ordered stages.

1. A search for culturally generated constraint or patterning in the distribution of funerary attributes.
2. The description of each differentiated subset of the funerary population in terms of the referent dimensions of age, sex, frequency, and spatial distribution.
3. The classification of each differentiated subset into general types of mortuary distinction—vertical, horizontal, and special status differentiation—using the referent dimensions and behavioral correlates.
4. The interpretation of each differentiated unit of the mortuary population, using behavioral correlates and appropriate models of social distinctions.

When these four steps are carried out, and all possible identifications have been made, the interrelationship of variously differentiated dimensions can be analyzed, residuals identified, and social inferences made.

Inelegant as it may seem, this procedure for the social analysis of funerary remains makes maximum use of the a priori knowledge of mortuary variability and of the isomorphisms existing between funerary and social differentiation. In addition, it allows for the recognition and testing of a wide range of behavioral distinctions that may appear in the funerary context.

The degree to which the variability in a given occurrence can be explained will depend, of course, on a number of factors beyond the control of this (or any) methodology, such as the level of idiosyncratic variation present in the funerary activities and the nature of the symbols used to designate social distinction. Yet, it does provide a procedure through which relatively precise statements concerning past societal organization can be formulated and tested.

This chapter has drawn upon previous studies of mortuary variability and considerations of archaeological formation and recovery processes in an effort to formulate an integrated framework for the archaeological study of mortuary variability. This framework provides a starting point for analysis, applying the a priori knowledge necessary for the formulation of research questions and for the selection of methodologies and analytical techniques that are most applicable to these research questions. Furthermore, it offers the potential not only to recognize known forms of social distinction but also to discover entirely new varieties of social differentiation for which ethnographic precedent may not exist. The value of this framework and the approach for the social analysis of funerary remains that it suggests must be determined ultimately by its usefulness in substantive archaeological research. The controlled archaeological investigations presented in the extended case study that follows offer a preliminary test of the framework and its explanatory procedures.

4

The Analysis of Mortuary Variability: Controlled Experiments

A major deficiency in the existing archaeological theory of mortuary variability has been the failure to test its propositions using archaeological data. In the second portion of this study, a series of controlled experiments using archaeological data is carried out to provide a preliminary test of the proposed framework for mortuary analysis. This chapter lays the groundwork for these experiments by documenting in successive sections the experimental design, the archaeological samples, the typology, and the analytical methods employed.

Experimental Design

This study is designed to consider three distinct aspects of mortuary variability in an archaeological context: (1) mortuary differentiation as an expression of social distinctions in the living society; (2) variation in a society's funerary treatment through time; and (3) the expression of ethnic distinction through mortuary practices.

To investigate these aspects of mortuary variability, it was necessary to establish an independent means for assessing the inferences drawn from archaeological analysis. This control is provided by the sample sites selected for analysis. The archaeological samples are drawn from a series of cemeteries produced by cultures for which the ethnic identity and social organization are documented from ethnohistoric and ethnographic sources. In this way, the ethnographic literature provides an independent check on the conclusions derived from archaeological analysis. The sample is further structured to include sites produced by the same culture but at slightly different times, as well as contemporary sites affiliated with distinct ethnic cultures. This configuration allows for controlled comparisons across both temporal and ethnic boundaries.

A total of six sites are included in the study. These sites were produced by the Pawnee, Omaha, and Arikara tribes in the late eighteenth and early nineteenth centuries and are located in the present-day states of Nebraska and South Dakota in the United States. The full documentation of the sites is presented in the section on the archaeological samples.

The analyses follow the methodology outlined in Chapter 3. After a consideration of the postdepositional and recovery factors that influence the observed archaeological samples, the basic constraint operating in each sample is evaluated, analyzing funerary treatment and artifact occurrence against the referents of age, sex, spatial distribution, and frequency. Multivariate techniques are employed to monitor more complex attribute interaction, with these results again being evaluated against the referent attributes. Once this procedure has been completed, the patterns of formal differentiation and artifact-based differentiation are integrated, and the isolated patterning classified (where possible) into vertical, horizontal, or special status distinctions. At this point the specific investigation of structural differentiation, temporal change, and ethnic distinctions can be addressed.

Site Descriptions and Sample Documentation

In addition to the considerations of sample selection discussed in the previous section, the choice of sample sites was constrained by two additional factors: (1) the need to select sites that were as close to contemporary as possible, to minimize diachronic distortion; and (2) the need to select sites of sufficient size and completeness to permit statistical analysis. In addition, selection was limited to those sites in which excavation had been sufficiently controlled to permit reliable analysis.

These criteria were best met by the Arikara sites, where numerous large, well-excavated cemeteries have been recovered by salvage projects connected with reservoir construction on the Missouri River in South Dakota. Of these, two were selected for analysis: the Larson site (39WW2) and the Leavenworth site (39CO9). The control on both of these excavations was generally good, and the extensive location of graves was enhanced by the use of heavy earth-moving equipment.

For the Pawnee, three sites met the sample requirements: the Clarks site (25PK1), the Linwood site (25BU1), and the Barcal site (25BU4). Although these sites are smaller than the Arikara cemeteries and have been less extensively explored, they are potentially useful in monitoring temporal change in funerary practices given their near contiguous time spans and their association with the same band division of the Pawnee.

The choice of comparable Omaha sites was difficult. Excluding isolated grave finds and the possible Omaha manifestation at the Blood Run site (Harvey 1971) and the Stanton site (Gunnerson n.d.), the only documented Omaha cemeteries excavated in recent times are the two burial areas associated with the historic Omaha settlement, Tonwontonga (the Big Village), known as the Ryan site (25DK2), and an unnamed site (25DK10). These two related sites were excavated in 1939 and 1940, respectively, and were combined to form the Omaha sample.

These sites comprise the sample on which the present analysis is based. Before describing the individual sites in more detail, it is necessary to consider the relevant effects of postdepositional processes and recovery techniques on these archaeological samples.

Postdepositional Effects

Postdepositional processes of both cultural and natural origin have affected the observed archaeological remains in the site sample. Natural postdepositional effects are relatively limited, beyond the expected decay of most perishable remains, given the undisturbed context of the sites and their relatively short time in the archaeological context (a maximum of 230 years). One further source of natural disturbance is rodent activity. Graves were frequently infested with rodents attracted to the more loosely packed earth. Rodent burrowing of this kind can distort the internal positioning of bones and artifacts, and occasionally may remove objects from association by bringing them to the surface. Rodent disturbance is a constant possibility in all graves, but only severe cases of disturbance can be recognized, given the limited documentation available for several of the test samples.

Postdepositional effects of cultural origin have resulted from the partial or total destruction of earlier graves by later interments (particularly a problem at the two Arikara sites) or the looting of graves by later inhabitants of the area. No evidence for systematic selection is observed among the graves destroyed by either activity, and, as such, it is unlikely that the loss of these cases from the sample will seriously distort the overall pattern of mortuary differentiation in the sample sites.

Graves that have been seriously disturbed by postdepositional factors have been excluded from the archaeological sample. This exclusion accounts in part for the discrepancy between the number of graves recovered from each cemetery and the number of graves used in the analysis.

Recovery Considerations

Although the specific excavation and recovery techniques employed at each site will be discussed later, certain more general considerations of recovery bias will be presented here.

A question of primary importance regarding the documentation of each site is how complete was recovery—that is, what proportion of the existing graves were actually found during excavation? In all of these excavations, entire block areas were exposed in an effort to locate graves and to define site boundaries. In no instance were surface indications relied upon as the sole criterion for burial discovery. In this sense, all the excavations were locally intensive and were very likely to have discovered all the interments that existed in the vicinity of excavation. The excavations vary, however, in their degree of area search. Both the Arikara samples are the result of extensive search, aided by earth-moving machinery. This procedure allowed the discovery of discontinuous burial zones. For the remaining sites, limited testing was performed, usually on adjacent hilltops. It is virtually certain in all these cases that additional burial zones were missed during excavation. From an analytical perspective, the absence of these other burial zones will, to a greater or lesser degree, bias the sample's representation of the culture's range of mortuary treatments. Distinctions that might be expected to employ spatial segregation as a symbolic designator, such as many types of horizontal differentiation, will be particularly vulnerable to this sample bias.

At a more specific level, two classes of interment were excluded from the study because of ambiguities in archaeological recovery: (1) graves containing multiple interments for which individual grave associations were not well defined; and (2) graves for which ambiguity existed in the excavation records. Although graves of the former type were not included in the analysis of artifact occurrence, multiple interment was noted as a variety of mortuary treatment.

Recovery limitations also necessitated the exclusion of several classes of funerary attributes from consideration. Organic remains, as mentioned in the discussion of postdepositional effects, had in large part decayed from the sample by the time of excavation. Yet, such artifacts were recovered occasionally. Since the actual presence or absence of these artifacts could not be determined in the majority of graves, they were necessarily excluded from analysis. An exception to this rule was made for the wood burial coverings. Although burial coverings were considerably larger and more substantial than other types of organic artifacts, their recovery was susceptible to similar sample bias. Therefore, such observations were used only with utmost caution and awareness of their potential bias.

Unmodified artifacts, including animal bone, stone, and small numbers of isolated pot sherds, were the second class of attributes affected by recovery processes. Because of the general difficulties in the excavation of mortuary remains and the lack of precise locational control in the earlier excavations, it was difficult to reliably distinguish objects of this type that had been intentionally placed in a grave from similar objects present in occupational debris that were unintentionally incorporated in the grave. This was a particular problem at the Larson site, where the cemetery was located immediately adjacent to the settlement. Artifacts of this type were disregarded as grave inclusions.

In addition to artifacts, the recovery of human osteological materials was in some cases seriously affected by postdepositional and recovery processes. In a few cases, poor preservation conditions completely destroyed skeletal material, precluding its observation or recovery. In many other instances, the bone was badly decayed and no attempt was made to recover it. In those cases where photographs or reliable field determinations were made, general estimates of age and sex have been obtained; otherwise no estimates were possible. The existence of graves for which age and sex is not known is a serious deficiency for social analysis, since these values are absolutely fundamental to social reconstruction. This problem is most serious in the Pawnee sample and less so for the Arikara and Omaha.

A final consideration of recovery pertains to the absolute quantities of small and numerous objects, such as trade beads and metal bangles. Since these objects are relatively small in size and since very limited screening was employed in these excavations, the absolute quantity of these two types is highly suspect, although their relative frequency is probably a valid and useful measure. However, as this study is concerned with only the occurrence and not the abundance of grave inclusions (see following section on typology), this is only of marginal concern in the present circumstance.

In general, where uncertainty has been introduced into the sample through postdepositional or recovery processes, affected cases or variables have been excluded from the analysis. This exclusion is to a certain extent wasteful of potential information, particularly given the already limited number of graves available in several of the samples. The inclusion of these cases or variables, however, would introduce further ambiguity into the samples and effectively increase the level of background "noise" against which cultural patterning in the samples must compete for recognition. For this reason it seems desirable to eliminate as much identifiable ambiguity as possible from the samples prior to analysis, to thereby increase the chance of detecting meaningful patterning in the mortuary area.

Pawnee Sites

Three Pawnee cemetery sites were analyzed in this study. Two are historic period sites of the Grand (Chaui) Pawnee band and represent the only pure Grand Pawnee occupations presently known (Wedel 1936:29). In both cases, the burial areas are in close association with village areas that have been partially excavated. The third site is protohistoric Pawnee (circa 1750) (Lower Loup phase), and, because of its geographic placement, is also probably Chaui (Grange 1968:133).

Linwood Site, 25BU1

The Linwood site is located 3 miles (5 km) south of the Platte River on an east terrace of Skull Creek in Butler County, Nebraska. The site occupies the western portion of an alluvial terrace running approximately three-quarters of a mile (1 km) along Skull Creek, bounded on the south, west, and east by high bluffs (Wedel 1936:29). Two known burial areas are situated on the bluffs to the immediate south (main burial area) and to the east (Walla Hill). Two occupation episodes at Linwood have been documented: Component A was located in the southwest portion of the site on the upper terrace and covers roughly 20 acres (8 ha). This component appears to have been occupied from as early as 1777 to approximately 1809 (Grange 1968:18) and was reported occupied by both Lewis and Clark (1893) and by Pike (Wedel 1936:17). Although Component A has yet to be extensively excavated, it has undergone a number of limited excavations, including the Nebraska Archaeological Survey, under the direction of W. D. Strong in 1930 (two houses and one burial), and the excavation of five houses, several caches, a ceremonial ring, and burials in 1939 by John L. Champe for the Nebraska State Historical Society (Champe 1939). Additional limited work has been carried out since this time by the highway salvage division of the Nebraska State Historical Society (see Carlson and Steinacher 1976:10–12).

Component B, covering approximately 40 acres (16 ha), is located northeast of Component A on the lower terrace. Wedel has identified Component B as the Grand Pawnee village visited by Oehler and Smith in 1851 (1914:22, 31) and abandoned in 1857 when the inhabitants moved to the Genoa site (Grange 1968:19). This component of the site has not been excavated, and the surface indications of lodges and a sod wall have been obliterated.

The occurrence of at least two occupational episodes at Linwood raises a potentially serious problem for an analysis of the funerary remains. If the same burial areas were used indiscriminately during these different periods, the mixed group of graves could provide misleading results, particularly for the analysis of temporal change in Pawnee funerary treatment. There is solid evidence to demonstrate at least some intermixing: an 1844 U.S. half dime recovered from a grave on Walla Hill. The overall content of the grave assemblages, however, corresponds overwhelmingly with a 1777–1809 date. Based on this observation, it appears that each occupation probably made use of distinct cemetery areas, although the cemeteries of earlier occupations were also used to a limited degree. The burials from both the main area and Walla Hill are therefore treated as deriving from the earlier component at Linwood, with the realization that a small number of later burials are almost certainly mixed among them. Given the provisional nature of the sample, the results produced using the Linwood material must be carefully screened to identify any potential distortion produced by such intermixing.

Burials associated with the Linwood site were discovered on two main bluffs overlooking the village sites. A total of 52 burials were excavated, 39 on the main burial hill and 13 on Walla Hill. Two additional burials were found in the village confines in cache pits. Tests were also carried out on the adjoining Barta Hill for additional burials, though none was discovered. Although the majority of the burials surviving on these two hills were probably recovered during the 1939 excavations, additional burials undoubtedly occur on other bluff tops not examined. Similarly, extensive activity by amateurs in the region had destroyed a number of graves in these two areas prior to excavation (John Champe, personal communication 1977). Of the 54 graves recovered, 51 met the criteria for inclusion in the present study.

Clarks Site, 25PK1

The Clarks site is located on a narrow terrace on the south side of the Platte River, near the present town of Clarks, Nebraska, in Polk County. The site encompasses an area of roughly 30 acres (12 ha), on a narrow terrace between the river and the bluffs that run parallel to the river in a northeasterly direction. The burials associated with this site are found on two adjacent bluff tops southeast of the main occupation area. Wedel has identified this site as the Grand Pawnee village occupied from about 1820 to 1845 (Wedel 1936:31).

The major excavation of the site was undertaken by Robert B. Cumming, of the Nebraska State Historical Society in 1940. These excavations unearthed three lodges, six caches, and approximately 70 burials (Cumming 1940). As with the Linwood site, it is unlikely that a complete sample of burial remains was recovered, both because of the limited testing of other areas during the 1940 excavations and the destruction caused by local amateurs. Of the 70 graves recovered in 1940, 65 met the inclusion criteria for the present study.

Barcal Site 25BU4

The Barcal site is located on a high terrace immediately west of Skull Creek and approximately 3 miles (5 km) south of the Linwood site. The site covers an area of about 25 acres (10 ha). Excavations carried out by John L. Champe in 1936 for the Nebraska State Historical Society, uncovered three houses, two midden areas, numerous pits, and 34 burials. The Barcal site represents a protohistoric manifestation of the Pawnee, taxonomically designated the Lower Loup phase. Given the lack of direct historical evidence, it is more difficult to specify the duration of occupation at the Barcal site or its precise band affiliation. On the basis of a ceramic seriation and the proportional occurrence of trade materials, Grange (1968:130) has dated the Barcal site within the broad range of A.D. 1650 to 1750, perhaps as late as 1770. The occurrence of specific trade types, such as both clasp and butcher knives, seems to confirm this dating. Current analysis of the site and its trade materials supports this general dating and argues for use during the later half of Grange's proposed time period. The median date of A.D. 1750 is used in this study. A tentative affiliation of the Barcal site with the Chaui division of the Pawnee is based on the geographic location of the settlement. Each of the Pawnee bands traditionally occupied a definite territory within central Nebraska; in the case of the Chaui, this was the area south of the Platte River (Wedel 1936:29). The location of the Barcal site would be associated with the south bands of the Pawnee, as opposed to the Skidi (Champe and Fenenga 1974:50), and very probably with the Chaui division (Grange 1968:113). In the analysis of the archaeological materials from the Pawnee sites, it will be necessary to scrutinize closely the evidence from the Barcal site to assure that observed variation between the Barcal and the later Chaui sites is not attributable to an initial misidentification of band affiliations. All 34 Barcal burials met the criteria for inclusion in the present study.

Omaha Sites

The two Omaha burial sites are both associated with an Omaha village located on Omaha Creek near the town of Homer, in northeastern Nebraska (O'Shea and Ludwickson n.d.). This village (known as Tonwontonga, or the Big Village [25DK5]) (J. O. Dorsey 1884:263), was occupied at the end of the eighteenth century and on several occasions in the nineteenth century, between 1794 and 1843 (Smith 1974:182–187). Although the multioccupational nature of the settlement presents a problem for precise dating, the remains from the two burial areas included in this study are likely to date from a period centering on 1811, based on the abundance of manufactured goods and the frequent occurrence of datable silver ornaments.

Ryan Site, 25DK2

The Ryan site is located on a high ridge overlooking the Missouri River, to the southeast of the village area. The site contains at least two components, an early component associated with Plains Woodland and Great Oasis, characterized mainly by disarticulated or bundled burials, and a later component of deeper, extended burials associated with the Omaha occupation. Three areal locations were specified at the time of excavation:

1. Area A, the main area, which contains 14 Omaha burials, 7 Woodland features (at least 50 individuals), the burial of a dog, and an articulated bison spine.
2. Area B, which contains a single Omaha burial feature with three individuals.
3. Area C, which contains no burials.

Although the site was originally identified by the presence of three moundlike structures, these do not appear to have been artificial in nature, although Woodland sherds were encountered in the fill of many graves (Champe 1946:117). The site was examined by the Nebraska Archaeological Survey in September 1939, under the direction of Earl Bell, and was excavated by Stanley Bartos, Jr. (Bartos 1939). Of the Omaha graves recovered, 11 met the entry criteria for the present study.

25DK10

25DK10, the other burial area associated with the Big Village, was excavated by John Champe in the summer of 1940. This site is located on the top of a bluff running due south, overlooking the river from directly behind the Omaha settlement.

It is highly probable that it was on this site that Bradbury briefly described the Omaha village and its cemetery in 1811 (Bradbury 1904:66). All the graves found at this site are attributable to the Omaha occupation, although an anomalous complete Great Oasis-type rim was encountered during the course of excavation (although not in association with any grave). Champe recovered a total of 36 graves from DK10 (Champe 1940), of which 24 were used in the present study.

Although it is likely that all the graves in this location were recovered, that additional graves exist throughout the area is almost certain.

Arikara Sites

Two Arikara sites were chosen for analysis. Both were extensively excavated as part of reservoir salvage efforts.

Larson Site, 39WW2

The Larson site, a large protohistoric site, is located on a high terrace on the east side of the Missouri River, in the state of South Dakota. The associated burial area was located approximately 100 yards (90 m) behind and at a slightly higher elevation than the village (Bass and Rucker 1976:36). The village was initially excavated by the River Basin Survey under the direction of Alfred Bowers in 1963 and 1964. Further excavations were carried out by J. J. Hoffman, also of the River Basin Survey, in 1966. The cemetery was excavated over three field seasons (1966–1968) by William Bass of the University of Kansas. Bass's excavations included the use of heavy earth-moving equipment to ensure nearly complete recovery of the burial features.

The occupation of the Larson site is bracketed by the dates of the Postcontact Variant of the Coalescent Tradition, A.D. 1675–1780 (Lehmer 1971:163). Within this time span, there is some disagreement as to the actual dating of the Larson occupation. Although several estimates have placed Larson in the later half of this time period (cf. Jantz 1973; Owsley 1975), recent seriation studies now support a dating in the range A.D. 1680–1740 (Craig Johnson personal communication, 1982), which is in good agreement with the specific trade materials found in the grave assemblages. These latter dates are provisionally employed as the most likely time of occupation for the Larson site.

Because of the frequent reuse of burial pits by the Arikara, it is difficult to give an exact number to the individuals recovered from the Larson site, although Bass and

Rucker (1976:37) refer to a "cleaned" sample of 410 individuals. The Larson settlement is of interest in that it also contained a large skeletal sample of unburied individuals recovered from the various lodge floors. The demographic implications of the village remains are dealt with by Douglas Owsley (1975). Of the grave features excavated at the Larson cemetery, 181 met the inclusion criteria for the present study.

Leavenworth Site, 39CO9

The Leavenworth site was a large double village located on the west bank of the Missouri River, and divided by Elk Creek, in the state of South Dakota. This site was occupied from about 1800 to 1832, although it was abandoned for at least 1 year following the 1823 reprisal attack on the village by troops under the command of Colonel Henry Leavenworth (Wedel 1955:80–81). The site was visited by a number of travelers during its approximately 28 years of use, including Lewis and Clark, Brackenridge, Bradbury, Catlin, and Maximillian Prince of Wied (Bass *et al.* 1971:22–29). The burial zone, which was located on the bluff tops behind the village area, was composed of five distinct areas. Of these five burial areas, four were found to the south of Elk Creek, while a single area (Area E) was located to the north of the creek (Bass *et al.* 1971:34–35).

A number of excavations have taken place at the Leavenworth cemetery, including W. H. Over of the University of South Dakota (1915, 1917); M. W. Stirling of the Smithsonian Institution (1923); W. D. Strong (1932), also of the Smithsonian Institution; James Caldwell, an amateur (1935); and finally the extensive excavations directed by William Bass of the University of Kansas (1965–1966) prior to the site's final immersion in the Oahe reservoir. In addition to these excavations, a relatively large-scale excavation of the village was completed by University of Nebraska field schools under the direction of Preston Holder in 1960 and 1961 (with additional fieldwork in 1962). The results of these excavations have been analyzed by Richard Krause (1972). The Leavenworth excavations, like those at the Larsen site, employed large earth-moving vehicles as a means of extensive excavation, recovering a total of 235 individuals, of which 151 met the entry criteria for this study. Thirty-three individuals were recovered by Stirling during his excavations; the details of these graves and artifact associations have been published by Wedel (1955:96–102). These graves were not incorporated into the present study.

Temporal Placement

The general chronological framework within which the present study is set has been discussed with reference to each particular site and is summarized in Figure 4.1. With the exceptions of the Larson site and the Barcal site, which were dated on

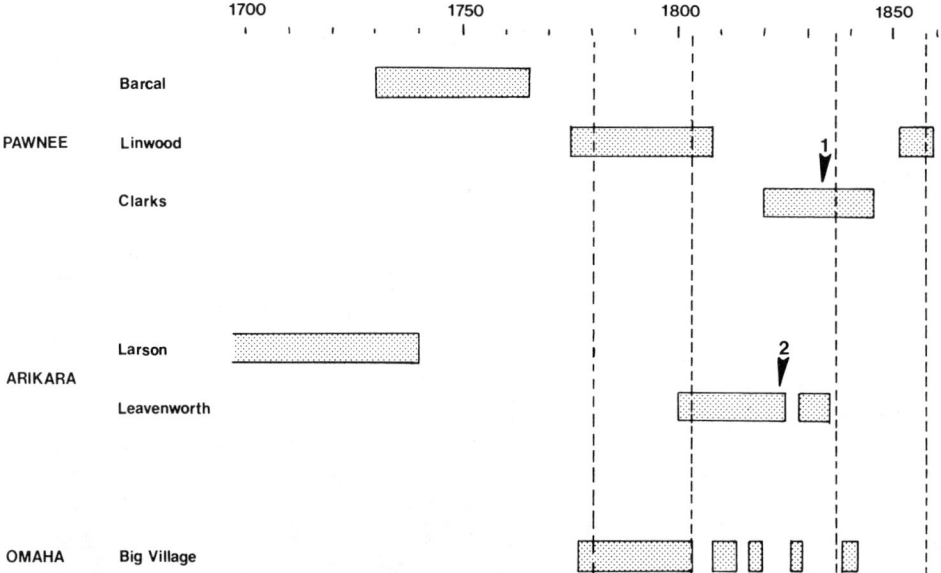

Figure 4.1. Relative temporal placement of the Omaha, Pawnee, and Arikara samples. 1, Village burned by Delawares, 1832; 2, village attacked by Col. Henry Leavenworth, 1823. Dashed lines indicate major epidemics.

archaeological grounds, the dating of the sites is based on ethnohistorical documentation. Although the sites have been selected so as to be as nearly contemporaneous as possible, some variation is inevitable because of the rapid rate of culture change during the historic period.

Typological Considerations

The formulation and application of a relevant typological scheme for the analysis of materials from the historic period is at once easier and more difficult than the similar task in a prehistoric context. It is easier in the sense that a large portion of the material assemblage is familiar and is made up of recognizable objects, whose name, function, and range of variation is known in the context of the investigator's own culture. Yet, simply because an artifact was designed for a particular function does not mean that it was perceived or used in that way by members of different native groups.

Typologies are arbitrary. Regardless of the derivation, be it cross-cultural indexes or techniques of numerical classification, they all emphasize a subset of the total attributes manifest in the artifacts or assemblage at the expense of other potential characteristics. The validity of a typology then rests, not on its ability to approach some ultimate "real" classification, but rather on the extent to which it permits the adequate measure of those variables that the analyst wishes to study (Voorripps 1982; Watson 1973). The goals of the study should determine the critical elements of the particular typology employed (Binford 1972:114).

In accord with the current research interests of the study, with emphasis on the structured use of artifacts as symbols within the mortuary ritual, and on the interplay of native and Euroamerican goods, three major distinctions were seen as relevant to the classificatory scheme: (1) artifact function; (2) the distinction between artifacts of native and Euroamerican manufacture; and (3) the raw material from which the artifact was fashioned. At a practical level, the building of the typology was also influenced by the need to keep the total number of variables manageable and to enhance comparability between graves and sites.

TABLE 4.1

86-Element Analytical Typology

Glass bottle	Tubular shell bead	Metal lace/braid
Ceramic pot	Wampum bead	Copper crimp/clip
Native glass pendant	Heavy shell bead	Sheet brass blade
Animal effigy	Rectangular shell bead	Lead ring/coil
Glass trade beads	Shell runtee	Lead band
Bear claw	Marine snail shell	Sheet silver bracelet
Animal teeth	Perforated shell pendant	Silver cross
Bird beak	Flat shell bead	Silver hair plate
Bird bone	Metal bracelet	Silver earring
Raptor talon	Metal bead/bangle	Small silver brooch
Small mammal cranium	Iron knife	Gunflint
Rib shaft wrench	Axe/wedge	Stone spear point
Squash knife	Scissors	Scoria abraider
Scapula hoe	Strike-a-light	Sandstone shaft smoother
Quill flattener	Metal eating implement	Whetstone
Cancellous paint applicator	Small metal hardware	Hammer stone
Awl	Horse gear	Stone sphere
Metatarsal flesher	Small iron tools	Stone projectile point
Elk horn scraper	Metal projectile point	Stone pipe
Bone/antler implement	Iron scraper	Petrified wood
Gun parts/accessories	Iron digging implement	Retouched flake
Pin game cup	Metal container	Unretouched flake
Polished bone tube	Metal buckle	Stone knife
Bone pendant	Finger ring	Plate chalcedony knife
Curved rib ornament	Metal button	Side scraper
Bone point	Large cast brass bell	End scraper
Mussel shell	Smaller brass bell	Pipestone ornament
Gorget	Thick wire coil	Gypsum
Shell hair pipe	Thin wire coil	

The typology follows the lead of several important studies of historic site remains, including Bell et al. (1974), Lehmer and Jones (1968), Quimby (1966), and Wedel (1936). In addition, the determination of artifact function was guided by discussions of material culture in J. O. Dorsey (1890, 1896) and Fletcher and La Flesche (1911). The typology consists of 86 artifact categories and is presented in Table 4.1. This classification differs from the descriptive typologies mentioned above in its tendency to lump together objects that are similar in kind, such as metal bracelets or beads, but that differ in small typological detail. This allows a clear definition of the social use of material culture as mortuary symbols, without the confusing influence of small-scale chronological variation in artifact shape or ornamentation. Although this typology is well suited for a study of mortuary symbolism, the disregard of detailed typological variation may make it unsuitable for other purposes.

In addition to this working typology, a second system of artifact classification was used. This second typology represents an extreme compression of the first and includes a total of six artifact categories. These are listed in Table 4.2, along with the component artifact types included within each category. As can be seen, this typology keys on the function of the artifact in very broad terms and on the source of manufacture. This classification allows the use of material culture in the mortuary ritual to be viewed on an even more general level and will allow the maximum comparability between individual graves and between sites.

Among the artifact types recognized in the 86-element analytical typology are a set of special artifacts that are referred to here as objects of sociotechnic importance (Binford 1962). These objects, including animal effigies, bird beaks (typically truncated premaxillae), bird bone (worked), small-mammal crania, large stone spear-points, stone pipes, and carved pipestone ornaments, constitute a set of artifacts for which special ritual or symbolic significance was frequently ascribed in Plains society. As such, they serve as initial indicators of special or elevated social standing within the mortuary populations.

The designation of types as likely sociotechnic objects does not preclude the use of other artifacts as social symbols. Nor does it necessarily mean that any one of these types necessarily was used in a given sample as a sociotechnic object or that the uses were equivalent and uniform between the three cultures under investigation. These, indeed, are relationships that will be examined through analysis, rather than strictly determined in advance. Yet, knowledge that these particular types were frequently used as special social symbols will aid in the classification and interpretation of the observable mortuary patterning. Attributes of this class also form specific expectations for specific classes of Plains social differentiation, as is shown in the ethnographic models of social differentiation within a mortuary context listed in Chapter 5.

Artifact occurrence was recorded in a presence–absence form for all artifact types. The abundance of each type was not considered in the present study. A preliminary analysis of attribute distribution showed that most types occur in a very uniform and

TABLE 4.2

Typology of Artifact Categories

Artifact class	Equivalent types
Trade-derived body ornaments	Gorget, shell hair pipe, wampum beads, heavy shell beads, rectangular shell beads, shell runtee, flat shell bead, metal bracelet, finger ring, large cast brass bell, smaller brass bell, thick wire coil, thin wire coil, metal braid, lead ring, lead band, sheet silver bracelet, silver cross, silver hair plate, silver earring.
Trade-derived clothing ornaments	Glass trade beads, metal bead/bangle, metal buckle, metal button, copper crimp/clip, small silver brooch.
Trade-derived implements	Glass bottle, gun parts/accessories, iron knife, axe/wedge, scissors, strike-a-light, metal eating implements, small metal hardware, horse gear, small iron tools, metal projectile point, iron scraper, iron digging implement, metal container, sheet brass blade, gunflint.
Native ornaments	Native glass pendant, bear claw, animal teeth, raptor talons, polished bone tube, bone pendant, curved rib ornament, tubular shell bead, marine snail shell, perforated shell pendant.
Native implements	Ceramic pot, rib shaft wrench, squash knife, scapula hoe, quill flattener, cancellous paint applicator, bone awl, metatarsal flesher, elk horn scraper, bone/antler implement, pin game cup, bone point, mussel shell, scoria abrader, shaft smoother, whetstone, hammer stone, stone sphere, stone projectile point, petrified wood, retouched flake, unretouched flake, stone knife, plate chalcedony knife, side scraper, end scraper, gypsum.
Sociotechnic objects	Animal effigy, bird beak, bird bone, small mammal cranium, stone spear point, stone pipe, carved pipestone ornament.

limited number across the sample graves. This type of frequency distribution suggests that simple occurrence is the primary unit of variation. A few types, such as trade beads and metal bangles, exhibit a more varied abundance distribution, and it is likely that for these types some information is being lost through the neglect of this abundance information. Although this study will concentrate on artifact incidence, the analysis of abundance variability could be significant in a more fine-grained study of any of these mortuary samples. Yet here, where concern is with relatively gross levels of social distinction, incidence analysis seems most appropriate.

Non-artifact-based observations varied in their manner of coding. Formal treatment attributes were recorded on a presence–absence basis, with the exception of grave dimensions and orientation. Sex was coded as male, female, or indeterminate, and age distinctions were coded as infant, child, adolescent, adult, mature adult, and old adult. For most analytical purposes, these age categories were further compacted into categories of adult and subadult.

Methods of Analysis

The object of the analysis is to generate information relevant to the understanding of the three aspects of mortuary variability described in the section on experimental design. The methods used in the present study are summarized below.

The analytical procedures used closely follow the steps for social analysis outlined in Chapter 3. Funerary differentiation is first considered as it appears in each of the sample sites. These findings then serve as a basis for evaluating the behavior of the three primary sources of mortuary variability: social differentiation, temporal variation, and ethnic distinction.

The search for patterning in the data sets is primarily a statistical operation, and the techniques used will be described in more detail shortly. The interpretation of mortuary variability proceeds by comparing observed patterning with idealized patterns produced by various types of social differentiation. The classification of a given aspect of differentiation as reflecting a vertical, horizontal, or special status dimension is realized by comparing the observed configuration of referent values with the characteristic patterns for each dimension. These characteristics are summarized in Table 4.3. The more detailed interpretation of mortuary distinctions likewise involves structured comparison, this time with the archaeological representation of specific social components drawn from the ethnographies of the three Plains tribes considered. Chapter 5 presents an ethnographic background for these tribes, along with their main categories of social differentiation as they would appear in an

TABLE 4.3

Expected Referent Variable Configurations for the Major Categories of Social Differentiation

Referent values	Vertical differentiation	Horizontal differentiation	Special status differentiation
Age/sex	Skewed distribution	Normal distribution	Variable
Frequency	Hierarchical pyramid	Variable but equal size	Low level of occurrence
Spatial distribution	Unlikely	Likely	Likely
Means of symbolic designation	Differential energy expenditure in treatment and grave goods	Equal levels of energy expenditure; use of non-valued symbols	Nonnormative treatments; low levels of energy expenditure

archaeological context (as per Chapter 3). Although in application these comparisons are self-explanatory, some further remarks are warranted on the statistical techniques employed.

The statistical analysis of mortuary data involves two main operations: (1) the discovery of relationships within a body of data; and (2) the evaluation of the significance of these relationships. The significance tests employed in the analyses are common to archaeological research. These tests are documented at their point of application and require no additional comment here. With the exception of the association tests described below, a 0.05 level of probability was employed as the critical test value for all significance testing. Three statistical procedures are central to this analysis. These include a measure of association, principal component analysis, and cluster analysis.

Chapter 3 noted the importance of determining the constraints operating on the distribution of attributes as measured against the primary referents of age and sex, as a first step in understanding the organization of observed mortuary variability. The relatively low frequency of occurrence of many artifact types typically found within the mortuary context presents a formidable problem for the identification of constraint on specific artifact distributions. In most cases there are simply too few occurrences of a given type to permit the effective use of contingency statistics. Yet some constant criterion for evaluating the significance of an observed distribution is highly desirable. One solution would be to accept as constrained only those types whose distribution was perfectly consistent; for instance, a type that occurred in 100 male graves and a single female grave would not be considered to be constrained. An equally inadequate solution would be to consider a type as associated with the particular age or sex group with which it occurred most frequently. The pragmatic solution adopted here, although by no means an ideal one, has been to employ a measure of association, Kendall's tau, for the evaluation of the significance of a distribution.

In these tests, a critical level of 0.1 is set as the minimum level of probability indicative of a constrained distribution. The less-stringent rejection level was employed in recognition of the numerous idiosyncratic factors that can affect artifact occurrence. Yet, even with such a procedure, it is frequently not possible to isolate many of the potentially meaningful constraints on association. Therefore, in addition to the statistical criterion, an additional rule was employed: Any type that occurred in two or more grave units and that had a constant age and/or sex association was considered to be constrained. Such a rule allows those types that behave consistently (although at a level below which the statistical significance can be evaluated) to be included as types with a restricted distribution. Both the statistical criterion and this limiting rule incorporate a certain degree of arbitrariness into the determination. Yet they can be justified on the ground that (1) as they are applied consistently in all cases, the measures obtained between sites will be consistent with one another, and thus interpretable; and (2) the criterion is nonabsolute, in the sense that it allows a degree of flexibility for idiosyncratic variation in type distribution, while retaining the ability to recognize most of the associational constraints present.

The demonstration of specific constraints is of interest, both to evaluate the degree of organization in the use of the material culture and to aid in the interpretation of the results of the multivariate analysis of artifact covariation.

The second technique used extensively is principal component analysis. This study employs principal component type factor analysis as a means of evaluating the covariation of sets of artifacts observed in the mortuary occurrence. Like other factor analytic techniques, component analysis begins with a matrix of correlation coefficients, but it differs from classical factor analysis in that unities are left in the principal diagonal of the correlation matrix.

For this study, phi coefficients (Hays 1973:744) were calculated for all pairs of variables. In order to minimize spurious correlation (see Cowgill 1968:372), a minimum level of occurrence was established for the inclusion of types in the analysis. Speth and Johnson (1976) have considered this problem in some detail. For the purpose of the present analysis, a type was included if it occurred in at least 5% of the graves. The choice of such a level is arbitrary and reflects a desire to eliminate infrequently occurring types on the one hand, and yet retain as much of the observed variation present in the occurrence on the other.

Types meeting the occurrence criteria were subjected to principal component analysis as implemented in the Statistical Package for the Social Sciences (SPSS) procedure Factor (Nie *et al.* 1975), and components with an eigenvalue greater than 1.0 were extracted. These components were not interpreted directly but were rotated in accord with varimax criteria. Varimax rotation attempts to simplify the columns of the factor matrix, such that each variable either loads strongly (in a negative or positive direction) on a given factor or loads at nearly zero (Harman 1976:290). This loading pattern permits an interpretation of the resulting factors consistent with the presence/absence form of the original variable and enhances the overall interpretability of the components (Cowgill 1977:129).

The loading of variables on the rotated factors generally takes the form of one of three generalized patterns, recognition of which can aid in the interpretation of the factors. The first is known as a *grouped* pattern (Harman 1976:100), in which a series of variables loads strongly in the same direction against a background of low loadings on other variables. The strong loading is typically positive, but it can also be negative.

A second pattern type is known as *bipolar* (Harman 1976:100) and occurs when both strong positive and negative loadings of variables occur on the same factor. Such factors express effectively inverse or mutually exclusive relationships, with either being diagnostic. The third general form has been termed a *specific* factor (Rummell 1970:326) and describes a factor that is defined by a strong loading on a single variable. This pattern is perhaps the least useful and frequently occurs in

TABLE 4.4

Factor Loading Patterns[a]

	Factor		
Variable	1 (Grouped)	2 (Bipolar)	3 (Specific)
Var01	<u>.900</u>	.010	−.006
Var02	<u>.875</u>	.105	−.057
Var03	<u>.910</u>	.076	.032
Var04	.001	<u>.875</u>	.105
Var05	−.001	<u>.870</u>	.007
Var06	.025	.036	<u>.945</u>
Var07	.120	<u>−.900</u>	.015
Var08	−.036	<u>−.913</u>	−.032

[a] Underlined values represent diagnostic factor loadings.

weakly structured data sets that include types with low communalities. Table 4.4 provides a hypothetical set of factor loadings illustrating these three generalized factor patterns.

In addition to this direct interpretation, the derived factors are also used for the calculation of factor scores. These scores provide a standardized numerical measure of the relative strength or importance of each factor for a given grave unit, based on the artifact assemblage present in it. These scores will form the basis for one of the two clustering procedures used in the study.

In addition to the visual inspection of factor results, it will be desirable to compare the different factor solutions numerically, particularly those from sites produced by a single ethnic group. The coefficient of congruence will be used for this comparison (Rummel 1970:461). This coefficient is defined as follows:

$$\delta_{lq} = \frac{\sum_{j=1}^{m} \alpha_{jl} \alpha_{jq}}{\left[\left(\sum \alpha_{jl}^2 \right) \left(\sum \alpha_{jq}^2 \right) \right]^{1/2}}$$

where: α_{jl} is the loading of variable X_j on factor S_l of one study; α_{jq} the loading of variable X_j on factor S_q of another study; m the number of variables common to both studies (Rummel 1970:462).

The value of this coefficient, like that of a correlation coefficient, "ranges from −1.0 (for perfect negative similarity) through zero (for complete dissimilarity) to 1.0 (for perfect similarity)" (Rummell 1970:461). In a geometric sense, the coefficient of congruence is the cosine of the angle formed by the two factors in the space of the m common variables.

In the comparisons using this coefficient, in which presence/absence data have been used, more emphasis will be placed on the absolute value of the coefficient than on the sign. Using this coefficient it will be possible to determine how similar two factor solutions actually are, a determination that is made difficult in visual inspection by the influence of somewhat different variable composition and the vagaries of small sample sizes.

Unlike principal component analysis, which focuses on the interaction of sets of artifacts (R-mode analysis), cluster analytic techniques are used to identify similarity and structure between sets of graves (Q-mode analysis). Two different cluster procedures are used, and each employs starting data of a different kind.

The first procedure, monothetic division, is a divisive technique that partitions the set of cases so as to maximize the dissimilarity between groups on the basis of the presence or absence of a given artifact type (Everitt 1974:20). The particular method employed here is known as *information analysis,* which uses an information measure as a means for determining the dissimilarity between groups (Sneath and Sokal 1973:241), as implemented in Clustan version 1-C (Wishart 1975).

Data from each site were supplied to the program in the form of attribute lists (Wishart 1975:15). All graves from each site, including empty graves (those with no artifact inclusions), were used in this analysis. Empty graves were given a dummy variable value, which was masked during the actual analysis.

Although some objections have been raised regarding the use of monothetic divisive techniques on formal grounds (cf. Jardine and Sibson 1971:115), the technique has proved of considerable use in the archaeological analysis of mortuary variability (cf. Peebles 1972; Tainter 1975b). In the present study, it is employed as a means of identifying major subdivisions of graves within each sample, focusing both on the types that serve to mark distinctions and on the referent characteristics of the subsets formed by this partitioning.

The second clustering procedure is of the agglomerative type, which seeks to combine those cases most similar to one another into common clusters. Ward's method, which progressively fuses those two clusters that result in the minimum increase in the error sum of squares (Everitt 1974:15), was used as implemented in Clustan 1-C (Wishart 1975).

The data for this analysis are the factor scores generated by principal component analysis. The use of factor scores, however, means that only the variables and cases used in the principal component analyses can contribute to the cluster solution.

Both clustering techniques, and both forms of data presentation, have certain advantages. The clustering of a raw incidence matrix allows all the artifact occurrence information to be utilized in the analysis, but it implicitly assumes that all these variables are of equal weight and importance, which often is not the case. The clustering of factor scores partially solves this weighting problem (cf. Christenson and Reed 1977; Reed and Christenson 1978), but, because of the range of spurious correlation (Cowgill 1968; Speth and Johnson 1976), it can include only those variables that occur frequently. The analysis here is structured, therefore, to use data in both forms, in a comparative manner. It is reasoned that, if the same or a complementary structure is derived using these substantially different techniques and data, it will argue for the reality of the identified structure.

At the present time, it is not possible to evaluate precisely the significance of a cluster solution or to determine whether a solution represents the best possible partitioning of a population. Furthermore, cluster analysis methods are largely heuristic and have value only to the extent that they provide insight into the organization of a particular data set. For these reasons, the interpretation of cluster results must remain thematic and attempt to extract the logic underlying the apparent divisions. This somewhat subjective examination of the cluster results is seen as more realistic and in the end more useful than a strict attempt to ascribe social meaning to each small cluster of graves produced by a particular cluster run. As with the other aspects of mortuary observation, the referent variables of age, sex, pervasiveness, and spatial occurrence will be examined for each grave set generated in the cluster analyses to assess its potential significance to the overall mortuary symbolism.

5

The Ethnographic Background

The *Great Plains*, as used in the present discussion, refers to a major geophysical subdivision of the North American continent, stretching from Canada in the north to Texas in the south, and from the Rocky Mountains eastward to the Missouri River (Wedel 1961:23). More specifically, the present study deals with the central subarea of this region, particularly certain portions of the states of Nebraska and South Dakota, with primary focus on the Missouri River and on the Platte and Loup Rivers (Figure 5.1).

The 100-year span of time represented by the sites analyzed in this study (A.D. 1750–1850) was a time of intense stress and change for all the native groups in this region, especially for the semisedentary villagers. Four major processes were in operation that disrupted and undermined the native lifeways: (1) the movement of new people onto the Plains; (2) the advent of virulent epidemic diseases derived from Euroamerican contact; (3) the progressing extermination of the bison; and (4) the rapid distribution of a wide variety of items of Euroamerican material culture, particularly the horse and firearms. These factors combined to produce a disintegration of the village lifeway and the temporary florescence of a nomadic equestrian culture based on hunting and raiding, and to pave the way for permanent Euroamerican settlement. It is not my purpose to provide a detailed account of these processes, as a number of excellent accounts have been written (cf. Holder 1970).

It is against this historical background that the present study is set. The mortuary remains of three Plains village groups are considered: the Pawnee of central Nebraska, the Omaha of northeastern Nebraska, and the Arikara of central South Dakota. All three groups employed a mixed economy based in varying degrees on riverine horticulture and hunting, manifesting all or most of the elements described by Willey (1966:320) as characteristic of the Plains Village Tradition. The native material cultural assemblages for all the groups were very similar, reflecting the basic unity of the Plains adaptation, but beyond this the cultures are distinct.

The remainder of this chapter provides a brief discussion of the major organizational characteristics of the three tribes and a comparative summary of organizational features affecting the patterns of mortuary variability.

The Pawnee

Pawnee Ethnohistory

The Pawnee, speakers of a Caddoan language, occupied a 120-mile (220 km) stretch of the Platte River and Loup River valleys from the north fork of the Loup River on the west to the confluence of the Platte and Elkhorn rivers in the east, in the present-day state of Nebraska (Grange 1968:8). Although this region formed the heartland of the Pawnee territory, the tribe moved over a much wider area of the Plains during the semiannual bison hunts and further into the Spanish Southwest on horse stealing expeditions (Wishart 1979:384). Prehistoric sites within this same

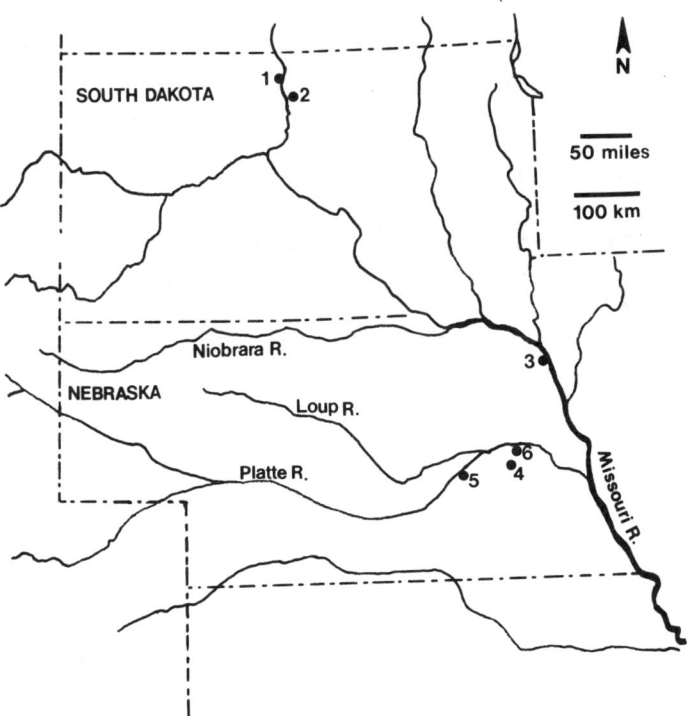

Figure 5.1 The six village sites employed in the analysis: the two Arikara sites, (1) Leavenworth and (2) Larson, in northern South Dakota; (3) the Omaha Big Village in northeastern Nebraska; and the three Pawnee settlements, (4) Barcal, (5) Clarks, and (6) Linwood, in eastern Nebraska.

region, known archaeologically as the Lower Loup phase, are generally associated with the Pawnee (cf. Grange 1968; Wedel 1938), and there is some evidence to suggest that the preceding Upper Republican and Loup River manifestations may represent a continuum of Pawnee/Caddoan-speaking occupation on the Plains dating as far back as A.D. 800 (Strong 1935; Wedel 1979).

Historically, the Pawnee tribe was divided into four bands that were autonomous and endogamous (Weltfish 1965:20), known as the Chaui, Pitahawirata, Kitkahahki, and Skidi. In earlier times each band comprised several villages (Champe and Fenenga 1974; Parks 1979b), although during historic times, each band tended to exist as a single village. In the nineteenth century, even these bands joined together into larger villages for mutual defense.

Pawnee Kinship

The basic organizational unit of Pawnee society was the household, which was also the main productive unit (Weltfish 1965:18–19). Residence was primarily matrilocal (Grinnell 1891:279), while descent was matrilineal (Weltfish 1965:20), although with some bilateral elements (Murdock 1949:233). Sororal polygyny was common among the Pawnee, as was, to a lesser extent, polyandry (Lesser 1930:100–101). There apparently were no clans among the Pawnee (but see Allis 1887:146), although each village was divided into northern and southern moieties (Lowie 1954:99). These moieties were crosscut by numerous men's societies, which were a primary vehicle for village ceremonialism and integration. These societies, however, were not strictly based on age–grade distinctions (Murie 1916:558).

The Pawnee village typically comprised 10–13 households and behaved as an endogamous unit, making it, in effect, a large, geographically localized, extended family (Weltfish 1965:20).

Pawnee Social Ranking

Pawnee social ranking was determined first on the basis of descent and secondarily through personal achievement, expressed via the accumulation and disposal of wealth and through war exploits. Pawnee society was divided into three stable ranked groups. The highest group was composed of the chiefs and priests. These positions were strictly hereditary, although an individual's desire and ability were important in affirming the position. The second rank category included the members of various men's societies and successful warriors. Membership in this rank tended to be hereditary (Murie 1916:643), although membership fluctuated through generations (Holder 1970:36–37). An individual's exploits and his ability to underwrite generous gifting played an important role in establishing membership in this second level. The third level, the commoners, included the remainder of the band's membership.

Besides hereditary office, there was the possibility of personal gain and achievement through various socieites, particularly the doctor's society, and through war exploits and raiding (Weltfish 1965:19). Special temporary positions were also known. For example, each band retained 24 young braves as police. Their tenure was limited to a year, and their authority generally was limited to maintaining order on the bison hunts.

Although there was the opportunity for social achievement, no amount of personal achievement could elevate an individual to the level of a hereditary position. Similarly, an individual with a hereditary right to an office of leadership had to prove himself worthy of the office through generous gifting and personal exploits (Dunbar 1880:261; Grinnell 1889:260).

Pawnee Mortuary Practices

The Pawnee practiced individual inhumation as their primary means of mortuary disposal (James 1823:281). The Reverend Samuel Allis, a missionary and interpreter for the Pawnee, gave the following account to Morgan: "They excavated a grave or trench and then dug an opening in one side large enough to insert the body under the disturbed earth, laid it horizontally, covered it with a mat, and deposited by its side a number of articles, filled up the trench and raised a mound over it" (Morgan 1959:136). A more detailed picture of Pawnee mortuary treatment, at least the treatment afforded warriors, was provided by a Skidi informant:

> In olden times, when a warrior was about to die, they brought all the things that he had worn when he was on earth, and they put them upon him. When he died a priest was hired to come and take the holy ointment and put it all over the body of the deceased. Then a buffalo robe was put over the dead man. Women were paid to dig a grave about two and a half feet deep. Then the women went to the timber and cut two forks and several poles. These they took up on the hill where the grave had been dug, set the forked poles, one at each end, and laid a pole across the two forks of the end poles. The people then brought the dead man, laid him in the grave and placed all his valuables in the grave. Then the poles were set up on each side of the pole lying across the forks, grass was piled on top of these at each end, and the women piled a lot of dirt upon the poles around the grave, so that it was like a house. . . . If the deceased had any ponies and the relatives knew that he liked any particular pony, they would kill the pony upon his grave, believing that he would ride the pony to the Spirit Land. If the people were told by the deceased not to kill any ponies upon his grave, then the relatives roached the pony and cut the hair from the pony's tail; then they spread the hair over the grave and kept the pony. (Dorsey 1904a:341)

Hughes (1968:356) noted a number of mourning prescriptions, including self-mutilation, fasting, haircutting, and name taboos, and Murray (1900:272) during his stay with the Pawnee, observed the use of small mourning lodges in which relatives of the deceased continued their lamentations after the band had moved on to a new location.

One aspect of Pawnee burial ritual that was constantly noted was the tendency to bury the dead on high promotories or bluffs: "The Pawnee bury their dead upon the summits of the bluffs, and for two or three miles above and below this town, the top of each hill is covered with graves" (Carleton 1943:74). Wedel (1936:91) has also noted that, although the mortuary customs of the different bands were apparently identical, when two bands occupied the same village (as happened with increasing regularity in the nineteenth century), each band maintained its own distinct cemetery area (see also Hyde 1974:262).

Little detailed ethnographic evidence dealing with Pawnee mortuary differentiation is available. Hughes (1968:356) suggests that the elaborateness of the burial ritual and of the mourning rites tended to vary with rank. Dorsey's informant noted two special categories of mortuary differentiation:

> There were other ways of burial among the Pawnee. When a poor woman died, the women would go to the side of a hill where they would cut a shallow hole, then they would roll the woman in a buffalo robe, place her in the hole, and cover her up with dirt. . . . If a chief's son died, he was buried in a sort of house, and the war ornaments of the chief were placed at the head of the grave. If the chief had any calumet pipe sticks, they were placed upon the grave. (Dorsey 1904a:341)

From these assertions, it appears that social rank and wealth were major determinates of the mortuary treatment that an individual received, and that such features as burial location, grave size, and burial architecture could be markers of social standing. The mention of locational distinctions between bands and the fact that the Pawnee employed a number of disposal areas could suggest that other social units, such as the moiety division, may also have been spatially differentiated.

Ethnohistorical evidence also suggests varieties of nonnormative burial treatment. Allis relates one such incident following an attack by the Sioux in June 1843: "The Pawnees were so badly frightened they threw their dead into corn caches and heads of ravines, covered them lightly, picked up some of their traps and left some in their lodges, crossed the river and went about three miles that night" (Allis 1887:155).

If one consults Pawnee folktales, a number of other examples of nonnormative burial treatment are suggested. These tales provide insight into the treatment of social deviants. Witches were buried in locations distinct from the normal cemetery area (Dorsey 1906:232), occasionally burned (Dorsey 1906:240), and, in at least one instance, decapitated prior to burial (Dorsey 1904a:218). Suicides were not buried in the regular cemetery either (Dorsey 1906:134). Other types of deviants, particularly those violating approved relations with the opposite sex, were occasionally not buried at all (Dorsey 1904a:90, 1906:432).

Folktales also provide further insight to the more normal aspects of Pawnee burial custom. Grave preparation was normally performed by females paid by the family of the deceased, although in the event of the death of a child the grave seems to have been the responsibility of the parents (Dorsey 1906:347). This also seemed to be the case for young, unmarried adult males (1904a:69). It is also noted that, if a child died and its mother had died sometime previously (although not necessarily immediately preceding the child's death), the grave might be opened and the child placed in the grave with the mother (Dorsey 1906:133). Folk traditions indicate that the placing of the graves on high promontories, the hiring of women for grave preparation, and the construction of mortuary coverings were normative practices that were received by most individuals (Dorsey 1906:126–127). From this evidence it is difficult to tell whether such treatment was denied only deviants and the extremely destitute, or whether such treatment was normative for only the individuals relating the tales, who, in most cases, would have come from the higher strata of Pawnee society.

In general, ethnographic and historical sources provide us with a normative view of Pawnee mortuary practices and an indication of some mortuary differentiation based on band affiliation and social standing. If the evidence from folktales is included, we get a more detailed view of the variability inherent in Pawnee death customs, particularly the treatment of social deviants, but this is a view that is difficult to evaluate and of unknown reliability. Even accepting all these sources of evidence, we must conclude either that the Pawnee exhibited considerably less differentiation in their mortuary customs than would be expected on the basis of the degree of rank differentiation present in the society, or that ethnographic and historical observations do not fully document the range and complexity of Pawnee mortuary ritual. Archaeological analysis will allow the opportunity to test these alternatives.

The Omaha

Omaha Ethnohistory

The Omaha tribe, speakers of a Dhegihan Siouan language, were relative newcomers to the Plains region. The earliest fairly certain location of the Omaha is on the Big Sioux River in northwest Iowa, circa A.D. 1700 (based on the Delisle map drawn following the descriptions of Le Sueur; see Smith 1974:21). Throughout the later historic period, the primary territory of the Omaha was on the west side of the Missouri River in the present state of Nebraska. The territory extended from the confluence of the Platte in the south to the confluence of the Niobrara in the northwest (J. O. Dorsey 1886:218). Despite their late arrival on the Plains, the Omaha adopted all the major features of the Plains villages, including the earth lodge and the mixed economy based on hunting and riverine horticulture.

Omaha Kinship

Omaha society was divided into two moieties, one associated with the earth and the other with the sky, each comprising five clans (Fletcher and La Flesche 1911:135). The clans and moieties were exogamous, with patrilineal descent (L. H. Morgan 1959:87) and virilocal residence (Fletcher and La Flesche 1911:39). Each clan was further divided into a varying number of subdivisions (Fletcher and La Flesche 1911:136–137). The customs of the levirate and sororate were practiced, as was sororal polygyny in some cases (Dorsey 1884). Societies crosscut the clan organization. These tended to be of two varieties: social and warrior societies, which were open to anyone who could perform the requisite acts of eligibility, and secret societies, in which membership was achieved by virtue of a dream or vision.

Omaha Social Ranking

Three major ranked grades were recognized among the Omaha: commoners, braves, and chiefs. Braves earned their position through war honors and prowess in the hunt. The designation of chief is a more complex issue. In a strict sense, chieftainship was not hereditary. Rank was achieved through the performance of graded, prescribed acts involving the distribution of wealth. The performance of these deeds constituted the necessary condition for a specific rank, although election then became only a possibility and was not automatic. Since the achievement of rank depended on a household's ability to produce quantities of surplus wealth, the system retained a strong hereditary aspect. (The importance of heredity in achieving chiefly rank is supported by Fletcher and La Flesche's claim [1911:202] that the shift from a hereditary to achieved rank membership took place only in recent times.) Two major grades of chief were recognized. The lower grade, the *shabe'*, was unlimited in membership, including all those who performed the basic level of prescribed acts. The second grade, the *Ni'kagahi' shabe'*, was more elevated and limited in membership. Furthermore, members of the higher grade elected individuals of the lower grade to their membership when a vacancy occurred through the death of a member. From this higher grade of chief came the council of seven chiefs, *Nini'baton*, the main administrative unit of the tribe, and from the council of seven chiefs were selected the two principal chiefs of the Omaha (Fletcher and La Flesche 1911:202–208). The office of principal chief closely followed hereditary lines. In addition, there were offices associated with the various clans, and some of these were hereditary, such as the keeper of the clan's specific ceremonies. Yet, neither these clan offices nor the clans themselves were political. Like other Plains groups, the Omaha recognized status through temporary leadership positions, such as the leader of the annual bison hunt, war chiefs, and soldiers who were chosen for the most dangerous missions and policing of the tribe on the bison hunts.

A final consideration concerns the European-inspired "paper chiefs." Paper chiefs were individuals who had not qualified for chiefly rank, but who were designated chiefs by traders, and who used the specific economic standing that this afforded to subvert the traditional avenues of rank acquisition (Smith 1974:105). The notorious Blackbird, who died in 1800, is probably the most prominent example of this pathway to rank among the Omaha (Fletcher and La Flesche 1911:82, 85).

Omaha Mortuary Practices

The existing ethnohistorical documentation for Omaha mortuary customs is extensive, with detailed accounts deriving from Thomas Say, of the Long expedition in 1819–1820 (James 1823), the observations of L. H. Morgan in 1860, and the ethnographic writings of Alice Fletcher and Francis La Flesche in 1889 and 1911. These detailed accounts can be supplemented with briefer commentaries from other nineteenth-century travelers, including George Catlin. For the most part, there is good agreement between these various sources.

Very soon after death, the body of the deceased was prepared for burial (Fletcher and La Flesche 1911:592). It is worth quoting La Flesche's account of the steps involved in preparation and interment in some detail, as it will be of interest as a basis for comparison with archaeological observation.

> Soon after death the corpse is placed in a sitting posture facing the east and dressed in gala costume, ornaments are put upon the hair and person, and sometimes the face painted in the same manner as the Hunga in the ceremony of the sacred pipes, that is if the deceased belonged to one of the gentes owning a sacred pipe. (La Flesche 1889:6–7)

> Goods are collected from the kindred, to be given to the poor at the time of interment. The grave, never more than four feet deep, is dug by a poor man who is paid for his labour. The body is bourne upon a stretcher made by binding two cross-sticks on two poles ten or twelve feet long. . . . The bed of the stretcher is woven of willow wands, on which a robe is spread, the hairy side uppermost, and pillows are used to keep the sitting corpse in position, the feet being covered with robes or blankets. . . . When the grave is reached the relatives gather around the opening, the corpse is lifted from the litter and held by the bearers while the robes on which it sat are arranged for its reception in the grave, where it is placed upon them, facing east, and the articles of value, chiefly ornaments worn by the person during life, are deposited beside the body. If the deceased be a man, his weapons are then laid by his side; if a woman, her sewing bag containing her awl, quills, and articles used for embroidery; if a child, its playthings are placed beside it. (La Flesche 1889:9)

Several sources deal with duties to the dead after burial. La Flesche mentioned one involving the placement of a symbol of a man's secret society on his grave (1889:10).

A second form of death duty refers to those elements of the formal mourning that continue after the kinsman's burial (cf. Morgan 1959:88), including the placement of food offerings at the grave and prescribed periods of mourning. Thomas Say mentions a prescribed period of mourning that lasted from 7 to 12 months, during which time the violent expressions of grief were gradually allowed to diminish (James 1823:2). Say's account and those of others (cf. Bushnell 1927:51) include varying prescriptions concerning the duties of a widow or widower, in terms of changing location of residence and the length of time that must pass before remarriage could take place.

In the event of the death of a chief or a brave warrior, there was a more general participation of the community in the mortuary ritual:

> For the death of a brave warrior or of a chief, the lamentation is more general, and many of those who visit the body previous to its removal, present to it blankets, bison robes, breechcloths, and moccasins, which are sometimes thus accumulated in considerable numbers; of these presents, part is retained by the orphans, if any, but the greater number is entombed with the body. Over the grave of a person of this description, a kind of roof or shelter is constructed of pieces of wood reared against each other, and secured at top, then sodded over with grass sod. (James 1823:2)

La Flesche also suggests mortuary differences when he notes that a warrior's horse was frequently killed on top of his grave (1889:9). It is also noted that, when the deceased individual was a member of one of the Omaha secret societies, the responsibility for much of the mortuary ritual shifted from the family to the society (Fletcher and La Flesche 1911:553–554; La Flesche 1889:7). Yet, despite the additional ritual carried out by the secret society, little or no evidence of it is manifested in the actual burial of the individual.

> All the regalia which the dead man had purchased the right to wear was removed from him at the proper time and returned to his lodge. Nothing of that character was buried with the dead. After the lodge had been dismissed in the manner already described, the dead body was removed and given the ordinary form of burial. (Fletcher and La Flesche 1911:553)

La Flesche observes that an individual struck by lightening is differentiated: "A man struck by lightening is buried where he fell, and in the position in which he died. His grave is filled with earth, and no mound is raised over one who is thus taken from life" (1889:10). It is also suggested that suicide victims and murderers may have been accorded differential burial.

Besides these cases, which could be classed together as deviant, Omaha oral tradition suggests another circumstance in which radically different mortuary preparations were employed. The tradition, as related by Fletcher and La Flesche, states that, while the Omaha (and the Ponca, who had not yet separated from them) were living in the vicinity of the Big Sioux River in present-day northwest Iowa, "a disastrous battle took place, and as a result this village seems to have been abandoned, after the dead had been gathered and buried in a great mound, around which a stone wall was built" (1911:73). It is possible that this village site is known archaeologically as the Rock Island site (also known as the Blood Run site, see Harvey 1971; M. Wedel 1981), which is dated to the period 1700–1725.

Finally, there is some evidence to suggest that the Omaha, on occasion, employed some sort of scaffold burial. George Catlin, the artist, who traveled up the Missouri in 1832, provides a detailed description of an Omaha custom of depositing their dead in the crotch or branches of trees (1876:10).

The assertion that tree burial was the normal procedure for Omaha burial is in direct contradiction to the accounts of both Say and Fletcher and La Flesche, as well as to the observations of Sergeant Ordway (1916:110) and John Bradbury (1904:66), who strolled by accident into the cemetery area at the Big Village. Yet, that it was employed on occasion has been supported by Bushnell (1927). He noted that, when the band was on its semiannual hunts and members died, especially infants or younger children, they were placed in crotches of trees (1927:51). (This was not always the case, see Fletcher and La Flesche [1911:84] referring to the death of Big Elk's son.) Further, the Omaha chief, Big Elk, in an eulogy address given at the death of the Sioux chief, Black Buffalo, in 1813, also makes mention of scaffold burial: "I shall be wrapped in a robe, (an old robe perhaps) and hoisted on a slender scaffold to the whistling winds, soon to be blown down to the earth—my flesh to be devoured by the wolves, and my bones rattled on the Plains by the wild beasts" (Bradbury 1904:222–223). Based on these sources, then, it seems likely that scaffold burial was an option that the Omaha did employ on occasion.

Among the Omaha, in addition to the normative burial practices, such as extended inhumation, constant orientation, and the construction of burial coverings, a number of social categories were recognized by differential treatment in the mortuary ritual. These included rank differences through community participation and the abundance of grave offerings; clan membership through the inclusion of symbolic or totemic artifacts; membership in societies through preinterment ritual; basic adult/subadult and male/female distinctions in dress and artifact inclusions; and several classes of alternative burial relating to special circumstances of death or to deviant social behavior on the part of the deceased.

Though the more complete documentation of Omaha mortuary practices reveals a spectrum of differential procedures in the disposal of the dead, there is still a considerable gap between the classes of mortuary distinction observed and the range of rank and kinship positions that could be recognized. Yet, ethnographic and historic sources do provide a more complete picture of the range and logic of Omaha mortuary ritual and the specific routes through which mortuary distinction was achieved. As such, it will provide a good base for comparison with the inferences derived from the analysis of the mortuary remains.

The Arikara

Arikara Ethnohistory

The Arikara, the northernmost Caddoan-speaking tribe, were a loosely organized confederacy of subtribes, each of which maintained a separate village (Fletcher 1908:86; Parks 1979b). In historic times the Arikara occupied a region centering on the Missouri River in South Dakota. The Arikara are close relatives to the Skidi band of the Pawnee; the folk traditions of both groups suggest only a recent split (Hyde 1974:52; Parks 1979a).

Arikara Kinship

The Arikara, perhaps more than either the Omaha or the Pawnee, were affected by the disruptive influences of Euroamerican contact, and, therefore, it is difficult to categorize precisely the elements of their social organization, since it was changing at a relatively rapid rate. It appears as though Arikara society was originally organized on much the same lines as their near relatives, the Skidi Pawnee, with a tendency toward matrilocal residence (Curtis 1970), matrilineal descent (with some bilateral elements), and sororal polygyny (Tabeau in Abel 1939:181–182), and, also, having a number of social and secret societies (Lowie 1916:656). The differences in social organization between the Pawnee and the Arikara seem to reflect the particular stress and environment that the Arikara experienced in the middle Missouri region (Deetz 1965:30). These include a shift toward nonsororal polygyny, with the concomitant weakening of matrilocal residence (Brackenridge 1962:253), and the tendency toward a kinship terminology emphasizing a generational system (Deetz 1965:27). All these effects can be seen as reflecting adaptations to stress and depopulation, as well as possible borrowing from the nearby Siouan-speaking village tribes, the Mandan and Hidatsa.

Arikara Social Ranking

Ranking, like other elements of Arikara kinship, bears considerable resemblance to ranking in Pawnee society, yet with significant differences. In earlier times, the Arikara claimed a governing system in which each village was semiautonomous, with a village bundle, a head chief, and three subordinate chiefs (Curtis 1970:149). On matters that concerned the tribe as a whole, there was a head chief (always of the Awa'hu band) and four assistant chiefs (Gilmore 1928:411; however, Curtis [1970:71] claims only a total of four chiefs). To hold the rank of chief, although some attention was paid to birth, it was necessary to prove oneself through gifting, prescribed deeds, and warfare (Brackenridge 1962:254; Denig 1961:62). As with the Omaha, although heredity was not strictly a necessary condition, chieftainship did tend to follow family lines, both through economic mechanisms and through a tendency toward endogamy among chiefly families (Holder 1970:60–61).

There were also mechanisms for acquiring rank and prestige through personal achievement that were open to all individuals. These included membership in the various societies, many of which maintained military activities (there were three women's societies as well [Curtis 1970:150]). Alternatively, one could participate in the doctors' societies. Although certain rites tended to be transmitted through hereditary links, many others could be obtained through an apprenticeship and the purchasing of ritual knowledge (Curtis 1970:151).

Arikara Mortuary Practices

Morgan, at Fort Clark in North Dakota in 1862, gives the following summary of Arikara funerary customs:

> Just out of the village is the burying ground. The Arickarees did not scaffold the dead but buried them in the ground. The most of the graves, and there are hundreds of them visible, are on the segment of a great circle. Others are grouped together. They wrapped up a body, dug a grave, and put it either in a sitting posture or doubled it up, I don't know which. I saw the size of some of the graves. They could not have extended the body and I could not tell whether it was an empty grave and timbered roof like the Omaha, or the earth was placed on the body. (Morgan 1959:162)

The actual burial procedure has been noted by several authors. Curtis provides the following account:

> The dead were dressed and painted by the parents and other close relations, and if no appropriate clothing had been left by the deceased they furnished it. The moment life had passed, the family hired some old woman to dig the grave, and at mid-forenoon of the following day her relations placed the body on a buffalo robe and carried it to the grave, where it was laid on its back wrapped in a robe, the head towards the east and resting on a pillow. (Curtis 1970:63)

This is in close agreement with the description mentioned by Prince Maximillian in 1834:

> Various things are sometimes cast into the grave of eminent men; the corpse is dressed in the best clothes, the face painted red, and sometimes a good horse is killed on the grave. If the deceased has left a son, he receives his father's medicine apparatus; if not, it is buried with him in the grave. (Thwaites 1906:411)

Fletcher (1908:86) suggests that only personal effects were interred and that all other property was distributed to the individual's relatives.

The suggestion that medicine apparatus was occasionally buried with the deceased is especially interesting and fits well with ethnographic accounts of the buying and selling of ritual knowledge and apparatus among the Arikara. The burying or disposal of medicine bundles is also mentioned by Gilmore (1927:349) and recently by Howard (1974:243). Curtis's informants, however, dispute Maximillian's claim of horse sacrifice, claiming that horses were never sacrificed, and also noting that weapons were never buried (Curtis 1970:63). There is evidence to support Maximillian's assertion that the burial procedure was varied according to the eminence of the individual, as in the involvement of "priests" in the mortuary ritual (Hughes 1968:356) or in special funerary monuments, as suggested by Morgan (1959:162).

Arikara folk traditions provide at least hints that suggest special mortuary treatments for various types of social deviants, including cremation (G. Dorsey 1904b:88) and exposure (i.e., where the body was simply left on the prairie and given no funerary treatment whatsoever [Dorsey 1904b:90]). Interestingly, these same folk traditions describe the mutilation and dismemberment of slain enemies, at least on the part of the Sioux (Dorsey 1904b:88). This practice appears to have been common among the Plains tribes (cf. Morgan 1953).

Finally, there is some ethnohistorical support for the assertion that the Arikara did employ scaffolding on occasion, at least as an intermediate stage before interment. Tabeau makes this assertion, claiming the dead were placed on a scaffold or in the trees (in Abel 1939:211–212).

Despite some disagreement in the ethnographic sources, there is evidence that the Arikara recognized rank or wealth differences in their ritual for the disposal of the dead in both (1) the amount of community participation in the mortuary ritual and (2) the specific grave inclusions and offerings placed with the deceased. It was further shown that personal belongings were interred with the dead, suggesting that such de facto differentiation in the possessions of differing classes of individuals, such as between children and adults or men and women, could be expected. These accounts also documented the use of several different disposal treatments that were employed under special circumstances.

Intertribal Relations

Throughout the eighteenth and nineteenth centuries, there are references to direct contact and relations between these three Plains groups. The Pawnee and the Arikara were most closely connected, having languages that were mutually intelligible and common folk traditions relating to an earlier time when the two tribes were one. Although the exact date of the split is open to some dispute, linguistic evidence (Parks 1979a) suggests the split occurred no longer than 500 years ago. Later contact, on a tribal level, took place in 1833–1835, when the Arikara moved to live with the Skidi in the vicinity of the Loup River (Hyde 1974:183–184; see also Wood 1955). After this stay, the Arikara returned to their traditional region along the Missouri River.

Important contact between the Omaha and the Arikara appears to have occurred primarily in the eighteenth century. Omaha traditions recount sporadic warfare between the two groups while the Omaha were still on the east side of the Missouri River. This resulted, ultimately, in the Arikara moving farther to the north and the Omaha occupying much of their previous territory on the west side of the Missouri (Fletcher and La Flesche 1911:75). The Omaha also credit the Arikara as the source for their earth lodge, and for knowledge of the use of maize, although it seems unlikely that the Omaha had no knowledge of maize before this time (Fletcher and La Flesche 1911:75–76).

Periodic trade and warfare have been documented between the Pawnee and the Omaha (Fletcher and La Flesche 1911:87, 406–408). In later historic times, under increasing pressure from the Sioux, the Pawnee and Omaha occasionally met for a joint bison hunt (Hyde 1974:246).

In addition to contact at a tribal level, the movement of individuals and small groups throughout the Plains was extensive, allowing at least potential for a great deal of cultural mixing and the emergence of pan-Plains traits.

Summary

The discussion so far has presented a general overview of the central Plains in the late eighteenth and earlier nineteenth centuries, and has summarized the major organizational features of Omaha, Pawnee, and Arikara societies. Despite differences in detail, one is struck by the underlying similarity of the organization of these three societies. This similarity is all the more striking when one considers the vast differences in the length of time the various groups occupied their historic regions. The Pawnee, whose Caddoan-speaking forebearers may date back as far as A.D. 800 in the region as the Upper Republican manifestation, contrast with the Omaha, who crossed the Missouri River after A.D. 1700. Eggan, in his study of Plains kinship makes a similar observation:

> The hypothesis proposed earlier that "tribes coming onto the Plains with different backgrounds and social systems ended up with similar kinship systems" can be tentatively extended to Plains' society as a whole, despite the variation noted. This is in large measure an internal adjustment to the uncertain and changing conditions of the Plains environment—ecological and social. (Eggan 1955:518–519)

Eggan's stress on change highlights the fact that, while for the purpose of review it has been necessary to describe the social organization of these groups as static, they were in fact dynamic. Deetz (1965) has discussed in some detail the trajectory of this change for the Pawnee and Arikara, and similar effects can be clearly documented among the Omaha. The possibility of relatively rapid adaptive change in the organizational aspects of Plains societies must be carefully considered in the analysis of their mortuary remains. The likelihood of such change is enhanced by the occurrence, in the 100-year span of time covered by the sample sites, of no fewer than four major epidemics.

Now that the major structural elements of Omaha, Pawnee, and Arikara social organization have been identified, their idealized configuration in an archaeological

TABLE 5.1
Archaeological Models for Categories of Plains Social Differentiation

Social category	Demographic attributes		Pervasiveness	Symbolic designation	Spatial element expected
	Sex	Age			
Vertical distinctions					
Chiefly office	Male	Adult	Low	Supralocal symbols. Most energy-intensive mortuary treatments. High level of personal wealth.	No
Hereditary ascription	—	Subadult	Very low	Treatment or artifacts normally limited to adult statuses.	No
Ritual office	—	Adult	Low	Sociotechnic objects, particularly implements. Imperfect correlation with personal wealth. May have a hereditary component.	No
Special prestige positions	Male (usually)	Adult	Low	Local sociotechnic or exotic items. Strong correlation with upper-level wealth standing.	No(?)
Wealth	—	Adult (usually)	Variable	Quantity and variety of artifacts in grave assemblage (particularly exotic trade items).	No
Horizontal distinctions					
Moiety membership	—	—	50%	Possible formal differentiation (location, orientation, etc.). Sociotechnic artifacts specific to each division. Cross section of vertical dimensions.	Yes(?)

Clan membership (Omaha)	—	—	10%	As above, each with specific sociotechnic markers.	Yes(?)
Society membership (non-kin based)	Variable	Adult	Low	Specific, local sociotechnic marker.	No
Male status	Male	Adult	—	Technomic artifacts relating to hunting and warfare. Gender-specific ornamentation.	No
Female status	Female	Adult	—	Technomic artifacts relating to gardening or primary manufacture. Gender-specific ornamentation.	No
Subadult status	—	Subadult	—	Possible small gender-specific artifacts or toys. Subadult ornamentation.	No
Special status distinctions					
Circumstance of death	—	—	Low	Nonnormative burial treatment. Individual may or may not be accorded normal grave assemblage.	?
Social deviant	—	Adult	Low	Nonnormative burial treatment. Interment away from usual burial areas. Atypical grave inclusions or absence of inclusions.	Yes

context can be modeled. This modeling is based on the description of these social elements and specifies those referent properties that will be archaeologically visible. For each social element, the demographic composition and expected frequency is specified, along with the likely classes of symbolic designators and possible spatial attributes. To be compatible with the archaeological analyses, these social features are grouped together as vertical, horizontal, and special status distinctions and are presented in Table 5.1.

These expected configurations will be directly comparable to similar descriptions generated through archaeological analysis. Although the rank models are quite similar for all three ethnic groups, the modeling of horizontal distinctions required additional group-specific definition. These models portray only the major elements of Plains social organization, and many small-scale status designations may also be represented in the archaeological occurrence. Yet, for the present study, these principal elements of social organization are the main focus of inquiry.

This chapter has attempted to provide an overview of the major features of Omaha, Pawnee, and Arikara social organization. As such, it can be used as a scale against which the results of the archaeological analysis can be evaluated. Yet the complementary nature of ethnographic observation should be kept in mind. Both ethnographic and archaeological observation stress those features that are most accessible to their sphere of observation. For this reason, although on a gross level the concept of using ethnohistorical observations as a control is useful, the specific data of both sources should be perceived as complementary and equally useful in the understanding of the patterning manifest by these historic groups.

6

Mortuary Differentiation and Social Distinction

As a test of the accuracy and reliability of social reconstructions based on funerary evidence, this chapter describes the archaeologically recovered evidence for mortuary patterning at the six Plains sites and attempts to infer from these observations the main features of Omaha, Pawnee, and Arikara social differentiation. Each group of sites belonging to a single ethnic group is considered separately (first the Pawnee, followed by the Arikara and the Omaha). For each site, the aspects of burial treatment and the composition of grave assemblages are analyzed. The data on artifact occurrence from these sites are presented in full in the appendix. The descriptions are followed by a summary of mortuary differentiation recognized at each site and its likely implications for the structure of social differentiation in the living community.

When all the sites associated with a single group have been presented, a summary of the results and an evaluation of the social reconstructions will be made, based on historical and ethnographic documentation. The final section of the chapter draws together these results with a discussion of their more general significance for the archaeological study of mortuary variability. The analyses presented in this chapter are also referred to in Chapters 7 and 8, which focus on the effects of temporal variation and ethnic differentiation on the interpretation of mortuary differentiation.

The Pawnee

Barcal Site

Formal Treatment

The single burial area associated with the Barcal site yielded a total of 34 graves. Because of soil conditions, bone preservation at the site was extremely poor. As a result, although age determinations were made on 27 of the 34 skeletons, reliable sex

TABLE 6.1
Barcal: Burial Descriptions

Grave number	Sex	Age[a]	Length	Width	Depth	Orientation	Posture[b]	Disarticulated	Multiple burial	Burial covering
1	—	3	91	61	107	W	Fx	—	—	+
2	F	4	137	91	137	W	Fx	—	—	+
3	—	8	76	51	76	W	Fx	—	—	—
4	—	8	69	56	74	—	—	—	—	—
5	—	8	119	56	86	W	—	—	—	+
6	—	3	132	97	97	—	—	—	—	—
7	F	4	109	107	114	W	Fx	+	—	+
8	—	4	140	91	97	W	Fx	+	—	—
9	—	—	102	84	51	W	—	—	—	—
10	—	9	114	99	112	W	—	+	—	—
11	—	9	97	76	86	W	Fx	+	—	+
12	M	9	109	76	109	W	Fx	—	—	+
13	—	8	114	89	112	W	Fx	—	—	+
14	—	8	97	66	89	—	—	—	—	+

#	Sex	Age				Dir	Fx			
15	—	5	122	94	114	—	—	+	—	+
16	—	4	74	56	91	E	Fx	—	—	—
17	—	4	122	76	109	W	Fx	—	—	—
18	—	9	152	127	114	SW	Fx	—	—	—
19	—	4	107	81	119	W	Fx	—	—	—
20	—	8	104	86	117	W	Fx	—	—	—
21	—	—	109	109	122	—	—	+	—	—
22	—	8	127	89	81	W	—	+	—	—
23	—	—	91	61	61	—	—	+	—	—
24	—	2	114	76	91	—	Fx	—	—	—
25	—	9	114	71	109	W	Fx	—	—	+
26	—	9	107	91	107	W	Fx	—	—	—
27	M	5	109	97	117	W	Fx	—	—	—
28	—	2	147	89	102	E	Fx	+	—	+
29	—	—	112	91	107	W	Fx	—	—	+
30	—	4	91	76	109	W	—	+	—	—
31	—	8	74	58	102	W	—	+	—	—
32	—	—	107	79	109	W	—	—	—	—
33	—	—	74	58	122	W	—	—	—	—
34	—	—	147	81	119	W	—	+	—	+

[a] 1 = 0–2 years, 2 = 3–12 years, 3 = 13–17 years, 4 = 18–30 years, 5 = 31–40 years, 6 = 41–50+ years, 8 = undifferentiated child, 9 = undifferentiated adult.
[b] Fx = flexed.

determinations were possible for only 4 of the 15 adult skeletons. It was therefore not possible to use sex as a primary referent in the Barcal analysis.

Primary inhumation was the normative burial treatment at the Barcal site. The dead were placed in a flexed posture, with the grave oriented along an east–west axis. The body was positioned with the head toward the west. In more than 40% of the cases (14/34), a wood burial covering was found. These coverings were of the "ridge-pole" type, forming a raised roof over the grave. Coverings of this type have already been described in the ethnographic discussion of Pawnee burial practices (Chapter 5). A complete summary of burial treatment at the Barcal site is presented in Table 6.1.

In addition to these normative practices, an alternative burial program was discovered at Barcal. At least nine burials were secondary interments, of which two varieties were observed (Table 6.2). In four cases, the majority of the bones were present in the grave, but in a disarticulated state. In one instance, this took the form of an articulated pelvis and lower limbs, but with the absence of any bone from the upper body (similar occurrences will be described in the other Pawnee cemeteries). In a second instance, the upper trunk of the individual was articulated, while the lower half of the body, although present, was disarticulated. In the other two cases, the majority of the bones were present, but the remains were completely disarticulated and scattered. The other variety of secondary interment involved the burial of only the cranium, without accompanying postcranial elements. This treatment was observed in five instances. Of those individuals receiving secondary burial, five were adults, two subadults, and two of indeterminate age. An equal number of adults and subadults received the skull-only burial, but only adults were disarticu-

TABLE 6.2

Barcal: Disarticulated Burial

Type and grave number	Sex	Age	Comments
Disarticulated			
7	Female	Adult	Upper half of the body articulated, lower half present but disarticulated.
15	—	Mature	Completely disarticulated.
26	—	Adult	Only pelvis and lower legs present, fully articulated.
34	—	—	Completely disarticulated.
Skull only			
6		Juvenile	
9	—	—	
10	—	Adult	
30	—	Adult	
31	—	Child	

TABLE 6.3

Barcal: Grave Dimensions by Age

	Adult average rank (N=15)	Subadult average rank (N=12)	U	Significance
Length	15.0	12.7	74.5	$p > .10$
Width	16.8	10.5	47.5	$p < .05$
Depth	17.6	9.5	36.0	$p < .01$

lated and buried with postcranial elements. Secondary interments were distributed over the entire cemetery area, with no evidence of spatial clustering.

A second differential use of burial treatment involved grave orientation. Three individuals were interred with their bodies oriented in a direction other than west: one to the southwest and two to the east. This group of individuals included both adults and subadults, and did not exhibit spatial clustering within the cemetery.

Grave size and depth were the only formal dimensions that distinguished adults from subadults at Barcal. Although there was no significant difference in average grave length between adults and subadults, the graves of adults were significantly wider and deeper than those of subadults (Table 6.3).

One final differential aspect of burial treatment at Barcal was the location of graves within the cemetery. Although only a single burial area was associated with the Barcal site, the placement of graves within it was sufficiently segregated to suggest the existence of two distinct grave clusters (Figure 6.1). This division produces northeast and southwest clusters that are very similar in size (northeast N = 15, southwest N = 16). The occurrence of age groups within the two clusters (Table 6.4) is somewhat skewed, with twice as many subadults in the northeast group and twice as many adults in the southwest group. This distribution is not so skewed, however, as to reflect factors other than chance. The fact that no other aspect of formal treatment was linked to this spatial division of the cemetery and the similarity in the cluster sizes may both argue that these groupings represent some form of horizontal social distinction, such as lineage groups.

One other aspect of the Barcal burial program that deserves comment is the occurrence of burial coverings, as they might indicate a form of burial elaboration. The frequent occurrence of the structures (42%) and their indiscriminate association with all age categories and burial types would seem to suggest that burial coverings were an element in the normative burial treatment that did not constitute a special elaboration. This being the case, the apparent absence of coverings from some graves could be explained, at least in most cases, as a failure of preservation with no social significance.

Little interaction was observed among the various aspects of burial treatment

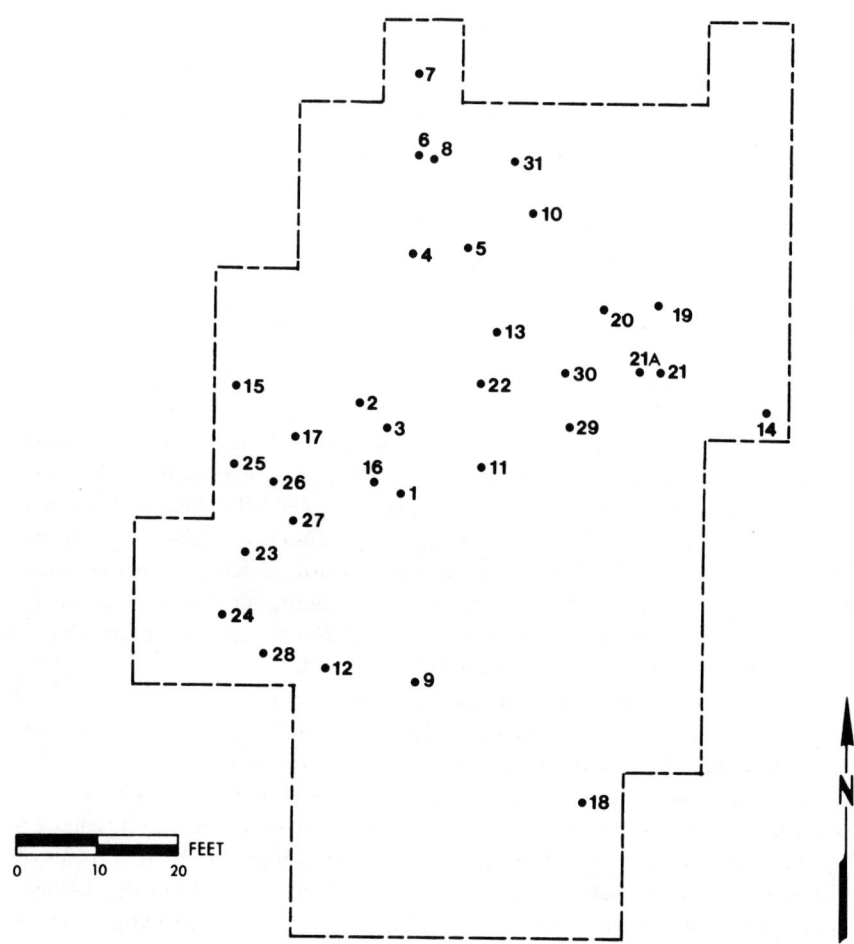

Figure 6.1 Plan of the Barcal site cemetery.

TABLE 6.4

Barcal: Demographic Composition of Burial Clusters[a]

Cluster	Adults	Subadults	Unknown	Total
Northeast	5	8	2	15
Southwest	$\underline{10}$	$\underline{4}$	$\underline{2}$	$\underline{16}$
	15	12	4	31

[a] $\chi^2 = 1.4$; $df = 1$; $p > .1$.

identified at the Barcal site. Formal treatment served to differentiate adults from subadults in grave size and may have marked two distinct kin or corporate groups through grave location within the cemetery. The significance of the alternative disposal program and of nonnormative orientation must await the consideration of artifact usage.

Artifact Occurrence

Twenty-five artifact types were observed in the burials at the Barcal site, the fewest of any of the six sites used in the analysis. These included 11 Euroamerican trade types and 14 types of native manufacture.

Although it was not possible to assess artifact association on the basis of sex, six types (24%) did exhibit distributions that were constrained by age. These types included iron knife, thick wire coil, sandstone shaft abraider, stone pipe, retouched flake, and end scraper. All these were limited in their distribution to adults and, with only one exception, represent implements rather than ornaments.

The total number of types occurring in the grave assemblages at Barcal ranged from 0 to 7 (Figure 6.2), reflecting a relatively continuous distribution. A compari-

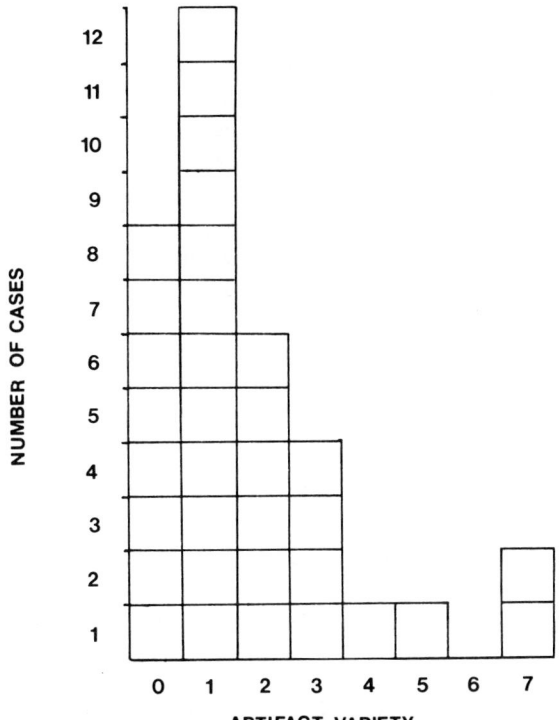

Figure 6.2 Number of different artifact types per grave assemblage at the Barcal site.

TABLE 6.5

Barcal: Artifact Class Association by Age

Artifact class	Average adult rank ($N=15$)	Average subadult rank ($N=12$)	U	Probability
Trade goods				
Body ornaments	15.5	12.1	67.5	.1276
Clothing ornaments	13.7	14.4	85.5	.7606
Implements	16.4	11.0	54.0	.0152
All trade items	16.9	10.3	46.0	.0193
Native goods				
Ornaments	14.0	14.0	90.0	.9999
Implements	15.5	12.1	67.0	.2191
Sociotechnic	14.8	13.0	78.0	.1971
All native items	15.7	11.9	64.5	.1748

son of the variety found in the graves of adults and subadults revealed that adults were buried with a significantly greater variety of grave goods than were subadults.

In addition to the basic occurrence of artifacts, structure was observed in the distribution of the six artifact classes. Table 6.5 contrasts the variety of each class of artifacts occurring in grave assemblages of adults and subadults. Adult grave assemblages exhibited a significantly greater variety of trade implements and of trade-derived items in general. Further, in no instance was a subadult buried with a sociotechnic object, although these types occurred too infrequently to permit a meaningful statistical test of their distribution. These results suggest that subadults had few hard restrictions regarding the kinds of goods placed in their grave assemblages, but that they consistently had fewer goods than did adults. This difference is most pronounced with reference to trade implements, which must have represented a relatively valuable object at the time of the Barcal occupation.

Principal Component Analysis

Because of the small number of artifact types occurring at Barcal, the 5% occurrence level for use in principal component analysis was retained, although this resulted in the inclusion of artifact types that occurred only twice. A total of 12 types met this entry criterion. Principal component analysis was conducted on the 26 graves containing artifact assemblages. Five factors were extracted with eigenvalues greater than 1.0, and these accounted for a total of 72.6% of the variance in the original correlation matrix. The rotated factor matrix is presented in Table 6.6 and a summary of the factor results in Table 6.7.

The five factors present a series of artifact sets that contrast artifact function and

TABLE 6.6

Barcal: Varimax Rotated Factor Matrix

Artifact type	Factor 1	Factor 2	Factor 3	Factor 4	Factor 5
Ceramic pot	0.68505	−0.09042	0.10097	0.21584	0.12281
Glass trade beads	0.39994	−0.45845	0.46043	0.12743	0.38502
Gun parts/accessories	0.01423	−0.05752	0.11669	−0.78462	0.12459
Mussell shell	0.03896	0.68512	−0.03402	−0.30090	0.19898
Iron knife	−0.04059	−0.12876	−0.89029	0.16485	0.15620
Metal container	0.90441	−0.05424	0.06737	−0.04751	−0.00370
Thick wire coil	0.32779	0.04650	0.44069	0.42389	0.39899
Lead band	−0.03507	−0.12854	0.12273	0.15340	−0.90288
Sandstone shaft smoother	0.81674	0.00507	0.06571	−0.47737	0.00897
Stone pipe	−0.05756	0.76549	0.18542	0.26850	0.11521
Retouched flake	0.56874	0.46321	−0.35931	0.28932	0.05792
End scraper	−0.04767	0.76562	0.00002	0.06449	−0.08269

source of origin. Factor 1 highlights both native and European containers, along with retouched flakes and sandstone shaft smoothers. Factor 2 presents a dichotomy between native and European goods, particularly implements. The positive loading of stone pipes may signal a linkage of these traditional implements with rank or prestige. Factors 3, 4, and 5 exhibit very strong, but negative, loadings on cutting

TABLE 6.7

Barcal: Factor Summary[a]

Factor number	Loading pattern	Percentage variance	Diagnostic positive loadings	Diagnostic negative loadings
1	Group	23.2	Ceramic pot Metal container Sandstone shaft smoother + Retouched flake +	
2	Bipolar	18.1	Whole mussel shell Stone pipe + End scraper +	Glass trade beads
3	Bipolar	11.4	Glass trade beads Thick wire coil +	Iron knife + Retouched flake +
4	Grouped	10.8	Thick wire coil +	Gun parts Sandstone shaft smoother Whole mussel shell
5	Specific	9.1		Lead band

[a]Constraints: + adult only.

implements (Factor 3), weaponry (Factor 4), and lead bands (Factor 5). In each case, a weaker positive loading on the factor is registered for thick wire coils and glass trade beads. These results seem to indicate that grave assemblages at Barcal did not form distinct sets. Rather, artifacts appear to have been used in a varied and overlapping manner.

Hierarchical Fusion Cluster Analysis

Hierarchical fusion cluster analysis was performed on the factor scores generated in the principal component analysis. As such, it was used to classify the 26 graves that contained at least one artifact type. The results of the six-cluster solution are presented graphically in Figure 6.3 and as cluster diagnostics in Table 6.8.

Considerable chaining is apparent in the dendrogram, reflecting the existence of

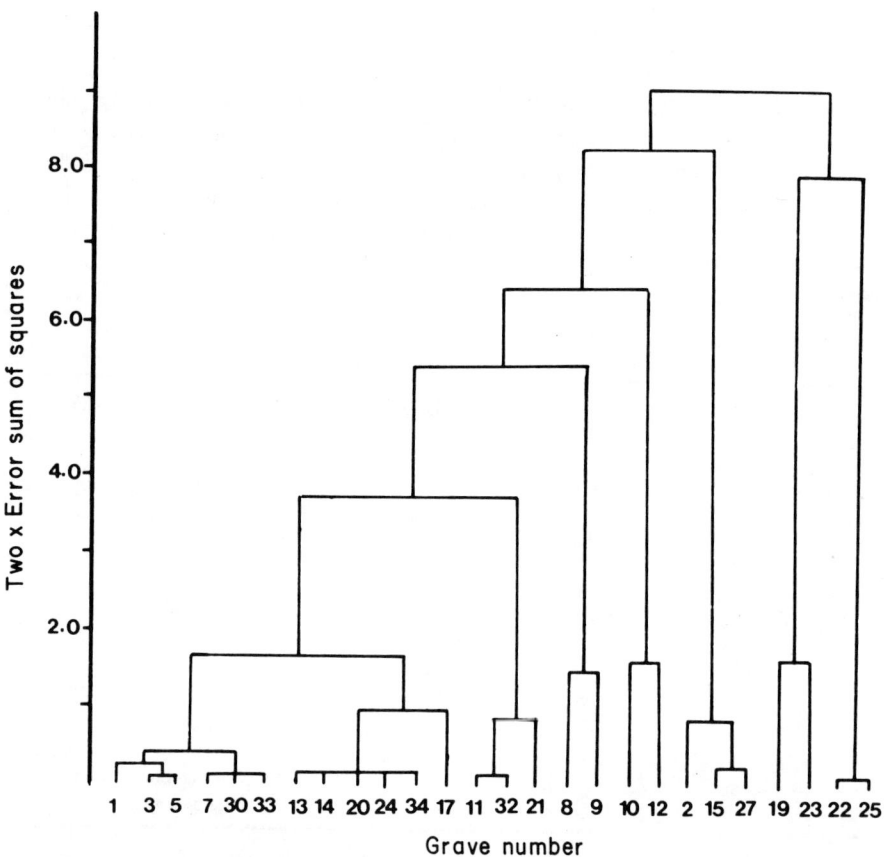

Figure 6.3 Dendrogram produced by the clustering of Barcal site factor scores.

TABLE 6.8

Barcal: Hierarchical Fusion Cluster Diagnostics

Cluster number	Factor number	Mean origin	S.D.	Factor number	Mean origin	S.D.
1	1	−.3521	.2863	4	.0963	.5675
	2	−.1679	.6907	5	.2172	.4467
	3	.2605	.4692			
	Number of individuals	15				
	Number of adults	3				
	Number of subadults	8				
	Cluster members	1,3,5,7,11,13,14,17,20,21,24,30,32,33,34				
2	1	−.1102	.4766	4	.4476	.5226
	2	−.3496	.3625	5	.4241	.1951
	3	−2.4172	.5083			
	Number of individuals	3				
	Number of adults	3				
	Number of subadults	0				
	Cluster members	2,15,27				
3	1	.0483	.6505	4	−2.6652	1.2732
	2	−.1954	.8559	5	.4232	.4596
	3	.3964	.4509			
	Number of individuals	2				
	Number of adults	1				
	Number of subadults	0				
	Cluster members	8,9				
4	1	−.1955	.5046	4	.9121	.1611
	2	2.6002	1.3644	5	.3913	.8808
	3	.6298	1.0430			
	Number of individuals	2				
	Number of adults	2				
	Number of subadults	0				
	Cluster members	10,12				
5	1	3.0721	1.3562	4	−.1614	1.0450
	2	−.1843	.7913	5	−.0126	.6479
	3	.2288	.0618			
	Number of individuals	2				
	Number of adults	1				
	Number of subadults	0				
	Cluster members	19,23				
6	1	−.1191	0	4	.5211	0
	2	−.4366	0	5	−3.0669	0
	3	.4169	0			
	Number of individuals	2				
	Number of adults	1				
	Number of subadults	1				
	Cluster members	22,25				

small, discrete groups of graves that lack any central structure. The fusion of such small-scale clusters tends only to water down the mean factor score values, producing amorphous and largely meaningless grave clusters.

The most distinct structure is the division of Clusters 5 and 6 from the rest (which would correspond to a two-cluster solution). Clusters 5 and 6 exhibit a strong positive loading on Factor 1 (graves with containers, retouched flakes, and shaft smoothers) and a strong negative loading on Factor 5 (graves with flat lead bands), respectively. The precise meaning of this division is not entirely clear, although some manner of temporal process may be responsible.

To consider the clusters individually: Cluster 2 is composed of graves with a strong negative loading on Factor 3 (i.e., graves that contain iron knives and retouched flakes); Cluster 3 showed a negative loading on Factor 4 (i.e., graves with gun parts, mussel shells, and shaft smoothers), and Cluster 4 exhibited a strong positive loading on Factor 2 (graves with mussel shells, stone pipes, and end scrapers). Cluster 1, by far the largest cluster ($N = 15$), represents primarily graves with relatively weak loadings on all five factors.

The clusters did exhibit some discrimination on the basis of age. All but one of the subadults were found in Cluster 1 (the exception was in Cluster 6). The remaining four clusters were composed exclusively of adults. Cluster 2 had individuals of both sexes, while little could be said concerning the distribution of sexes among the

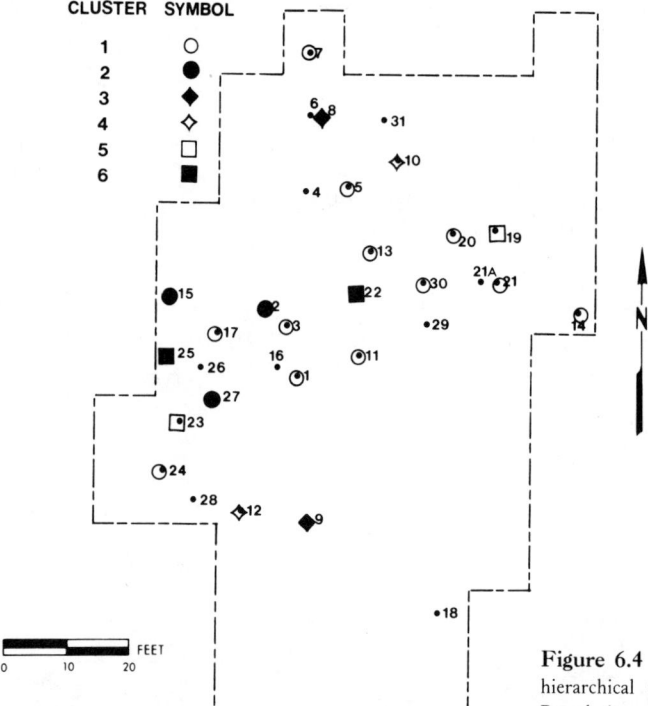

Figure 6.4 Spatial distribution of hierarchical fusion clusters at the Barcal site.

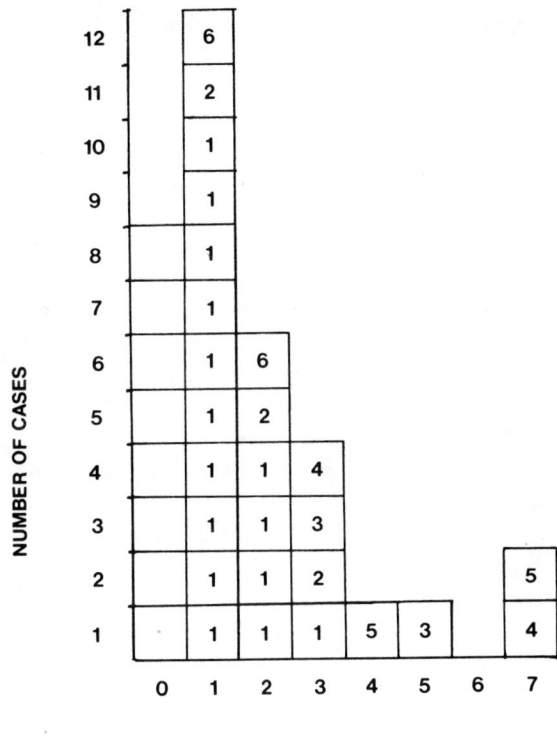

Figure 6.5 Comparison of cluster membership with variety of artifact types in the grave assemblage at the Barcal site.

remaining clusters. Cluster 4 was the sole group to contain sociotechnic items, stone pipes, and of the two members in this cluster, one was a male. This raises the possibility that pipe ownership may have been restricted to males at Barcal.

The spatial distribution of cluster members was remarkably uniform over the two burial areas (Figure 6.4). Of the four clusters that contained only two members (Clusters 3, 4, 5, and 6), each had one member in the northeast burial group and one in the southwest burial group. Only Cluster 2 (graves containing iron knives and retouched flakes) exhibited a restricted spatial distribution, with all three members located in the southwestern grave group. Although the extent of spatial clustering is insufficient to reject chance as the cause ($\chi^2 = 1.34$, $df = 1$, $p > .1$), the close placement of these three graves and their occurrence in a single burial group may suggest some relationship between these individuals.

These results suggest that variation in the composition of grave assemblage does form a kind of rank scale, with those assemblages containing implements and sociotechnic objects at one end of the scale and graves with only ornaments, particularly such cheap trade ornaments as glass trade beads, at the other end. Another aspect of this ordering can be seen by comparing the variety of artifact types occurring in each grave assemblage, with the assemblage's cluster assignment. As Figure 6.5 illustrates, members of Clusters 3, 4, and 5 have the highest values for artifact variety among the burial population. It should be remembered that only 12 of the 25 types occurring at Barcal were used in the principal component analysis, whereas all 25 types were considered in the construction of Figure 6.5. This may suggest the existence of even a third rank level, made up of those eight cases (24%) interred with no grave offering.

The results of hierarchical fusion analysis, then, do suggest some manner of vertical differentiation in the burial population. This ranking is expressed, not through the exclusive occurrence of specific artifact types, but rather in terms of the occurrence of "expensive" implements or sociotechnic objects as grave offerings and by the number of different types included within the grave assemblage. Following this scheme, individuals in Clusters 3, 4, and 5 would appear to be in the highest level (one that could not be held by subadults); individuals in Clusters 1, 2, and 6 would appear to be in the lower level, along with those individuals who were interred without grave offerings.

Monothetic Division Cluster Analysis

All 34 grave assemblages and 25 artifact types were employed in the monothetic divisive cluster analysis. The main partitioning of the population required three divisions, resulting in four terminal clusters. A summary of the cluster results is presented in Table 6.9 and Figure 6.6. The population was split first on the presence or absence of glass trade beads. Those graves lacking trade beads were divided by the occurrence of mussel shells, and the graves with mussel shells were further subdivided by the presence of iron strike-a-lights.

Little structure is apparent in the age or sex composition of these clusters. With the exception of Cluster 2 (which contained only a single member, an adult male), all the clusters exhibit a relatively even representation of adults and subadults. Both of the identified females occur in Cluster 3, as did one of the two identified males, so little can be said concerning sex-based distinctions.

None of the clusters exhibit a distinguishable pattern of spatial occurrence (Figure 6.7). In fact, the distribution of cluster members is strikingly even between the two burial zones within the cemetery.

What is perhaps best illustrated from this analysis is the relative simplicity of artifact usage in the Barcal mortuary treatment. Monothetic division, in this instance, distinguishes graves with trade beads from graves with mussel shells and both from graves with neither. The lack of any age patterning in these clusters, and their broad level of occurrence, might suggest the operation of some variety of horizontal social distinction. The absence of any clear correspondence between cluster membership and artifact variety would also support this conclusion. The precise

TABLE 6.9

Barcal: Monothetic Division Cluster Diagnostics

	Cluster[a]			
	1	2	3	4
Glass bottle	0	0	0	0
Ceramic pot	2	0	0	0
Native glass pendant	0	0	0	0
Animal effigy	0	0	0	0
Glass trade beads	9	0	0	0
Bear claw	0	0	0	0
Animal teeth	0	0	0	0
Bird beak	0	0	0	0
Bird bone	0	0	0	0
Raptor talon	0	0	0	0
Small mammal cranium	0	0	0	0
Rib shaft wrench	1	0	0	0
Squash knife	0	0	0	0
Scapula hoe	0	0	0	0
Quill flattener	0	0	0	0
Cancellous paint applicator	1	0	0	0
Awl	0	0	0	1
Metatarsal flesher	0	0	0	0
Elk horn scraper	0	0	1	0
Bone/antler implement	0	0	0	0
Gun parts/accessories	1	0	0	1
Pin game cup	0	0	0	0
Polished bone tube	0	0	0	0
Bone pendant	0	0	0	0
Curved rib ornament	0	0	0	0
Bone point	0	0	0	0
Mussel shell	2	1	0	9
Gorget	0	0	0	0
Shell hair pipe	0	0	0	0
Tubular shell bead	0	0	0	0
Wampum bead	0	0	0	0
Heavy shell bead	0	0	0	0
Rectangular shell bead	0	0	0	0
Shell runtee	0	0	0	0
Marine snail shell	0	0	0	0
Perforated shell pendant	0	0	0	0
Flat shell bead	0	0	0	0
Metal bracelet	0	0	0	0
Metal bead/bangle	0	0	1	0

(*continued*)

TABLE 6.9 Continued

	Cluster[a]			
	1	2	3	4
Iron knife	0	0	2	1
Axe/wedge	0	0	0	0
Scissors	0	0	0	0
Strike-a-light	0	1	0	0
Metal eating implement	0	0	0	0
Small metal hardware	0	0	0	0
Horse gear	0	0	0	0
Small iron tools	0	0	0	0
Metal projectile point	0	1	0	0
Iron scraper	0	0	0	0
Iron digging implement	0	0	0	0
Metal container	2	0	0	0
Metal buckle	0	0	0	0
Finger ring	0	0	1	0
Metal button	0	0	0	0
Large cast brass bell	0	0	0	0
Smaller brass bell	0	0	1	0
Thick wire coil	3	0	0	1
Thin wire coil	0	0	0	0
Metal lace/braid	0	0	0	0
Copper crimp/clip	0	0	0	0
Sheet brass blade	0	0	0	0
Lead ring/coil	0	0	0	0
Lead band	0	0	2	0
Sheet silver bracelet	0	0	0	0
Silver cross	0	0	0	0
Silver hair plate	0	0	0	0
Silver earring	0	0	0	0
Small silver brooch	0	0	0	0
Gunflint	0	0	0	0
Stone spear point	0	0	0	0
Scoria abraider	0	0	0	1
Sandstone shaft smoother	2	0	0	1
Whetstone	0	0	0	0
Hammer stone	0	0	0	0
Stone sphere	0	0	0	0
Stone projectile point	1	0	0	0
Stone pipe	0	1	0	1
Petrified wood	0	0	0	0
Retouched flake	1	1	1	0
Unretouched flake	0	0	0	0
Stone knife	0	0	0	0
Plate chalcedony knife	0	0	0	0

TABLE 6.9 *Continued*

	Cluster[a]			
	1	2	3	4
Side scraper	0	1	0	0
End scraper	0	1	0	1
Pipestone ornament	0	0	1	0
Gypsum	0	0	0	0

[a] Cluster composition:

Cluster number		
1	Number of individuals	9
	Number of adults	2
	Number of subadults	3
	Cluster members	1,3,5,9,11,19,21,23,32
2	Number of individuals	1
	Number of males	1
	Number of adults	1
	Cluster member	12
3	Number of individuals	15
	Number of males	1
	Number of females	2
	Number of adults	8
	Number of subadults	5
	Cluster members	2,4,6,7,16,18,22,25,26,27,28,29,30,31,33
4	Number of individuals	9
	Number of adults	4
	Number of subadults	4
	Cluster members	8,10,13,14,15,17,20,24,34

type of horizontal distinction that this pattern of artifact occurrence might signal, however, is not immediately clear.

Barcal Mortuary Differentiation

When the mortuary distinctions reflected in artifact usage and burial treatment are combined, we find them interlocking in a complementary fashion, with grave assemblages tending to communicate vertical distinctions and treatment attributes signaling horizontal and special status distinctions. Only rarely was a single social feature marked by both grave artifacts and treatment. Table 6.10 summarizes the main types of mortuary differentiation identified at the Barcal site.

Several varieties of vertical differentiation were recognized. A dimension termed *achieved wealth* was observed, particularly in the results of the principal component analysis and the corresponding hierarchical fusion cluster analysis. Two levels were apparent: an upper level composed solely of adults with the greatest variety of grave goods, particularly trade implements; and a lower level comprising both adults and

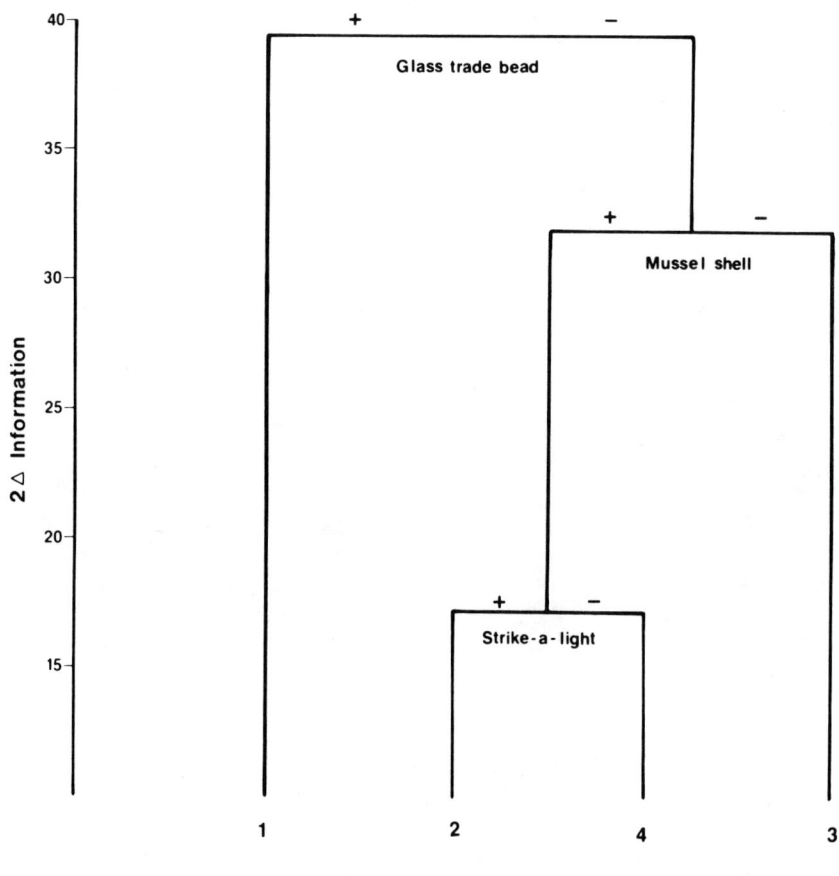

Figure 6.6 Dendrogram produced by monothetic divisive clustering of the Barcal grave assemblages.

subadults with more modest grave assemblages. The division between these two levels was not distinct; rather it appears that achieved wealth existed as a continuum with two clear modes.

The second vertical dimension was a restricted social position, which might correspond to a chiefly political office. This distinction was marked by burial with a stone pipe and was observed in only two cases (one an adult male, the other an unsexed adult). These individuals had grave assemblages from the upper wealth stratum, and both were interred with mussel shells (see below). No form of grave elaboration was associated with this distinction, but the uniform spatial distribution of the graves, one in each of the two burial clusters, tends to confirm the uniqueness of the position held by these two individuals.

The clearest horizontal distinction at Barcal was the division of the burial population into two, equal-sized groups of spatially distinct graves. Adults and subadults occurred in both burial groups. In addition, this division was crosscut by both of the vertical dimensions already discussed. One stone pipe owner was found in each of the burial areas, and both groups contained a mixture of upper and lower wealth level grave assemblages. Given these properties, it seems likely that the two burial clusters marked some manner of kin or corporate group membership. Although the limited number of cases available for analysis precludes a more precise determination of this social unit, some variety of lineage group would seem the most probable unit of social differentiation symbolized.

Adult versus subadult status was communicated through both burial treatment and artifact occurrence. The graves of adults were significantly larger and deeper than those of subadults. Similarly, a number of age-specific artifact types were identified. In addition, adults on average had a significantly greater number of trade implements and all trade goods, and a greater variety of goods in their grave assemblages. The correspondence of artifact quantity with both age and wealth seems to accentuate the "achieved" character of the Barcal system of social ranking, at least as it was symbolically expressed in the mortuary ritual.

A final element of horizontal differentiation was observed in the frequent occur-

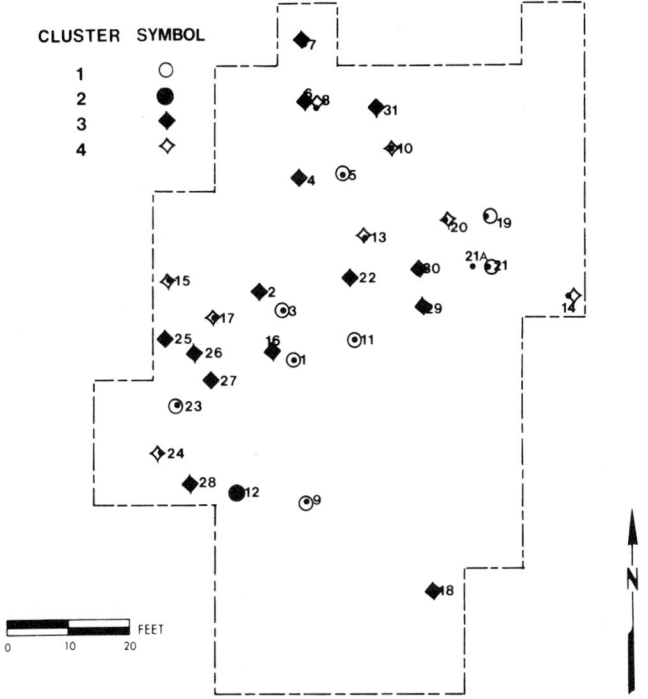

Figure 6.7 Spatial distribution of monothetic division clusters at the Barcal site.

TABLE 6.10

Barcal: Mortuary Differentiation

Social distinction	Number	Sex	Age	Formal differentiation	Artifact differentiation	Comments
Vertical distinctions						
Achieved wealth						
Upper level	11	—	Adult		Greater artifact variety Emphasis on implements	
Lower level	15	—	—		Less variety, fewer goods	
Elevated social position (Chiefly office)	2	Male(?)	Adult		Pipe ownership Upper wealth level Burial with mussel shell	One in each of the two burial areas.
Horizontal distinctions						
Corporate group (lineage)	15/16	—	—	Grave location		Crosscuts vertical distinctions.
Society membership	10	—	—		Burial with mussel shell	Crosscuts corporate group distinction.
Adult/subadult	15/11	—	—	Grave size and depth	Age-specific artifacts Variety of artifacts	
Special status distinctions						
Circumstances of death						
Location of death?	5	—	—	Skull-only burial		No wealth correlation
Season of death?	4	—	Adult	Disarticulated burial		No wealth correlation
?	2	—	—	Nonnormative orientation	No grave goods	

rence of mussel shells in the Barcal grave assemblages. Gilmore (1927:339) noted the use of mussel valves as dishes to hold consecrated tobacco among the Arikara. The shell found in the Barcal grave assemblages may have served a similar function. Shells occurred in about a third of the graves, were distributed evenly between the two burial clusters, and occurred with both adults and subadults. The frequent occurrence of shells and their tendency to crosscut both kin group and wealth boundaries would suggest they may have functioned to mark membership in some manner of sodality or totemic group. Yet, their close association with traditional goods, and particularly stone pipes (as illustrated in the results of the principal component analysis), may suggest they are linked with some manner of rank distinction as well. This is perhaps as good a case as any to illustrate the fact that the world does not always fall neatly into predetermined categories and, indeed, that some patterns of mortuary symbolism may well be recognized but uninterpretable.

Several special status distinctions were reflected in the Barcal mortuary occurrence. The two forms of disarticulated burial most probably reflect the location or the time of an individual's death. It would appear either that these individuals died away from the main settlement and their remains were transported back for burial, or that they died during the winter and could not be buried until the ground thawed in the spring. This explanation seems more probable than rank-based differentiation, because of the frequent and somewhat indiscriminate occurrence of the alternative treatment and the lack of any additional treatment or artifact inclusion to mark the distinction. Although no association between disarticulated burial and grave assemblage wealth was apparent, the demographic breakdown of the occurrences may offer some insight into the application of the two alternative forms of disarticulated burial. Although both adults and subadults could receive the skull-only burial, only adults were found to receive complete disarticulated burial. This may suggest that the latter treatment was reserved for individuals of greater social importance, since the additional manipulation or transportation of the *in toto* remains seems to imply the willingness of the community or relatives to expend an extra measure of effort in the funerary treatment.

An additional special status distinction was marked by the interment of two individuals in a nonnormative westerly orientation. The infrequent occurrence of this treatment, the nonvaluable channel used to communicate the distinction, and the total lack of grave offerings would seem to indicate either that these individuals were social deviants or that they experienced some peculiar circumstance at death. Since they were included in the community cemetery, and as one is a child, some circumstance of death would seem the more likely explanation.

To summarize the observed Barcal mortuary symbolism, funerary treatment and grave assemblage tended to perform complementary tasks in mortuary differentiation. Treatment tended to symbolize horizontal and special status distinctions, whereas the composition of the grave assemblage seemed to be the primary medium for the expression of vertical differentiation. The lack of redundancy in the symbolic marking of social distinctions may be noteworthy, particularly in the ranking of vertical distinctions. The pattern of artifact usage in the mortuary treatment suggests that trade implements were perceived as valuable commodities but that trade materials had not yet come to dominate the material culture. Indeed, native goods, in the form of stone pipes and mussel shells, carried much of the load as symbolic markers in the mortuary ritual. Overall, the grave assemblages tended to reflect the achieved personal status of each individual. Although achieved wealth is expressed, marked mortuary elaboration is not really observed at Barcal, even among the individuals holding elevated social positions. This suggests that the ranking system was probably quite weak, with little absolute difference between the individuals within it.

Linwood Site

Formal Treatment

As was the case at the neighboring Barcal site, bone preservation at Linwood was poor. For this reason, although ages could be assigned to most of the individuals in the sample, sex determinations were not possible in many instances. A complete summary of formal burial treatment at the Linwood site is presented in Table 6.11.

The normative burial treatment at Linwood was primary inhumation of the dead in a flexed posture. The graves were rectangular in shape and located in one of at least three burial areas, all of which overlooked the settlement.

Formal treatment served to differentiate several segments of the Linwood mortuary population. In addition to the normative corpse preparation treatment, an alternative disposal program was observed. In 11 cases, the dead were found in a disarticulated or semidisarticulated state. Individuals of either sex could receive this treatment. Although subadults were accorded disarticulated burial on two occasions, the treatment appears to have been restricted primarily to adults. In all but one instance, disarticulated burial took the form of a scattered mass of bone within the grave, often with a number of skeletal elements being absent. Occasionally, an anatomical subunit, such as an arm or a leg, was found intact, along with the disarticulated remains.

The exception to this pattern was found in Grave 42, in which the articulated lower half of a body was encountered (including pelvis, legs, and feet), but without any remains of the upper skeleton. In addition, the intact bones of a fetus were found positioned within the pelvis. Although the cases listed in Table 6.11 definitely represent disarticulated burials, it is possible that additional individuals received secondary burial, but in a rearticulated form. Reexamination of the osteological remains, currently in progress, promises to clarify the actual extent of secondary burial among the Pawnee.

A second aspect of the treatment that differentiated adults from subadults was grave size. The graves of adults were significantly longer than those of subadults

TABLE 6.11

Linwood: Burial Descriptions

Grave number	Sex	Age[a]	Length	Width	Depth	Orientation	Posture[b]	Disarticulated	Multiple burial	Burial covering
Area A
1	M	4	—	30	76	—	—	—	—	—
2	—	—	124	79	81	N	—	—	—	—
3	—	1	102	74	97	W	Fx	—	—	—
4	—	1	107	91	102	NE	Fx	—	—	—
5	—	2	—	—	137	NE	Fx	—	—	—
6	—	2	81	56	152	SE	Fx	—	—	—
7	—	1	122	81	76	E	Fx	—	—	—
8	M	6	155	130	163	SW	Et	—	—	+
9a	—	9	—	—	122	—	—	—	—	—
9b	—	1	91	46	142	—	—	+	—	—
10	—	9	—	—	76	—	—	+	—	—
11	—	9	—	—	132	—	—	+	—	—
17	—	9	163	74	99	—	Fx	—	—	—
24	—	2	127	79	160	NE	Fx	—	—	+
25a	M	4	—	—	—	—	—	+	—	—
25b	M	6	—	—	165	—	—	—	—	—
28	—	2	—	—	112	—	—	+	—	—
29	—	—	112	89	112	—	—	+	—	—
30	—	9	168	102	160	—	—	—	—	—
31	—	1	—	—	137	—	—	—	—	—
32	—	—	91	76	114	—	—	—	—	[c]
33	—	1	—	—	107	—	—	—	—	—
34	—	1	—	—	—	—	—	—	—	—

(*continued*)

TABLE 6.11 *Continued*

Grave number	Sex	Age[a]	Length	Width	Depth	Orientation	Posture[b]	Disarticulated	Multiple burial	Burial covering
35	M	4	179	76	155	W	Et	—	—	—
36	—	1	91	76	137	—	—	—	—	—
37	M	9	130	86	170	W	Fx	—	—	—
38	—	1	91	71	132	SE	Fx	—	—	—
Area B										
12	—	2	122	91	91	NE	Fx	—	—	—
13	—	8	152	122	112	—	—	+	—	—
14	—	1	81	81	91	SE	Fx	—	—	—
15	—	8	94	74	94	NE	Fx	—	—	—
16	—	1	102	76	76	—	—	—	—	—
18	—	8	104	66	109	—	—	—	—	—
19	—	—	168	61	147	—	—	—	—	—
20	M	4	—	—	99	—	—	—	—	—
21	F	4	—	—	124	—	—	—	—	—
22	—	2	152	122	147	W	Fx	—	—	—
23	—	—	91	61	112	—	—	—	—	—
26	—	1	130	97	142	NE	Fx	—	—	—
27	—	9	150	91	152	—	—	—	—	—

Walla Hill

39	F	4	—	—	—	—	—	—	—	—	
40	F	4	—	—	—	—	Fx	—	—	—	
41	—	—	112	76	135	E	Fx	+	—	—	
42	F	9	—	—	—	E	Fx	—	—	—	—d
43	—	1	107	61	163	W	—	—	—	—	
44	—	9	—	—	137	—	—	+	—	—	
45	—	9	—	—	51	—	Fx	—	—	—	
46	—	1	69	48	64	NE	—	+	—	—	
47	M	5	142	76	117	—	—	—	—	—	
48	F	4	117	76	69	E	Fx	+	—	—	
49	—	8	122	112	66	—	—	—	—	—	
50	—	—	84	64	89	—	—	—	—	—	—c
51	F	5	119	71	71	—	—	—	—	—	
52	—	8	97	66	84	NW	—	—	—	—	+

[a] 1 = 0–2 years, 2 = 3–12 years, 3 = 13–17 years, 4 = 18–30 years, 5 = 31–40 years, 6 = 41–50+, 8 = undifferentiated child, 9 = undifferentiated adult.
[b] Fx = flexed; Et = extended.
[c] No skeletal remains.
[d] Intact fetal remains *in situ*.

112   6. Mortuary Differentiation and Social Distinction

TABLE 6.12

Linwood: Grave Dimensions by Age

	Adult average rank	Subadult average rank	U	Significance
Length	21.9 (8)	11.5 (20)	20.5	$p<.05$
Width	16.4 (9)	14.4 (20)	77.5	$p>.10$
Depth	22.8 (18)	20.6 (24)	193.5	$p>.10$

(Table 6.12), although grave width and depth were not significantly different. The data available were insufficient to permit a meaningful test of sex-based differences in grave size.

Grave orientation seems to have been used to differentiate males (oriented toward the west) from females (oriented toward the east) (Figure 6.8). If subadults are considered relative to this orientation pattern, two-thirds exhibit a female orientation. This might indicate that an infant's apparent viability was a precondition to receiving male status.

The placement of graves in at least three distinct burial areas represents another differential component of the Linwood funerary treatment (Figure 6.9). These burial zones—Area A, Area B, and Walla Hill—contain 27, 13, and 14 interments, respectively. The demographic composition of the three zones was somewhat skewed (Table 6.13), with a relative preponderance of subadults in Area B, and of females at Walla Hill. Neither of these tendencies was sufficiently extreme, however, to be statistically significant. Nevertheless, the restrictive composition of these three areas may suggest that they were not symbolizing a horizontal distinction. This will be discussed in detail later.

In addition to these distinctions, two aspects of mortuary treatment were observed that seem to constitute special elaboration. Two individuals were interred in a nonnormative extended burial posture. Both were adult males, and both graves exhibited a size and depth at the upper end of the observed range. Only three graves were found to have a wood burial covering. Two of these were the graves of adult males, and the third of a subadult (if the burial orientation of this grave is considered, it would suggest that this child was also a male). Although both of these

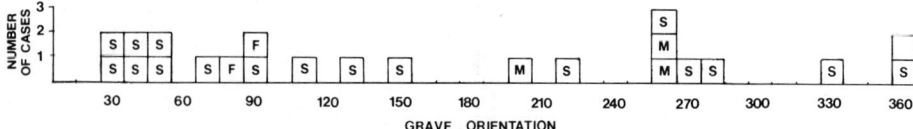

Figure 6.8 Grave orientations in the Linwood site cemeteries. Orientations are presented as degrees east of north. F, female; M, male; S, subadult.

The Pawnee 113

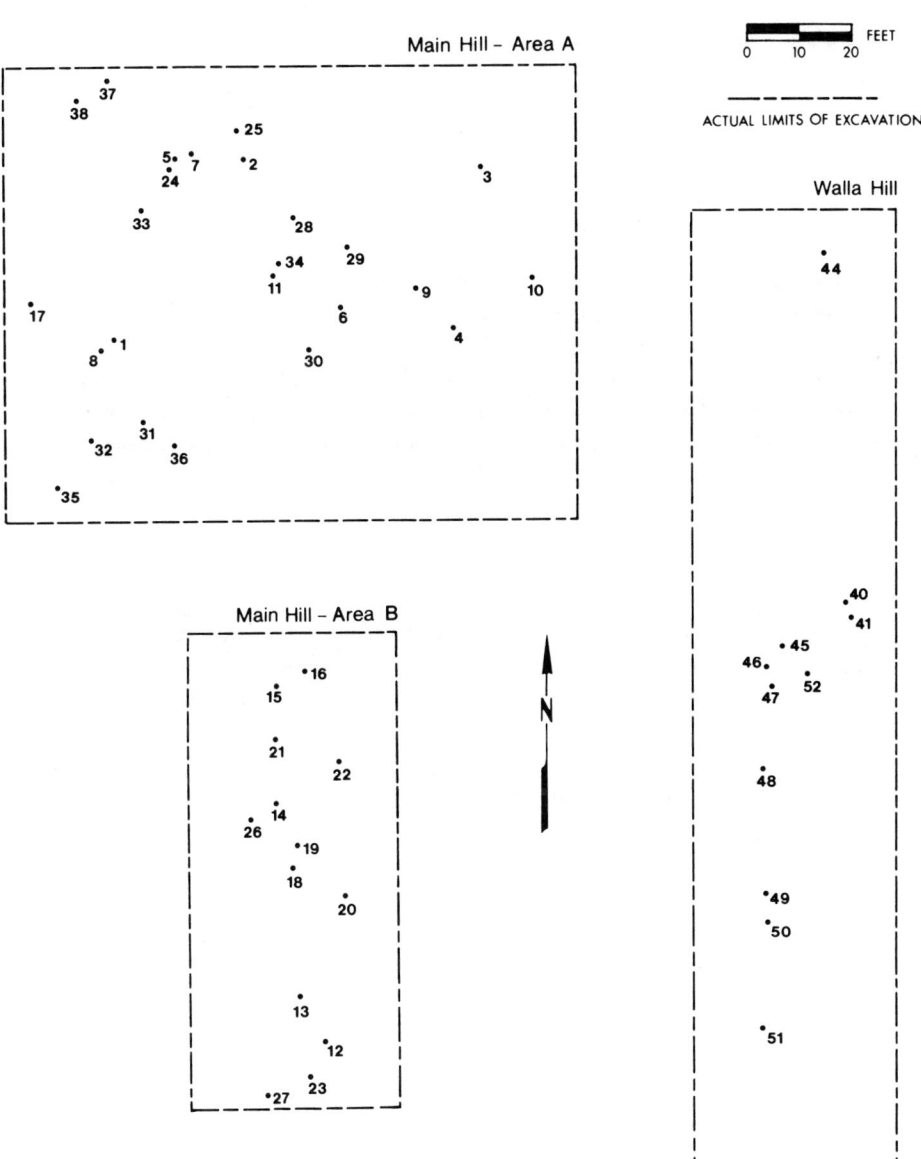

Figure 6.9 Plan of the Linwood site cemeteries.

TABLE 6.13

Linwood: Age and Sex Breakdown by Burial Area

Location	Male	Female	Adult	Subadult	Total
Area A	6	0	11	13	27
Area B	1	1	3	8	13
Walla Hill	1	5	8	4	14
	8	6	22	25	

treatments might represent special elaboration, confirmation must await a consideration of artifact usage in the Linwood mortuary treatment.

Several social dimensions appear to be expressed in the mortuary treatment. Age was distinguished by differences in grave length and the likelihood of receiving the alternative burial treatment, whereas sex was marked by grave orientation. The occurrence of distinct burial areas may be indicative of vertical social distinction. Both possible varieties of mortuary elaboration, burial coverings and extended burial, are more frequent in Area A (both instances of extended burial, and two of the three cases of burial coverings). The fact that Area A is also the nearest of the three areas to the village may suggest some ranking function in burial location. The more complete definition of this distinction, and of the alternative disposal program, must await a consideration of artifact usage in the funerary treatment.

Formal channels at Linwood carry a wide variety of social messages, including

TABLE 6.14

Linwood: Artifact Type Associations

Female	Male
—	Glass trade beads
	Tubular shell beads
	Metal bead/bangle
	Small metal hardware
	Metal buckle
	Finger ring
	Whetstone
	Stone pipe
Subadult	Adult
Metal projectile point	Iron knife
Metal button	Small metal hardware
Lead ring/coil	Metal buckle
	Smaller brass bell
	Sheet brass blade
	Gunflint
	Whetstone

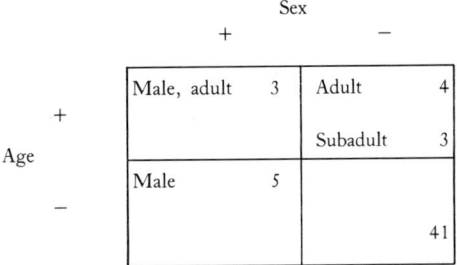

Figure 6.10 Age and sex constraints on artifact occurrence at the Linwood site.

relatively basic age and sex differences, and also various aspects of rank differentiation.

Artifact Occurrence

A total of 56 types were recovered from the Linwood burials, including 24 native types and 32 trade types. Fifteen of the 56 types (27%) exhibited some manner of constraint in their distribution; 7 by age, 5 by sex, and 3 by both age and sex (Table 6.14 and Figure 6.10). All but one of these constrained types were either trade items or artifacts for use with trade implements (such as a whetstone for sharpening a metal tool). Stone pipe was the only constrained type of native manufacture. The occurrence of these restricted artifact types was markedly asymmetrical, with no female-linked equivalents for the eight types associated exclusively with males. Of the male-restricted types, several were not constrained by age, notably the stone pipes.

TABLE 6.15

Linwood: Artifact Class Associations by Sex

Artifact class	Average male rank ($N=6$)	Average female rank ($N=6$)	U	Probability
Trade goods				
Body ornaments	7.8	5.2	10.5	.1520
Clothing ornaments	8.5	4.5	6.0	.0419
Implements	8.0	5.0	9.0	.1073
All trade items	8.3	4.7	7.0	.0719
Native goods				
Ornaments	8.5	4.5	6.0	.0190
Implements	7.7	5.3	11.0	.2123
Sociotechnic	8.0	5.0	9.0	.0578
All native items	9.2	3.8	2.0	.0074

TABLE 6.16

Linwood: Artifact Class Associations by Age

Artifact class	Average adult rank ($N=13$)	Average subadult rank ($N=20$)	U	Probability
Trade goods				
Body ornaments	16.4	17.4	122.5	.7473
Clothing ornaments	18.2	16.2	114.5	.5409
Implements	17.9	16.4	118.0	.6352
All trade items	17.8	16.5	120.0	.7088
Native goods				
Ornaments	16.9	17.5	129.0	.9633
Implements	19.8	15.2	94.0	.1202
Sociotechnic	17.9	16.4	118.0	.5095
All native items	19.3	15.5	100.0	.2440

TABLE 6.17

Linwood: Varimax Rotated Factor Matrix

Artifact type	Factor 1	Factor 2	Factor 3	Factor 4	Factor 5
Glass bottle	−0.08204	0.09836	0.82546	−0.04639	0.00215
Glass trade beads	0.05012	0.07539	0.00661	0.13233	−0.16405
Small mammal cranium	−0.07401	0.09803	−0.06073	0.15745	−0.03191
Gun parts/accessories	0.58550	0.11181	−0.00693	0.09122	0.29451
Mussel shell	−0.11190	−0.10118	0.77461	−0.01396	−0.19230
Tubular shell bead	−0.16145	−0.31957	−0.14194	0.05276	−0.23902
Metal bracelet	−0.07077	0.03615	−0.02220	0.12468	0.80829
Metal bead/bangle	−0.02627	0.83968	0.18934	−0.01147	0.15081
Iron knife	0.65124	−0.21261	−0.16304	0.28961	−0.22530
Metal eating implement	−0.08435	−0.10218	0.05438	0.10746	−0.15891
Small metal hardware	0.04498	0.12376	0.07697	0.59108	0.17582
Horse gear	0.07708	−0.02030	−0.07371	0.16284	−0.03485
Metal projectile point	0.38562	0.62673	−0.18506	−0.08132	−0.34273
Metal container	0.09349	−0.12944	0.14414	−0.09885	−0.24521
Metal buckle	0.25985	−0.04376	0.08893	0.87716	0.07661
Finger ring	−0.00108	0.05482	0.66820	0.21803	0.06639
Metal button	−0.01487	−0.07157	0.02384	0.12136	−0.04584
Smaller brass bell	−0.04531	0.06759	−0.00417	−0.31158	0.44186
Lead ring/coil	−0.07104	−0.02036	−0.28348	−0.17585	0.59898
Silver earring	−0.08632	0.07609	−0.14674	0.01128	0.02347
Gunflint	0.78133	0.08266	0.17673	0.19348	0.10366
Sandstone shaft smoother	−0.10295	0.18014	−0.19121	0.60115	−0.24769
Whetstone	0.56027	0.24525	0.29527	0.21130	0.12433
Stone projectile point	0.84462	−0.13780	−0.09489	−0.03814	−0.08934
Stone pipe	−0.03803	0.83775	−0.07635	0.12785	0.00236
Unretouched flake	0.85844	0.03126	−0.04909	−0.08873	0.09031
Stone knife	0.79699	0.26544	−0.16400	0.07724	−0.22910

If the occurrence and quantity of artifact categories are considered, a similar pattern is observed. Trade-derived clothing ornaments, native ornaments, and sociotechnic objects all occur in significantly greater quantities among males than among females (Table 6.15). Similarly, the overall occurrence of all types and of all types of native manufacture are skewed toward male grave assemblages. No significant difference in the occurrence of any class of artifact was observed between age groups (Table 6.16).

Principal Component Analysis

Principal component analysis included all graves that contained at least one artifact type and all types that occurred in at least three graves (7.5% level of occurrence). This produced a sample of 40 cases and 27 variables. A total of 11 factors were extracted with eigenvalues greater than 1.0, which jointly accounted for 82.6% of the original variance. Factor loadings are presented in Table 6.17 and summarized in Table 6.18.

Factor 1 groups a series of trade and related native implements into a single

Factor 6	Factor 7	Factor 8	Factor 9	Factor 10	Factor 11
−0.04671	−0.09163	0.09541	−0.20821	−0.02148	0.13746
−0.11265	0.02811	0.12640	−0.06333	0.85093	0.20576
0.88734	−0.06507	−0.18607	0.18486	−0.00747	−0.09046
−0.02664	0.55786	0.24698	0.17689	0.18207	0.08937
0.21587	−0.17098	−0.07766	0.15186	−0.08265	0.03519
0.15510	0.57237	0.22325	0.05685	0.24449	−0.28209
−0.10902	0.05083	−0.11882	−0.17559	−0.07760	−0.09458
0.06060	−0.08073	0.21232	−0.02633	0.00022	0.05803
0.22136	−0.05117	0.13237	0.07684	−0.05440	−0.16157
−0.00261	0.13045	−0.06973	0.11156	0.14278	0.85480
−0.15084	0.15761	0.49556	0.26451	0.25720	0.19705
0.00021	0.14497	0.88299	0.08512	0.12702	−0.10599
−0.14053	−0.11909	−0.08347	0.01560	−0.17087	−0.12142
0.67719	−0.02220	0.33052	−0.27433	−0.07667	0.17240
0.13006	0.11955	0.04892	−0.00346	0.10209	0.13486
−0.19406	0.10645	−0.23803	0.19401	0.38815	−0.32648
0.02476	0.08910	0.08802	0.90537	0.00868	0.10302
0.22985	−0.19935	0.17474	0.20872	0.56624	−0.15220
−0.09688	−0.04337	0.18500	0.38978	−0.04231	−0.10990
−0.08656	0.80989	0.05095	0.04755	−0.13120	0.18732
−0.00866	0.34607	0.06053	−0.22786	0.04577	−0.10127
0.13443	−0.32574	0.18467	0.14694	−0.20631	−0.19529
0.49358	0.16818	0.02399	−0.22470	−0.04102	−0.05281
0.00745	−0.10514	−0.12736	−0.12561	0.01723	0.05730
0.07389	0.17587	−0.18561	−0.06370	0.22020	−0.13631
−0.05171	−0.11401	0.25187	0.25879	0.04002	0.05776
−0.09504	−0.14550	−0.13590	−0.02578	−0.04286	−0.06436

TABLE 6.18

Linwood: Factor Summary[a]

Factor number	Loading pattern	Percentage variance	Diagnostic positive loadings	Diagnostic negative loadings
1	Group	16.8	Gun parts Iron knife + Gunflint + Whetstone M+ Stone projectile point Unretouched flake Stone knife	
2	Bipolar	10.8	Metal bead/bangle M Metal projectile point − Stone pipe M	Tubular shell bead M Iron knife +
3	Bipolar	9.4	Glass bottle Whole mussel shell Finger ring M	Lead ring/coil −
4	Bipolar	8.9	Small metal hardware M+ Metal buckle M+ Sandstone shaft smoother	Smaller brass bell +
5	Bipolar	7.3	Metal bracelet Lead ring/coil −	Tubular shell bead M Iron knife + Metal projectile point − Metal container Sandstone shaft smoother Stone knife
6	Group	6.3	Small mammal cranium Metal container	
7	Bipolar	5.8	Gun parts Tubular shell bead M Silver earring	Sandstone shaft smoother

[a] Constraints: +, adult only; −, subadult only; M, male only; F, female only.

integrated male tool kit, with an apparent emphasis on hunting (and perhaps warfare). Factors 4 and 8 also appear to group functionally related sets of implements. Factor 2 is of interest because of the positive loading on stone pipes. Yet, this factor does not seem to reflect a set of ritual goods; instead it loads with two small trade types, metal bangles and metal projectile points, and exhibits a strong negative loading on a series of processing and food preparation tools. The factor perhaps may best be interpreted as distinguishing a set of male (regardless of age) items from a series of possibly female-related food processing tools. The remaining factors define body ornament sets for subadults (Factors 5 and 9) and for general usage (Factor 10) and two sets of domestic implements (Factors 6 and 11) that might be expected to have a female association. Factor 7 seems to mark a set of valuable trade items, again with a clear male association.

The factor results illustrate the complete integration of trade materials into Pawnee material culture. Trade as well as native-made artifacts seem to perform symbolic functions in the mortuary ritual. These results emphasize the asymmetrical symbolic definition of male and female roles in the Linwood funerary treatment.

Hierarchical Fusion Cluster Analysis

The clustering of factor scores produced from the principal component analysis revealed a relatively weak overall organization of material culture in the Linwood mortuary occurrence. The lack of a strong central structure of artifact occurrence is evident in the clear tendency for chaining in the dendrogram (Figure 6.11). The cluster diagnostics are presented in Table 6.19, and the spatial distribution of cluster members in Figure 6.12.

The overall pattern suggested by this cluster result is a series of grave assemblages that are loosely formed into a rank ordering, reflecting some manner of achieved wealth. If this interpretation is correct, Clusters 2 and 5 would represent

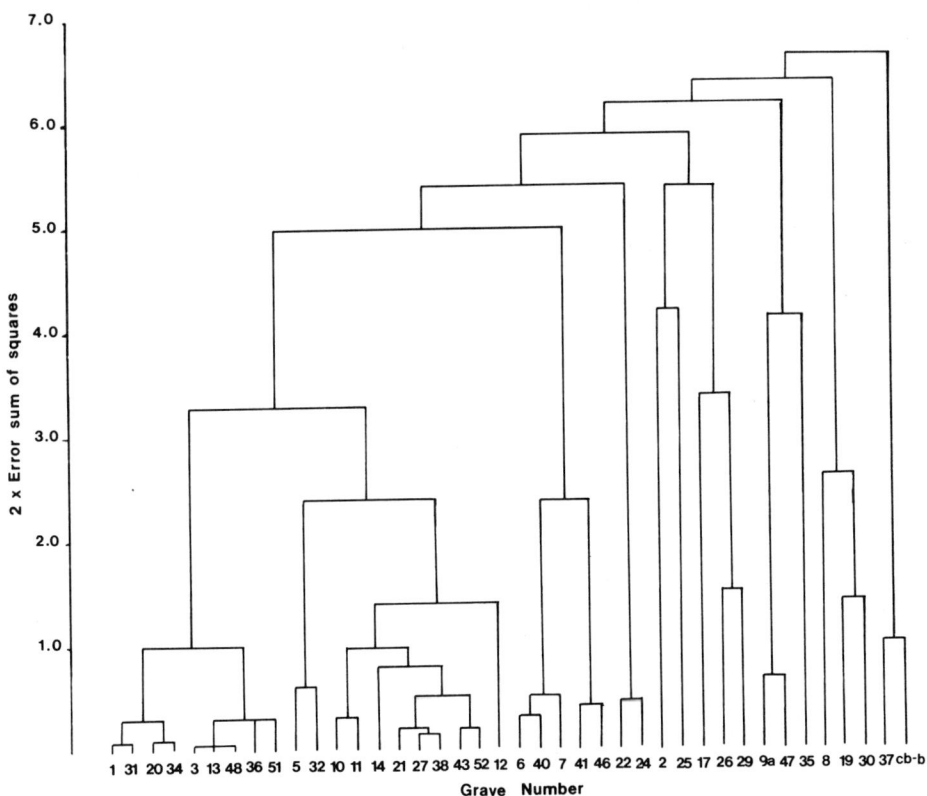

Figure 6.11 Dendrogram produced by the clustering of Linwood site factor scores.

TABLE 6.19

Linwood: Hierarchical Fusion Cluster Diagnostics

Cluster number	Factor number	Mean origin	S.D.	Factor number	Mean origin	S.D.
1	1	−.2790	.2206	7	−.2496	.6056
	2	−.0477	1.0001	8	−.1046	.4183
	3	−.1327	.8571	9	−.2588	.6034
	4	−.2543	.3997	10	−.2189	.9261
	5	.0275	1.0190	11	.1032	.8939
	6	−.2436	.4862			
	Number of individuals	27				
	Number of males	2				
	Number of females	4				
	Number of adults	6				
	Number of subadults	15				
	Cluster members	1,3,5,6,7,10,11,12,13,14,20,21,22,24,27,31,32,34 36,38,40,41,43,46,48,51,52				
2	1	.0240	.5668	7	1.3242	2.0201
	2	.0634	.8105	8	1.6510	1.9921
	3	−.4569	.5320	9	.6713	1.8308
	4	.5737	1.9225	10	.4950	.3573
	5	−.1268	.9769	11	.3155	1.6968
	6	−.1324	.4600			
	Number of individuals	5				
	Number of males	1				
	Number of females	0				
	Number of adults	1				
	Number of subadults	1				
	Cluster members	2,17,25,26,29				
3	1	−.2567	.2143	7	−.2257	.7332
	2	.3400	1.5826	8	−.6453	.0380
	3	−.2107	.6000	9	.6410	1.2281
	4	.5460	1.5879	10	−.0259	1.6634
	5	−.1106	.7838	11	−.3137	.5232
	6	3.0769	.4558			
	Number of individuals	3				
	Number of males	1				
	Number of females	0				
	Number of adults	1				
	Number of subadults	0				
	Cluster members	8,19,30				

TABLE 6.19 *Continued*

Cluster number	Factor number	Mean origin	S.D.	Factor number	Mean origin	S.D.
4	1	−.0038	.4754	7	.3692	.6962
	2	.1901	1.3886	8	−.8254	.5019
	3	2.3170	.2961	9	.6728	1.7767
	4	.7561	1.8426	10	1.3460	.7449
	5	.2303	1.7339	11	−1.1321	.7468
	6	−.6730	.2095			
	Number of individuals	3				
	Number of males	2				
	Number of females	0				
	Number of adults	2				
	Number of subadults	1				
	Cluster members	9a,35,47				
5	1	4.0968	.1897	7	−.1555	.1897
	2	−.3102	.8790	8	−.5093	.5779
	3	−.2262	.0912	9	−.1556	.3129
	4	.0462	1.4912	10	−.2620	1.2063
	5	−.2341	.7315	11	−.0133	.3450
	6	.0141	.2292			
	Number of individuals	2				
	Number of males	1				
	Number of females	0				
	Number of adults	2				
	Number of subadults	0				
	Cluster members	37, Cache Burial B				

the most highly ranked, Clusters 3 and 4 an intermediate level, and Cluster 1 the lowest and least differentiated category. The ranking is not sharply defined. Instead, a continuous distribution of wealth is partitioned by the apparent "cost" of the trade goods placed with the deceased. Cluster 5 exhibited a strong loading on Factor 1, the male implement set that included gun parts, iron knife, whetstone, stone knife, and stone projectile point. The other upper-level wealth cluster was number 2, which loaded on Factor 7 (gun parts, shell beads, and silver earring) and on Factor 8 (horse gear). The middle-level clusters, 3 and 4, although containing a number of trade items, did not possess the larger, more expensive implements, or silver. Instead, they emphasized sets of small metal ornaments (Cluster 4) and metal containers (Cluster 3). As Clusters 2, 4, and 5 all share a marked male emphasis, these results would suggest that the upper levels of achieved wealth were restricted primarily to males. Cluster 1 is an unmistakable composite that contains all the known female grave assemblages and the majority of subadults. This cluster primarily is made up of those assemblages with relatively weak loadings on all the factors. It also contains several small sets of graves that share high loadings on other

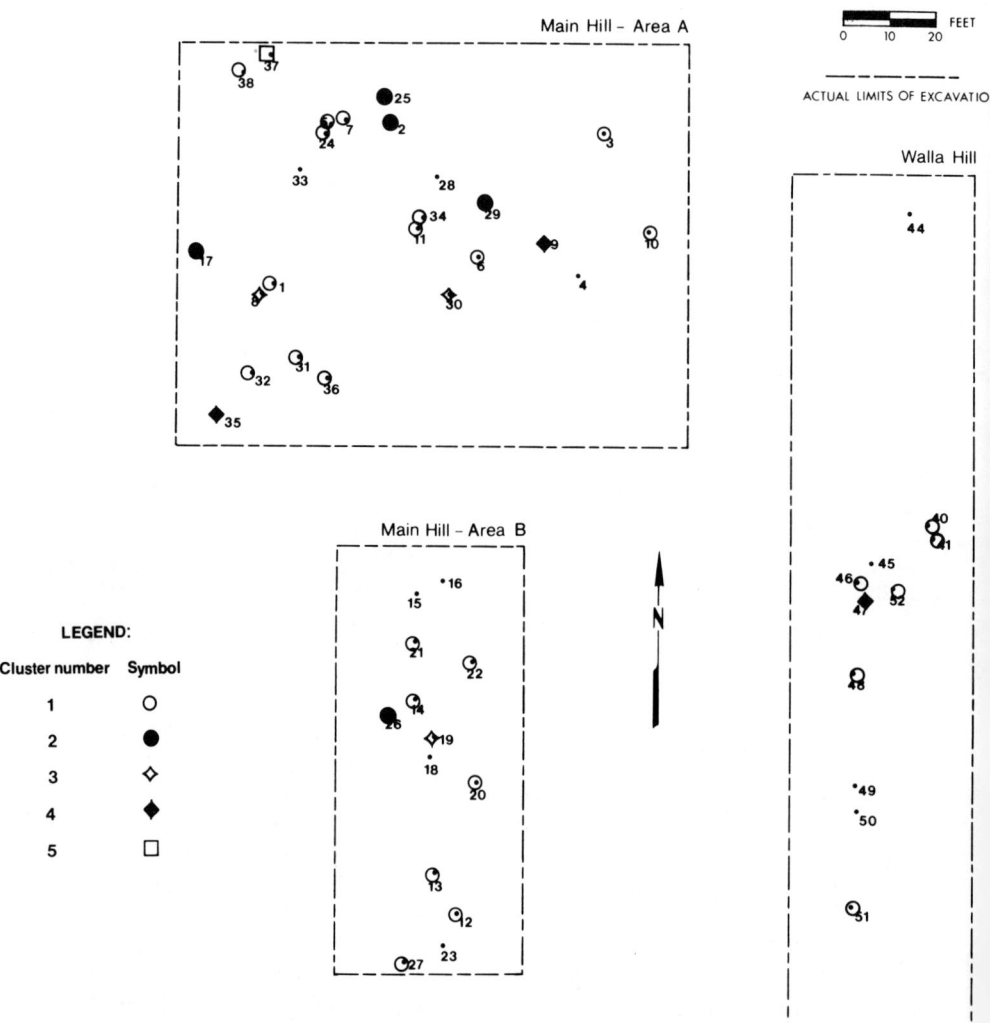

Figure 6.12 Spatial distribution of hierarchical fusion clusters at the Linwood site cemeteries.

factor combinations. A good example is those graves with a positive loading on Factor 2, which includes stone pipe.

A comparison of cluster membership with the number of artifact types in the grave assemblage supports the conclusion that this cluster result primarily represents a dimension of wealth (Figure 6.13). When all artifacts are considered, Clusters 2 and 5 again contain the greatest quantities, Clusters 3 and 4 have intermediate numbers, and Cluster 1 has the least number, as observed previously.

Some further suggestion of rank order underlying this cluster result is found in the spatial distribution of cluster members. Cluster 1 members, representing the lowest wealth level, dominated the occurrences in Area B and at Walla Hill, whereas Clusters 2 and 5, representing the highest wealth level, were limited in their occurrence to Area A (Figure 6.12). Such a correspondence between wealth and burial area would suggest that the privilege of burial in the nearest and most prominent cemetery area was controlled, at least in part, by personal or family wealth standing.

Two more general observations can be drawn from this cluster analysis. The emphasis on trade materials as markers of wealth would indicate a basic change in the character of Pawnee material culture. It also may suggest that participation in trade was an important vehicle for the acquisition of wealth among the Linwood Pawnee.

The lack of close correspondence between wealth and stone pipe ownership is also of interest. This imperfect fit, coupled with the lack of age constraint in pipe ownership, seems to indicate that the pipe marked a hereditary position or privilege that was not directly tied to personal achievement or wealth. The use of trade materials as wealth indicators is even more pronounced in the results from monothetic divisive cluster analysis.

Monothetic Division Cluster Analysis

Monothetic divisive cluster analysis was performed on all 51 of the Linwood graves and produced a partitioning of the cemetery population very similar to that derived from the cluster analysis above. These results are summarized in Table 6.20

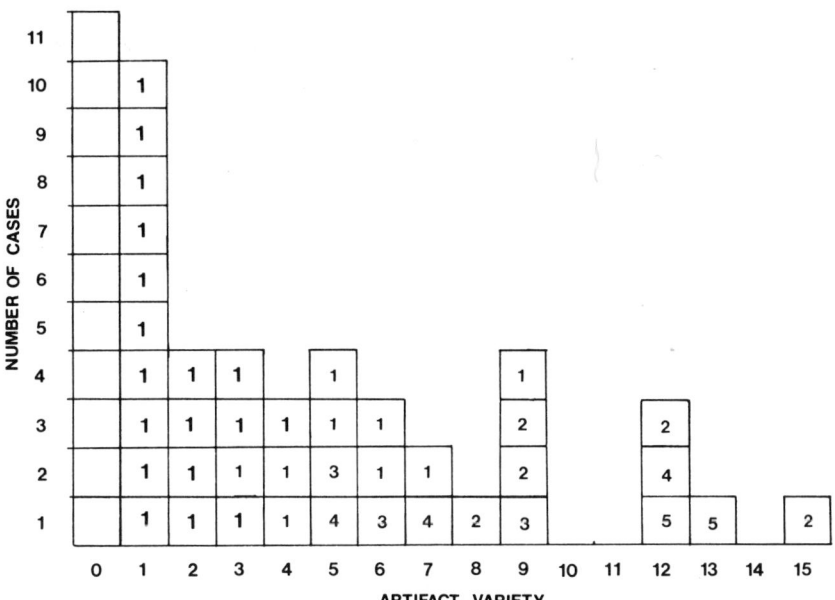

Figure 6.13 Comparison of hierarchical fusion cluster membership with variety of artifact types in the grave assemblage at the Linwood site.

TABLE 6.20

Linwood: Monothetic Division Cluster Diagnostics

	Cluster[a]			
	1	2	3	4
Glass bottle	0	4	2	1
Ceramic pot	0	0	1	0
Native glass pendant	0	0	0	0
Animal effigy	0	0	0	0
Glass trade beads	1	7	9	5
Bear claw	0	0	0	2
Animal teeth	0	0	1	0
Bird beak	0	0	0	0
Bird bone	0	1	0	1
Raptor talon	0	0	0	1
Small mammal cranium	0	3	0	0
Rib shaft wrench	0	0	1	0
Squash knife	0	0	1	0
Scapula hoe	0	0	0	0
Quill flattener	0	0	1	0
Cancellous paint applicator	0	0	0	0
Awl	0	0	1	0
Metatarsal flesher	0	0	0	0
Elk horn scraper	0	0	0	0
Bone/antler implement	0	0	0	0
Gun parts/accessories	2	0	0	6
Pin game cup	0	0	0	0
Polished bone tube	0	0	1	0
Bone pendant	0	0	0	0
Curved rib ornament	0	0	0	0
Bone point	0	0	0	0
Mussel shell	0	4	2	0
Gorget	0	2	0	0
Shell hair pipe	0	0	0	0
Tubular shell bead	0	4	3	4
Wampum bead	0	0	0	0
Heavy shell bead	0	0	0	0
Rectangular shell bead	0	0	0	0
Shell runtee	0	0	0	0
Marine snail shell	0	0	0	0
Perforated shell pendant	0	1	0	0
Flat shell bead	0	0	0	0
Metal bracelet	0	0	4	2
Metal bead/bangle	0	3	3	2
Iron knife	2	2	0	0
Axe/wedge	0	1	0	0

TABLE 6.20 *Continued*

	Cluster[a]			
	1	2	3	4
Scissors	0	0	0	2
Strike-a-light	1	0	0	1
Metal eating implement	0	2	0	1
Small metal hardware	0	1	0	3
Horse gear	0	1	0	2
Small iron tools	0	0	0	1
Metal projectile point	1	0	2	0
Iron scraper	0	0	0	0
Iron digging implement	0	2	0	0
Metal container	1	12	0	2
Metal buckle	1	2	0	2
Finger ring	0	0	2	1
Metal button	0	1	2	2
Large cast brass bell	0	0	0	1
Smaller brass bell	0	1	3	2
Thick wire coil	0	0	0	0
Thin wire coil	0	0	1	1
Metal lace/braid	0	0	0	0
Copper crimp/clip	0	0	0	0
Sheet brass blade	1	1	0	0
Lead ring/coil	0	0	4	3
Lead band	0	0	0	1
Sheet silver bracelet	0	1	0	0
Silver cross	0	0	1	0
Silver hair plate	0	0	0	0
Silver earring	0	0	2	3
Small silver brooch	0	0	0	1
Gunflint	2	0	0	2
Stone spear point	0	0	0	0
Scoria abraider	0	0	0	0
Sandstone shaft smoother	0	2	2	0
Whetstone	2	3	0	2
Hammer stone	0	0	0	0
Stone sphere	0	0	0	0
Stone projectile point	2	1	0	0
Stone pipe	0	1	2	2
Petrified wood	0	0	0	1
Retouched flake	2	0	0	0
Unretouched flake	2	0	0	1
Stone knife	2	0	1	0
Plate chalcedony knife	0	0	0	0
Side scraper	1	0	0	0
End scraper	2	0	0	0

(*continued*)

TABLE 6.20 *Continued*

		Cluster[a]			
		1	2	3	4
Pipestone ornament		0	0	0	0
Gypsum		0	0	0	1

[a] Cluster composition:

Cluster number		
1	Number of individuals	2
	Number of males	1
	Number of females	0
	Number of adults	2
	Number of subadults	0
	Cluster members	37, Cache Burial B
2	Number of individuals	12
	Number of males	2
	Number of females	1
	Number of adults	3
	Number of subadults	6
	Cluster members	6,7,8,19,25,30,31,34,36,40,41,46
3	Number of individuals	31
	Number of males	3
	Number of females	5
	Number of adults	10
	Number of subadults	13
	Cluster members	1,3,4,9a,10,11,12,13,14,15,16,18,20,21,22, 23,24,27,28,32,38,39,42,43,44,45,47,48,50, 51,52
4	Number of individuals	6
	Number of males	1
	Number of females	0
	Number of adults	1
	Number of subadults	2
	Cluster members	2,5,17,26,29,35

and Figure 6.14. The first two divisions distinguished graves with gun parts and then divided those graves lacking gun parts by the presence or absence of metal containers. This seems to provide the most essential level of structure in artifact usage at the Linwood cemetery. The third division further separated graves with gun parts by the presence of iron knives. As in the hierarchical fusion analysis, all the variables responsible for these critical divisions were trade items.

The results of this analysis highlight the clear distinction between those graves with few, if any, grave goods (Cluster 3) and those with quantities of offerings. The demographic composition of the clusters provides further definition to this structuring of the mortuary population. Clusters 1 and 4 both appear to be male grave assemblages. Of these, Cluster 1 isolates an adult male assemblage, while Cluster 4 appears to lack any age qualifications. Cluster 2 is open to either sex and all ages. Although the assemblages in this cluster exhibit a range of sociotechnic objects and trade materials, the average number of artifacts in the grave assemblage was lower than that of Clusters 1 and 4 (Figure 6.15). Cluster 3 burial assemblages contained the fewest grave offerings. Assemblages of this type were not restricted by age or sex. Despite the relative paucity of grave goods in these assemblages, they did contain an occasional sociotechnic object. The spatial distribution of grave assemblages was also similar to that obtained through the earlier cluster analysis. The great majority of the graves in both Area B and Walla Hill belonged to Cluster 3, whereas the majority of the richer grave assemblages were restricted to Area A (Figure 6.16).

The results from monothetic divisive analysis are consistent with our expectations for the designation of a vertical social distinction. An individual's rank along this dimension would seem to be expressed through the richness of the grave assemblage and particularly by the occurrence of expensive trade items. The highest of these levels was limited to males, whereas membership in the intermediate or lower level was open to individuals of either sex.

It is important to note that this ranking is not sensitive to the presence of

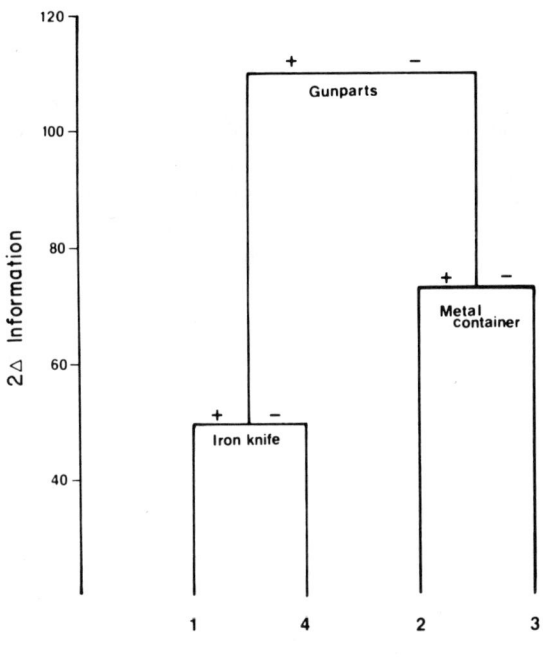

Figure 6.14 Dendrogram produced by monothetic divisive clustering of the Linwood grave assemblages.

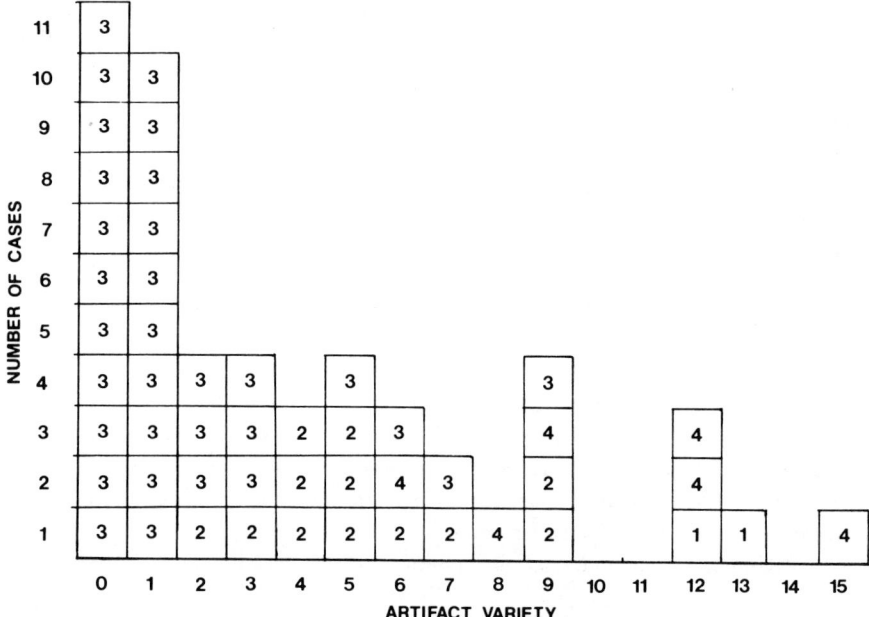

Figure 6.15 Comparison of artifact variety with monothetic divisive cluster membership at the Linwood site.

sociotechnic objects in the burial assemblage. Since this dimension seems to reflect a type of personal wealth distinction, it seems that the prerogative of burial with these other social symbols, particularly stone pipes, reflects a distinct social dimension not tied to wealth. The occurrence of stone pipes with impoverished subadult grave assemblages would seem to support this conclusion and perhaps argue for the hereditary transmission of such distinction.

Artifacts in the Linwood mortuary complex served principally to mark vertical types of social distinctions. The constraint on artifact occurrence, particularly the asymmetry in the symbolic representation of male and female tasks, seems to reflect an enhanced importance of male roles in the Linwood social organization. Since artifact occurrence is closely tied with the symbolic designation of distinctions, this may indicate that males had preferential access to wealth, perhaps through participation in the Euroamerican trade.

The multivariate analyses highlighted the importance of trade goods in the Linwood mortuary symbolism and illustrated how completely they had been integrated into Pawnee material culture. An individual's economic standing or access to wealth was expressed through the range and type of ornaments worn by the deceased and by the implements that were placed with the dead in the grave. In addition to wealth, the occurrence of sociotechnic artifacts marked further distinctions, most importantly stone pipe ownership. Pipes occurred among both young and old (although limited to males), regardless of the individual's personal wealth. This pattern of occurrence is characteristic of a social distinction that is ascribed rather than achieved, and seems to reflect a vertical distinction independent of personal wealth. The interrelationship of these vertical dimensions will be clarified in the next section when considered in light of the corresponding variables of mortuary treatment.

Linwood Mortuary Differentiation

When the mortuary distinctions expressed through burial treatment and artifact occurrence are combined, a clear and well-integrated system of mortuary symbolism is apparent. This system of mortuary differentiation is summarized in Table 6.21.

Three main types of vertical distinction were expressed. The economic standing, or wealth, of an individual was expressed through the content of the burial assemblage and by the location of the grave among the three burial areas. Three

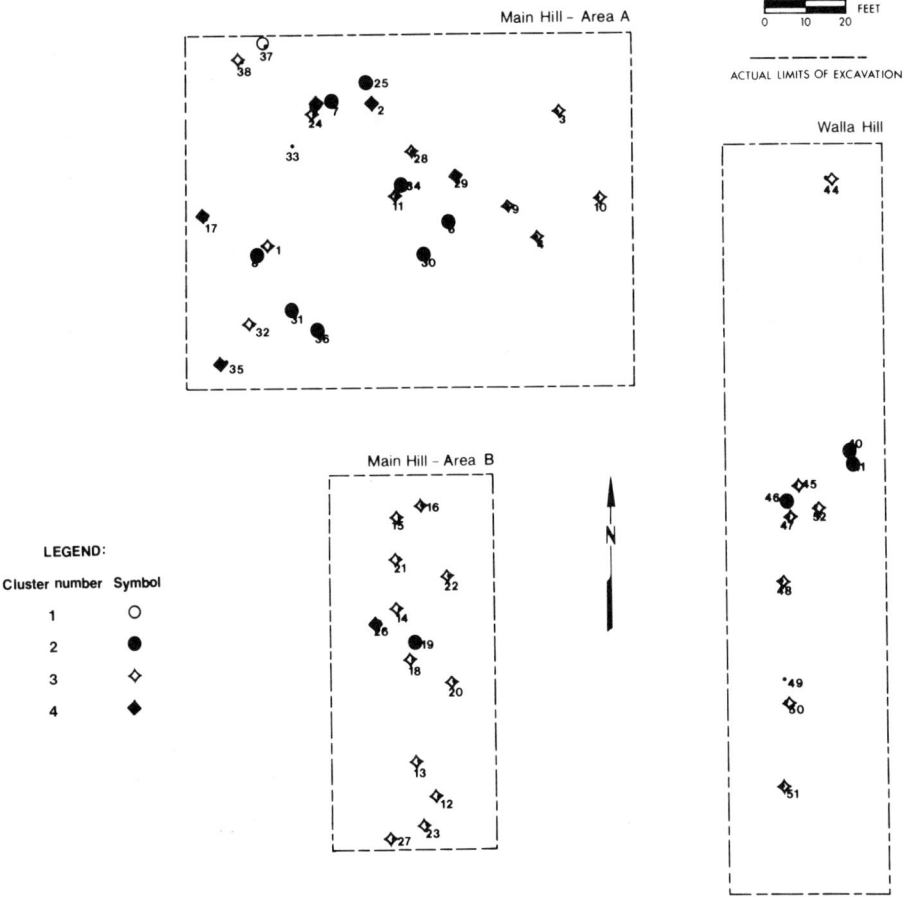

Figure 6.16 Spatial distribution of monothetic divisive clusters at the Linwood site cemeteries.

TABLE 6.21

Linwood: Mortuary Differentiation

Social distinction	Number	Sex	Age	Formal differentiation	Artifact differentiation	Comments
Vertical distinctions						
Achieved wealth						Grave location criterion is not absolute for these wealth levels
Upper level	8	Male	—	Burial in Area A	Greatest artifact variety. Emphasis on expensive trade goods	
Middle level	12	—	—		Fewer valuable trade goods	
Lower level	31	—	—	Burial in Area B or Walla Hill	Few if any grave goods	
Elevated social position						
Chiefly office	2	Male	Adult	Burial in Area A. Extended burial posture	Pipe ownership. Upper wealth level	
Hereditary ritual office	4	Male	—	Burial in Area A	Pipe ownership	Imperfect correlation with achieved wealth, particularly among subadults.
Horizontal distinctions						
Adult/subadult	16/21	—	—	Grave size	Age-specific artifacts	
Male/female	7/6	—	—	Grave orientation	Gender-specific artifacts	
Special status distinctions						
Circumstances of death						
Location or season of death	11	—	Adult	Disarticulated burial	Few grave goods	
Remains not recovered for burial	2	—	—	Symbolic grave	Few grave goods	Most frequent in Area A.

distinct levels of wealth could be identified. The uppermost level contained graves with the greatest quantity of artifacts and particularly the occurrence of valuable trade goods, such as gun parts, silver ornaments, and iron knives. Individuals in this category were buried in Area A, the nearest to the village. Only males could achieve this highest wealth level. The second level contained an intermediate number of types in its grave assemblages, again with an emphasis on trade items, such as metal containers. Membership in this middle level was open to both males and females, and these individuals also were most frequently buried in Area A. The lowest wealth level includes those graves with few, if any, grave offerings. These individuals tended to be buried in the more distant areas, Area B and Walla Hill.

The occurrence of wood burial coverings corresponded, to a degree, with personal wealth. Two of the three individuals found with such coverings were adult males of the uppermost wealth category. The third, however, was a subadult from the lowest wealth level. Given the uncertainty inherent in the recovery of these coverings, no firm conclusion can be drawn from these occurrences.

The second vertical dimension is consistent with the designation of an individual who held a position of social and political leadership within the community that might be termed *chiefly office*. These individuals, all adult or mature males, were buried in an extended posture and were located in Burial Area A. In addition, both individuals had grave assemblages that identified them as members of the uppermost wealth stratum. Both individuals also were stone pipe owners.

The third rank distinction symbolized at Linwood was seen in pipe ownership. Pipe ownership was limited to males (but without age restriction) buried exclusively in Area A (despite the fact that not all were members of the upper wealth stratum). Given the imperfect association between achieved wealth and pipe ownership, and the pattern of grave location, it appears that this position may have been a hereditary ritual office. It is also informative to note that all the pipe owners with poor grave assemblages were subadults! Given the close relationship between pipes and trade, and the importance of trade goods in the accumulation of wealth at Linwood, pipe ownership may reflect a hereditary right to conduct trade. The grave assemblages of the subadults would then reflect their potential, although unfulfilled, to participate in such trade activities.

The horizontal distinctions symbolized at Linwood are limited to the simple differentiation of adults from subadults and males from females. Age-based distinctions are less pronounced and were marked by significantly longer adult graves and by a series of age-specific artifact types. Sex distinctions were symbolized by grave orientation and by sex-specific artifact types.

Considerable asymmetry was observed in the designation of male versus female roles. Although a number of artifact types were exclusively associated with males of any age, no equivalent female types were observed. Females also received grave assemblages with consistently fewer native implements and fewer types overall. This may reflect a greater emphasis on male roles and activities resulting from the increased importance of trade and trade goods to the Linwood Pawnee.

Two special status distinctions were recognized at Linwood. The first was indicated by an alternative burial treatment, disarticulated burial. This status was significantly, but not exclusively, associated with adults. Individuals who received this treatment typically possessed relatively poor burial assemblages and yet were most often interred in burial Area A. The most likely explanation is that this alternative treatment marks individuals who died while the tribe was away from the main village and whose remains were returned for burial. This probably was not done in all cases. The location of the burials suggests that this was more likely to occur in the case of important or wealthy individuals.

The second special distinction was indicated by "symbolic" graves, graves with normal dimensions and modest grave assemblages that gave no evidence that a body was placed in the grave. A possible explanation for this occurrence is that they represent the death of individuals whose remains could not be recovered for burial. Clearly, symbolic graves were not constructed for every individual whose remains were not recovered; there must have been many. These individuals must have represented in some sense special cases.

Both special status distinctions seem to present a contradiction in Linwood mortuary symbolism. In both cases, the community seems willing to expend extra effort in the mortuary treatment of these individuals, and yet all have rather modest grave assemblages. In these instances, the circumstances of death seem to take precedence over the designation of an individual's specific social standing. There may also be a practical reason for the poorer grave assemblages. Much of the grave assemblage comes to the grave as a result of being worn by the deceased at the time of burial or as an identifiable accessory. In the case of disarticulated burial, or when there is no body, many of these elements would have been unnecessary or even inappropriate on purely practical grounds and as such are not found archaeologically in the grave assemblage. This would seem to be a case where the qualitative distinction far outweighs the quantitative one.

In all, mortuary symbolism at the Linwood site is well integrated and redundant. Most of the social distinctions symbolized in the mortuary ritual are reflected both by aspects of treatment and by the content of the grave assemblage. Perhaps the two most striking aspects of the mortuary symbolism are the relatively weak definition of age-based distinctions and the marked emphasis on male roles and activities relative to female roles.

Clarks Site

Formal Treatment

The normative burial treatment at the Clarks cemetery was primary inhumation of the dead in a flexed posture. The graves were of variable oblong shape and located in at least five distinct burial areas on the bluff tops overlooking the village. Graves tended to be oriented in a northerly direction (Table 6.22).

TABLE 6.22
Clarks: Burial Descriptions

Grave number	Sex	Age[a]	Length	Width	Depth	Orientation	Posture[b]	Disarticulation	Multiple burial	Burial covering
Burial Hill 1										
1	M	4	119	69	147	N	Fx	—	—	—
2	M	6	160	66	109	N	Fx	—	—	—
Burial Hill 2										
1	M	4	124	74	155	N	Fx	—	—	—
2	M	4	152	81	112	NE	Fx	—	—	—
4	—	1	58	51	81	NE	Fx	—	—	—
5	—	4	135	84	102	NE	—	+	—	—
6	—	8	79	38	94	NE	Fx	—	—	—
7	—	1	53	33	61	NW	Fx	—	—	—
8	—	—	122	46	86	NE	Fx	—	—	—
9	F	4	127	76	76	NW	Fx	—	—	—
10	F	4	114	79	36	NE	Fx	—	—	—
11	—	9	—	53	107	N	—	—	—	—
14	—	8	74	51	94	—	—	+	—	+
15a	—	—	—	—	—	NE	Fx	—	—	—
15b	—	9	130	61	114	N	Fx	—	—	+
17	M	5	160	84	99	NE	Fx	—	—	—
18	—	9	112	66	147	E	Et	—	—	—
19	—	3	114	53	122	NE	Fx	—	—	—
20	—	8	97	64	84	NE	—	+	—	—
21	—	8	119	84	122	E	—	+	—	—
22	—	9	127	109	86	NE	Fx	—	—	—
23	M	9	127	102	86					

(continued)

TABLE 6.22 *Continued*

Grave number	Sex	Age[a]	Length	Width	Depth	Orientation	Posture[b]	Disarticulation	Multiple burial	Burial covering
24	F	4	130	69	86	NW	Fx	—	—	—
25	—	8	—	—	—	—	—	—	—	+
26	F	4	137	86	89	N	Fx	—	—	—
27	—	9	140	104	94	SE	Fx	—	—	—
28	—	8	84	43	84	W	Fx	—	—	—
29	—	—	112	79	66	—	—	+	—	—
30a	—	8	84	43	99	W	Fx	—	—	—
30b	—	8	102	86	—	—	—	—	—	+
31	M	4	145	91	61	W	—	+	—	—
Burial Hill 5										
1	—	1	114	53	86	E	Fx	—	—	+
2	—	8	99	53	112	NE	—	—	—	+
3	—	1	91	79	107	NE	Fx	—	—	—
4a	—	1	114	74	97	NE	Fx	—	—	+
4b	—	1	51	28	46	NE	—	—	—	—
5	—	1	94	36	84	N	Et	—	—	—
6	—	1	89	43	79	N	Fx	—	—	—
7	F	4	132	102	122	SE	Fx	—	—	—
8	—	1	86	56	76	NE	Fx	—	—	—
9	—	2	91	53	163	E	Fx	—	—	—
10	M	9	168	61	119	NE	—	+	—	—
11	M	4	135	91	97	NE	Fx	—	—	+

12	—	2	102	53	102	E	Fx	—	—	—
13	—	1	86	56	107	SE	Fx	+	—	—
14	—	9	142	99	157	NW	Fx	—	—	+
15	M	2	94	46	132	NE	Fx	—	—	—
16	—	4	170	86	145	NE	Fx	+	—	+
17	M	8	99	76	56	E	—	—	—	—
18	—	5	142	91	89	N	Et	+	—	—
19	—	1	107	107	124	E	Fx	—	—	—
21	—	1	91	46	104	E	Fx	+	—	+
22	—	1	104	69	99	W	—	—	—	—
F-1	—	—	—	—	—	—	—	—	—	[c]
BP-3	—	8	—	—	—	—	—	—	—	—
Burial Hill 6										
1	M	6	198	71	132	NE	Fx	—	—	—
2	—	1	—	—	—	—	—	—	—	—
3	—	—	—	76	—	—	—	—	—	—
4	—	2	122	114	91	—	Fx	—	—	+
BP-3	M	4	122		102	NW	—	+	—	—
Burial Hill 7										
1	—	—	—	—	—	—	—	—	—	—
2	—	2	—	—	—	—	—	—	—	+
3	—	9	122	91	142	NE	Fx	—	—	—
4a	—	8	122	122	91	E	—	—	—	—
4b	—	1	107	—	—	E	—	—	—	+
5	—	1	91	91	102	NE	Et	—	—	+

[a] 1 = 0–2 years, 2 = 3–12 years, 3 = 13–17 years, 4 = 18–30 years, 5 = 31–40 years, 6 = 41–50+ years, 8 = undifferentiated child, 9 = undifferentiated adult.
[b] Fx = flexed; Et = extended.
[c] No skeletal remains.

TABLE 6.23

Clarks: Grave Dimensions by Age

	Adult values		Subadult values				
	Mean	S.D.	Mean	S.D.	t	df	Significance
Length	54.6	7.9	36.7	6.9	8.8	52	$p < .001$
Width	33.3	5.9	23.7	8.9	4.6	51	$p < .001$
Depth	42.6	12.0	38.0	9.6	1.5	50	$p > .05$

Treatment variables also were used to differentiate segments of the mortuary population. The right to burial in the community cemetery may itself represent the most fundamental level of mortuary differentiation. Although there is no evidence to suggest differential burial on the basis of age, such a difference is suggested with regard to an individual's sex. Of the 28 adults in the sample, 19 could be identified by sex; 14 were males and 5 females ($p = .032$, binomial test, Seigel 1956:38). Indeed, if all the unsexed adults were females, this would still increase their numbers only to the level of the identified males. This skewed occurrence may be the result of some systematic bias in the identification or preservation of female remains, but the possibility that it is the result of intentional differentiation on the part of the Clarks Pawnee must be considered.

Grave size served to differentiate adults from subadults in length and width, but not in grave depth (Table 6.23). No difference was observed in the average size or depth of graves by sex. Although grave size did distinguish adults from subadults, the simple physical needs for accommodating the body undoubtedly played some role in this distinction.

The location of burial among the five identified areas was another differential aspect of the funerary treatment (Table 6.24). Of these, two were heavily utilized, Burial Hill 4 ($N = 33$) and Burial Hill 5 ($N = 24$); while the other three contained

TABLE 6.24

Clarks: Age and Sex Breakdown by Burial Area

Location	Males	Females	Adults	Subadults	Total
Burial Hill 1	2	0	2	0	2
Burial Hill 4	5	4	15	13	28
Burial Hill 5	4	1	6	17	23
Burial Hill 6	3	0	4	2	6
Burial Hill 7	0	0	1	4	5
	14	5	28	36	64

The Pawnee 137

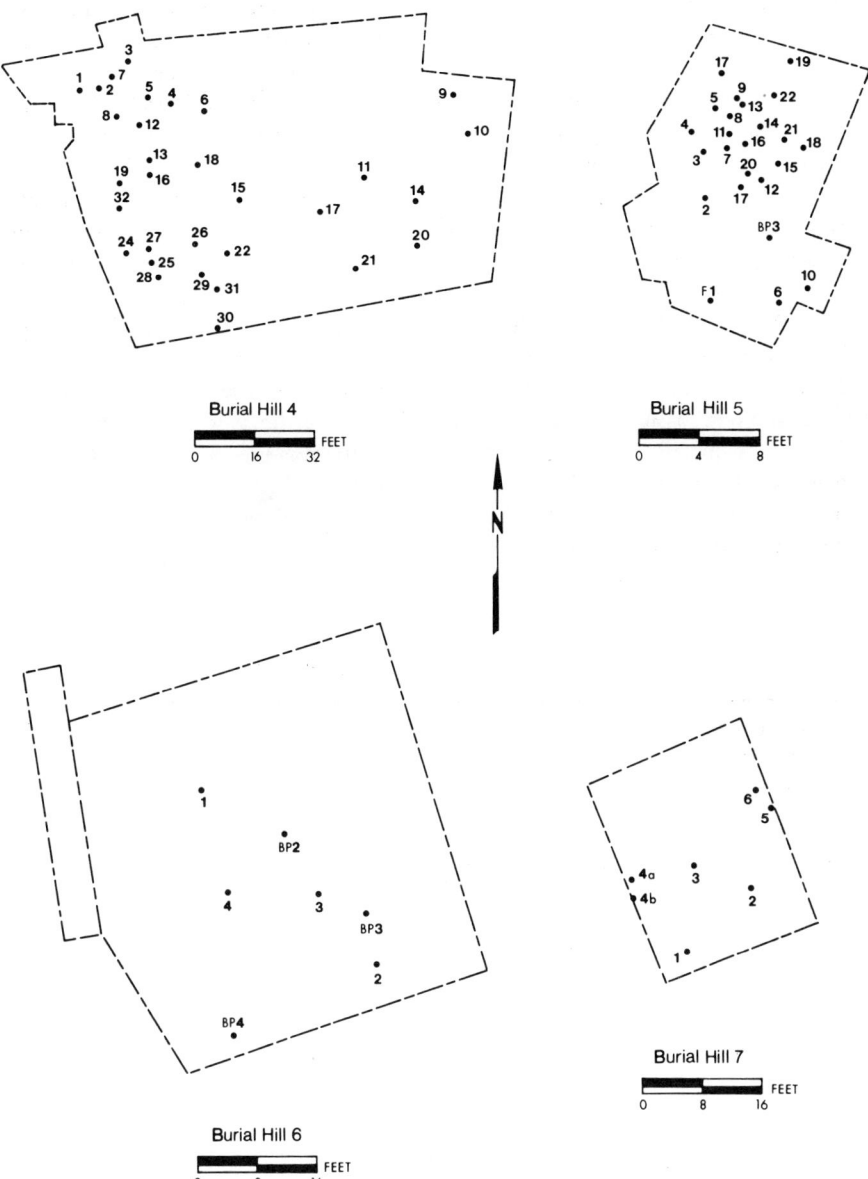

Figure 6.17 Plan of the Clarks site cemeteries. Dashed lines indicate limits of excavation.

considerably fewer interments, Burial Hill 1 ($N = 2$), Burial Hill 6 ($N = 7$), and Burial Hill 7 ($N = 7$) (Figure 6.17). Although these values are relatively accurate, it should be remembered that not all possible burial locations were tested during excavation and that some graves had been destroyed by looters prior to excavation. There is the suggestion of preferential interment of subadults in Burial Hill 5, but this is not statistically significant. The further understanding of these burial areas must await a consideration of artifact usage.

In addition to the normative body treatment, an alternative program of treatment, disarticulated burial, was observed. Two varieties of disarticulated burial were in evidence. In four cases, the body was found in a state of complete disarticulation. Two adults and one subadult, along with one individual of unknown age, were given this treatment. Three of the four individuals were interred in Burial Hill 4. The second class of treatment can be characterized as semiarticulated burial. Four different varieties of semiarticulation were observed: complete articulation but with hands and feet absent from the grave; articulated lower limbs without other skeletal elements, complete articulation with upper limbs missing, and articulated with torso, hands, and feet missing (Table 6.25). Despite the preponderance of adults, the occurrence of alternative treatment was not significantly limited by age or associated with burial hill location.

TABLE 6.25

Clarks: Disarticulated Burial

Type and location	Sex	Age	Marks	Comments
Disarticulated				
BH-4:21	—	Child	?	Skull and ribs only.
BH-4:29	—	—	?	Many bones absent.
BH-4:31	Male	Adult	+	Completely disarticulated; cut marks on mandible.
BH-6:Burial Pit 3	Male	Adult	+	Completely disarticulated; numerous cut marks.
Semiarticulated				
BH-4:5	—	Adult	?	Arm missing.
BH-4:11	—	Adult	?	Legs articulated; rest of the skeleton absent.
BH-4:22	—	Adult	?	Legs articulated; rest of the skeleton absent.
BH-5:10	Male	Adult	+	Legs below knees and hands absent.
BH-5:13		Child	—	Hands and feet absent.
BH-5:18	Male	Mature	+	Feet, skull, and torso absent; right arm present but disarticulated.
BH-5:21	—	Child	—	Hands and feet missing; preservation good.

Some comment is necessary on this alternative treatment. In an earlier discussion of the site (O'Shea 1981), it was concluded, along with the excavators, that the apparent disarticulation was the result of recent pot hunting, and indeed several of the graves at the Clarks site do bear clear evidence of plundering. However, the preliminary results of a reanalysis of the Clarks osteological remains now indicates that these 11 occurrences were the result of intentional dismemberment. Six of the 11 cases of disarticulation have been reexamined and, with the exception of the two subadults (complete skeletons missing only the hands and feet), all gave clear evidence of dismemberment, indicated by deep cut marks in the bone. Also, in at least one instance, an apparently articulated burial also exhibited deep cut marks on the midshaft of the right femur (Grave 23, BH-4). Although other causes are possible, the potential for rearticulated burial cannot be rejected.

As was the case in the two Pawnee cemeteries considered earlier, these alternative treatments probably reflect an individual's time and circumstance of death, rather than an intentional type of mortuary elaboration. This is suggested by the unrestricted occurrence of the treatment among individuals of all ages and both sexes. This assertion will be further supported in the next section when artifact occurrence is analyzed.

The occurrence of wood burial coverings at Clarks raises the possibility of grave elaboration. At least two forms of covering were observed, the traditional pole and gable type, and a second variety in which a child's cradle board was used as a covering. In addition to these, several other graves gave evidence of additional covering types, such as a wooden bowl placed over the head of the deceased or the use of woven matting. The occurrence of grave coverings are summarized in Table 6.26. Out of a total of 66 cases where observation could be made, 21% of the graves were covered (excluding graves with matting or bowls as coverings). In the absence of any correlation of coverings with other mortuary variables, it would appear that the coverings were part of the normative treatment at Clarks and were not a special grave elaboration. It can also be seen that, although both adults and subadults could receive the gable-type covering, only subadults were covered with cradle boards.

The final category of treatment at Clarks was represented by four individuals who were interred in a nonnormative, extended burial posture. All these individuals were subadults, and the graves exhibited no spatial clustering within the cemetery. In all probability this posture was the result of expedience, applied idiosyncratically to the young, and did not carry any additional symbolic meaning. This hypothesis will be tested against the distribution of artifacts within the cemetery.

Taking all aspects of funerary treatment together, we find that treatment variables were primarily normative in character and served to differentiate only a limited number of basic social distinctions. Adults were differentiated from subadults by grave size and the use of cradle boards as burial coverings. Circumstance of death was also indicated by way of an alternative disposal program. Excluding the possibility that females were less frequently buried at the Clarks cemetery, no evidence

140   6. Mortuary Differentiation and Social Distinction

TABLE 6.26

Clarks: Burial Coverings

Type of covering and location	Sex	Age
Gabled covering		
BH-4:17	Male	Mature
BH-4:30b	—	Child
BH-5:1	—	Infant
BH-5:11	Male	Adult
BH-5:14	—	Adult
BH-5:16	Male	Adult
BH-5:22	—	Infant
BH-7:3	—	Adult
Cradle board covering		
BH-4:15a	—	Child (?)
BH-4:25	—	Child
BH-5:2	—	Child
BH-5:4a	—	Infant
BH-7:4b	—	Infant
BH-7:5	—	Infant

for a male–female distinction was observed in the burial treatment, nor was there any clear indication of elevated social standing or grave elaboration. It is possible that grave location may reflect some manner of horizontal distinction, but the possibility must be considered in the light of artifact usage in the Clarks mortuary complex.

Artifact Occurrence

A total of 49 types were observed at the Clarks site, 19 of native manufacture and 30 of Euro-American origin. The distribution of these types was highly structured, with 29 of the 49 types exhibiting a restricted distribution on the basis of age or sex (Table 6.27 and Figure 6.18). Distinct male and female types were recognized, as were age-specific types. A significant level of constraint also was observed in the occurrence of artifact classes, with subadults having a greater variety of trade-derived body ornaments and with adults possessing greater varieties of native-made implements and sociotechnic objects and a greater average number of native-made types overall (Tables 6.28, 6.29). This high level of constraint in artifact distribution at Clarks also is evident in the multivariate analysis of artifact occurrence.

Principal Component Analysis

Principal component analysis was performed on the 55 graves that contained at least one artifact. Twenty-seven variables were used in this analysis. Each variable

TABLE 6.27

Clarks: Artifact Type Associations

Female	Male
Awl	Gun parts/accessories
Metatarsal flesher	Tubular shell bead
Iron scraper	Metal bracelet
	Strike-a-light
	Small iron tools
	Metal projectile point
	Metal lace/braid
	Sandstone shaft smoother
	Whetstone
	Stone projectile point
	Stone pipe
	Pipestone ornament
Subadult	**Adult**
Glass trade bead	Bird beak
Metal eating implement	Awl
Iron digging implement	Gun parts/accessories
Finger ring	Mussel shell
Large cast brass bell	Metal bead/bangle
Lead ring/coil	Iron knife
	Axe/wedge
	Small iron tool
	Iron scraper
	Metal projectile point
	Metal buckle
	Gunflint
	Sandstone shaft smoother
	Whetstone
	Stone projectile point
	Stone pipe
	Side scraper
	Pipestone ornament

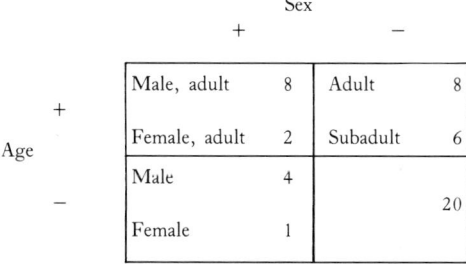

Figure 6.18 Age and sex constraints on artifact occurrence at the Clarks site.

TABLE 6.28

Clarks: Artifact Class Associations by Sex

Artifact class	Average male rank (N=9)	Average female rank (N=5)	U	Probability
Trade goods				
Body ornaments	7.9	6.8	19.0	.6133
Clothing ornaments	8.8	5.1	10.5	.0792
Implements	7.8	7.0	20.0	.7314
All trade items	8.1	6.4	17.0	.4553
Native goods				
Ornaments	8.1	6.5	17.5	.2726
Implements	8.1	6.5	17.5	.4851
Sociotechnic	8.3	6.1	15.5	.2753
All native items	8.6	5.5	12.5	.1732

occurred in at least four graves, constituting a 7% occurrence level for inclusion. A total of nine factors were extracted, which accounted for 67.8% of the original variance in the correlation matrix. The varimax rotated factor matrix is presented as Table 6.30 and is summarized in Table 6.31.

The factor results highlight distinct task kits and ornament sets. Factors 1 and 6 represent male tool kits, with Factor 6 possibly representing a specialized arrow making kit; Factor 4 and possibly Factor 8 appear to define female-oriented task

TABLE 6.29

Clarks: Artifact Class Associations by Age

Artifact class	Average adult rank (N=23)	Average subadult rank (N=32)	U	Probability
Trade goods				
Body ornaments	22.4	32.0	240.0	.0196
Clothing ornaments	26.5	29.1	334.0	.5304
Implements	30.8	26.0	304.0	.2538
All trade items	28.1	27.9	366.0	.9725
Native goods				
Ornaments	25.6	29.7	312.5	.1856
Implements	36.3	22.1	178.0	.0002
Sociotechnic	31.5	22.8	288.0	.0062
All native items	35.3	22.8	200.5	.0025

TABLE 6.30

Clarks: Varimax Rotated Factor Matrix

Artifact type	Factor 1	Factor 2	Factor 3	Factor 4	Factor 5	Factor 6	Factor 7	Factor 8	Factor 9
Glass bottle	0.29041	−0.12348	−0.25735	0.26802	0.32214	0.04088	0.24866	−0.44631	−0.17530
Glass trade beads	0.08014	0.17887	−0.67573	−0.14846	0.11956	0.00039	0.00231	−0.03035	0.13313
Bird beak	−0.11988	0.66874	0.15101	0.28406	−0.27269	0.22195	0.05230	−0.14962	0.22629
Elk-horn scraper	0.02700	−0.19339	0.04031	0.19220	0.04926	0.00617	−0.02942	0.72980	0.00154
Gun parts/accessories	0.78795	0.18561	0.19055	0.14302	0.03257	0.02182	−0.02047	0.23688	0.14320
Mussel shell	0.24101	−0.06744	0.14849	0.83844	−0.08794	0.05328	0.01668	0.08778	0.04111
Tubular shell bead	0.11348	0.00324	−0.28874	−0.05739	0.56659	0.33011	−0.24877	0.15065	0.15600
Metal bracelet	0.15174	0.23980	0.29837	−0.16442	0.12664	0.00249	−0.63398	−0.03836	0.02794
Metal bead/bangle	0.16529	0.05126	0.19287	0.09054	0.33219	0.12667	0.61863	0.14783	0.42358
Iron knife	0.42471	0.17649	0.25213	0.29987	0.04482	0.44820	−0.23573	−0.04640	−0.24008
Metal eating implement	0.16082	0.03410	−0.27366	−0.15669	0.21426	−0.16406	−0.31779	−0.22184	0.27144
Small metal hardware	0.75390	−0.14556	0.01307	0.00473	−0.04017	−0.12190	0.13452	−0.17804	−0.14622
Metal projectile point	0.01527	−0.20010	−0.10014	0.10691	0.18500	0.74150	0.20005	0.14891	−0.01904
Iron scraper	−0.10605	0.10258	−0.01616	0.74286	0.16718	0.02193	0.06788	0.13330	0.00036
Metal container	0.15200	0.22919	0.28355	0.30631	0.62859	−0.16730	0.03958	−0.01154	−0.11159
Finger ring	−0.15260	−0.03501	−0.07972	−0.03397	0.79901	0.01240	0.04037	0.01354	−0.09807
Metal button	−0.00015	0.81173	0.01932	−0.07865	0.16679	−0.09362	−0.11380	−0.05617	0.07242
Smaller brass bell	0.06875	0.37154	−0.33141	0.38883	−0.24049	−0.27557	0.13866	−0.06966	0.06197
Lead ring/coil	−0.52734	0.13084	−0.06239	0.11197	0.05536	−0.38851	0.13771	0.10681	−0.14475
Silver earring	−0.03903	0.06990	−0.09250	0.03066	−0.11473	−0.06361	0.03137	−0.03851	0.82259
Gunflint	0.16653	0.29674	0.48843	−0.35682	−0.05116	−0.05659	0.39477	0.08063	0.23425
Sandstone shaft smoother	−0.01208	0.42261	0.18016	−0.07552	−0.20567	0.72945	−0.03373	−0.07014	−0.11238
Whetstone	0.49149	0.05606	0.62853	0.13133	0.10005	0.19697	0.09628	0.32333	0.08272
Stone projectile point	0.44001	0.37338	0.13990	−0.14136	−0.02356	−0.02121	0.58033	−0.15745	−0.10330
Stone pipe	0.23949	0.17693	0.75370	−0.05521	0.00131	0.01649	−0.08410	−0.09753	−0.01250
Retouched flake	0.42450	0.50778	−0.09881	0.20992	0.10967	0.08088	0.02883	0.41186	−0.16721
Side scraper	−0.07947	0.44344	−0.11892	−0.01624	0.16061	0.11894	0.22793	0.49076	−0.26872

TABLE 6.31

Clarks: Factor Summary[a]

Factor number	Loading pattern	Percentage variance	Diagnostic positive loadings	Diagnostic negative loadings
1	Bipolar	15.4	Gun parts/accessories M+ Small metal hardware Iron knife +	Lead ring/coil −
2	Bipolar	9.2	Bird beak + Metal button Retouched flakes Glass trade beads − Smaller brass bell	Elk horn scraper Metal projectile point M+
3	Bipolar	8.1	Whetstone M+ Stone pipe M+ Gunflint +	Glass bottle Glass trade beads − Tubular shell bead M Smaller brass bell
4	Bipolar	7.2	Whole mussel shell + Iron scraper F+ Smaller brass bell	Gunflints +
5	Bipolar	6.9	Tubular shell bead M Metal container Finger ring − Glass bottle	Bird beak + Smaller brass bell Sandstone shaft smoother M+
6	Bipolar	6.3	Metal projectile point M+ Sandstone shaft smoother M+ Iron knife +	Smaller brass bell Lead ring/coil −
7	Bipolar	5.6	Metal bead/bangle + Stone projectile point M+ Lead ring/coil −	Tubular shell bead M Metal bracelet M Iron knife + Metal eating implement −

[a]Constraints: +, adult only; −, subadult only; M, male only; F, female only.

sets. Modal ornament sets can also be identified: Factor 2 representing adult ornamentation, along with one of the two sociotechnic symbols (bird beaks); Factors 5 and 7 representing male ornament sets that lack age restrictions; and Factor 9 representing a series of co-occurring ornaments that were not constrained by either age or sex. Factor 3 is made up of a series of implements, including stone pipes, that are limited in their occurrence to adult males. These implements may function as a prestige set, both in occurrence and by the less-valuable artifact types that are negatively associated with the factor.

These results suggest a highly patterned use of artifacts in the mortuary ritual at the Clarks site. Grave assemblages tend to emphasize the age and sex of the dead,

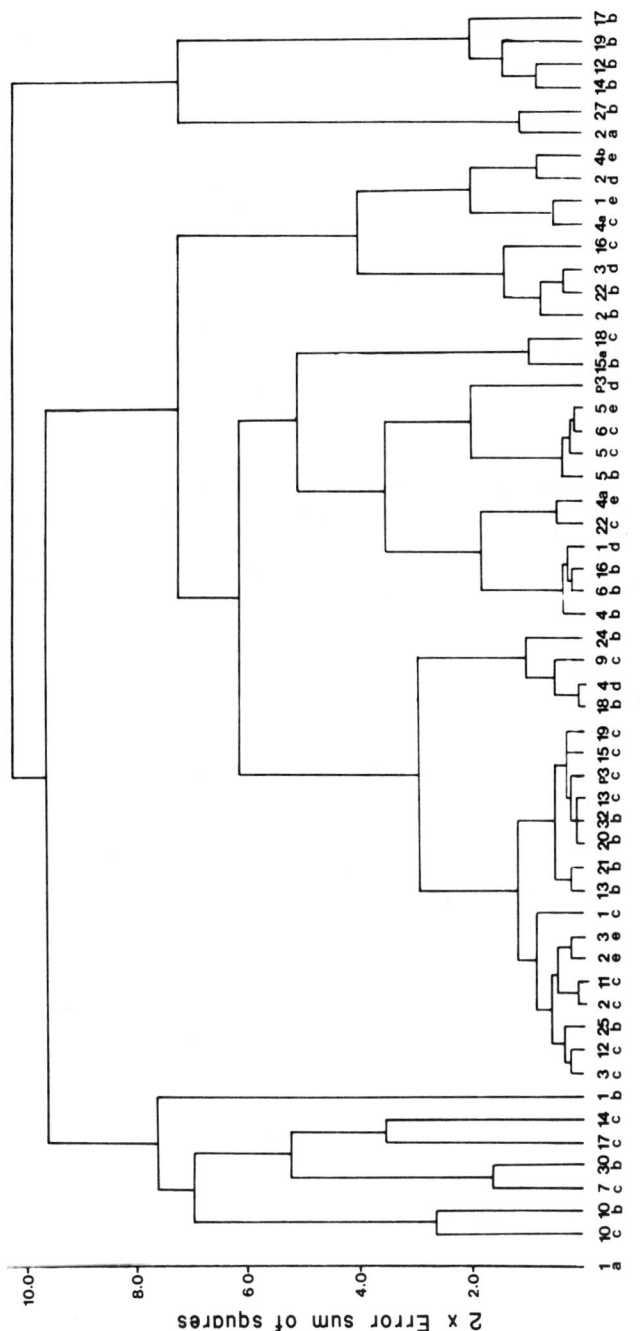

Figure 6.19 Dendrogram produced by the clustering of factor scores. Burial area is indicated for each case by a letter designation below the grave number: a, Burial Hill 1; b, Burial Hill 4; c, Burial Hill 5; d, Burial Hill 6; and e, Burial Hill 7.

146   6. Mortuary Differentiation and Social Distinction

highlighting male and female implements and age-specific use of various combinations of ornaments.

Hierarchical Fusion Cluster Analysis

The clustering of graves by their factor scores yielded a relatively clear partitioning of the population at the level of seven clusters. This result is presented in Figure 6.19 and cluster diagnostics in Table 6.32. Clusters 1 and 2 represent adult male assemblages, with an emphasis on implement sets and sociotechnic objects, loading on Factors 2, 3, and 6 or Factors 1, 3, and 7, respectively. Clusters 4, 5, and 7 reflect adult implement assemblages; Clusters 5 and 7 are female kits, and 4 is a male kit. Cluster 6 is made up of those individuals with unconstrained ornaments, and Cluster 3 represents graves with weak loadings on all factors.

The parallelism between Clusters 1 and 2 is particularly interesting. Although they seem very similar in composition, they occur at opposite sides of the dendrogram, suggesting perhaps a structural opposition between individuals with these two grave assemblages.

This cluster result reflects a clear rank ordering of the mortuary population. If one considers the total number of artifact types in each grave (as distinct from the factor scores on which the cluster analysis was based), the three clusters on the left side of the dendrogram (adult male Cluster 1 and adult female Clusters 5 and 7) contain by far the greatest variety of artifacts (Figure 6.20). Cluster 2, the parallel of Cluster 1 on the right side of the dendrogram, also exhibits a large variety of types, whereas the rest of the right-side clusters have considerably fewer types. This configuration suggests that Clusters 1 and 2 both reflect males of high, but distinct, rank. One aspect of this distinction would seem to be that Cluster 1 represents individuals who are both of special rank and wealthy in economic terms, whereas Cluster 2 individuals lack this wealth. Clusters 5 and 7 would be ranked females. Although they are not in a position equivalent to the males with sociotechnic objects, they do seem to be of high economic standing and their nearness to Cluster 1 in the dendrogram would seem to confirm this. Clusters 4 and 6 reflect intermediate levels of social or economic importance, whereas Cluster 3 is composed of those members of the population holding the lower status positions.

One final aspect of the hierarchical fusion result is the spatial component of the clusters (Figure 6.21). Overall, the members of each cluster are distributed evenly across the five burial areas, although two clusters do have patterns that are at least suggestive of purposeful segregation. Burial Hill 1 seems to contain a disproportionate number of high-ranking males, although the remaining members of Clusters 1 and 2 are distributed uniformly across the other burial areas. Unfortunately, the frequency of occurrence of these individuals is too low to permit a meaningful test of its significance. Alone among the clusters, members of Cluster 6 occur in only one burial area, Burial Hill 4. Why this relatively unnoteworthy cluster of individuals

TABLE 6.32

Clarks: Hierarchical Fusion Cluster Diagnostics

Cluster number	Factor number	Mean origin	S.D.	Factor number	Mean origin	S.D.
1	1	.2811	1.0160	6	1.9349	.5233
	2	3.3259	.0315	7	−.2362	1.9071
	3	1.0841	2.2775	8	−.2059	.7536
	4	−.6767	.0770	9	−.5382	1.1098
	5	−1.1408	.1903			
	Number of individuals	2				
	Number of males	2				
	Number of females	0				
	Number of adults	2				
	Number of subadults	0				
	Cluster members	BH-1:1,BH-5:10				
2	1	1.4063	1.5134	6	−.8106	.3635
	2	.4997	.5926	7	2.8894	.0297
	3	2.1234	1.6505	8	−.2341	.4150
	4	−1.3849	.2536	9	.8509	.1418
	5	.7318	.1281			
	Number of individuals	2				
	Number of males	1				
	Number of females	0				
	Number of adults	2				
	Number of subadults	0				
	Cluster members	BH-1:2,BH-4:27				
3	1	−.2195	.7642	6	−.3203	.5233
	2	−.2515	.5180	7	−.3213	.7654
	3	.0784	.7828	8	.1204	.6886
	4	−.1401	.6335	9	−.2217	.3996
	5	−.1287	.8873			
	Number of individuals	34				
	Number of males	5				
	Number of females	2				
	Number of adults	10				
	Number of subadults	21				
	Cluster members	BH-4:1,4,5,6,13,15a,16,18,20,21,24,25,32; BH-5: 1,2,3,5,6,9,11,12,13,15,18,19,22,BP-3; BH-6:1,4,BP-3; BH-7:2,3,4a,5				
4	1	.1679	.6825	6	1.3482	1.4028
	2	−.6961	.3304	7	.3787	.7393
	3	−.5101	.6825	8	−.6836	.6346
	4	−.1886	.5511	9	−.2150	.3565
	5	.4908	1.3220			
	Number of individuals	8				
	Number of males	2				
	Number of females	0				
	Number of adults	3				
	Number of subadults	3				
	Cluster members	BH-4:2,22; BH-5:4a,16; BH-6:2,3; BH-7:1,4b				

(continued)

TABLE 6.32 *Continued*

Cluster number	Factor number	Mean origin	S.D.	Factor number	Mean origin	S.D.
5	1	.5261	2.3120	6	−.7281	.5912
	2	1.3248	1.5471	7	.3588	.6445
	3	−.7920	1.1878	8	−.4340	1.6585
	4	1.9511	1.5650	9	−.8770	.9796
	5	.1046	.6155			
	Number of individuals	4				
	Number of males	0				
	Number of females	2				
	Number of adults	2				
	Number of subadults	2				
	Cluster members	BH-4:10,30; BH-5:7,17				
6	1	−.1381	.9740	6	−.2251	.5227
	2	.2473	.5482	7	.1110	1.0674
	3	−.3273	.7077	8	−.1363	.4868
	4	.1084	1.3633	9	2.9102	.9014
	5	−.4059	.7345			
	Number of individuals	4				
	Number of males	1				
	Number of females	0				
	Number of adults	1				
	Number of subadults	2				
	Cluster members	BH-4:12,14,17,19				
7	1	1.1922	0	6	1.6696	0
	2	.1756	0	7	.7101	0
	3	−.5225	0	8	4.5359	0
	4	2.1582	0	9	.4981	0
	5	2.4714	0			
	Number of individuals	1				
	Number of adults	1				
	Cluster member	BH-5:14				

(those with unconstrained ornament sets) should exhibit this limited spatial distribution is not clear.

In general, the results of hierarchical fusion cluster analysis suggest two dimensions of social ranking, one based on the occurrence of prestige goods and sociotechnic objects among adult males, and the other indicative of economic ranking.

Monothetic Division Cluster Analysis

Monothetic division was performed on the full 65 grave sample from the Clarks site. The four-cluster solution is summarized in Figures 6.22 and 6.23, and Table 6.33. The division of the mortuary population occurred first on the presence of whetstones; graves lacking whetstones were further divided by the occurrence of metal containers and glass trade beads. These clusters present a picture of rank organization similar to that observed in the clustering of factor scores. Based on their composition, as well as the average number of types per grave and the distribution of sociotechnic objects, it appears that these clusters rank order the grave assemblages. At the highest level are the individuals in Cluster 1. This cluster is limited to adult males (with one exceptional subadult) and has the highest average number of artifact types per grave, as well as the greatest number of sociotechnic objects. In addition to the critical occurrence of whetstones, graves in this cluster tend to possess substantial numbers of trade and native implements. In addition, they tend not to contain less expensive trade items, such as glass beads. The middle rank level is observed in Clusters 2 and 3. In Cluster 2, individuals tend to have a combination of expensive trade goods, particularly clothing and body ornamentation. All ages and both sexes are represented in Cluster 2. Cluster 3 is the lower end of the middle rank level, including graves with less expensive trade ornaments, particularly trade beads, along with an irregular scattering of other types. This cluster is made up mostly of males, without age restrictions. The base level is represented by Cluster 4, which iis made up of graves that either are devoid of any grave inclusion (50%) or have a small number of irregularly occurring types. All ages and both sexes are found within this cluster.

Two aspects of this cluster solution are of particular interest. These results suggest

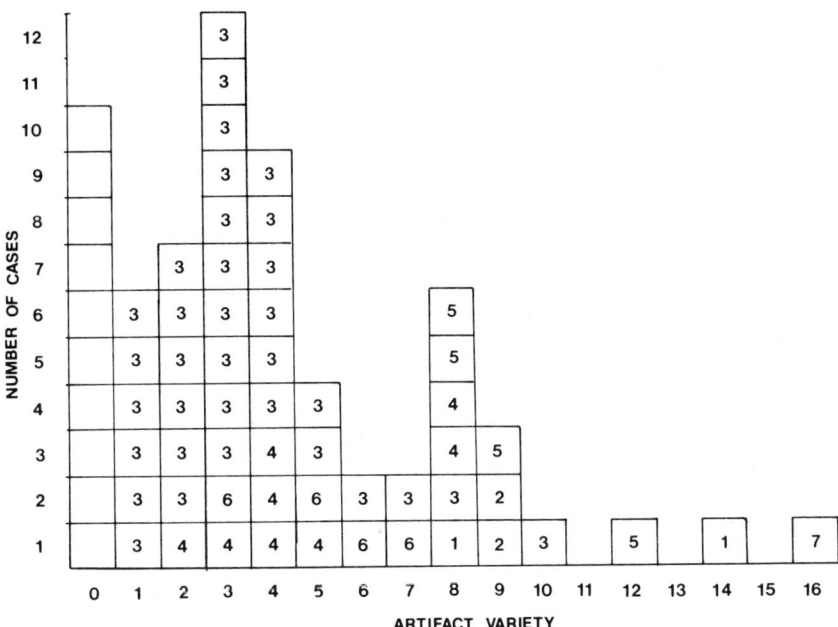

Figure 6.20 Comparison of artifact variety with hierarchical fusion cluster membership at the Clarks site.

150   6. Mortuary Differentiation and Social Distinction

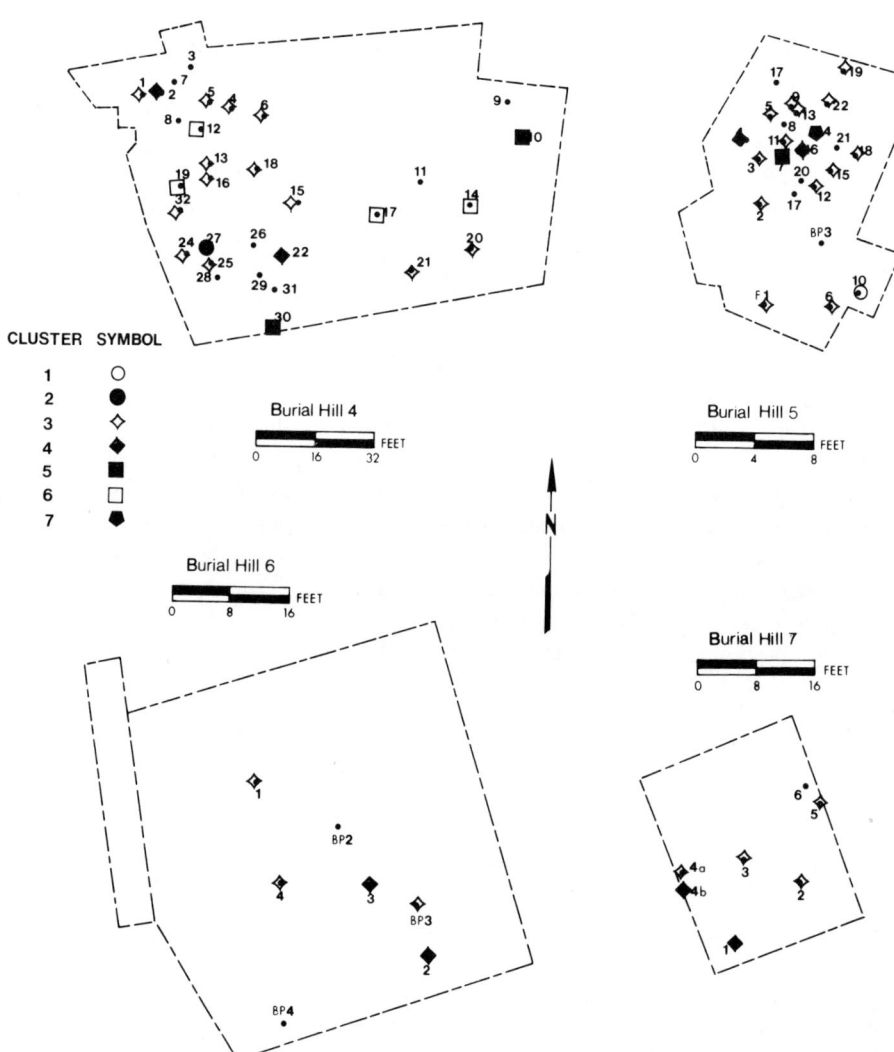

Figure 6.21 Spatial distribution of hierarchical fusion clusters at the Clarks site cemeteries.

the existence of institutionalized social ranking systems for both males and females that, although employing different specific artifacts as symbols, share the same structural form. In both, the occurrence of expensive implements and artifact variety are used as a means of expressing high economic standing. In this sense, the rank standing of males and females are comparable, with the exception that females cannot occupy the highest rung on the scale (i.e., males can occupy one of three rank levels, whereas females, and subadults in most cases, can occupy only two). The fact that subadults may hold this middle rank standing (or even the highest) may suggest a hereditary element in the determination of rank standing.

A second aspect of the cluster result relates to the distribution of sociotechnic objects. Although pipes and bird beaks might normally be assumed to be associated in the form of a calumet, this is not the case at Clarks, where pipe ownership and bird beak ownership are mutually exclusive. If we assume the monothetic divisive clusters to primarily reflect economic standing, the distribution of these two types is informative. Three of the four pipe owners are members of Cluster 1, while the fourth is found in Cluster 2. This suggests that pipe ownership is strongly, although imperfectly, correlated with economic standing. By contrast, bird beaks occur with equal frequency in all four of the clusters, illustrating a virtual lack of connection between this symbol and wealth. This suggests that the symbolic function, or the positions that these symbols mark, are qualitatively different. One further relationship can be inferred from these occurrences. Although subadults regularly occur in the middle as well as the lower wealth level, they are in no instance interred with sociotechnic objects. This would seem to indicate that these symbols mark the actual holding of a ritual or political office and not the potential to hold office. Given the ascriptive element noted in economic standing, it is unlikely that these offices were solely achieved, particularly since "poor" individuals could own bird beaks. Rather, it seems that burial with the symbol required that the office actually be held prior to death. This greater emphasis on generational features is in contrast to the pattern observed at the other Pawnee sites and will be considered in more detail in the next chapter.

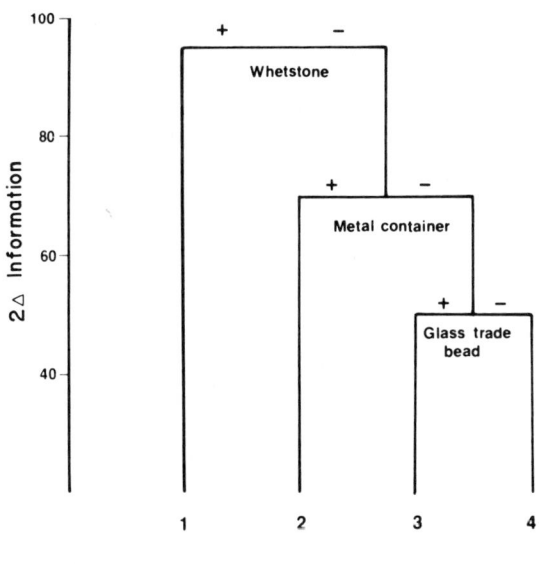

Figure 6.22 Dendrogram produced by monothetic divisive clustering of the Clarks grave assemblages.

152 6. Mortuary Differentiation and Social Distinction

Figure 6.23 Spatial distribution of monothetic divisive clusters at the Clarks site cemeteries.

Clarks Mortuary Differentiation

Taken together, mortuary differentiation at the Clarks site presents a well-integrated set of distinct mortuary statuses (Table 6.34). There is little redundancy in the symbolic marking of these distinctions through variables of treatment and variables of grave inclusion.

Aside from the differentiation of adults from subadults through restricted grave assemblages and grave size, and of males and females on the basis of grave artifacts, and possibly on the basis of inclusion in the cemetery, only one horizontal social

TABLE 6.33

Clarks: Monothetic Division Cluster Diagnostics[a]

	Cluster			
	1	2	3	4
Glass bottle	0	3	2	0
Ceramic pot	0	0	1	0
Native glass pendant	0	0	0	0
Animal effigy	0	0	0	0
Glass trade beads	2	9	24	0
Bear claw	0	0	0	0
Animal teeth	0	0	0	0
Bird beak	1	1	1	1
Bird bone	0	0	0	1
Raptor talon	0	0	1	0
Small mammal cranium	0	0	0	0
Rib shaft wrench	0	0	0	0
Squash knife	0	0	0	0
Scapula hoe	0	0	0	0
Quill flattener	0	0	0	0
Cancellous paint applicator	0	0	0	0
Awl	0	1	0	1
Metatarsal flesher	0	3	0	0
Elk horn scraper	2	0	1	1
Bone/antler implement	0	0	0	0
Gun parts/accessories	5	1	1	0
Pin game cup	0	0	0	0
Polished bone tube	0	0	0	0
Bone pendant	0	0	0	0
Curved rib ornament	0	0	0	0
Bone point	0	0	0	0
Mussel shell	5	3	3	1
Gorget	0	1	0	0
Shell hair pipe	0	0	0	0
Tubular shell bead	2	4	5	1
Wampum bead	0	0	1	0
Heavy shell bead	0	0	0	0
Rectangular shell bead	0	0	0	0
Shell runtee	0	0	0	0
Marine snail shell	0	0	0	0
Perforated shell pendant	0	0	0	0
Flat shell bead	0	0	0	0
Metal bracelet	2	2	2	1
Metal bead/bangle	3	0	1	1
Iron knife	5	4	3	1
Axe/wedge	1	1	0	0

(continued)

TABLE 6.33 *Continued*

	Cluster			
	1	2	3	4
Scissors	0	1	0	0
Strike-a-light	1	1	1	0
Metal eating implement	0	2	3	1
Small metal hardware	3	1	2	1
Horse gear	1	0	1	0
Small iron tools	2	0	1	0
Metal projectile point	2	0	3	1
Iron scraper	1	2	1	0
Iron digging implement	0	1	1	1
Metal container	6	13	0	0
Metal buckle	1	0	0	1
Finger ring	1	6	2	1
Metal button	2	5	2	0
Large cast brass bell	0	1	2	0
Smaller brass bell	0	3	2	2
Thick wire coil	0	0	0	0
Thin wire coil	0	0	0	0
Metal lace/braid	1	1	0	1
Copper crimp/clip	0	0	0	0
Sheet brass blade	0	0	0	0
Lead ring/coil	0	5	6	5
Lead band	0	0	0	0
Sheet silver bracelet	0	0	0	0
Silver cross	1	0	0	0
Silver hair plate	0	0	1	0
Silver earring	0	1	2	1
Small silver brooch	0	0	0	0
Gunflint	3	0	1	1
Stone spear point	0	0	0	0
Scoria abraider	0	0	0	0
Sandstone shaft smoother	2	0	2	0
Whetstone	8	0	0	0
Hammer stone	0	0	0	0
Stone sphere	0	0	0	1
Stone projectile point	2	1	1	0
Stone pipe	3	1	0	0
Petrified wood	0	0	0	0
Retouched flake	2	2	0	0
Unretouched flake	1	0	0	0
Stone knife	0	0	0	0
Plate chalcedony knife	1	0	0	0
Side scraper	1	2	1	1

TABLE 6.33 *Continued*

	Cluster			
	1	2	3	4
End scraper	0	0	0	0
Pipestone ornament	2	0	0	0
Gypsum	0	0	0	0

*a*Cluster composition:

Cluster number		
1	Number of individuals	8
	Number of males	4
	Number of females	0
	Number of adults	6
	Number of subadults	1
	Cluster members	BH-1:2; BH-4:15a,27; BH-5:9,10,14,16,18
2	Number of individuals	13
	Number of males	1
	Number of females	2
	Number of adults	4
	Number of subadults	9
	Cluster members	BH-4:5,6,10,14,30; BH-5:5,7,17,22; BH-6:BP3; BH-7:4a,4b,5
3	Number of individuals	24
	Number of males	4
	Number of females	0
	Number of adults	6
	Number of subadults	14
	Cluster members	BH-1:1; BH-4:1,2,4,12,13,16,18,19,20,21,22, 25,32; BH-5:1,2,3,4a,11,13,15,BP3; BH-6:2; BH-7:1
4	Number of individuals	20
	Number of males	3
	Number of females	3
	Number of adults	8
	Number of subadults	9
	Cluster members	BH-4:7,8,9,15a,17,23,24,26,28; BH-5:4b,6,8, 12,19,21; BH-6:1,3,4; BH-7:2,3

distinction was observed. This distinction, probably reflecting corporate group or lineage membership, was expressed through the use of distinct areas for burial. These burial areas, although different in size, seemed to contain age and sex compositions that were natural in their proportions. In addition, most other classes of mortuary differentiation did crosscut this spatial boundary. The uneven number of occurrences in these areas, and the propensity for ranked individuals to be interred in Burial Hill 1, may suggest that spatial location expressed more than a single meaning, although the horizontal distinction would be the most basic of those

TABLE 6.34

Clarks: Mortuary Differentiation

Social distinction	Number	Sex	Age	Formal differentiation	Artifact differentiation	Comments
Vertical distinctions						
Achieved wealth						
Upper level	8	Male	Adult		Greatest artifact variety; emphasis on native implements and expensive trade goods	
Middle level	37	—	—		Expensive trade goods and quantities of inexpensive trade ornaments	
Lower level	20	—	—		Few if any grave goods	
Elevated social position						
Chiefly office	4	Male	Adult		Pipe ownership; upper wealth level	
Ritual office?	4	—	Adult		Bird beak ownership	Not wealth correlated.
Horizontal distinctions						
Corporate group (Lineage)	Variable	—	—	Location of burial		
Adult/subadult	28/36	—	—	Grave size	Age-specific artifacts	
Male/female	14/5	—	—		Gender-specific artifacts	
Special status distinctions						
Circumstances of death						
Location or season of death	11	—	—	Disarticulated burial		
Remains not recovered for burial	1	—	—	Symbolic grave	Normal grave assemblage	
Alternative subadult treatment	4	—	Subadult	Extended burial		May be idiosyncratic.

meanings. It should also be remembered that not all possible burial locations were tested, and given the small sizes of several of the known areas, this interpretation must remain somewhat tentative.

A number of vertical distinctions were recognized and were expressed almost exclusively through the content of the burial assemblage. Three wealth levels were observed. The highest level of personal wealth was limited to adult males. These individuals possessed the greatest number of grave artifacts, and tended to have assemblages composed of native implements and expensive trade items. In addition, there was also the tendency for these graves *not* to contain less expensive trade items. The middle level was open to individuals of both sexes and of all ages. Individuals in this level tended to have some expensive trade item, such as a metal container, and to have a variety of cheaper trade ornaments. The final rank level was composed of those individuals with few if any grave goods. This resulted in a three-tier wealth system for males and a two-tier system for females and subadults.

The occurrence of sociotechnic objects served to denote two further vertical categories that are distinct from personal wealth. Pipe ownership corresponded with the holding of chiefly rank and was limited to a small number of adult males. Individuals occupying this position tended to be of the paramount wealth level and were evenly distributed among the varied burial areas, perhaps as lineage or corporate group heads. These individuals also possessed large quantities of expensive trade items, which may suggest some manner of connection with or control of the Euro-American trade.

The other position was marked by bird beak ownership. This distribution was mutually exclusive with pipe ownership and could be held by adult males or females. This social distinction was also evenly distributed among the different burial areas, but unlike pipe ownership, it was not strongly correlated with personal wealth. Indeed, bird beak owners could be of any of the three wealth levels. Of these two vertical dimensions, pipe ownership probably reflects sociopolitical authority, such as holding a chiefly office, whereas bird beak ownership reflects a less economically tied ritual position. Although neither position could be held by subadults, there may have been a hereditary aspect to the vertical ranking among the Clarks population. Since subadults could possess grave assemblages of either the middle or lower wealth level, it seems likely that infants did inherit, at least partially, the right to a particular wealth category or social position.

At least three and perhaps four types of special status distinctions were identified at Clarks. The circumstance of an individual's death, be it the time of year or perhaps the location of death, seems to have been reflected in the use of disarticulated burial as an alternative treatment program. This distinction was not limited by age or sex and did not correlate with any particular type of burial assemblage. Possibly related to this special status distinction was the occurrence of a symbolic grave, which contained a normal grave assemblage but no trace of human remains. The composition of this assemblage, which was not included in the numerical analysis, may be of some significance. It contained the following items, which were apparently wrapped in woven matting: 1 iron knife, 2 eagle talons, 1 iron file, 1 brass gun sideplate, 1 flintlock hammer, a pair of sandstone shaft abraiders, 1 strip brass knife, 2 brass buttons, numerous glass trade beads, several pieces of worked wood, and red, yellow, green, and white paint. On the basis of its composition, this would be the assemblage of an adult male, in the upper half of the middle wealth stratum. The most likely explanation for the occurrence is the death of an individual whose remains could not be recovered for burial. Although this must have been a common happening for the Pawnee, given the constant warfare of the nineteenth century, the contents of the grave assemblage may indicate that such treatment was only accorded to individuals of some wealth and importance.

The final special status distinction was an alternative burial posture, extended burial, which several subadults received. This pattern of occurrence did not correspond to any other category of treatment or grave assemblage variable, and probably reflects an idiosyncratic variation in funerary treatment for subadults, particularly young infants.

Notably absent from the set of mortuary distinctions observed at the Clarks site are instances where both treatment and assemblage variations were used to mark the same distinction. By and large, treatments served to distinguish adults from subadults, circumstance of death, and group affiliation. All other aspects of funerary treatment retain a normative character and were extended to all members of the population. Correspondingly, the contents of the grave assemblage served to differentiate virtually all the observed vertical distinctions. The organization of social distinctions symbolized in the Clarks mortuary ritual is consistent with that of a highly structured population with distinguishable wealth and nonwealth axes of vertical differentiation, but where the paramount levels of wealth converge with sociopolitical leadership.

Pawnee Results

Archaeological Reconstructions

The results of archaeological analysis on the three Pawnee samples are in good agreement with the known characteristics of Pawnee social organization. The comparison of known attributes with those recognized through archaeological analysis is presented in Table 6.35.

Vertical social distinctions were readily and consistently observed in the Pawnee samples. The full range of expected rank elements was recognized at both the Linwood and Clarks sites, while at Barcal a nearly complete set was obtained. The results from the three Pawnee sites actually provide a more detailed representation of the rank organization of the population than is reflected in Table 6.35. Not only were highly ranked individuals recognized, but the intermediate and lower rank

TABLE 6.35

Pawnee: Comparison of Ethnographic and Archaeological Observations of Mortuary Differentiation

	Source of observations				
	Ethnographic		Archaeological		
Type of differentiation	Society	Mortuary	Barcal	Linwood	Clarks
Vertical					
Chiefly office	+	—	+	+	+
Achieved wealth	+	+	+	+	+
Hereditary ascription	+	—	—	+	+
Ritual office	+	—	—	+	+
Special prestige positions	+	—	—	—	—
Horizontal					
Moiety membership	+	—	+(?)	—	+(?)
Matrilineal residence/descent	+	—	—	—	—
Society membership	+	—	+(?)	—	—
Male/female	+	+	?	+	+
Adult/subadult	+	+	+	+	+
Special status					
Circumstance of death	+	+	+	+	+
Social deviant	+	+	—	—	—
Alternative subadult treatment	+	+	—	—	+

strata could also be identified and their relative sizes and compositions compared. Three distinct wealth levels were visible at both Linwood and Clarks, while two were distinguished at Barcal. These rank levels and their mode of expression in the funerary ritual coincide with the ethnographic descriptions of rank strata in Pawnee society (see Chapter 5).

Horizontal social distinctions were much more ambiguous in their archaeological expression than were the vertical distinctions. Elementary differences, such as age and gender distinctions, were observed in all three of the sites examined. Yet, none of the more general features of horizontal organization, such as corporate group membership, descent orientation, moiety affiliation, or society membership, could firmly be demonstrated from the mortuary samples. Evidence suggestive of such distinctions was observed, however, in several instances. Possible indicators of corporate group affiliation were observed at both Barcal and Clarks. An indicator of society membership was also suggested at Barcal. Yet, neither moiety membership nor the matrifocus of descent could be discerned from any of the mortuary samples. Furthermore, no evidence for *any* higher-order horizontal distinction was found at the Linwood site.

Special status distinctions were recognized consistently in the archaeological samples. In all cases, these were attributed to treatments reflecting special circumstances of death, particularly death at a time or place that precluded immediate burial and in cases of mutilation and dismemberment resulting from warfare. Although the special status character of the treatments is clear, the interpretation of their specific meanings is still hypothetical and warrants further specific testing. The ascription of these treatments to the category "circumstance of death," and not to "social deviancy," is based on the fact that burial was within the community cemetery, an occurrence that would be unlikely in the case of serious social deviants (see accounts of treatment of deviants among the Pawnee, Chapter 5). It should be noted, however, that special death circumstances might also result in an individual's burial in some location other than the community cemetery, such as the Pawnee practice of burying war dead in disused cache pits.

Although the overall agreement between the known social features and the archaeological reconstruction is quite good, archaeologcal analysis was not able to distinguish the main features of horizontal organization in Pawnee society, nor did it reveal the existence of special treatments for social deviants. To assess the significance of these findings, the consistency of findings between sites must be considered, along with the limitations imposed on the analysis by the particular samples used.

Two major limitations were recognized in the Pawnee samples: (1) small sample size and (2) an inadequate number of sexed individuals. Both deficiencies would be expected to introduce additional spurious variation into the results and to reduce the number of distinct social categories that could be recognized. The level of agreement that is observed from the analyses, seen in this light, is remarkable; certainly the inconsistencies that do exist are not major. Had the sample size been larger, the ambiguity in the recognition of horizontal distinctions might have been reduced, although this is far from a foregone conclusion. Had more reliable sex determinations been available, the primary improvement would have been in the fine-grained definition of social features, but this probably would not have materially altered the coarse distinctions evaluated in this study.

One further aspect of the samples that should be considered is their placement in time. As was noted in Chapter 5, the social organization of these Plains groups was not static during the eighteenth and nineteenth centuries. There is, therefore, a possibility that some of the discrepancies in the site results are the product of social change among the Pawnee and not of archaeological error. In those instances where an early–late distinction can be drawn, as in the close agreement in vertical distinctions between Linwood and Clarks, and the somewhat-less-well-expressed vertical distinctions at Barcal, temporal change should be considered as the source of variation. (This is addressed in more detail in Chapter 7.) Not all discrepancies, however, can be explained in this fashion. Temporal change is an unlikely source for the disagreement on elements of horizontal differentiation, where the earliest and latest sites are in the best agreement and no definable early–late trend can be identified. Seen in light of these considerations, the ambiguity and inconsistency in the recognition of higher-ordered horizontal features of social organization would seem to be the single most serious deficiency in the archaeological reconstructions.

Ethnographic Accounts of Mortuary Practices

Ethnographic accounts of Pawnee mortuary custom provide a good view of the normative funerary treatment and also some insight into differential practices (Table 6.35). Of the differential practices, vertical distinctions were the most completely documented, with indications of special treatment for wealthy individuals, ranked males, and ranked subadults. These accounts do not, however, mention differential treatment for chiefs or holders of ritual office. Compared with the archaeological findings, the ethnographic documentation of vertical mortuary differentiation is incomplete.

Horizontal differentiation, beyond simple age and sex distinctions, was not recorded ethnographically. In this, ethnographic documentation is not markedly different from the archaeological results, where such distinctions were observed in an inconsistent and ambiguous fashion.

Only in the case of special status distinctions were the ethnographic accounts more complete than the archaeological reconstructions. Special treatments accorded individuals with abnormal circumstances of death were recorded, along with a variety of treatments for various forms of social deviance (see Chapter 5). The superior documentation of special status distinctions should be tempered by one additional observation. Few of these observations were derived from standard ethnographic sources; rather they were gleaned from catalogs of Pawnee folktales. This is not really surprising, since these special treatments would occur only rarely and as such might be missed by an observer, while their very novelty makes them a likely subject for oral history. Yet, if one employed only the formal ethnographic accounts of the Pawnee and ignored the folktales, the list of differentiated mortuary categories would shrink by half.

Ethnographic accounts of Pawnee funerary activity are most complete in their detailing of the normative aspects of funerary treatment and are secondarily concerned with gross levels of rank differentiation. If folktales are included, a rich assortment of special status differentiations is added. Taken as a whole, the view of Pawnee mortuary practices provided by ethnography is somewhat less detailed than that obtained through archaeological investigations and falls well short of documenting the full range of differential practices expected for Pawnee society.

The Arikara

Larson Site

Larson is the earliest site included in the analysis and is also the site with the longest apparent period of use. It overlaps in time the occupation of the Barcal site, some 500 km to the south. A plan of the cemetery is presented in Figure 6.24.

162 6. Mortuary Differentiation and Social Distinction

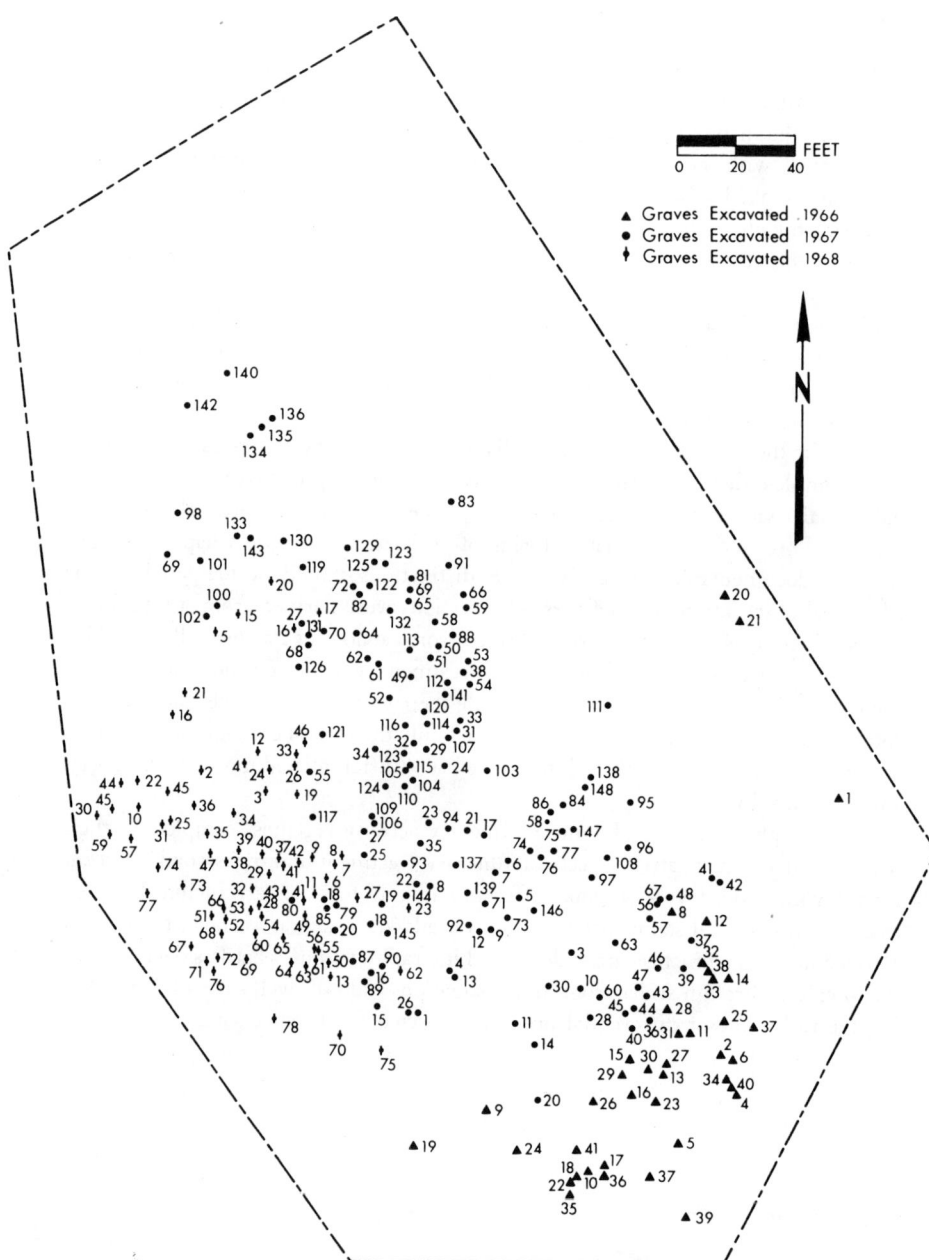

Figure 6.24 Plan of the Larson site cemetery.

Formal Treatment

The normative burial treatment at Larson was primary, single inhumation. The body was placed in a flexed posture and oriented with the head toward the northwest. The grave was closed with a simple wood covering, often taking the form of poles or planks placed flat across the opening of the grave and at right angles to its long axis. Although mortuary preparation was extremely homogeneous within the cemetery, a degree of variation was observed in each aspect of the treatment.

The analysis of burial treatment was hampered by the practice of stratifying interments above, and frequently through, existing graves. The practice is understandable given the technological limitations of bison bone implements, yet such stratification does pose considerable problems, since it frequently disturbed and scattered existing graves. An analysis of grave sequencing did not provide evidence for internal patterning of grave deposition by age or sex. This result suggests that grave superimposition probably was a haphazard rather than a systematic occurrence.

Because of superpositioning problems, all stratified graves were excluded from the analysis of grave size and depth, as were those recovered from the water's edge or beyond. This left a sample of 117 individual graves. No significant difference was observed in grave dimension between males and females. A comparison of adult and subadult graves, however, revealed that graves of adults were significantly larger and deeper than those of subadults (Table 6.36). As a further test, the adult category was divided into two groups, distinguishing mature individuals (age = 40+) from the rest. The results of this additional test were negative; although both adult groups exhibited average grave dimensions that were larger than those of subadults, they were not significantly different from one another.

Grave orientation at Larson was overwhelmingly skewed toward the northwest quadrant. A full 96% of all graves for which orientation could reliably be determined ($N = 420$) fell within this sector (Table 6.37). Graves with other orientations are listed in Table 6.38. There was no significant association of these alternative orientations with any age or sex category, nor do they cluster within the cemetery.

TABLE 6.36

Larson: Grave Dimensions by Age

	Adult values		Subadult values				
	Mean	S.D.	Mean	S.D.	t	df	Significance
Length	143.3	21.3	82.3	27.4	9.59	98	$p < .001$
Width	94.5	18.3	57.9	21.3	7.81	98	$p < .001$
Depth	82.3	30.5	57.9	21.3	4.37	107	$p < .001$

TABLE 6.37

Larson: Grave Orientation

Orientation	Frequency	Percentage
North	159	37.9
Northwest	168	40.0
West	78	18.6
Southwest	4	1.0
South	3	.7
Southeast	2	.5
East	2	.5
Northeast	4	1.0
	420	

Burial posture exhibited a similarly limited range of variation. Of the 410 cases for which burial posture could be determined, 382 (93%) were flexed. Among the flexed inhumations, no preference for the left or right side was observed. In those cases where a flexed posture was not used, the corpse was placed on its back in an extended posture, with the positioning of the legs varying from fully extended to a kind of trapezoidal configuration, where the legs were widely splayed at the knees and together at the ankles. The instances of nonnormative body posture are summarized in Table 6.39. No significant association by age or sex was noted for alternative burial posture, nor do these cases cluster within the cemetery.

TABLE 6.38

Larson: Nonnormative Grave Orientation

Grave number		Sex	Age (years)	Orientation
F101	20a	—	Birth–1	SW
	28a	—	3–6	SW
	38b	—	Birth–1	NE
F102	10	—	Birth–1	NE
F103	1	—	7–12	S
F201	30b	—	3–6	E
	30g	—	3–6	NE
	43a	F	40+	SW
	75a	M	30–40	NE
	77	—	1–2	E
	92a	—	Birth	S
	124g	M	30–40	S
F301	8b	—	Infant	SW
	46c	M	Adult	SE
	72b	—	Infant	SE

TABLE 6.39

Larson: Nonnormative Posture

Grave number		Sex	Age (years)	Posture
F101	23	—	Birth–1	Extended
	22b	—	Birth–1	Trapezoidal
	29a	—	Birth–1	Trapezoidal
	40b	M	30–40	Trapezoidal
F103	2	F	Adult	Extended
F201	10b	—	1½–2	Extended
	11a	—	Birth–1	Extended
	14e	—	Birth–1	Extended
	18	—	Birth–1	Trapezoidal
	23c	—	1–2	Extended
	48	—	1½–2	Trapezoidal
	55b	—	1½–2	Extended
	55g	M	20–25	Extended
	55i	M	20–30	Extended
	61a	—	Birth	Extended
	94a	M	30–40	Extended
	96	—	Birth–2	Trapezoidal
	99	—	1–2	Extended
	115	—	3–5	Extended
	144	—	Birth–1	Trapezoidal
	145b	—	Birth–1	Extended
F301	4	—	Infant	Trapezoidal
	19b	—	Adolescent	Extended
	38c	—	Child	Trapezoidal
	51b	—	Infant	Extended
	53	—	Child	Trapezoidal
	54e	F	Adult	Trapezoidal
	60a	—	Infant	Extended

Wood burial coverings were numerous, being observed in 62% of the subadult graves, 69% of the adult male graves, and 89% of the adult female graves. These percentages are likely to underrepresent the actual occurrence because of the frequent destruction of coverings with grave superpositioning. This high frequency of occurrence makes it unlikely that the coverings were used as a form of grave elaboration and suggests rather that they were employed as a basic element in the burial ritual. It is possible, of course, that the failure to receive a covering may have carried social significance. Unfortunately, it was impossible to determine which graves were not covered, compared to those for which the covering did not survive for archaeological recovery.

Two additional varieties of differential treatment were observed at Larson: multi-

TABLE 6.40

Larson: Artifact Type Associations

Female	Male
—	Native glass pendant
	Bird beak
	Small mammal cranium
	Rib shaft wrench
	Polished bone tube
	Curved rib ornament
	Bone point
	Perforated shell pendant
	Stone spear point
	Stone projectile point
	Retouched flake
	Plate chalcedony knife
	End scraper
	Gypsum
	Pipestone ornament
Subadult	Adult
Ceramic pot	Bird beak
Glass trade beads	Rib shaft wrench
Animal teeth	Quill flattener
Gun parts/accessories	Mussel shell
Heavy shell bead	Bone/antler implement
Rectangular shell bead	Curved rib ornament
Flat shell bead	Bone point
Metal bracelet	Perforated shell pendant
	Metal container
	Stone spear point
	Scoria abraider
	Sandstone shaft smoother
	Hammer stone
	Stone projectile point
	Petrified wood
	Retouched flake
	Unretouched flake
	Stone knife
	Plate chalcedony knife
	Side scraper
	End scraper
	Gypsum

ple interment and partial disarticulation. In a few instances, more than one individual was found to occupy a single grave. These "true" multiples are distinguished from instances where graves were closely overlapped at differing times. Although it was impossible to determine the precise number of true multiple graves, they appear to compose only a small portion of the mortuary population. It also seems that the most frequent pattern of occurrence was for a young adult female to be interred with a subadult. This pattern might suggest a type of special status distinction, marking a linkage between two individuals in their approximate time of death, or perhaps a kin tie, such as a mother or other close female relative with the child. Although such an explanation is appealing and consistent with the observed occurrences, it is not possible to test this hypothesis on the basis of the available archaeological evidence.

Disarticulated burial was rare at Larson (Owsley, personal communication 1982) and did not seem to function as a distinct, alternative disposal program of the kind observed among the Pawnee. Two adult males (F201 84a and 55g) had both been decapitated, but these were the only instances where disarticulation could be demonstrated. Other apparent cases of disarticulation seem to be the result of postinterment disturbances, produced by the construction of later graves. It also has been suggested (Ubelaker and Willey 1978) that the Arikara occasionally exposed the dead in the grave prior to its closing, and similar suggestions have been found in the ethnohistorical literature (Orser 1980), but the detailed osteological assessment needed to test this possibility was beyond the scope of the present study.

In summary, treatment variables were overwhelmingly employed as normative indicators. Only in grave size and depth was a regular age-based distinction expressed. In those instances where nonnormative grave orientation or burial posture was observed, no association with an age or sex category was detected, nor did these occurrences exhibit any tendency to cluster spatially. Furthermore, there was little redundancy in the occurrence of nonnormative treatments. In only a single instance did an interment exhibit more than one nonnormative treatment—Grave F201 55g, where the individual was decapitated and interred in an extended burial posture. These nonnormative treatments will be considered further in the light of artifact usage in the Larson mortuary treatment.

Artifact Occurrence

The analysis of artifact occurrence was difficult at Larson because of the frequent postinterment disturbances of the graves. This made the analysis of empty graves (i.e., graves with no associated artifacts) particularly ambiguous. For this reason, the analysis of grave assemblages was confined to those 166 graves with clearly associated artifacts.

Of the 86 artifact types, 53 occur in the Larson cemetery. As befits its early date, there is a greater emphasis on native-made artifacts than on trade materials, with 19 of the 42 possible trade types and 34 of the 44 possible native-made types observed. As can be seen from Table 6.40 and Figure 6.25, the distribution of types was

	Sex +	Sex −
Age +	Male, adult 11	Adult 11 / Subadult 8
Age −	Male 4	19

Figure 6.25 Age and sex constraints on artifact occurrence at the Larson site.

highly constrained; 64% of the artifact types exhibited a significant distributional association by age or sex. What is perhaps most interesting about the configuration of constrained types is the asymmetry in the expression of male and female related artifacts. Whereas a total of 15 types are limited in their occurrence to males, no types exhibit a similar association with female grave assemblages. It is also interesting to note the relatively large number of types ($N = 8$) that are associated with subadults. That this set of types should include a number of presumably expensive trade types, such as gun parts and metal bracelets, is particularly interesting.

A similar pattern of artifact occurrence was observed when the distribution of artifact classes was considered (Tables 6.41 and 6.42). Mann–Whitney U tests conducted on artifact class occurrence by age and sex exhibited the same asymmetry between male and female associated artifact classes and confirmed the existence of a definite set of goods associated with subadults. These latter results, in particular, seem to indicate that many of the trade materials acquired by the Larson Arikara were perceived simply as colorful ornaments, lacking major wealth or status signifi-

TABLE 6.41

Larson: Artifact Class Associations by Sex

Artifact class	Average male rank ($N=39$)	Average female rank ($N=25$)	U	Probability
Trade goods				
Body ornaments	32.8	32.0	474.0	.7580
Clothing ornaments	31.4	34.2	444.5	.4884
Implements	32.3	32.8	480.0	.8489
All trade items	31.5	34.1	447.5	.5401
Native goods				
Ornaments	36.4	26.4	335.0	.0140
Implements	34.8	28.9	397.0	.1905
Sociotechnic	36.4	26.4	336.0	.0068
All native items	37.9	24.1	278.5	.0024

TABLE 6.42

Larson: Artifact Class Associations by Age

Artifact class	Average adult rank (N=72)	Average subadult rank (N=94)	U	Probability
Trade goods				
Body ornaments	73.0	91.5	2631.0	.0017
Clothing ornaments	76.8	88.6	2905.0	.0789
Implements	86.4	81.3	3178.5	.1780
All trade items	74.2	90.6	2713.0	.0203
Native goods				
Ornaments	84.0	83.1	3346.5	.8850
Implements	102.5	69.0	2017.5	.0001
Sociotechnic	90.7	78.0	2869.0	.0168
All native items	101.5	69.7	2087.0	.0001

cance. Further clarification of this orderly use of material culture in the funerary process is observed in the principal component analysis.

Principal Component Analysis

Given the large number of cases and the highly structured pattern of artifact occurrence, the entry criterion for component analysis was relaxed to allow any type occurring in at least five graves (3%) to be included in the analysis. Thirty-one types were employed, from which 11 components with eigenvalues greater than 1.0 were derived. These components jointly accounted for 65.1% of the original variance. The rotated factor matrix is presented in Table 6.43, and its major features are summarized in Table 6.44.

These factors highlight a series of tightly structured implement sets and ornament combinations. Factors 2 and 3 represent adult male tool kits, one relating to arrow manufacture and the other to more general purpose activities. Factor 4 is another adult tool kit, but one that may be more closely associated with female activities. Factors 5 and 6 are contrastive ornament sets that both exhibit an association with subadults. The role of trade materials is clearly expressed by Factors 1 and 7; Factor 1 with positive loadings on most trade-derived items; and Factor 7 with strong negative loadings on a range of traditional goods. This pattern suggests that trade goods were not well integrated into the total artifact assemblage. Similar patterns were observed in the later factors; Factors 8 and 11 are additional task sets, and Factor 9 is a male ornament set. Factor 10 is a somewhat specialized factor, loading principally on the large bifacially worked spear points that occur in a small number of male graves. The moderate strength positive loading of other sociotechnic goods,

TABLE 6.43

Larson: Varimax Rotated Factor Matrix

Artifact type	Factor 1	Factor 2	Factor 3	Factor 4	Factor 5
Ceramic pot	0.22873	−0.07951	−0.06724	−0.09480	−0.10642
Glass trade beads	0.25329	0.02822	−0.21793	0.04335	0.50752
Bird beak	0.17443	−0.12431	0.51461	−0.05482	0.00072
Bird bone	−0.16276	0.08542	0.17275	0.10893	0.04315
Small mammal cranium	−0.10215	−0.00307	−0.17131	0.02737	−0.06177
Rib shaft wrench	0.17235	0.72021	−0.00674	0.32897	0.05490
Squash knife	0.00234	−0.03282	0.02533	−0.02419	−0.07865
Quill flattener	0.14078	0.09041	−0.05857	−0.01096	−0.12834
Tubular shell bead	0.04598	0.09020	−0.01119	0.17767	0.76907
Heavy shell bead	0.06891	−0.03191	−0.01403	0.00785	−0.00042
Shell runtee	−0.02796	−0.02310	0.03473	0.19127	0.12515
Marine snail shell	−0.08304	0.07210	−0.06145	0.01383	−0.00448
Perforated shell pendant	0.27991	0.25085	−0.12821	0.01685	−0.06332
Flat shell bead	−0.08145	−0.07145	0.03249	−0.12225	0.71543
Metal bracelet	0.71919	−0.07764	0.10128	0.05157	−0.03785
Metal bead/bangle	0.32769	−0.24323	−0.07018	0.24689	0.04086
Metal projectile point	0.69592	0.24767	0.06515	0.03701	0.17069
Metal container	0.02093	0.58819	0.08103	−0.07153	−0.00642
Copper crimp/clip	0.59712	0.26108	−0.15797	−0.21091	−0.12263
Sheet brass blade	0.56612	−0.01990	0.24773	0.18714	0.23080
Bifacial spear point	0.08069	0.01876	0.04254	0.10303	−0.02010
Scoria abraider	0.09759	0.14195	0.12102	0.84350	−0.01956
Sandstone shaft smoother	−0.04386	0.77919	0.14706	0.04911	−0.03100
Stone projectile point	0.06629	0.52028	0.33431	0.04696	0.00268
Retouched flake	0.09498	0.23413	0.58246	0.35814	−0.01198
Unretouched flake	−0.01040	0.37699	0.43878	0.24975	−0.14700
Stone knife	0.08429	0.01436	0.72346	0.17325	−0.01915
Plate chalcedony knife	0.29680	0.51691	0.06803	0.12208	0.06520
Side scraper	0.09126	0.08190	0.11030	0.82754	0.07533
End scraper	0.04484	0.47142	0.64768	−0.14522	0.03742
Pipestone ornament	0.73857	0.05096	0.10095	0.17268	−0.02517

such as bird beaks, with this factor emphasizes the special nature of this particular grave inclusion.

Overall, the factor results provide further evidence of the highly structured use of grave offerings at Larson. Trade goods, both ornaments and implements, appear to occupy a relatively marginal role in the symbolic mortuary usage and are not well integrated into the Larson material culture complex.

Hierarchical Fusion Cluster Analysis

The clustering of factor scores resulted in a somewhat confused picture of assemblage organization that seems to contradict the indications of strong artifact

TABLE 6.43 *Continued*

Factor 6	Factor 7	Factor 8	Factor 9	Factor 10	Factor 11
0.38928	−0.36695	−0.02877	0.10032	−0.09593	−0.08009
0.32878	0.35879	−0.11269	−0.17562	0.04222	−0.07056
−0.05123	−0.10339	−0.10505	0.17378	0.47074	−0.09032
−0.01197	0.10755	−0.03106	0.77217	−0.00407	−0.01191
0.10956	0.34298	0.17910	−0.03671	0.41524	0.47787
−0.13217	−0.10413	−0.07902	0.02577	0.12127	−0.03489
−0.04711	0.01273	−0.12467	−0.04894	−0.11799	0.79694
−0.04122	−0.04229	0.71486	−0.04307	0.12262	−0.11502
−0.32191	−0.01332	−0.10430	0.06971	0.04727	−0.01602
−0.61476	0.20812	−0.08776	−0.18080	−0.24913	−0.25584
0.65176	0.10008	−0.07363	−0.15446	−0.14565	−0.14385
0.05673	−0.80746	0.00932	−0.08656	0.04540	−0.02280
0.00763	−0.07379	0.00806	0.62645	−0.04842	−0.04659
0.29945	−0.01599	0.01394	−0.01490	−0.10090	−0.05904
−0.07978	0.07669	0.01158	−0.03990	0.11642	−0.17620
−0.00359	0.21284	0.50152	0.23031	−0.23010	0.15993
0.00183	−0.07731	0.03509	0.01696	0.07987	0.41020
0.02257	0.01541	0.54118	−0.10574	−0.13431	−0.00237
0.14752	0.17823	0.03445	0.17274	−0.11305	−0.04905
0.21043	−0.08486	0.32568	−0.11771	0.02746	0.05125
−0.02896	0.01083	0.01785	−0.11054	0.76705	−0.04013
0.02912	−0.03275	−0.16450	0.05391	0.04448	−0.01937
0.01306	0.07042	0.02104	0.31517	−0.05215	−0.03665
0.01483	−0.11226	0.02660	0.27161	0.47829	−0.05604
0.06271	0.02588	0.33881	0.08572	−0.06714	−0.05805
0.23972	0.21517	−0.24528	−0.10717	−0.06367	−0.01483
−0.09804	0.02225	−0.12500	0.04452	0.06126	0.02307
−0.03542	−0.18126	0.28792	0.21086	0.00978	0.29334
0.10202	0.06399	0.24475	0.08067	0.09148	0.01856
0.12773	0.05940	0.13814	−0.08575	0.05850	0.05326
−0.06618	−0.03613	0.12129	0.02051	0.04709	0.00654

patterning previously observed. The summary statistics and dendrogram from the analysis are presented in Table 6.45 and Figure 6.26. The six-cluster solution lumps a full 66% of the assemblages into an amorphous Cluster 1, in which virtually all strong loadings are washed out. The one diagnostic feature of the cluster is the low variance associated with a negative loading on Factor 1 (i.e., trade goods). Clusters 2–6 provide various small-scale contrasts; Clusters 2 and 5 consist of assemblages, mainly those of subadults, that are dominated by trade materials, Cluster 2 with trade beads (Factor 5) and Cluster 5 by the ornament and implement set of Factor 1. Cluster 3 presents the uneasy combination of assemblages loading on Factor 8 (quill flatteners and metal containers) and Factor 10 (large stone spear

TABLE 6.44

Larson: Factor Summary[a]

Factor number	Loading pattern	Percentage variance	Diagnostic positive loadings	Diagnostic negative loadings
1	Group	15.5	Metal bracelet − Metal projectile point Copper crimp/clip Sheet brass blade Pipestone ornament M	
2	Bipolar	8.1	Rib shaft wrench M+ Metal container + Sandstone shaft smoother + Stone projectile point M+ Plate chalcedony knife M+	Metal bead/bangle
3	Bipolar	6.5	Bird beak M+ Retouched flake M+ Unretouched flake + Stone knife + End scraper M+	Glass trade beads −
4	Bipolar	5.5	Scoria abraider + Side scraper +	Copper crimp/clip
5	Group	5.0	Glass trade beads − Tubular shell bead Flat shell bead −	
6	Bipolar	4.8	Shell runtee Ceramic pot −	Heavy shell bead − Tubular shell bead
7	Group	4.4		Ceramic pot − Marine snail shell

[a] Constraints: +, adult only; −, subadult only; M, male only; F, female only.

points). Cluster 4 loads exclusively on Factor 11 (squash knife and small mammal cranium), and Cluster 6 loads consistently on Factor 4 (scoria abraider and side scraper). None of the clusters exhibits the rigid age and sex structuring that was expected based on the bivariate analysis and principal component analysis. The dendrogram suggests that the grave assemblages are not lacking in structure, but rather that they are structured at a very fine scale. Yet, even when the results were evaluated at the level of 18 clusters, there was still little indication of the general logic underlying Larson mortuary inclusions.

For contrast, the raw dichotomous data were transformed into a matrix of distance coefficients and were similarly clustered using Ward's method. The results from this run are presented in Table 6.46 and Figure 6.27. The clusters of raw data including all 53 types, begin to suggest a general structure for the mortuary complex. Unfortunately, not all of the observed structure can be attributed to intentional mortuary symbolism.

TABLE 6.45

Larson: Hierarchical Fusion Cluster Diagnostics

Cluster number	Factor number	Mean origin	S.D.	Factor number	Mean origin	S.D.
1	1	−.1924	.2842	7	−.1771	.9650
	2	−.0771	.5026	8	−.2449	.4505
	3	.0753	1.0626	9	.0011	.9948
	4	−.0719	.5123	10	−.1966	.4409
	5	−.2372	.4965	11	−.1740	.3482
	6	.0559	1.0045			
	Number of individuals	110				
	Number of males	21				
	Number of females	18				
	Number of adults	45				
	Number of subadults	65				
	Cluster members	F101: 2,12b,15,19,22b,29e,32d, 32e,33b,33e,35a,38c,40a; F201: 2d,3a,3f,8d,10a,10b,11a,11d,14c,19d,27a, 27d,30e,30g,31,32c,34b,35c,38b,40, 44,46,47e,49,52a,52b,54a,54b, 58,61a,62,63a,64c,68a,69b, 69c,71a,78,80b,81,82a,84c, 91,93d,94b,95,96,97g,100,101a,102g,104,106, 107,113c,117,119,122b,124a,124b, 127b,128,130c,134,136a,`142,`145d,146b; F301: 2f,4,5,8b,8c,11,13,15,19c,20,21,`33c, 38c,39c,40,41a,43a,45,47,50e,55b,55c,58e,58f, 59c,60a,60b,68a,72a					
2	1	−.1810	.4198	7	.2120	.4821
	2	−.2353	.3702	8	−.0269	.5610
	3	−.2405	.1980	9	.0605	.3512
	4	−.2483	.3480	10	−.2713	.3872
	5	2.5211	.9530	11	−.0799	.4854
	6	−.6143	1.2058			
	Number of individuals	15				
	Number of males	3				
	Number of females	1				
	Number of adults	4				
	Number of subadults	11				
	Cluster members	F101: 11,27c; F201: 30c,53,99,109a,110a,110b,116a,133c; F301: 9b,22a,50b,50f,67b					
3	1	−.4901	.3785	7	.3675	1.1841
	2	.3082	1.5324	8	1.4680	1.7696
	3	−.2343	.8106	9	−.2349	.8189
	4	−.0726	.9146	10	1.3855	1.8134
	5	−.3462	.3953	11	.1075	.9248
	6	.1068	.4521			

(continued)

TABLE 6.45 *Continued*

Cluster number	Factor number	Mean origin	S.D.	Factor number	Mean origin	S.D.
	Number of individuals	21				
	Number of males	11				
	Number of females	4				
	Number of adults	16				
	Number of subadults	5				
	Cluster members	F101: 17b;				
		F201: 8c,55g,55i,75a,84a,85,94a,101b,125,126a, 132;				
		F301: 16,19b,29c,32,49b,50g,50h,62b,78				
4	1	.0132	.6288	7	.0719	.5292
	2	−.1857	.2454	8	−.7053	.6067
	3	.1433	.5695	9	−.2768	.2437
	4	−.1369	.0919	10	−.6676	.5703
	5	−.4449	.5702	11	4.5084	1.8322
	6	−.2665	.2272			
	Number of individuals	5				
	Number of males	1				
	Number of females	0				
	Number of adults	2				
	Number of subadults	3				
	Cluster members	F103: 1; F201: 6a,131; F301: 7,62a				
5	1	2.7509	1.7859	7	.8115	.8972
	2	.2679	2.4879	8	.0622	1.2506
	3	−.3590	.6422	9	.1667	.9081
	4	−.6196	.6812	10	−.2387	.6776
	5	−.4322	.6114	11	−.4878	1.0548
	6	.0559	1.0972			
	Number of individuals	11				
	Number of males	1				
	Number of females	1				
	Number of adults	2				
	Number of subadults	9				
	Cluster members	F201: 29,50,55f,65,88; F301: 14,31,60c,61,65,70				
6	1	.9620	2.6351	7	−.1744	1.7005
	2	.8787	2.5111	8	−.1611	1.1857
	3	.8701	2.2817	9	.8636	3.0885
	4	5.1608	.4956	10	.6403	2.5742
	5	.6302	1.6900	11	−.1327	.6696
	6	.3844	1.9232			
	Number of individuals	4				
	Number of males	2				
	Number of females	1				
	Number of adults	4				
	Number of subadults	0				
	Cluster members	F201: 63c; F301: 3h,42,66				

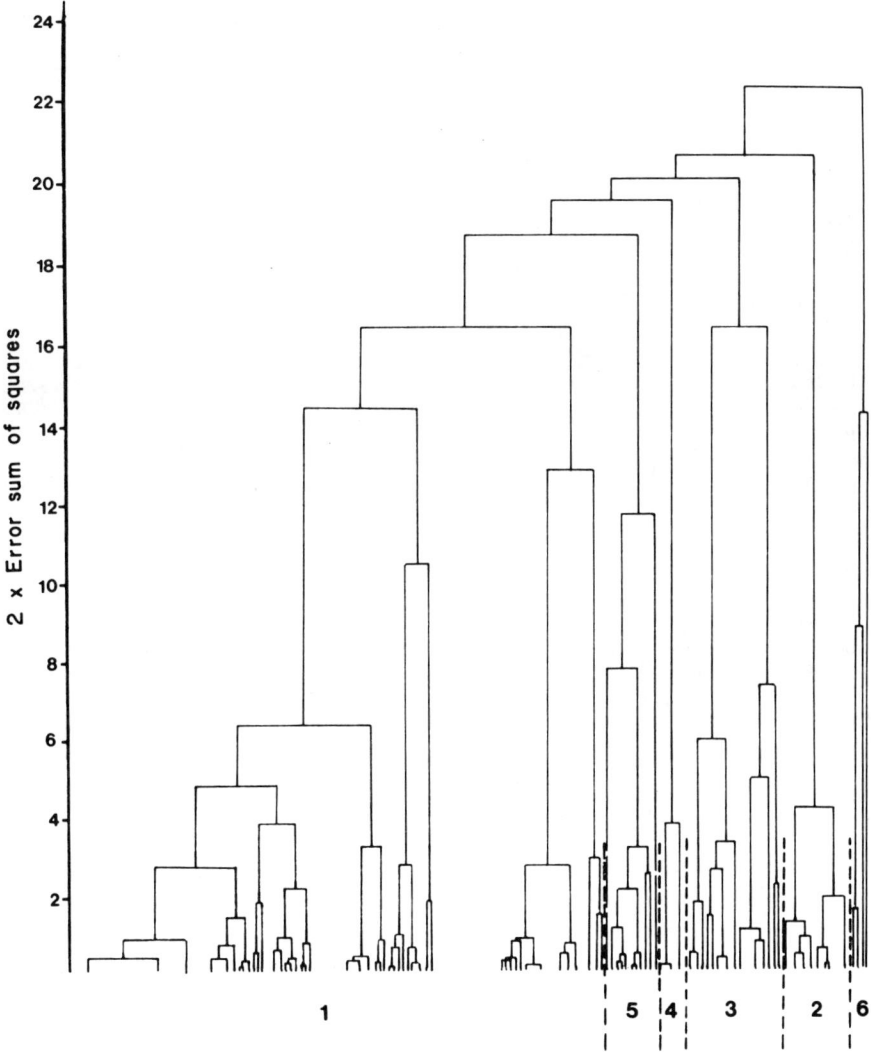

Figure 6.26 Dendrogram produced by the clustering of Larson site factor scores. Due to the large number of cases, the dendrogram has been truncated at its base to preserve legibility. The six-cluster solution is designated by the numerals below the dendrogram.

TABLE 6.46

Larson: Hierarchical Fusion Cluster Diagnostics (Raw Data)

	Cluster[a]					
	1	2	3	4	5	6
Glass bottle	0	0	0	0	0	0
Ceramic pot	0	0	7	0	1	1
Native glass pendant	0	0	1	0	1	1
Animal effigy	0	0	0	0	0	0
Glass trade beads	38	10	1	6	9	3
Bear claw	0	0	0	0	0	1
Animal teeth	0	0	3	0	0	0
Bird beak	0	1	4	0	1	3
Bird bone	0	0	4	0	0	2
Raptor talon	0	0	0	0	0	0
Small mammal cranium	4	2	1	0	0	0
Rib shaft wrench	0	0	2	1	0	4
Squash knife	0	1	4	0	0	0
Scapula hoe	0	1	2	0	0	0
Quill flattener	0	2	6	0	0	2
Cancellous paint applicator	0	0	0	0	0	0
Awl	0	2	0	1	0	1
Metatarsal flesher	0	0	0	0	0	0
Elk horn scraper	0	0	0	0	0	0
Bone/antler implement	0	0	1	0	0	2
Gun parts/accessories	0	0	1	0	0	1
Pin game cup	0	0	0	0	0	0
Polished bone tube	0	1	0	0	0	1
Bone pendant	0	0	2	0	0	0
Curved rib ornament	0	0	3	0	0	1
Bone point	1	0	1	0	0	0
Mussel shell	0	0	0	2	0	2
Gorget	0	0	0	0	0	0
Shell hair pipe	0	0	0	0	0	0
Tubular shell bead	7	2	1	2	0	2
Wampum bead	0	1	0	0	0	0
Heavy shell bead	0	3	1	18	0	0
Rectangular shell bead	1	1	1	1	0	0
Shell runtee	3	1	0	0	2	0
Marine snail shell	5	0	24	0	2	2
Perforated shell pendant	0	0	6	0	0	3
Flat shell bead	7	1	0	0	2	0
Metal bracelet	0	3	0	1	1	2
Metal bead/bangle	1	17	3	0	0	1
Iron knife	0	0	0	0	0	0
Axe/wedge	0	0	0	0	0	0

TABLE 6.46 *Continued*

	Cluster[a]					
	1	2	3	4	5	6
Scissors	0	0	0	0	0	0
Strike-a-light	0	0	0	0	0	0
Metal eating implement	0	0	0	0	0	0
Small metal hardware	0	0	0	0	0	0
Horse gear	0	0	0	0	0	0
Small iron tool	0	0	0	0	0	0
Metal projectile point	1	2	0	0	0	3
Iron scraper	0	0	0	0	0	0
Iron digging implement	0	0	0	0	0	0
Metal container	0	2	0	0	0	3
Metal buckle	0	0	0	0	0	0
Finger ring	0	0	0	0	0	0
Metal button	0	0	0	0	0	0
Large cast brass bell	0	0	0	0	0	0
Smaller brass bell	0	0	0	0	0	0
Thick wire coil	0	0	0	0	0	0
Thin wire coil	1	1	0	0	0	0
Metal lace/braid	1	0	0	0	0	0
Copper crimp/clip	0	3	0	0	0	2
Sheet brass blade	0	2	0	0	1	2
Lead ring/coil	0	0	0	0	0	0
Lead band	0	0	0	0	0	0
Sheet silver bracelet	0	0	0	0	0	0
Silver cross	0	0	0	0	0	0
Silver hair plate	0	0	0	0	0	0
Silver earring	0	0	0	0	0	0
Small silver brooch	0	0	0	0	0	0
Gunflint	0	0	0	0	0	1
Bifacial spear point	0	0	5	0	1	1
Scoria abrader	0	2	1	0	2	2
Sandstone shaft smoother	0	0	0	0	1	4
Whetstone	0	0	0	0	0	1
Hammer stone	0	0	0	0	0	2
Stone sphere	0	0	0	0	0	0
Stone projectile point	0	0	5	0	0	6
Stone pipe	0	1	2	0	0	0
Petrified wood	1	0	0	0	0	2
Retouched flake	0	3	3	1	1	8
Unretouched flake	0	2	1	3	19	6
Stone knife	0	1	0	1	1	3
Plate chalcedony knife	0	2	3	0	0	6
Side scraper	0	4	0	0	0	2
End scraper	1	0	1	0	3	7

(continued)

TABLE 6.46 *Continued*

	Cluster[a]					
	1	2	3	4	5	6
Pipestone ornament	1	5	0	0	0	3
Gypsum	0	0	0	0	0	3

[a]Cluster composition:

Cluster number		
1	Number of individuals	39
	Number of males	5
	Number of females	2
	Number of adults	8
	Number of subadults	31
	Cluster members	F101: 2,12b,17b; F201: 31,34b,53,54b,62,71a, 78,99,101a,104,107,109a,110a,110b,113c,116a, 119,124a,125,126a,133c; F301: 5,8b,8c,13,15, 19b,20,22a,40,43a,50b,55c,60a,67b,70
2	Number of individuals	19
	Number of males	3
	Number of females	5
	Number of adults	9
	Number of subadults	10
	Cluster members	F101: 11,27c; F201: 30c,50,55f,63c,84c,85,88, 91,100,101b,122b; F301: 7,14,31,32,65,66
3	Number of individuals	62
	Number of males	21
	Number of females	9
	Number of adults	33
	Number of subadults	29
	Cluster members	F101: 15,19,22b,33e,40a; F103: 1; F201: 3a,6a, 8c,8d,10a,10b,11d,14c,19d,27d,30e,30g,35c, 38d,40,44,49,52a,52b,54a,55g,55i,64c,68a, 69b,71a,81,93d,94b,95,96,97g,102g,128,130c, 131,132,145d,146b; F301: 4,11,16,29c,39c, 49b,50e,50g,50h,55b,58e,59c,60b,62a,62b, 72a,78
4	Number of individuals	18
	Number of males	0
	Number of females	2
	Number of adults	4
	Number of subadults	14
	Cluster members	F101: 29e,32e,33b,38c; F201: 46,47e,58,63a, 80b,82a,134; F301: 9b,19c,21,41a,47,50f,61
5	Number of individuals	19
	Number of males	4
	Number of females	6
	Number of adults	10
	Number of subadults	9
	Cluster members	F101: 32d,35a; F201: 2d,3f,11a,27a,61a,65,84a, 106,117,124b,136a,142; F301: 33c,38c,45, 58f,68a
6	Number of individuals	9
	Number of males	6
	Number of females	0
	Number of adults	8
	Number of subadults	1
	Cluster members	F201: 29,32c,75a,94a,127b; F301: 2f,3h,42,60c

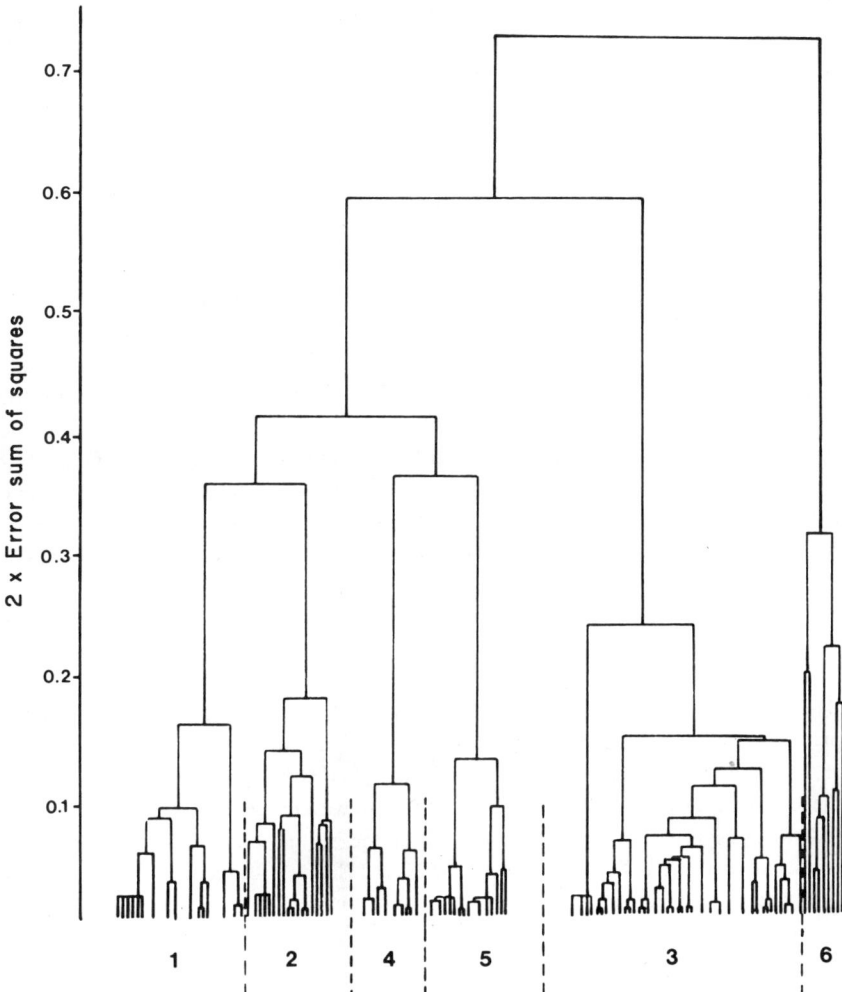

Figure 6.27 Dendrogram produced by the clustering of Larson site raw incidence scores. To preserve legibility the base of the dendrogram has been truncated. The six-cluster solution is designated by the numerals immediately below the dendrogram. A complete listing of cluster membership is presented in Table 6.47.

The first four clusters on the left of the dendrogram (Clusters 1, 2, 4, and 5) are defined by the presence or absence of frequently occurring trade ornaments (particularly glass beads) and by the average number of types in the grave assemblage. Cluster 1 is composed primarily of the graves of subadults ($\chi^2 = 11.2$, $df = 1$, $p < .05$), which contain almost exclusively glass beads. The graves in this cluster have the second lowest average number of types (1.9). Cluster 2 contains an equal number of adults and subadults and is defined primarily by the occurrence of metal beads, although 50% of the assemblages also contain glass trade beads. This cluster had the second highest average number of types (4.2) and contained a total of six sociotechnic objects (five pipestone ornaments and one stone pipe). Clusters 4 and 5 exhibit an organization parallel to that of Clusters 1 and 2. Cluster 4 has three times as many subadults as adults ($\chi^2 = 2.8$, $df = 1$, $p > .05$) and is defined by the presence of heavy shell beads. Cluster 5 has an equal number of adults and subadults, with unretouched flakes as the main diagnostic artifact. Both clusters have a relatively low average number of types (2.1 for Cluster 4 and 2.5 for Cluster 5), and both are composed of graves with few, if any, trade goods. This distinction between graves with and without trade goods mirrors Cluster 1 in the clustering based on factor scores.

The remaining two clusters are more complex. Cluster 3 represents a composite of at least three distinct assemblages. As a whole, graves in this cluster contain the lowest average number of types (1.6) and nearly no trade goods. The first clue to the composite nature of the cluster is the fact that the most commonly occurring artifact type, marine snail shell beads, occurs in only 30% of the assemblages. The three cluster components are (1) graves containing solely marine snail shell beads (2 males, 4 females, 12 subadults; the cases on the left side of the cluster); (2) a series of primarily male assemblages containing irregular sets of native implements, among which occur four bird beaks and two stone pipes; and (3) a small set of adult males interred with large spear points.

These last individuals have been interpreted as high-status male "warriors" by Bass and Rucker (1976:41), on the assumption that the finely made points were prestige markers. Examination of the osteological remains and the artifacts, however, indicated that, in at least one case (Grave F301 50H), the point may have been the cause of death, as a fragment of the tip was found still embedded in the individual's vertebra. Furthermore, two of these individuals were decapitated; a similar occurrence is known from Burial 25 at 25DK10 (see section on the Omaha).

Cluster 6 is composed of a series of mature male grave assemblages. It is the smallest of the six clusters, with only nine members, and had the greatest average number of types per grave (11.3). These assemblages are set apart by two features: they all contain an elaborate array of stone and bone tools (often associated with arrow manufacture), and all possess some form of likely sociotechnic object. The demographic composition of the cluster is also significant. Five of the nine individuals are mature males, and three more are adults of undetermined sex (presumably male). The remaining individual is a child. The skewing of ages toward older males highlights the importance of the cluster, while the inclusion of a single subadult may be suggestive of the character and transmission of the symbolized position.

These results seem to have a two-fold logic. On the one hand, assemblages are differentiated along the lines of age and quantity of grave inclusions. On the other hand, the cluster structure clearly divides the population by the presence or absence of trade ornaments, particularly glass trade beads. This latter division resulted in the appearance of parallel assemblage types—that is, pairs of clusters with similar demographic attributes, but with one marked by a native ornament and the other by an equivalent trade ornament. Cluster 1 compared with Clusters 3 and 4 seems to illustrate this pattern. Structurally, the assemblages are identical, only the source of the beads is different. The strong association of all these ornaments with subadults, and the similar demographic composition of the clusters, suggests that the difference is not the result of intentional mortuary differentiation, but rather reflects changes in the source and kinds of beads available to the Larson Arikara during the site's use.

Similarly, it has been suggested, based on the distribution of trade goods (particu-

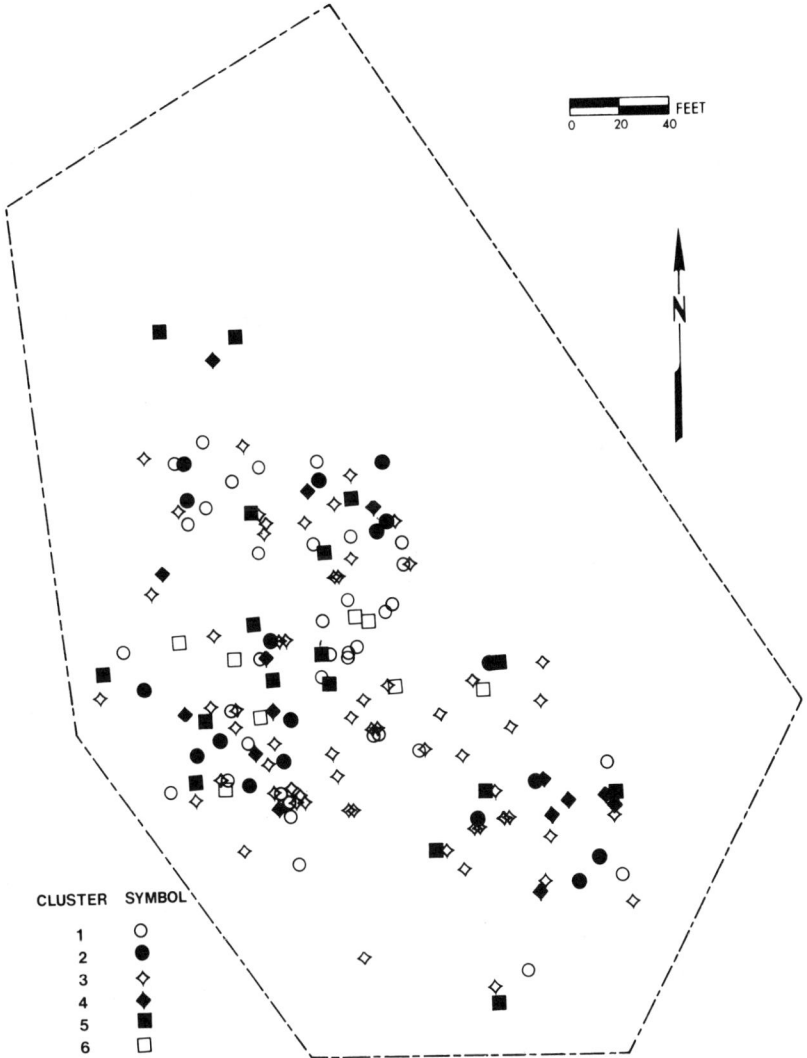

Figure 6.28 Spatial distribution of raw score hierarchical fusion clustering at the Larson site cemetery.

larly glass beads), that a horizontal stratigraphy can be observed at Larson, with earlier graves in the southeast and later graves in the north and west. Despite the temporal effects mentioned previously, the cluster results (Figure 6.28) do not support this claim. The apparent pattern is produced mainly by Cluster 1 graves (assemblages with only glass trade beads), which are overwhelmingly subadults. Clusters 2–5, those with trade goods and those without, are spread evenly over the site. This suggests that some manner of age- (rather than time-) dependent segregation of graves is responsible for the observed spatial pattern. Members of Cluster 6 also exhibit a restricted pattern of occurrence, concentrating in the central portion of the cemetery. If grave location were primarily the result of site growth over time, a more even demographic and social representation of the population would be expected in the various parts of the cemetery.

In general, the results of this raw data hierarchical fusion analysis suggests a system of mortuary differentiation that distinguished individuals by age, sex, and size and composition of the burial assemblage. A high level of redundancy in grave assemblage components was not observed; most graves contained a single artifact, and even among the few large assemblages, individuals rarely had more than a single sociotechnic object.

In addition to the rank and special status distinctions already mentioned, the cluster analyses also highlighted the changing artifact inventory of the Arikara, which adds an additional, although spurious, dimension to the social analysis.

Monothetic Division Cluster Analysis

Monothetic divisive analysis provides a similar view of the structure of Larson mortuary differentiation, but one that highlights even more dramatically the temoral effect in artifact occurrence. These results are presented in Table 6.47 and Figure 6.29. Despite the large number of age- and sex-specific types, only two of the eight clusters exhibited significant demographic skewing: Cluster 2 showed a clear adult, male selection ($\chi^2 = 6.2$, $df = 1$, $P < .05$), while Cluster 7 contained a significantly greater than expected number of subadults ($\chi^2 = 8.9$, $df = 1$, $p < .05$). Both clusters have counterparts in the hierarchical fusion analysis previously discussed.

The population was divided initially by the occurrence of glass trade beads. Those with beads, on the left side of the dendrogram, were further divided by the presence of retouched flakes (Cluster 1) and by the presence (Cluster 3) or absence (Cluster 7) of metal bead–bangles. Cluster 7 highlights grave assemblages, primarily of subadults, that contain only glass beads. Among graves lacking glass beads, graves with end scrapers (Cluster 2) were first distinguished. The remaining assemblages were then divided using marine snail shell beads, metal bead/bangles and unretouched flakes. The distribution of the eight clusters is plotted on a plan of the cemetery in Figure 6.30. No clear spatial component to the clusters is apparent, except the northwest–southeast distribution of glass trade bead assemblages mentioned previously.

TABLE 6.47

Larson: Monothetic Divisive Cluster Diagnostics

	Cluster[a]							
	1	2	3	4	5	6	7	8
Glass bottle	0	0	0	0	0	0	0	0
Ceramic pot	1	0	0	2	0	0	2	4
Native glass pendant	0	1	0	0	0	1	0	1
Animal effigy	0	0	0	0	0	0	0	0
Glass trade bead	6	0	7	0	0	0	54	0
Bear claw	0	1	0	0	0	0	0	0
Animal teeth	0	0	0	1	0	0	0	2
Bird beak	1	2	0	1	0	1	1	3
Bird bone	1	1	0	0	1	0	0	3
Raptor talon	0	0	0	0	0	0	0	0
Small mammal cranium	0	1	1	0	1	0	3	1
Rib shaft wrench	2	2	0	0	0	0	1	2
Squash knife	0	0	1	0	0	1	0	3
Scapula hoe	0	0	0	0	0	0	1	2
Quill flattener	2	1	0	1	1	0	0	5
Cancellous paint applicator	0	0	0	0	0	0	0	0
Awl	1	0	1	0	1	0	1	0
Metatarsal flesher	0	0	0	0	0	0	0	0
Elk horn scraper	0	0	0	0	0	0	0	0
Bone/antler implement	1	1	0	0	0	0	0	1
Gun parts/accessories	1	0	0	0	0	0	0	1
Pin game cup	0	0	0	0	0	0	0	0
Polished bone tube	0	1	0	0	1	0	0	0
Bone pendant	0	0	0	1	1	0	0	0
Curved rib ornament	0	2	0	1	0	0	0	1
Bone point	0	0	0	1	1	0	0	0
Whole mussel shell	2	0	0	0	0	0	1	1
Gorget	0	0	0	0	0	0	0	0
Shell hair pipe	0	0	0	0	0	0	0	0
Tubular shell bead	2	0	0	1	2	0	9	0
Wampum bead	1	0	0	0	0	0	0	0
Heavy shell bead	0	0	0	1	3	3	6	9
Rectangular shell bead	0	0	1	0	0	0	2	1
Shell runtee	1	0	0	0	0	0	5	0
Marine snail shell	1	1	0	24	0	0	7	0
Perforated shell pendant	2	1	0	2	2	0	0	2
Flat shell bead	0	0	1	0	1	0	8	0
Metal bracelet	2	0	1	0	1	0	3	0
Metal bead/bangle	3	0	7	1	11	0	0	0
Iron knife	0	0	0	0	0	0	0	0
Axe/wedge	0	0	0	0	0	0	0	0
Scissors	0	0	0	0	0	0	0	0
Strike-a-light	0	0	0	0	0	0	0	0
Metal eating implement	0	0	0	0	0	0	0	0

(continued)

TABLE 6.47 *Continued*

	Cluster[a]							
	1	2	3	4	5	6	7	8
Small metal hardware	0	0	0	0	0	0	0	0
Horse gear	0	0	0	0	0	0	0	0
Small iron tool	0	0	0	0	0	0	0	0
Metal projectile point	2	1	2	0	0	0	1	0
Iron scraper	0	0	0	0	0	0	0	0
Iron digging implement	0	0	0	0	0	0	0	0
Metal container	1	3	1	0	0	0	0	0
Metal buckle	0	0	0	0	0	0	0	0
Finger ring	0	0	0	0	0	0	0	0
Metal button	0	0	0	0	0	0	0	0
Large cast brass bell	0	0	0	0	0	0	0	0
Smaller brass bell	0	0	0	0	0	0	0	0
Thick wire coil	0	0	0	0	0	0	0	0
Thin wire coil	0	0	0	0	1	0	1	0
Metal lace/braid	0	0	0	0	0	0	1	0
Copper crimp/clip	1	1	2	0	0	0	1	0
Sheet brass blade	3	0	1	0	0	0	1	0
Lead ring/coil	0	0	0	0	0	0	0	0
Lead band	0	0	0	0	0	0	0	0
Sheet silver bracelet	0	0	0	0	0	0	0	0
Silver cross	0	0	0	0	0	0	0	0
Silver hair plate	0	0	0	0	0	0	0	0
Silver earring	0	0	0	0	0	0	0	0
Small silver brooch	0	0	0	0	0	0	0	0
Gunflint	0	1	0	0	0	0	0	0
Bifacial spear point	1	0	0	0	0	0	1	5
Scoria abraider	3	0	0	0	1	2	0	1
Sandstone shaft smoother	1	3	0	0	0	1	0	0
Whetstone	1	0	0	0	0	0	0	0
Hammer stone	1	1	0	0	0	0	0	0
Stone sphere	0	0	0	0	0	0	0	0
Stone projectile point	2	4	0	2	0	0	1	2
Stone pipe	0	0	1	0	0	0	0	2
Petrified wood	1	1	0	0	0	0	1	0
Retouched flake	6	5	0	0	1	1	0	3
Unretouched flake	4	5	0	0	1	13	8	0
Stone knife	1	2	0	0	1	2	0	0
Plate chalcedony knife	3	3	1	2	1	0	0	1
Side scraper	4	0	0	0	2	0	0	0
End scraper	2	9	0	0	0	0	1	0
Pipestone ornament	2	1	1	0	3	0	2	0
Gypsum	3	0	0	0	0	0	0	0

*a*Cluster composition:

Cluster number		
1	Number of individuals	6
	Number of males	1
	Number of females	2
	Number of adults	4
	Number of subadults	2
	Cluster members	F201: 29,101b,136b; F301: 3h,42,66
2	Number of individuals	9
	Number of males	7
	Number of females	0
	Number of adults	8
	Number of subadults	1
	Cluster members	F201: 32c,54a,75a,94a,124b,125,127b; F301: 2f,60c
3	Number of individuals	7
	Number of males	1
	Number of females	1
	Number of adults	3
	Number of subadults	4
	Cluster members	F201: 88,122b; F301: 7,14,22a,31,32
4	Number of individuals	24
	Number of males	5
	Number of females	4
	Number of adults	9
	Number of subadults	15
	Cluster members	F101: 15,19; F201: 8c,8d,10a,10b,11d,19d,30e, 35c,38b,40,49,52a,64c,93d,94b,96,146b; F301: 4,29c,39c,58e,59c
5	Number of individuals	11
	Number of males	4
	Number of females	1
	Number of adults	5
	Number of subadults	6
	Cluster members	F101: 11,27c; F201: 30c,30g,63c,69b,84c,85, 91,100; F301: 65
6	Number of individuals	13
	Number of males	2
	Number of females	4
	Number of adults	7
	Number of subadults	6
	Cluster members	F101: 32d,35a; F103: 1; F201: 2d,3f,11a,27a,82a, 134; F301: 21,33c,38c,58f
7	Number of individuals	54
	Number of males	6
	Number of females	6
	Number of adults	14
	Number of subadults	40
	Cluster members	F101: 2,11,17b; F201: 31,34b,50,53,54b,55f,58, 61a,62,65,69c,78,84a,99,101a,104,106,107, 109a,110a,110b,113c,116a,117,119,124a,126a, 133c,142; F301: 5,8b,8c,9b,13,15,19b,19c,20, 40,41a,43a,45,50b,50e,50f,55c,60a,61,67b, 68a,70

(*continued*)

Cluster number		
8	Number of individuals	42
	Number of males	13
	Number of females	7
	Number of adults	23
	Number of subadults	19
	Cluster members	F101: 22b,29e,32e,33b,33e,38c,40a; F201: 3a,6a, 14c,27d,44,46,47e,52b,55g,55i,63a,68a,71a, 80b,81,95,97g,102g,128,130c,131,132,145d; F301: 11,16,47,49b,50g,50h,55b,60b,62a,62b, 72a,78

The hierarchical structure of the mortuary population is much less clear than in the previous cluster analysis results. This is due, in large part, to the temporal effect on artifact occurrence. The methodological constraint of selecting a single type that most efficiently divides the population, as the basis of monothetic divisive analysis, seems to be particularly vulnerable to change in the artifact inventory. The fact that the first division of the population was made on the basis of glass trade beads, a frequently occurring but relatively insignificant and time-dependent type, seems to confirm this suggestion.

Before ending the discussion of artifact usage at Larson, the unique character of sociotechnic objects in the Larson mortuary symbolism should be considered. Because of the extremely fine-grained character of mortuary symbolism at Larson, the present analysis could not hope to chart it completely. At a more detailed level of analysis one finds, for example, a series of infant graves containing only an antelope hoof and another set linked by the occurrence of a fox head. For present purposes, it is sufficient to note that the range of artifacts acting as sociotechnic items seems broad, including such items as curved rib ornaments, bear claws, spear points fashioned from exotic Knife River flint, and various types of animal remains. Whatever the specific meaning of these objects, relatively strict rules of occurrence and combination were observed. With only two exceptions, sociotechnic objects did not occur together. The exceptions were bird beaks, which apparently could occur with any other sociotechnic object, and the large spear points, which on one occasion occurred with a bobcat cranium. Aside from these instances, sociotechnic objects did not co-occur. Although the possible meaning of these symbols will be discussed in the next section, their pattern of occurrence suggests they functioned as distinct and self-contained statements, independent of the other aspects of the mortuary assemblage.

Artifact occurrence at the Larson site, then, was a means to express age and sex distinctions, to denote relative rank, and to signal numerous smaller-scale status distinctions. The interaction between artifact occurrence and funerary treatment in the Larson mortuary complex will be presented in the next section.

Larson Mortuary Differentiation

Little interaction was observed between the use of burial treatment and artifacts in Larson mortuary differentiation. Treatment variables in most cases were used to express normative or unifying aspects of the mortuary population and special status distinctions, whereas the contents of the burial assemblage expressed a broad range of primarily vertical distinctions. The major categories of mortuary differentiation observed at Larson are presented in Table 6.48.

Several vertical distinctions were recognized at Larson. A dimension of achieved wealth was expressed in the composition and size of an individual's burial assemblage. This distinction divided the population into two groups: a lower level made up of those grave assemblages with two or fewer types and an upper level with three or more types. As bead varieties appear to have been used interchangeably as mortuary inclusions, regardless of their source or type, they all were combined for

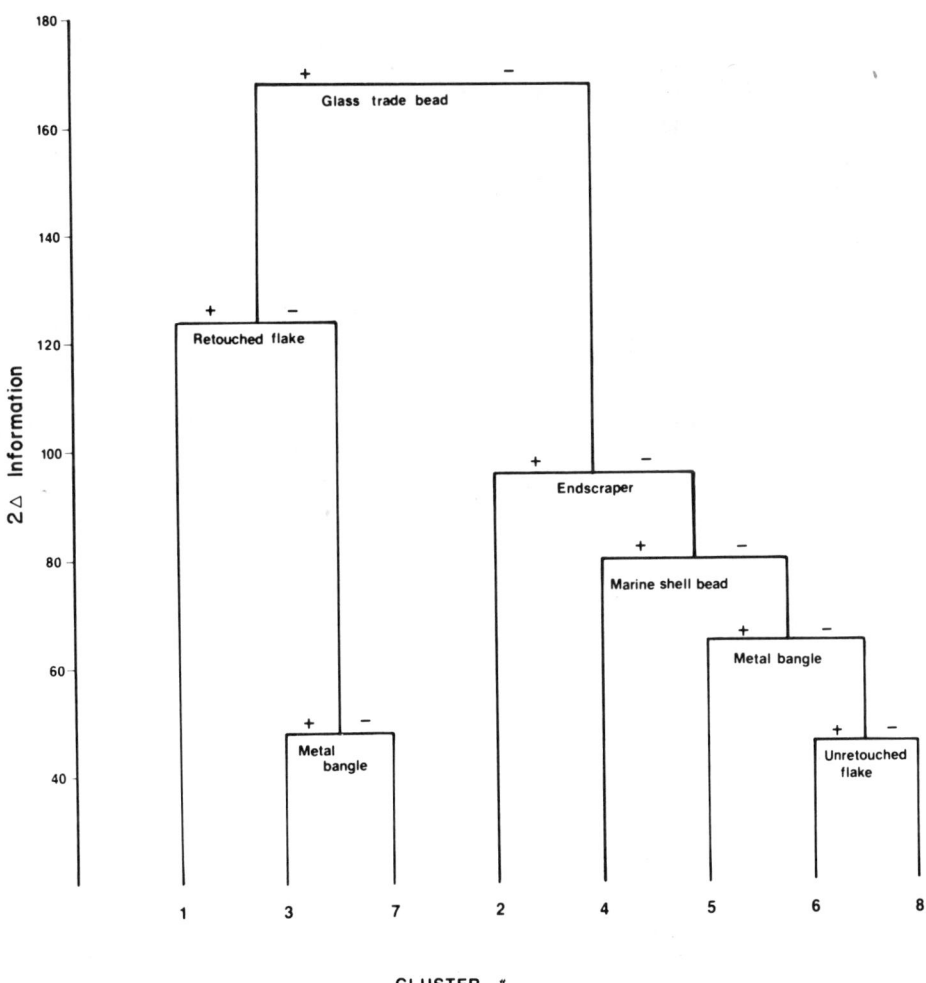

Figure 6.29 Dendrogram produced by monothetic divisive clustering of the Larson grave assemblages.

188   6. Mortuary Differentiation and Social Distinction

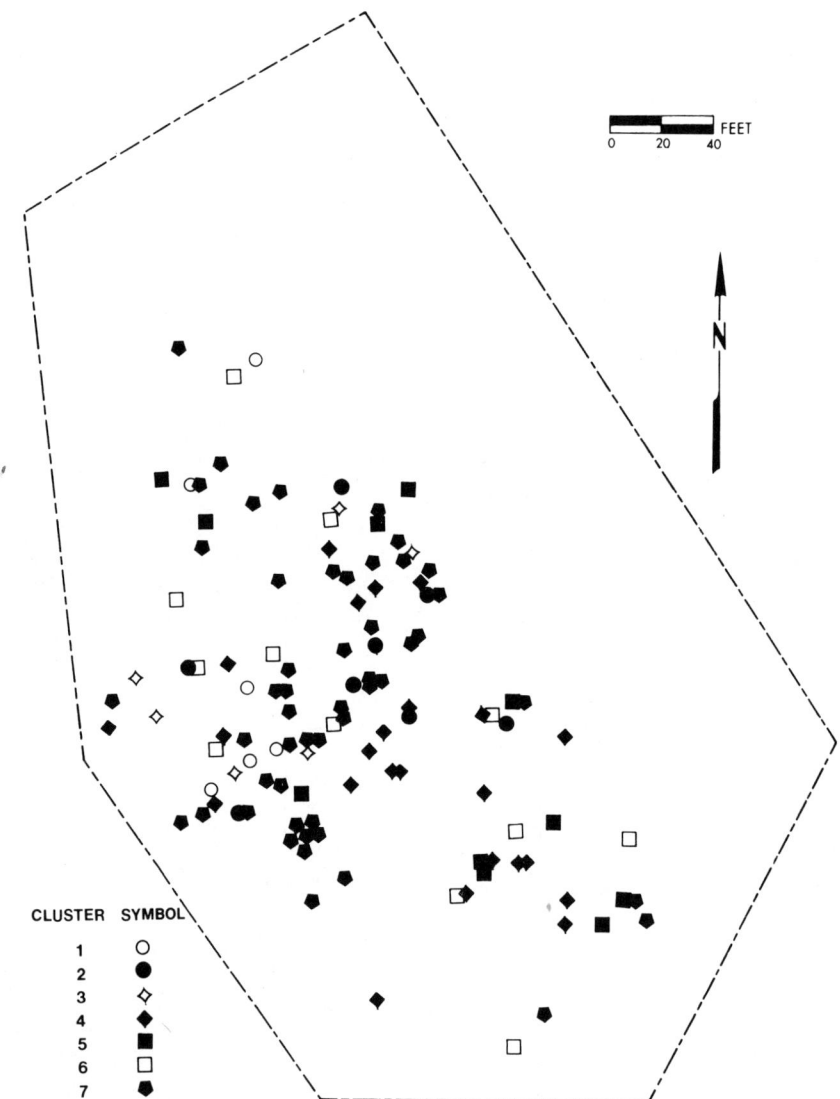

Figure 6.30 Distribution of monothetic division clusters at the Larson site cemetery.

the purpose of assessing the relative wealth of a given assemblage. This distinction placed approximately 90% of the burial population in the lower level and the remaining 10% in the upper wealth level. The lower wealth level contained most of the subadults and many females, whereas the upper level was composed of more adults and males. Individuals of any age and of both sexes did, however, occur in both wealth levels.

TABLE 6.48

Larson: Mortuary Differentiation

Social distinction	Number	Sex	Age	Formal differentiation	Artifact differentiation	Comments
Vertical distinctions						
Achieved wealth						Adults and males more common in upper level, females and subadults in lower.
Upper level	18	—	—		Three or more types	
Lower level	163	—	—		Two or fewer types	
Elevated social position						
Chiefly office	9	Male	Mature	Burial in the central portion of cemetery	Arrow maker's kit Sociotechnic object Upper wealth level	One subadult was included in this group.
Ritual office?	3	Male	—		Pipe ownership	
	9	Male	Adult		Bird beak ownership	
Special prestige position	9	Male	—		Pipestone ornament Upper wealth level	
	4	Male	Adult		Curved rib ornament Upper wealth level	
Horizontal distinctions						
Male/female	39/24	—	—		Gender-specific artifacts	Implement versus ornament dichotomy.
Adult/subadult	72/94	—	—	Grave size	Age-specific artifacts	
Special status distinctions						
Circumstances of death						
?	15	—	—	Nonnormative orientation		
?	28	—	—	Nonnormative posture		
Time of death?	?	—	—	Multiple interment		Typically female with subadult(s).
Surrogate warrior	7	Male	Adult	Decapitation or nonnormative posture	Large spear point	Spear point as likely cause of death.

A second vertical dimension, indicative of elevated social standing, was observed that may be equated with a position of chiefly power or authority. The position was marked by burial with the elaborate arrow maker's kit and with other sociotechnic objects. In addition, all the grave assemblages were classified as belonging to the upper wealth stratum. A total of nine individuals were accorded this treatment, and all but one were mature males. The remaining individual was a child. The graves of all these individuals were located in the central portion of the cemetery area.

The nature of this distinction is consistent with the expectation for chiefly status, with the elaborate tool kit serving as a unifying sociotechnic marker. The occurrence of a single child, buried with the total adult assemblage, suggests at least a tendency for hereditary transmission of this social position.

In addition to these two dimensions, at least four sociotechnic objects served to mark further varieties of vertical differentiation: Burial with a stone pipe or a bird beak marked what appear to be ritual offices, while a pipestone ornament or curved rib ornament was indicative of special prestige positions.

Pipe ownership does not appear to have reached the integrative significance at Larson that it attained in later times. Only one of the three owners had an assemblage of the upper wealth stratum, and none held a position of chiefly rank. One of the three individuals was a subadult (buried with a miniature pipe). Bird beak ownership, although significantly associated with adult males, also occurred with a subadult and with a single female. The position marked by bird beaks seems to have been more integrative (among the higher rank levels) and one that could be held in combination with other positions. Among the four types of special markers, only bird beaks occurred in combination with the other symbols. Despite this, membership in the upper wealth stratum was not a necessary condition for burial with a bird beak.

The two special prestige markers, pipestone ornaments and curved rib ornaments, seem simply to have served to amplify the wealth ranking of particular individuals. Although not limited to this use, the pipestone ornaments often were employed to mark wealthier adolescents, perhaps signifying their presumptive future position of wealth and prestige.

Few horizontal distinctions were observed at Larson, in terms of either treatment or artifact variables. Some of the small-scale distinctions recognized, such as burial with an antelope hoof or fox head, may have represented horizontal components, but no global features of horizontal differentiation were observed. Indeed, age and sex were the only categories of horizontal differentiation recognized at Larson. Adults were differentiated from subadults both by larger and deeper graves and by artifact sets specific to each group. In addition, there was a tendency for ornaments to be more commonly associated with subadults and implements of all kinds to be more commonly associated with adults. Although not distinguished in formal treatment, artifact sets were clearly delineated by sex. The mortuary symbolism associated with gender at Larson, however, is not wholly consistent with the working of a horizontal social dimension. The extreme asymmetry observed between male- and female-associated types, as well as the unequal representation of females in the upper wealth level, all seem to elevate male status, while placing female and subadult statuses at a lower level.

A number of special status distinctions also were recognized at Larson. Most spectacular were the individuals buried with the large spear points. In addition to the six persons who occupied this status, one other grave contained a spear point, although the point was much smaller in size and with a wholly inconsistent burial assemblage. This individual may have been connected with the particular status or its attendant ritual, but it is unlikely that he actually occupied that special status. As was noted in the previous section, in at least one case, the spear points were the probable cause of death, and most exhibited impact fractures characteristic of use. This seems to indicate that the implements were used either to kill the individual or to mutilate the body after death. In addition, these individuals had a higher probability of receiving nonnormative burial treatments (Table 6.49). Two of the six were interred in an extended burial posture, and two were decapitated (while a third exhibited cut marks on a cervical vertebra). In addition, several of their grave assemblages also contained sociotechnic objects. One association that emerges is that individuals receiving nonnormative treatment seem to have a greater quantity of spear points and were more likely to have special prestige markers. This suggests a degree of internal ranking among these individuals.

The symbolism of this special status distinction seems somewhat contradictory. The range of special treatments, sociotechnic objects, and the elaborate spear points (fashioned from exotic flint) all are indicative of a relatively energy-intensive treatment in death. This contrasts with the fact that the individuals appear to have been either killed or mutilated with the very symbols that marked their special position. The killing or mutilation of individuals might mark them as war captives, but their burial in the community cemetery and the elaboration of their burial assemblage suggests them to be individuals of some importance. Two possible interpretations can be offered: (1) these individuals represent high-ranked enemies slain by the

TABLE 6.49

Larson: Individuals Buried with Large Spear Points

Grave number	Number of spear points	Posture	Dismemberment	Sociotechnic symbols
F201				
55g	4	Extended	Decapitated	Eagle maxilla
55i	3	Extended	—	Bobcat cranium
84a	4	Flexed	Decapitated	—
F301				
50e	2	Flexed	—	—
50g	1	Flexed	—	—
62b	1	Flexed	—	Wolf bone

Arikara who were then accorded a "proper" burial; and (2) these are slain war captives who have been buried "in place of" important Arikara warriors whose remains could not be recovered for interment. Other interpretations are clearly possible, but these two seem the most consistent with the configuration of mortuary symbolism and treatment. Although it may not be possible to test between these two possibilities, metric analysis of the osteological remains could be used to test independently whether these individuals were members of the local Arikara community. In any event, the practice was not a frequent one. If the Larson cemetery was used continuously from 1680 to 1740 (i.e., for 60 years), this practice would have been employed on average only once every 10 years. The tendency for groups of these graves to cluster together in the cemetery, however, may indicate that such events were episodic. Several enemy war chiefs might have been slain in a successful raid (or defense) and buried in this manner. It might have been another 30 years before such a success was repeated.

The meaning of the other nonnormative burial treatments in the Larson mortuary symbolism is not clear. Persons of any age or either sex could be buried in an abnormal posture or orientation, as could members of either wealth level. It also is possible that nonnormative burial postures or orientations may have meant different things depending on the age, sex, and other characteristics of the deceased. Among these, nonnormative orientation might reflect some circumstance of death. Multiple interment seems to be yet another circumstantial status, perhaps linking related females and children who died at proximal times. This is another case where human biological analysis could provide a crucial independent test for an archaeologically derived inference.

In a general sense, the Larson mortuary population was highly differentiated. Although few horizontal distinctions were detected, a number of vertical and special status distinctions were recognized. The actual mortuary symbolism at Larson exhibited little redundancy. Each object appears to have had a precise and unique symbolic meaning, both in the highly constrained and structured pattern of artifact usage and in the general lack of interaction between identified sociotechnic markers. This highly organized and specific pattern of mortuary differentiation is in stark contrast to that observed at the later, Leavenworth site, which is considered in the next section.

Leavenworth Site

The Leavenworth cemetery is composed of five discrete burial areas, four on the bluff tops immediately behind the upstream half of the village and one small area (Area E) behind the downstream village. Plans of the major burial areas are presented in Figure 6.31.

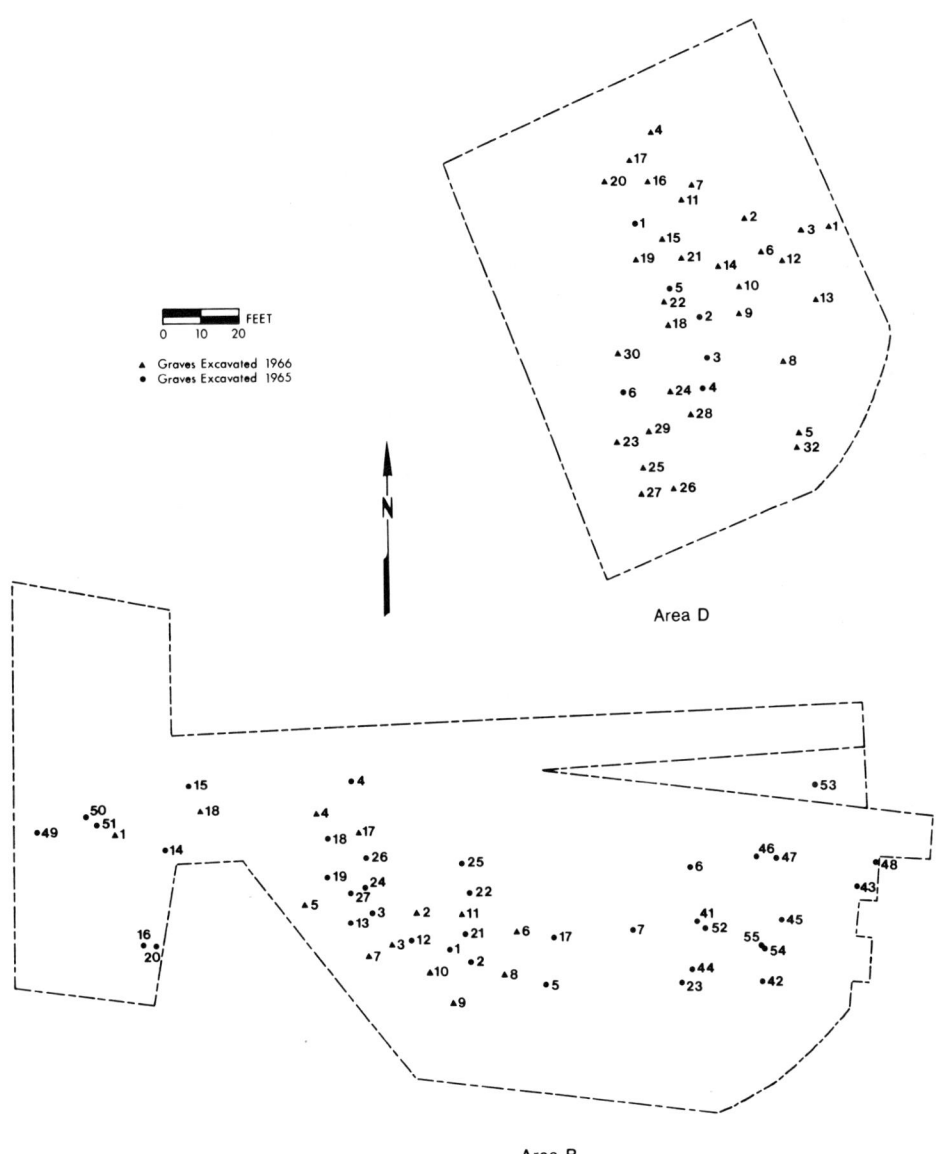

Figure 6.31 Plan of the Leavenworth site cemeteries.

194   6. Mortuary Differentiation and Social Distinction

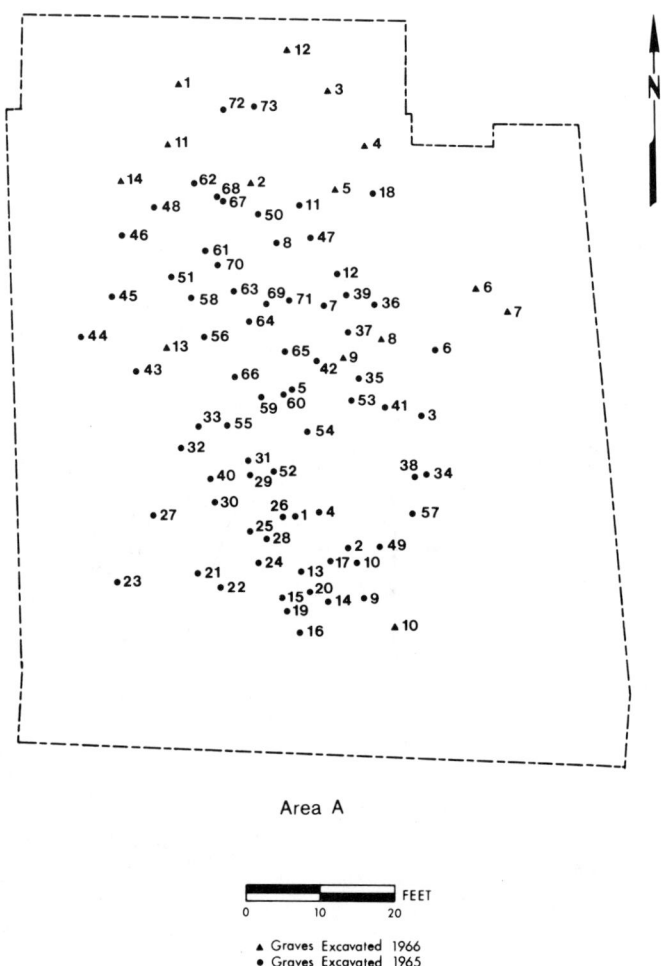

Area A

▲ Graves Excavated 1966
● Graves Excavated 1965

Figure 6.31 (*continued*)

Formal Treatment

The normal means of mortuary disposal at the Leavenworth site was primary inhumation. The body was flexed, often wrapped in robes of bison hide or fiber, and frequently was topped with some type of wooden covering. The analysis of burial treatments was hampered by the already mentioned Arikara practice of stratifying burials, which tended to destroy evidence from earlier interments (such as the presence of burial coverings), to enhance the apparent number of multiple interments, and to make ambiguous any evidence regarding the burial of disarticulated remains.

TABLE 6.50

Leavenworth: Nonnormative Burial Posture

Grave number	Sex	Age	Posture
F101 3b	Male	22–26 years	Extended
17	—	2–3 years	Extended
29	—	Birth	Extended
31b	—	Birth	Extended
38d	—	Birth	Extended
41	—	Premature	Extended
59	—	6 months	Extended
60	—	6 months	Extended
F201 7c	—	Birth	Extended
24a	—	1 year	Extended
41b	—	1–2 years	Extended
53b	—	Birth	Extended
F202 5c	—	4–5 years	Extended
7	—	2–3 years	Trapezoidal
F203 14	—	Birth–1 year	Trapezoidal
F220 46	—	1 year	Trapezoidal

Variability in mortuary treatment was limited. Tests of grave size and depth revealed no significant differences on the basis of sex, with a difference only in average length between the graves of adults and subadults.

In those cases where burial posture could be determined ($N = 160$), 90% were flexed, but with no preference for aspect. Of the 16 nonflexed burials, 15 were subadults and 1 was an adult male (Table 6.50). As at Larson, these nonflexed postures included both extended and trapezoidal burial postures. A chi-squared test confirmed the significant association of this treatment with subadults ($\chi^2 = 7.5$, $df = 1$, $p < .05$).

Grave orientation at Leavenworth was unconstrained. The orientation of graves varied over 360°, with slightly more individuals oriented in a northerly direction (Table 6.51). No significant association between sex or age was observed in grave orientation, nor did any of the burial areas exhibit a distinct pattern of orientation (Table 6.52).

Multiple interment also was observed at Leavenworth. Here again, however, the stratification of graves posed problems. Bass *et al.* (1971:155) record 107 individuals found in multiple graves of a total of 285 individuals (38%). Re-analysis of the excavation documentation, with a close eye to actual multiple interment, as opposed to incidental or circumstantial multiples, indicates only 19 graves (42 individuals) as true multiple graves (15% of total population, see Table 6.53). Of these true multiples, the most frequent configuration was for two or more subadults

TABLE 6.51

Leavenworth: Grave Orientation by Burial Area

Area[a]	Direction of orientation								Total
	N	NE	E	SE	S	SW	W	NW	
A	25	7	12	5	15	1	8	5	78
B	9	12	14	2	7	3	6	0	53
C	10	5	3	1	4	4	3	1	31
D	2	0	2	1	0	0	0	0	5
	46	24	31	9	26	8	17	6	167

[a] Area E not included; no intact burials.

to occur together. Occasionally an adult was buried with a subadult. In such cases, the adult could be of either sex, although females were slightly more frequent. In only one instance (Feature 101 Grave 27) were two adults placed in a single grave. In four instances, all involving subadults, a nonnormative burial posture was also employed.

Wood burial coverings at Leavenworth were, in most cases, considerably more simple than those seen among the Omaha and Pawnee, being composed of branches or planking laid flat across the top of the burial pit. Such coverings were observed in 69% of the Leavenworth graves. Given the destruction of coverings from decay and grave stratification, the actual percentage probably was considerably higher. It is unlikely, therefore, that such coverings represented a form of burial elaboration. As was the case at Larson, it is possible that burial *without* a covering carried social meaning, but this possibility cannot be tested with present data.

Another possible category of differential treatment is disarticulated burial. In 40% of the graves, the body was disarticulated, disturbed, or of undetermined

TABLE 6.52

Leavenworth: Grave Orientation by Age and Sex

Category	Direction of orientation								Total
	N	NE	E	SE	S	SW	W	NW	
Male	9	5	6	1	5	2	1	0	29
Female	8	3	6	1	6	2	5	0	31
All adults	18	8	12	2	12	6	7	0	65
Subadults	28	16	19	7	14	2	10	6	102
	46	24	31	9	26	8	17	6	167

TABLE 6.53

Leavenworth: Multiple Interment

Grave number	Number in grave	Sex	Age
F101 18	2	—	Premature
		—	Premature
21	2	—	Infant
		—	Infant
22	2	—	Infant
		—	Child
27	2	Female	Adult
		—	Adult
31	2	Male	Adult
		—	Infant
38	3	—	Infant
		—	Infant
		—	Child
50	2	Female	Adult
		—	Infant
54	2	Female	Mature
		—	Infant
F102 3	2	—	Infant
		—	Infant
5	3	Female	Adult
		—	Infant
		—	Child
11	2	Female	Adult
		—	Infant
18 (a,b)	2	—	Infant
		—	Child
F102 18 (c,d)	2	Male	Adult
		—	Infant
24	2	—	Child
		—	Child
53	2	—	Infant
		—	Child
F201 7	2	—	Infant
		—	Child
F202 5	3	—	Infant
		—	Infant
		—	Child
17	3	Female	Adult
		—	Infant
		—	Infant
F203 17	2	—	Adult
		—	Infant

posture. Although most are undoubtedly the result of postdepositional factors, it is not impossible that a portion were actual disarticulated burials, resulting either from intentional dismemberment or as a result of exposure prior to burial (cf. Ubelaker and Willey 1978). In one case (Feature 102 Grave 20), there is good evidence for the burial of a decapitated individual. This individual, a mature male, was buried in a normal flexed posture, but with the cranium out of anatomical position at the foot of the grave.

Choice of location in one of the five Leavenworth burial areas constitutes a final class of differential treatment. All five areas had a normal demographic composition and were of sizes that might correspond with distinct social subdivisions, such as bands. Bass et al. (1971:35) have suggested that Area E, the only region located behind the downstream village, may have been a scaffolding area used by visiting Cheyenne, because of the large number of fragmentary and disturbed remains found there. Such an explanation would seem to offer indirect support for the assertion that the other burial areas also represent distinct social units, although presumably Arikara. A consideration of artifact occurrences may clarify the significance of burial location at Leavenworth.

In summary, few differential uses of funerary treatment were observed at Leavenworth. Adults were distinguished from subadults only by grave length and by being less likely to be interred in an extended burial posture or multiple burial. No distinctions based on gender were observed. At one level this indicates possible use of funerary treatment to emphasize unifying symbolism. At the same time, there is a lesser degree of organization overall. The very lack of constraint in certain aspects of burial treatment, such as grave orientation, may itself be significant.

Both nonnormative treatments, extended burial and multiple interment, most directly affected subadults. There is, therefore, the possibility that these treatments may have carried different meanings when applied to adults. Extended burial of subadults may represent merely an expedient, particularly if one function of the flexed posture was to minimize the required grave dimensions. Similarly, multiple interment of subadults may represent an additional expedient employed in the event of closely spaced infant deaths. The high levels of infant mortality seen at Leavenworth may have made such an option attractive. If this was the case, both nonnormative treatments for subadults would constitute minor special status distinctions, indicating the circumstance of death. It seems likely that extended burial and multiple interment (and decapitated burial) may also represent adult special status distinctions, but they may reflect other relevant circumstances.

The level of interaction between nonnormative treatments was low. In four cases, one subadult within a multiple interment was also in extended posture. In no case did the co-occurrence of nonnormative treatments involve an adult. No other interaction between treatment variables was observed.

Funerary treatment at Leavenworth served to highlight a limited set of distinctions, differentiating individuals by age, marking a series of small-scale special status distinctions, and possibly denoting the existence of distinct horizontal social subdivisions within the burial population.

Artifact Occurrence

As at the Larson site, the frequent stratification and disturbance of graves made the determination of burial assemblage composition ambiguous in many cases. Therefore, only those graves with clearly defined assemblages were included in the artifact analysis. Similarly, graves lacking artifact inclusions were also excluded.

A total of 56 types were observed in the Leavenworth burials, 25 of native manufacture and 31 of Euroamerican origin. A total of 22 types (11 trade and 11 native) exhibited some manner of positive association in their occurrence by age or sex (Table 6.54 and Figure 6.32). Both sex- and age-specific types were present. An asymmetry was observed, however, in the occurrence of types exhibiting constraint by both age and sex. Three types were limited in their occurrence to adult males; no equivalent adult female types were observed.

Little constraint was seen in the distribution of artifact classes (Tables 6.55 and 6.56). Only trade-derived clothing ornaments exhibited differential occurrence by sex (females), while trade-derived implements were the only category to exhibit similar constraint by age (adult). No significant differences were observed in the quantity of trade or native goods, or in the total variety of artifacts included within the burial assemblage.

TABLE 6.54

Leavenworth: Artifact Type Associations

Female	Male
Animal teeth	Native glass pendant
Horse gear	Polished bone tube
	Iron knife
	Scissors
	Small metal hardware
	Metal lace/braid
	Stone pipe
	End scraper
Subadult	Adult
Glass bottle	Raptor talon
Ceramic pot	Small metal hardware
Metal bead/bangle	Finger ring
Metal eating implement	Metal lace/braid
Small iron tool	Stone spear point
Lead ring/coil	Scoria abraider
	Stone sphere
	Petrified wood
	End scraper

6. Mortuary Differentiation and Social Distinction

		Sex	
		+	−
Age	+	Male, adult 3	Adult 6
			Subadult 6
	−	Male 5	34
		Female 2	

Figure 6.32 Age and sex constraints on artifact occurrence at the Leavenworth site.

The occurrence of potential sociotechnic objects also was unconstrained. Of the range of possible sociotechnic symbols, only two types, stone pipes and stone spear points, exhibited a restricted distribution (Table 6.54), stone pipes occurring with males and spear points with adults. All the other types exhibit a random mixing of ages and sexes, which may suggest that they did not serve to mark vertical social distinctions. The role of sociotechnic objects in the Leavenworth mortuary ritual will be further examined through multivariate analysis.

Principal Component Analysis

As at the Larson site, the large number of cases allowed a relaxed entry threshold for variables in the principal component analysis. Any type that occurred in at least five graves (4%) was included in the analysis; 23 types met this criterion. The analysis resulted in the extraction of nine factors, which jointly accounted for 63.9%

TABLE 6.55

Leavenworth: Artifact Class Associations by Age

Artifact class	Average adult rank ($N=55$)	Average subadult rank ($N=77$)	U	Probability
Trade goods				
Body ornaments	69.3	64.5	1963.0	.3682
Clothing ornaments	61.2	70.3	1827.0	.0972
Implements	75.2	60.3	1637.0	.0091
All trade items	68.9	64.8	1983.5	.5175
Native goods				
Ornaments	64.3	68.1	1995.5	.5108
Implements	70.7	63.5	1885.0	.1471
Sociotechnic	69.2	64.6	1970.0	.2641
All native items	69.2	64.6	1969.5	.4641

TABLE 6.56

Leavenworth: Artifact Class Association by Sex

Artifact class	Average male rank ($N=28$)	Average female rank ($N=19$)	U	Probability
Trade goods				
Body ornaments	24.8	22.9	244.5	.5842
Clothing ornaments	21.4	27.8	194.5	.0421
Implements	25.9	21.2	213.0	.2026
All trade items	24.3	23.5	257.0	.8388
Native goods				
Ornaments	24.2	23.7	260.5	.8905
Implements	23.3	25.0	246.5	.6069
Sociotechnic	24.4	23.4	245.5	.7160
All native items	24.3	23.5	256.6	.8287

of the original variance. The varimax rotated factor matrix is presented in Table 6.57 and factor summaries are provided in Table 6.58.

The resulting factors provide a number of distinct artifact combinations, but these sets are without clear age or sex association. Factors 1 and 3 represent implement sets, with Factor 1 combining all weaponry with bird beaks and small mammal crania. Ordinarily this would be considered characteristic of an adult male tool kit, but at Leavenworth no such clear association was found. The other implement set, Factor 3, does exhibit an adult male orientation, combining iron knives and small metal hardware. Female-associated ornamentation weighs negatively on this factor. Factor 4 also expresses an equipment set, including the presumed sociotechnic objects, bird bone, along with raptor talons and bear claws (and also a moderate loading on bird beaks). This factor has a weak adult orientation and weaker negative loadings on a number of male- and subadult-associated trade ornaments.

Three factors represent ornament sets. Factor 6 combines three varieties of "strung" ornaments that overlap in their occurrence relative to males and females. Factors 7 and 9 highlight a trade-derived ornament. Factor 7 isolates metal bracelets and small brass bells against a negative loading background of implements and native ornaments, while Factor 9 distinguishes metal bangles, an ornament associated with subadults, from a variety of other goods.

The remaining three factors link ornaments with an implement. Factor 2 combines two varieties of clothing ornamentation (marine snail shells and smaller brass bells) with metal containers. Although no distinct age or sex associations were noted for these individual types, the artifacts loading negatively on this factor (see Table 6.57) tend to reflect male and adult associations. Factors 5 and 8 are even more ambiguous, each combining a single trade ornament with a native implement.

TABLE 6.57

Leavenworth: Varimax Rotated Factor Matrix

	Factor 1	Factor 2	Factor 3	Factor 4	Factor 5	Factor 6	Factor 7	Factor 8	Factor 9
Native glass pendant	0.06232	0.04982	−0.00136	0.03276	0.08909	0.77349	0.05882	−0.04041	0.01444
Glass trade beads	−0.09486	−0.01048	0.10198	−0.05075	−0.18377	0.48168	−0.03191	0.15207	−0.45316
Bear claw	0.21946	−0.15573	0.21453	0.39035	−0.39161	0.00796	0.25736	0.21136	−0.12453
Animal teeth	0.00923	0.21409	−0.20907	0.17430	−0.21234	0.34298	−0.00500	0.30213	−0.06993
Bird beak	0.54295	0.02833	−0.05915	0.42292	−0.29293	−0.28323	0.20718	0.00452	−0.15444
Bird bone	−0.08392	0.18309	0.04673	0.80965	0.14458	0.05435	0.15686	−0.07322	−0.04153
Raptor talon	0.29667	−0.10421	−0.05703	0.77601	0.02541	0.05449	−0.14625	−0.05649	−0.03048
Small mammal cranium	0.78634	−0.03254	0.04452	−0.12557	0.02468	0.02385	0.21778	0.07351	−0.05372
Cancellous paint applicator	0.12795	−0.12667	0.00999	0.15569	0.80376	−0.00260	0.07587	0.20733	0.02571
Gun parts/accessories	0.65568	0.03075	0.17815	0.20173	0.00447	0.06554	0.06797	0.09153	0.06033
Marine snail shell	−0.13381	0.70861	−0.12212	0.04851	0.01844	−0.00502	−0.09165	0.15284	−0.02941
Metal bracelet	0.08460	−0.00934	−0.00318	0.08330	0.06462	0.03415	0.81064	−0.02126	0.19920
Metal bead/bangle	−0.05343	−0.02676	−0.09732	−0.12053	−0.02171	−0.00431	0.13584	−0.00801	0.85935
Iron knife	0.20634	0.02801	0.73097	−0.14425	0.13480	0.12009	−0.16310	−0.07018	−0.04372
Small metal hardware	−0.01530	−0.10430	0.75468	0.14389	−0.09223	−0.10343	0.08545	0.00196	−0.12893
Metal projectile point	0.40952	−0.11871	0.12690	0.26070	−0.20387	0.35130	−0.35525	−0.07516	0.25132
Metal container	0.19809	0.63343	0.47160	0.02808	−0.05925	0.08379	0.10409	−0.03075	0.17514
Finger ring	−0.04540	0.33644	0.17435	−0.02088	0.41359	−0.02979	0.12685	−0.45976	−0.11181
Metal button	0.02875	0.03496	−0.16608	−0.11330	0.12892	−0.02075	0.12605	0.66173	−0.21443
Smaller brass bell	0.09773	0.51745	−0.12995	−0.01508	−0.11822	0.26580	0.40042	−0.05445	−0.22978
Gunflint	0.63560	−0.08740	0.06796	0.16635	0.21248	0.12359	−0.20147	−0.02797	−0.00973
Sandstone shaft smoother	0.10272	0.23263	0.34976	−0.03095	0.13151	0.04228	−0.16612	0.67386	0.17717
Stone projectile point	0.61962	0.46856	−0.08537	−0.09178	−0.08926	−0.35876	−0.08651	−0.00463	0.01794

TABLE 6.58

Leavenworth: Factor Summary[a]

Factor number	Loading pattern	Percentage variance	Diagnostic positive loadings	Diagnostic negative loadings
1	Group	14.0	Bird beak Small mammal cranium Gun parts/accessories Metal projectile point Gunflint Stone projectile point	
2	Group	8.0	Marine snail shell Metal container Smaller brass bell	
3	Bipolar	7.7	Iron knife M Small metal hardware M+	Animal teeth F
4	Group	7.2	Bird bone Raptor talon + Bear claw	
5	Bipolar	6.5	Cancellous paint applicator Finger ring +	Bear claw Animal teeth F Bird beak Metal projectile point
6	Bipolar	5.7	Native glass pendant M Glass trade bead Animal teeth F	Bird beak Stone projectile point
7	Bipolar	5.2	Metal bracelet Smaller brass bell	Metal projectile point Gunflint

[a]Constraints: +, adult only; −, subadult only; M, male only; F, female only.

Although most of the factors are interpretable as ornament or implement sets, clear age or sex association with these factors is lacking. The results do illustrate an effectively complete integration of Euroamerican materials into the native artifact complex. A certain level of contrast between the occurrence of ornaments and implements also is apparent. These patterns will be further explored via cluster analysis.

Hierarchical Fusion Cluster Analysis

The six-cluster hierarchical fusion analysis results are presented in Table 6.59 and Figure 6.33. Cluster 1 contains over half the cases in the sample and exhibits weak loadings on all nine factors (but with the lowest cluster variance associated with Factor 6, glass trade beads, native glass pendants, and animal teeth). Of the remaining clusters, Cluster 2 weighs positively on Factor 9 (metal bangles) and negatively on all other factors except Factors 2 and 7. Cluster 3 weighs positively on both

TABLE 6.59

Leavenworth: Hierarchical Fusion Cluster Diagnostics

Cluster number	Factor number	Mean origin	S.D.	Factor number	Mean origin	S.D.
1	1	−.1727	.3728	6	.1546	.9140
	2	−.3141	.4430	7	−.1643	.6024
	3	−.2966	.3181	8	.0960	.6637
	4	−.1224	.5259	9	−.4660	.4632
	5	−.2512	.4586			
	Number of individuals	69				
	Number of males	13				
	Number of females	9				
	Number of adults	29				
	Number of subadults	40				
1a	1	−.2274	.3290	6	−.2874	.4775
	2	−.3944	.2534	7	−.0692	.5153
	3	−.1929	.2197	8	.1300	.6269
	4	−.2023	.3443	9	−.5500	.3161
	5	−.2684	.4264			
	Number of individuals	50				
	Number of males	9				
	Number of females	6				
	Number of adults	20				
	Number of subadults	30				
	Cluster members	Area A, F101: 1a,7,12,28,30,36,38c,38d, 42,45,46,47,48a,55,56,57,58,60,63, 64,67; F201: 1,7b,8,10,11,13; Area B/C, F102: 4,17,43,46,49,53a,55; F202: 5a,9, 14,17a,17b; Area D, F103: 2; F203: 2,7,9,17a,25, 26,31,32; Area E, F120: 1,5				
1b	1	−.0261	.4481	6	1.3410	.7278
	2	−.0986	.7117	7	−.4195	.7478
	3	−.5747	.3766	8	−.0049	.7648
	4	−.0918	.8153	9	−.2407	.6864
	5	−.2049	.5458			
	Number of individuals	19				
	Number of males	4				
	Number of females	3				
	Number of adults	9				
	Number of subadults	10				
	Cluster members	Area A, F101: 14,15,25,32,66,69; F201: 3,5a; Area B/C, F102: 20,24b,25; F202: 1,3,8a,10a,12; Area D, F203: 4,27,30				

TABLE 6.59 *Continued*

Cluster number	Factor number	Mean origin	S.D.	Factor number	Mean origin	S.D.
2	1	−.2781	.4655	6	−.2011	.7022
	2	.0811	.8143	7	.2475	.9750
	3	−.8170	.3726	8	−.1900	.3688
	4	−.1926	.1885	9	1.3777	.9746
	5	−.2181	.3034			
	Number of individuals	28				
	Number of males	5				
	Number of females	5				
	Number of adults	13				
	Number of subadults	15				
2a	1	−.2874	.5204	6	−.3341	.4717
	2	.2779	.8508	7	−.2682	.4005
	3	−.1622	.4014	8	−.2279	.3936
	4	−.1801	.2090	9	1.4154	.9966
	5	−.2581	.3128			
	Number of individuals	21				
	Number of males	5				
	Number of females	3				
	Number of adults	9				
	Number of subadults	12				
	Cluster members	Area A, F101: 3b,17,18a,24,26,41,51,59,68,73; F201: 4; Area B/C, F102: 1,24a,52,54; F202: 5b,13; Area D, F103:5; F203: 18,28; Area E, F220: 4b				
2b	1	−.2502	.2671	6	.1978	1.1088
	2	−.5095	.1745	7	1.7945	.1429
	3	−.2615	.2813	8	−.0761	.2627
	4	−.2298	.1102	9	1.2645	.9714
	5	−.0981	.2564			
	Number of individuals	7				
	Number of males	0				
	Number of females	2				
	Number of adults	4				
	Number of subadults	3				
	Cluster members	Area A, F101: 9,19,61; Area B/C, F102: 51; F202: 10b; Area D; F203: 8,21				
3	1	2.3663	1.9964	6	−1.1593	1.1598
	2	.5958	1.1625	7	.1158	2.3840
	3	−.4340	1.4357	8	−.3409	.4668
	4	1.2997	2.8372	9	−.2535	.5141
	5	−.6189	1.0847			

(continued)

TABLE 6.59 *Continued*

Cluster number	Factor number	Mean origin	S.D.	Factor number	Mean origin	S.D.
	Number of individuals	8				
	Number of males	2				
	Number of females	2				
	Number of adults	5				
	Number of subadults	3				
	Cluster members	Area A, F101: 6,35,40;				
		Area B/C, F102: 21,42; F202: 6,17c;				
		Area D, F203: 23				
4	1	−.2199	1.2229	6	.3479	1.1407
	2	.6523	1.8401	7	.8437	1.2491
	3	.0112	.6124	8	−.7364	1.1447
	4	.5907	1.6088	9	−.3001	.6113
	5	1.9224	1.6672			
	Number of individuals	13				
	Number of males	4				
	Number of females	2				
	Number of adults	8				
	Number of subadults	5				
	Cluster members	Area A, F101: 11,31a; F201: 5b,12;				
		Area B/C, F102: 3d,12a,16,18d,22; F202: 5c,7;				
		Area D, F203: 17b,20				
5	1	−.1903	.4826	6	−.3901	.3025
	2	1.5520	2.2647	7	−.8797	.6147
	3	.7650	.6517	8	3.7008	1.0223
	4	−.0581	.3213	9	.8929	1.2311
	5	.9178	1.7755			
	Number of individuals	4				
	Number of males	0				
	Number of females	1				
	Number of adults	1				
	Number of subadults	3				
	Cluster members	Area A, F101: 34,54a; Area B/C, F102: 31,33				
6	1	.3773	1.5132	6	.1244	1.5354
	2	.0295	1.0587	7	−.4225	.6101
	3	2.9182	1.2465	8	−.4339	1.1440
	4	−.4314	.4199	9	−.3994	.7918
	5	−.0025	.5839			
	Number of individuals	9				
	Number of males	4				
	Number of females	0				
	Number of adults	4				
	Number of subadults	5				
	Cluster members	Area A, F101: 65; F201: 15;				
		Area B/C, F102: 28,36b; F202: 4;				
		Area D, F203: 1,6,11,15				

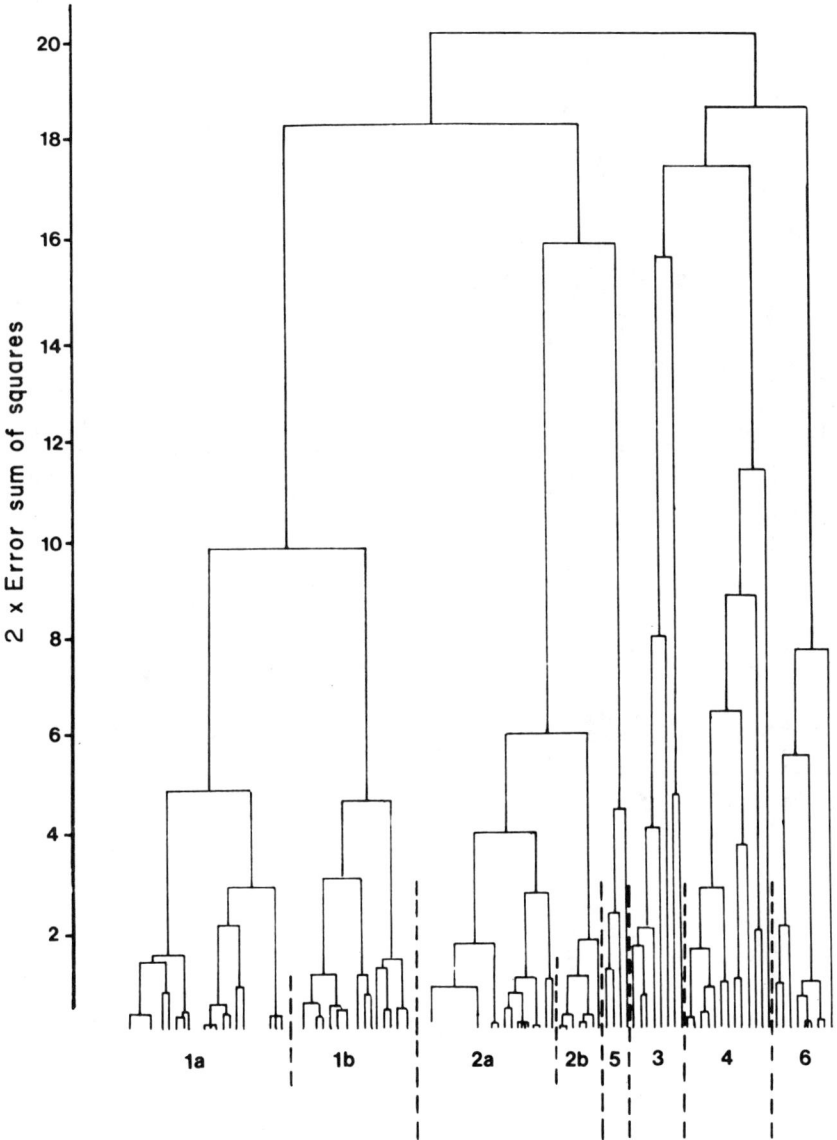

Figure 6.33 Dendrogram produced by the clustering of Leavenworth site factor sources. To preserve legibility, the base of the dendrogram has been truncated. The six-cluster solution, along with the subdivision of Clusters 1 and 2 is designated by the numerals below the dendrogram. A complete listing of cluster membership is presented in Table 6.59.

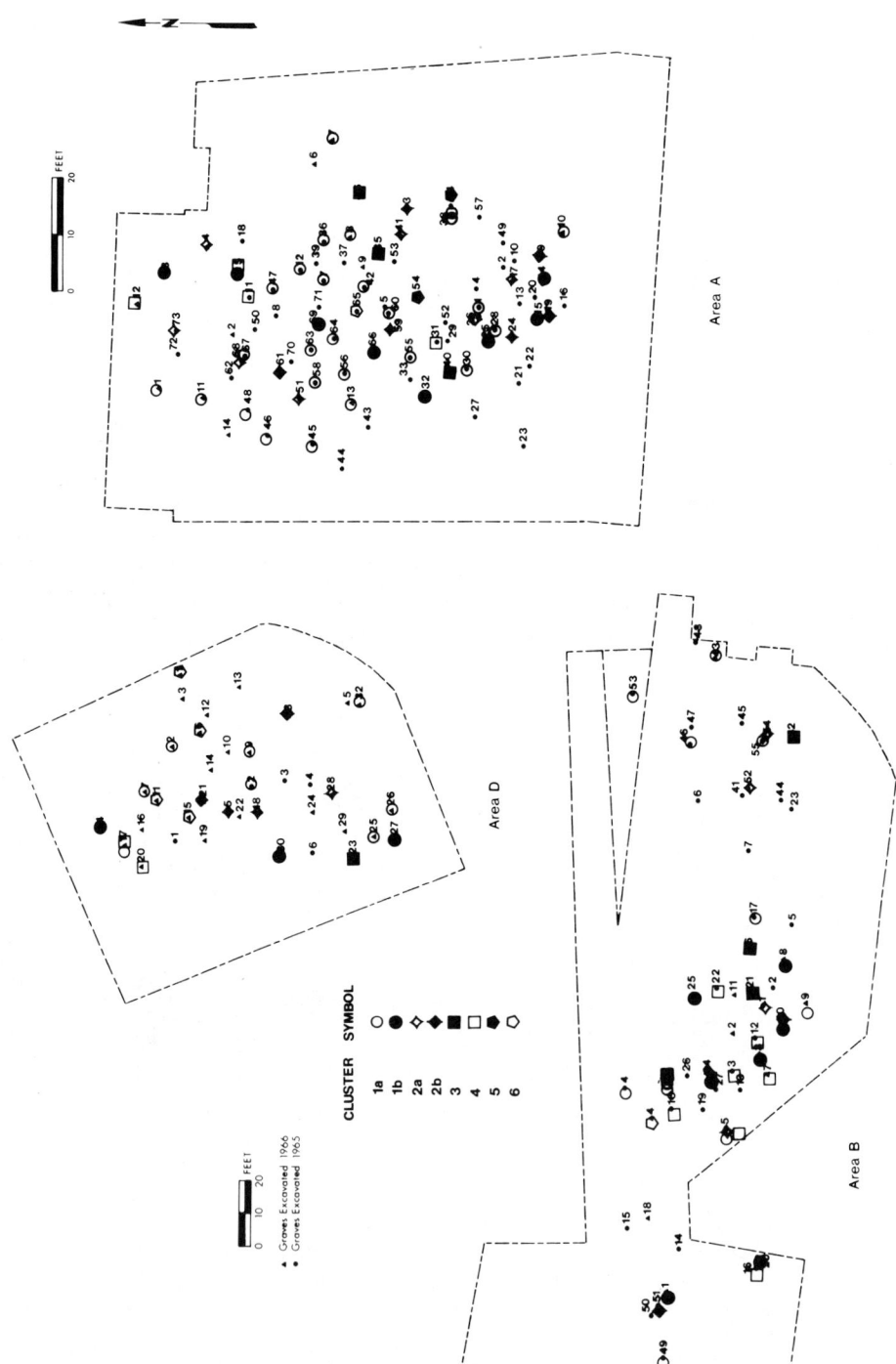

Figure 6.34 Spatial distribution of hierarchical fusion clusters at the Leavenworth site cemeteries.

Factor 1 (weaponry, bird beaks, and small mammal crania) and Factor 4 (bird beaks, bird bone, raptor talons, and bear claws). Cluster 5 is defined by strong positive values for Factor 8 (metal button and shaft smoother) and Factor 2 (marine snail shell beads, metal containers, and smaller brass bells). Finally, Cluster 6 includes those graves with strong positive loadings on Factor 3 (iron knives and small metal hardware). None of the six clusters exhibits significant association relative to age or sex, or to any of the five burial areas (Figure 6.34).

Excluding the hopelessly composite Cluster 1, the underlying structure of the clusters seems to primarily mark the occurrence of pervasive yet contrastive sets of ornaments and implements. Perhaps the most fundamental distinction can be seen by contrasting the two final clusters. The graves on the left side of the dendrogram (Clusters 1, 2, and 5) contain relatively few types (mainly beads, bangles, and other trade-derived ornamentation), whereas the 29 cases on the right side (Clusters 3, 4, and 6) typically contain a greater number of artifacts, particularly trade derived and native tools. Furthermore, although neither stone pipes nor stone spear points met the threshold requirement for inclusion in the principle component analysis, and therefore had no effect on the cluster outcome, they occur on the right side of the dendrogram in all cases.

Cluster 6 is the one cluster that may reflect a more fundamental aspect of the Leavenworth social structuring. In addition to the fact that no females were included among the eight cluster members ($p > .05$, however), most individuals possess relatively elaborate grave assemblages. All three of the stone pipe occurrences are also found with members of this cluster. Yet, despite these indications of elevated social standing, the equal number of adults and subadults in this group remains difficult to explain. If these burials were in some way indicative of elevated social standing, why were subadults included? In all probability, Cluster 6 is a composite of two distinct symbolic statements: (1) a variety of wealthy or elaborated male assemblages; and (2) an elevated social position marked by burial with an elaborate assemblage and a stone pipe. The occurrence of stone pipes with a subadult as well as with the adults indicates some manner of hereditary ascription for this position.

In all, the hierarchical fusion cluster analysis amplifies the basic conclusions derived from the principal component analysis—that is, that distinct sets of objects did occur in the burial assemblages at the Leavenworth site, but that they did not tend to be used to distinguish identifiable social subunits of the population. The burials in Cluster 6 may represent the one exception to this generalization.

Monothetic Division Cluster Analysis

Monothetic division highlighted a different aspect of the burial organization at Leavenworth. The diagnostics for the analysis are presented in Table 6.60 and Figure 6.35.

The population was first divided by the presence or absence of gun parts. Those clusters with gun parts (left side of the dendrogram) were further divided by the

TABLE 6.60

Leavenworth: Monothetic Division Cluster Diagnostics

	Cluster[a]							
	1	2	3	4	5	6	7	8
Glass bottle	1	0	1	0	0	0	0	0
Ceramic pot	0	0	0	0	0	1	1	0
Native glass pendant	1	2	16	0	0	0	0	2
Animal effigy	0	1	0	0	1	0	0	1
Glass trade beads	4	14	15	3	8	0	55	9
Bear claw	1	0	1	3	1	2	4	2
Animal teeth	0	1	2	1	1	0	3	1
Bird beak	1	0	0	3	1	2	0	0
Bird bone	0	0	2	2	0	1	1	0
Raptor talon	1	0	1	2	0	1	1	1
Small mammal cranium	2	0	0	1	0	1	1	1
Rib shaft wrench	1	0	0	0	0	0	1	0
Squash knife	0	0	0	0	0	0	0	0
Scapula hoe	0	0	0	0	0	0	0	0
Quill flattener	0	0	1	0	0	0	1	1
Cancellous paint applicator	0	0	0	0	0	2	1	2
Awl	0	0	0	1	0	0	0	0
Metatarsal flesher	0	0	0	0	1	0	0	0
Elk horn scraper	0	0	0	0	0	0	0	0
Bone/antler implement	0	0	0	0	0	0	1	0
Gun parts/accessories	4	0	0	3	0	0	0	12
Pin game cup	0	0	0	0	0	0	0	0
Polished bone tube	0	0	0	0	0	1	1	2
Bone pendant	0	0	0	0	0	0	0	0
Curved rib ornament	0	0	0	0	0	0	0	0
Bone point	0	0	0	0	0	0	0	0
Mussel shell	0	0	1	0	0	0	0	1
Gorget	0	0	0	1	0	0	2	0
Shell hair pipe	1	1	1	0	0	0	1	0
Tubular shell bead	0	0	0	0	0	0	1	0
Wampum bead	0	0	0	0	0	0	0	0
Heavy shell bead	0	0	0	0	0	0	0	0
Rectangular shell bead	0	0	0	0	0	0	0	0
Shell runtee	0	0	0	0	0	0	0	0
Marine snail shell	0	1	2	0	1	1	3	0
Perforated shell pendant	0	1	0	0	0	0	1	1
Flat shell bead	0	0	0	0	0	0	0	0
Metal bracelet	0	4	1	2	0	3	3	2
Metal bead/bangle	0	21	0	0	0	0	0	3
Iron knife	3	0	1	0	0	1	2	0
Axe/wedge	0	0	0	0	0	0	0	0
Scissors	2	0	1	0	0	0	0	0

TABLE 6.60 *Continued*

	Cluster[a]							
	1	2	3	4	5	6	7	8
Strike-a-light	0	0	0	0	0	0	0	0
Metal eating implement	0	0	0	0	0	0	2	0
Small metal hardware	1	0	0	1	0	1	4	0
Horse gear	2	0	0	0	0	0	1	0
Small iron tool	1	0	0	0	0	0	0	0
Metal projectile point	2	1	2	1	0	0	2	2
Iron scraper	0	0	0	0	0	0	0	0
Iron digging implement	0	0	0	0	0	0	0	0
Metal container	3	3	3	2	1	0	3	1
Metal buckle	0	1	0	1	0	0	0	0
Finger ring	1	1	2	0	0	2	4	0
Metal button	0	0	2	0	8	2	0	2
Large cast brass bell	0	0	0	0	0	0	0	0
Smaller brass bell	0	0	2	1	0	0	2	1
Thick wire coil	1	0	0	0	0	0	2	0
Thin wire coil	0	0	0	0	0	0	0	1
Metal lace/braid	0	0	0	0	0	0	1	1
Copper crimp/clip	0	0	0	0	0	0	0	0
Sheet brass blade	0	0	0	0	0	0	0	0
Lead ring/coil	0	1	0	0	0	0	1	1
Lead band	0	0	0	0	0	0	0	0
Sheet silver bracelet	0	0	0	0	0	0	0	0
Silver cross	0	0	0	0	0	0	0	0
Silver hair plate	0	0	0	0	0	0	0	0
Silver earring	0	0	0	0	0	0	0	0
Small silver brooch	0	0	0	0	0	0	0	0
Gunflint	3	0	0	1	0	1	2	2
Bifacial spear point	0	0	0	2	0	0	0	0
Scoria abraider	2	0	0	0	0	1	0	0
Sandstone shaft smoother	1	1	0	0	2	0	0	1
Whetstone	0	0	0	0	0	0	0	0
Hammer stone	0	0	0	0	0	0	0	0
Stone sphere	0	1	0	0	0	0	1	0
Stone projectile point	2	0	0	1	1	2	0	2
Stone pipe	2	0	0	0	0	0	1	0
Petrified wood	4	0	0	0	0	0	0	0
Retouched flake	0	0	0	0	0	0	0	0
Unretouched flake	1	0	0	0	0	0	1	0
Stone knife	3	1	0	0	0	0		0
Plate chalcedony knife	0	0	0	0	0	0	0	0
Side scraper	0	0	0	0	0	0	0	0
End scraper	1	0	0	0	0	0	0	1

(continued)

TABLE 6.60 *Continued*

	Cluster[a]							
	1	2	3	4	5	6	7	8
Pipestone ornament	0	0	0	1	0	0	0	0
Gypsum	0	0	0	0	0	0	1	0

[a]Cluster composition

Cluster		
1	Number of individuals	4
	Number of males	2
	Number of females	1
	Number of adults	3
	Number of subadults	1
	Cluster members	Area A, F101: 35,63; Area B/C, F202: 4; Area D, F203: 1
2	Number of individuals	21
	Number of males	4
	Number of females	5
	Number of adults	9
	Number of subadults	12
	Cluster members	Area A, F101: 3b,9,17,18a,19,24,26,41,51,73; F201: 4; Area B/C, F102: 24a,33,51,52,54; F202: 5b,10b,13; Area D, F203: 30; Area E, F220: 4b
3	Number of individuals	16
	Number of males	4
	Number of females	1
	Number of adults	7
	Number of subadults	9
	Cluster members	Area A, F101: 14,25,32,66,69; F201: 3; Area B/C, F102: 3d,17,18d,20,24b; F202: 3,10a; Area D, F203: 4,6,17b
4	Number of individuals	3
	Number of males	1
	Number of females	1
	Number of adults	2
	Number of subadults	1
	Cluster members	Area B/C, F102: 27,42; F202: 17c
5	Number of individuals	8
	Number of males	0
	Number of females	2
	Number of adults	3
	Number of subadults	5
	Cluster members	Area A, F101: 38c,46,54a,56; F201: 13; Area B/C, F102: 31; F202: 14; Area D, F203: 17a
6	Number of individuals	13
	Number of males	1
	Number of females	4
	Number of adults	7
	Number of subadults	6
	Cluster members	Area A, F101: 6,31a; Area B/C, F102: 12a,43,55; F202: 6,7; Area D, F203: 15,21,23,25; Area E, F120: 1,5
7	Number of individuals	54
	Number of males	10
	Number of females	8
	Number of adults	23

	Number of subadults	31	
	Cluster members		Area A, F101: 1a,7,11,12,28,30,36,38d,42,45,47,48a,55,57,58,60,61, 63,64,67,68; F201: 1,5a,7b,8,10,12,15; Area B/C, F201: 1,4,16, 22,25,28,36b,46,49,53a; F202: 1,5a,5c,8a,9,17a,17b; Area D, F203: 7,11,18,20,26,27,28,31,32
8	Number of individuals	12	
	Number of males	4	
	Number of females	0	
	Number of adults	6	
	Number of subadults	6	
	Cluster members		Area A, F101: 15,34,40,59; F201: 5b,11; Area B/C, F202: 12; Area D, F103: 2,5; F203: 2,8,9

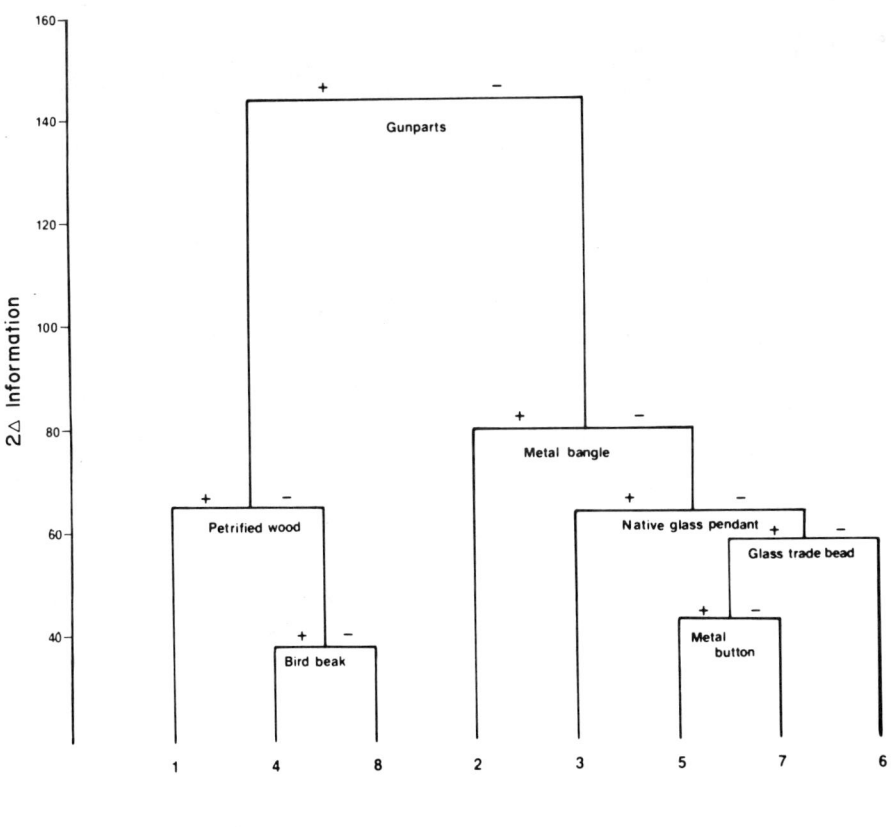

Figure 6.35 Dendrogram produced by monothetic divisive clustering of the Leavenworth grave assemblages.

occurrence of petrified wood (Cluster 1) and by the presence (Cluster 4) or absence (Cluster 8) of bird beaks. The clusters on the right half of the dendrogram were divided first by the occurrence of metal bangles (Cluster 2). Graves lacking bangles were further subdivided by the occurrence of native glass pendants (Cluster 3), glass trade beads, and metal buttons (Clusters 5, 7, and 6).

The results of this analysis do not suggest a great deal of structure in the use of grave offerings. None of the eight clusters exhibited a greater than expected number of any age or sex category, nor did any show a preferential distribution in the five burial areas (Figure 6.36). The one clear correspondent with cluster membership is the variety of goods in the burial assemblage. The amount decreases from left to right across the dendrogram, with Cluster 1 having the highest average value (mean = 13.0) and Cluster 6 having the lowest (mean = 1.9). If the initial division of the population is considered, graves with gun parts (left side of the dendrogram) contained on average 9.6 different types, whereas those lacking gun parts (right half of the dendrogram) had an average of 2.7 types.

The distribution of possible sociotechnic objects confirms the previous assertion that they were less constrained in occurrence. Although two of the three stone pipes and both spearheads occur in the left-side clusters, the remaining types are distributed at an approximately even density throughout the clusters. Cluster 4 has the highest overall occurrence of such types (mean = 4.3), whereas Cluster 2 contained none. The distribution of potential sociotechnic objects, particularly bird beaks, bird bone, raptor talons, and bear claws, seems to indicate that they were not functioning as specific social symbols. Their unconstrained distribution relative to age and sex and their tendency to be somewhat more prevalent in elaborate assemblages (contrast the monothetic division results with those of the hierarchical fusion analysis) argue that they probably were treated as valued or expensive objects, but not as distinct social markers. The two exceptions to this generalization were stone pipes and stone spear points.

On the basis of this analysis, it appears that few of the types used in the Leavenworth cemetery had qualitative significance. Rather, most inclusions behaved as quantitative indicators of economic standing. It is also likely that some objects were value graded. Gun parts, which so effectively divided the population into large and small grave assemblages, may have represented one of a class of "expensive" goods, as may some of the sociotechnic objects. There is, however, little evidence for structuring beyond this basic economic level. Although most individuals receiving nonnormative burial treatments were buried with either no artifacts or assemblages of the lower wealth level, a sufficient mix of wealths are observed among the cases to confirm the independence of these special status distinctions from wealth standing.

Although a number of mortuary distinctions were identified at Leavenworth, the overall level of organization within the population was low; fewer aspects of formal treatment were constrained, and fewer artifact types exhibited patterned associations either in terms of age and sex or in terms of strong correlation between sets of co-

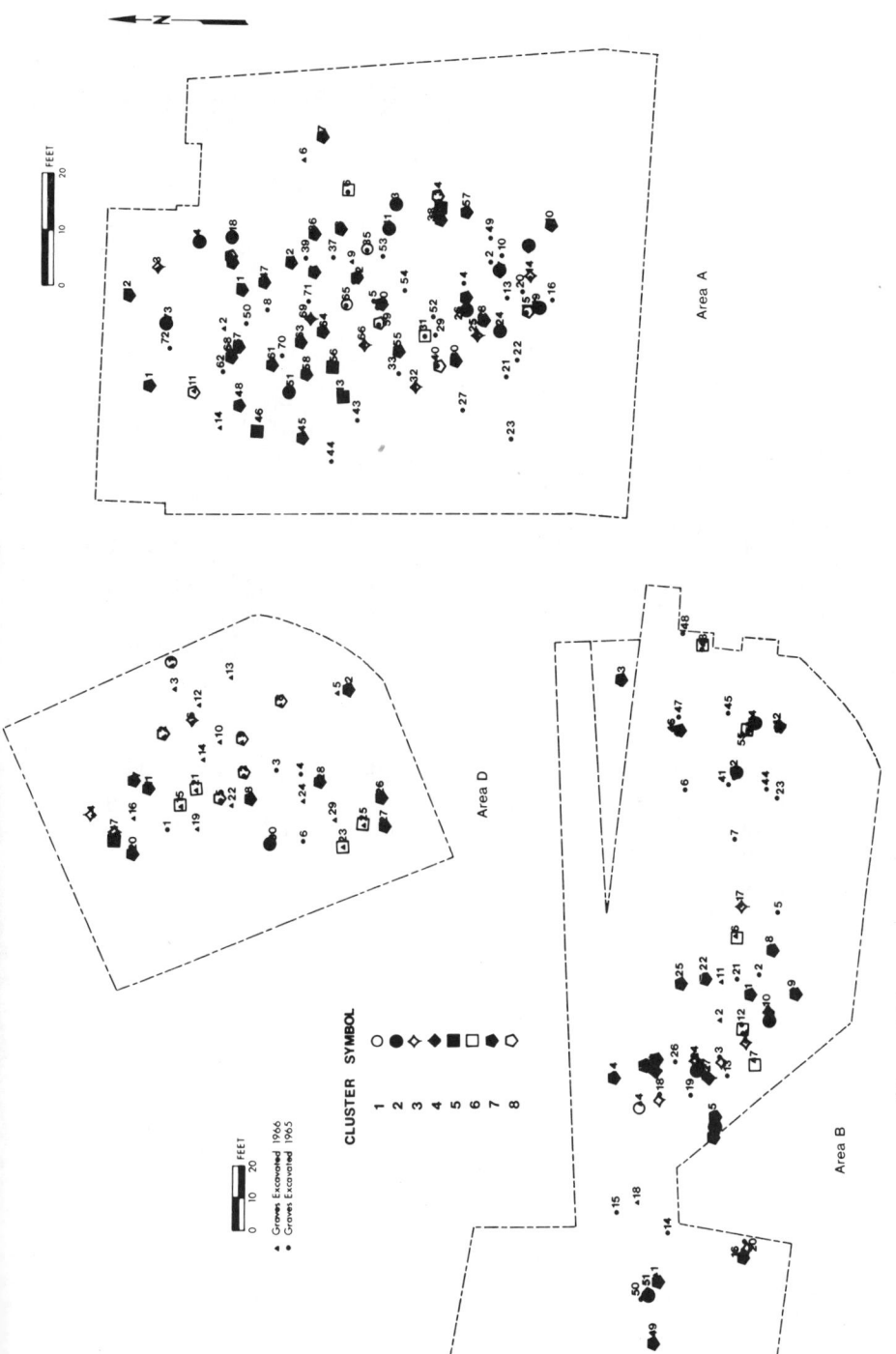

Figure 6.36 Spatial distribution of monothetic division clusters at the Leavenworth site cemeteries.

occurring artifacts. The primary axis of mortuary differentiation at Leavenworth was the quantity of artifacts buried with each individual. Few artifacts functioned as qualitative symbolic indicators. Both trade and native-made goods derived their primary symbolic importance from their rank worth as well as the quantity of such goods interred with the deceased. This pattern of artifact use is consistent with a deritualization of the mortuary symbolism, particularly in the use of artifacts as grave offerings.

Leavenworth Mortuary Differentiation

Little interaction was observed between the differential aspects of burial treatment and grave assemblage composition at the Leavenworth site. In only one instance (age-based differentiation) was a particular social distinction marked by both treatment and artifact occurrence. The basic categories of mortuary differentiation identified at the Leavenworth site are presented in Table 6.61.

Three categories of vertical distinction were recognized. The first has been termed *wealth*, although this distinction is not the exact equivalent of the category "achieved wealth" discussed in the previous analyses. Wealth at Leavenworth, as was most clearly seen in the results of monothetic divisive cluster analysis, was expressed through the elaborateness and size of the burial assemblage. The cases spread along this dimension in a continuous fashion, but with two distinct modes; for convenience, it will therefore be treated as a two-tier system. This distinction differs from others in the demographic compositions of the two levels. Both levels have normal demographic compositions. If the distinction were strictly achieved, one would expect many, if not all, subadults to be found in the lower level, but this is not the case. The observed pattern is suggestive of a hereditary class-type system, although it lacks the rigid hierarchy of symbols that normally is associated with such a system. The more likely explanation is that the wealth of an individual's family or corporate group was reflected in the burial assemblage, rather than the individual's own achieved wealth.

The second vertical distinction observed at Leavenworth reflects an *elevated social position*, which may connote chiefly authority or prerogative. The social position was limited to individuals of the upper wealth level and was symbolized by burial with a stone pipe. Two of the three holders of the position were adult males, while the third was an infant. The raw material of which the pipes were manufactured may provide additional insight into the nature of the social position and its transmission. Both adults were interred with pipes fashioned from red pipestone (catlinite) that was obtained through aboriginal exchange networks, whereas the infant's pipe was made from locally available limestone. This may be indicative of the presumptive nature of the subadult's status. Although these individuals occur in two of the five burial areas, it is unclear why holders of the position were not found in the other burial zones.

TABLE 6.61

Leavenworth: Mortuary Differentiation

Social distinction	Number	Sex	Age	Formal differentiation	Artifact differentiation	Comments
Vertical distinctions						
Achieved wealth						
Upper level	20	—	—		Five or more types	
Lower level	112	—	—		Fewer types	
Elevated social position						
Chiefly office	3	Male	Adult		Pipe ownership; upper wealth level	One subadult is included among these.
Special prestige position	2	—	Adult		Spear point ownership Bird beak ownership Upper wealth level	
Horizontal distinctions						
Corporate group (Bands?)	Variable	—	—	Location of burial		
Adult/subadult	55/77	—	—	Longer graves		
Male/female	29/22	—	—		Age-specific artifacts Gender-specific artifacts	
Special status distinctions						
Circumstances of death						
?	1	—	Adult	Nonnormative posture	Lower wealth level	
?	1	Male	Adult	Decapitation	Lower wealth level	
Time of death?	1	—	Adult	Multiple interment	Lower wealth level	
Alternative subadult treatment						
?	18	—	Subadult	Multiple interment		Both of these may represent expedient treatments.
?	15	—	Subadult	Nonnormative posture		

A more ambiguous social position was marked by the occurrence of a stone spearhead. Two adults, one male and one female, held this position. Both individuals also had upper-level wealth assemblages. These factors marked this as a vertical distinction; probably indicative of a special prestige position, although the occurrence of bird beaks may suggest a degree of merging with some ritual usage or function. There was no indication that these spear points were associated with the death or dismemberment of the owners as at the Larson site.

A rather more limited set of horizontal distinctions was observed at Leavenworth. The five burial areas are suggestive of a band-type distinction, because of their size, discrete spatial occurrence, and normal demographic composition. Unfortunately, no other class of evidence was found that corresponded with the spatial distinction. The only other horizontal distinctions recognized were male versus female, which was expressed via a series of sex-specific artifact types, and adult versus subadult, which was reflected in grave length and age-specific artifact types. It is possible that the distribution of various other artifact types, such as bird beaks and small mammal crania, may have served as markers for small-scale horizontal distinctions, but it seems more likely that these types were simply valuable goods.

A series of special status distinctions, all apparently reflecting circumstances of death, was observed. All were designated by nonnormative funerary treatment. Multiple burial and nonnormative extended burial posture were used to mark both adults and subadults, although the meaning of the treatment seems to have been determined by age. Both treatments, when applied to subadults, appear to have been essentially expedient behaviors. Multiple interments would occur in the event of the closely spaced death of two or more subadults and when a subadult died very near the time of an adult death. Whether such multiple burials are indicative of biological relatedness cannot be assessed on archaeological grounds.

Burial in an extended posture also was used for subadults, particularly young infants, again presumably as an expedient. For adults, both of these treatments occurred more rarely and appear to represent some more specific circumstances of death, although the identification of the specific meaning is not possible. It also is possible, however, that these isolated adult cases simply represent idiosyncratic variation in the normal mortuary treatment. A similar caution applies to the one observed instance of decapitation. This case may have resulted from a special circumstance at death, or it may have been the result of other random factors.

Arikara Results

Archaeological Reconstructions

Archaeological analysis of the two Arikara samples produced differing results. The analysis of the Larson site isolated a number of differential treatments that reflected the range of social features characteristic of Arikara social organization.

Fewer examples of these categories, however, were differentiated (or observed) at the Leavenworth site. The comparison of known social features with those inferred from archaeological analysis is presented in Table 6.62.

Vertical social distinctions were marked in both samples. At Larson, the full range of vertical distinctions was recognized. At Leavenworth, however, special ritual positions were not identified. Unlike the Larson site, no evidence for ranking independent of basic wealth was observed in the Leavenworth mortuary population.

Although the Larson results are in very good agreement with ethnographic descriptions of Arikara rank organization, the Leavenworth results, with its simpler rank structure, provides a poorer fit.

Major horizontal distinctions were not recognized in either of the two Arikara samples. Although basic age and sex distinctions were marked at both sites, no further horizontal elements were observed at Larson, while a possible band subdivision was detected at Leavenworth. No evidence for descent orientation or for the numerous documented social and secret societies was observed in the funerary remains at either site.

Special status differentiation was recognized at both sites. Most were indicative of

TABLE 6.62

Arikara: Comparison of Ethnographic and Archaeological Observations of Mortuary Differentiation

	Source of observations			
	Ethnographic		Archaeological	
Type of differentiation	Society	Mortuary	Larson	Leavenworth
Vertical				
Chiefly office	+	+	+	+
Achieved wealth	+	+	+	+
Hereditary ascription	+	—	+	+
Ritual office	+	+	+	—
Special prestige position	+	—	+	+
Horizontal				
Band membership	+	—	—	+(?)
Matrilineal residence/descent	+	—	—	—
Society membership	+	—	—	—
Male/female	+	+	+	+
Adult/subadult	+	+	+	+
Special status				
Circumstance of death	+	+	+	+
Social deviant	+	—	—	—
Alternative subadult treatment	+	—	+	+
Other	+	—	+	—

special circumstances at death, particularly among subadults. An additional distinction, probably resulting from the mutilation and burial of enemy warriors, was observed at Larson. No evidence for the burial of social deviants was encountered.

These results are similar to those from the Pawnee sites, in that the main vertical structures of the population were readily inferred through archaeological analysis, whereas the higher-order horizontal structure of the population and the treatment of social deviants could not be documented. Unlike the Pawnee study, however, the reconstructions resulting from the two Arikara cases were not consistent.

Two aspects of the Arikara samples adversely affected archaeological analysis: (1) the destruction or disassociation of many graves due to stratification and (2) the very low incidence of status markers. The first limitation resulted in an inability to assess possible alternative disposal treatments, such as disarticulated burial, and necessitated the exclusion of a number of cases from the sample because of ambiguity in the content of their grave assemblages. Yet, both samples were sufficiently large that the loss of these cases should not materially have affected the social reconstructions. Furthermore, any bias introduced by this factor would presumably have been consistent in its effects at the two sites. The low incidence levels were more problematic, particularly at a methodological level. At both sites, but particularly at Larson, possible evidence for a very fine-grained social symbolism was observed, yet the assessment of such symbols and their relative significance proved nearly impossible. This was particularly true since the symbols often did not resolve into any clear higher-level structure.

Yet, neither of these limitations would seem to account for the lack of horizontal structuring in the mortuary populations or for the inconsistency in results between the two samples. Despite the larger sample sizes (compared with the Pawnee and Omaha cases) and the more numerous age and sex determinations, little in the way of horizontal differentiation could be defined. Indeed, the only evidence for such structuring was the existence of discrete burial areas at Leavenworth.

Nor can the discrepancies between the archaeological results be attributed to sample limitations or data deficiencies. The divergent findings from the two Arikara sites must therefore be indicative of an inherent unreliability in social reconstructions based on funerary evidence or be the result of a shift in the Arikara funerary complex during the time between the use of the two sites. Change was observed in the detail of the Larson funerary complex and almost certainly must have continued during the years separating the two sites. It will be argued in the next chapter that the differences found in the two Arikara sites result not from archaeological deficiencies but rather from major structural changes in Arikara society that are accurately reflected in their mortuary treatment.

Ethnographic Accounts of Arikara Mortuary Practices

Ethnographic accounts of Arikara funerary activities provide good documentation for normative treatments and for vertical distinctions (Table 6.62). Indeed, the description of artifact usage and its rank connotations (see Chapter 5) were in good agreement with the archaeological results. Ethnographic sources, however, did not provide evidence for the expression of horizontal distinctions in the mortuary treatment or for a number of observed special status distinctions. The sole special status distinction mentioned was scaffold burial (which may ultimately have resulted in disarticulated burial). Ethnographic accounts were mute on the special status distinctions that were observed in the archaeological study. Neither ethnography nor archaeology documented any special treatment for social deviants.

Overall, ethnographic descriptions of Arikara funerary treatment provide a similar although less-detailed picture of mortuary differentiation, falling well short of documenting the full range of differential practices expected in Arikara society.

The Omaha

Big Village Site

Formal Treatment

The normative burial treatment at Big Village consisted of single, primary inhumation. The dead were placed on their backs in an extended posture with arms placed at their sides. Occasionally, the floor of the grave was sloped, so that the shoulders and upper portion of the body were elevated to something approaching a sitting posture. All graves were oriented with the head in a northwesterly direction (Table 6.63).

In addition to this normative program, funerary treatment also served to differentiate various components of the mortuary population. Grave size and depth (Table 6.64) differentiated adults from subadults, with adult graves tending to be longer, wider, and deeper than those of subadults. No systematic difference was observed in any grave dimension by sex (Table 6.65).

Three alternative programs of corpse treatment were in evidence at Big Village. Grave 20 at DK2 was a cremation burial. The individual, a young male, was set in the grave in an extended posture and burned in place. Grave offerings were placed in the grave prior to incineration and evidenced charring, with the exception of four human crania without mandibles (trophy skulls?) and a red painted horse skull. These latter offerings were placed on a small raised platform at the foot of the grave after burning. As cremation occurred in only a single instance, it is difficult to infer the social rules or circumstances that governed its use.

A second type of alternative treatment was observed in two instances, Feature 17b at DK10 and Feature 10 at DK2. In both cases the remains (both adolescent males) were found in a semi-disarticulated state. The bones were found in a jumbled mass, but in a good state of preservation, and with anatomical subunits, such as hands and feet, still in articulation. Both interments included grave offerings and lacked any evidence of postdepositional disturbance. Although these occurrences may reflect

TABLE 6.63
Big Village: Burial Descriptions

Grave number	Sex	Age[a]	Length	Width	Depth	Orientation	Posture[b]	Disarticulated	Multiple burial	Burial covering
25DK2a										
3	—	1	104	58	114	N	Et	—	—	—
7	F	4	246	102	160	N	Et	—	—	—
8	M	5	183	84	81	N	Et	—	—	—
9a	—	4	—	—	117	N	Et	—	+	—
9a	—	1	—	—	117	N	—	—	+	—
10	M?	3	122	79	163	—	Et	+	—	+
11	M	4	173	71	173	N	Et	—	—	—
14	F	4	147	107	163	W	Et	—	—	+
17	M	5	206	81	201	NW	Et	—	—	—
20	M	4	168	107	168	NW	Et	—	—	—[c]
22a	F	3	137	99	142	—	Et	—	+	—[d]
22a	—	2	137	99	56	—	Fx	—	+	—
23	F	4	137	53	179	NW	Et	—	—	—
24	—	2	112	51	157	W	Et	—	—	—
25	—	8	160	89	127	NW	Et	—	—	—
25DK2b										
2a	—	1	183	140	112	NW	Et	—	—	—
2b	M	4	183	140	124	NW	Et	—	+	—
2b	—	1	183	140	124	NW	Et	—	+	—
2b	—	1	183	140	124	NW	Et	—	+	—
2b	—	1	183	140	124	NW	Et	—	+	—
25DK10										
1a	—	1	—	—	61	—	—	—	—	—
1b	—	1	66	41	157	NW	Et	—	+	+
1b	—	2	66	41	157	—	—	—	+	+

2	—	8	—	—	61	—	Et	—	—	+
3	F	4	157	74	142	NW	—	—	—	—
4	F	4	—	—	—	—	—	—	+	—
5a	F	6	—	—	—	—	—	+	+	—
5a	—	8	—	—	—	—	—	+	+	—
5a	—	8	—	—	—	—	—	+	+	—
6a	M	6	112	46	107	NW	Et	—	+	+
6a	F	1	112	18	42	NW	Et	—	+	+
7a	F	6	—	—	—	—	—	—	+	—
7a	M	1	—	—	—	—	—	+	—	—
8a	F	6	—	—	—	—	—	+	+	+
8a	—	6	—	—	—	—	—	—	—	—
9	—	1	122	79	107	N	Et	—	—	—
11	—	1	107	51	69	N	Et	—	—	—
12	—	1	—	—	86	—	Et	—	—	—
13	—	2	107	46	74	—	Et	—	—	—
14	M	1	—	—	—	—	—	—	+	+
15a	—	6	—	—	—	—	—	—	+	+
15a	M	1	—	—	—	—	Et	—	+	—
16	M	4	244	137	201	NW	Et	—	—	—
17a	M?	1	—	—	157	NW	—	—	—	—
17b	M	3	165	56	152	—	Et	—	+	—
18	—	5	—	—	165	NW	Et	+	+	—
19a	—	2	102	64	132	NW	Et	—	+	—
19a	—	8	102	64	52	NW	Et	—	+	—
20/21a	F	5	152	—	152	N	Et	—	+	—
b	—	9	—	—	165	NW	—	—	+	—
a	—	1	152	—	152	W	—	—	+	—
a	—	2	—	—	165	—	—	—	—	—
b	F	3	152	—	152	—	—	—	—	—
22	—	1	—	—	—	—	—	—	—	—
23/24	M	9	—	91	—	W	Et	—	—	—
25	M	6	193	91	147	NW	Et	+	—	+

(continued)

TABLE 6.63 Continued

Grave number	Sex	Age[a]	Length	Width	Depth	Orientation	Posture[b]	Disarticulated	Multiple burial	Burial covering
26	—	1	—	—	—	N	Et	—	—	—
27	F	4	—	—	130	NW	Et	—	—	—
28a	F	6	183	122	179	NW	—	—	+	—
28a	—	1	183	122	179	NW	Et	—	+	—
29a	M	4	183	76	147	N	Et	—	+	—
29a	—	8	183	76	147	N	Et	—	+	—
30a	—	1	132	76	142	N	Et	—	+	—
30a	—	1	132	76	142	—	Et	—	+	—
30a	—	1	132	76	142	—	—	—	+	—
31	—	—	—	—	124	—	—	—	—	—
32	—	1	—	—	152	N	Et	—	+	—
33	—	1	94	58	114	NW	Et	—	+	—
34a	—	3	198	122	—	NW	Et	—	+	—
34a	—	2	198	122	—	NW	Et	—	+	—
34a	—	1	198	122	—	—	—	—	—	—
35a	—	1	—	102	—	—	—	—	+	—
35a	—	1	—	102	—	—	—	—	+	—
35a	—	1	—	102	—	—	—	—	+	—

[a] 1 = 0–2 years, 2 = 3–12 years, 3 = 13–17 years, 4 = 18–30 years, 5 = 31–40 years, 6 = 41–50+ years, 8 = undifferentiated child, 9 = undifferentiated adult.
[b] Fx = flexed; Et = extended.
[c] Cremation.
[d] Trophy skull.

TABLE 6.64

Big Village: Grave Dimensions by Age

	Adult average rank	Subadult average rank	U	Significance
Length	13.1 (12)	4.6 (7)	4.5	$p < .001$
Width	12.2 (12)	6.2 (7)	15.5	$p < .05$
Depth	17.6 (14)	8.7 (12)	26.5	$p < .01$

some special class of mortuary treatment, it seems more likely that they are the result of the well-known Plains practice of dismembering war victims (see Chapter 5). If such was the case, these individuals represent Omaha war dead whose remains had been recovered for burial. The treatment, then, would reflect the special circumstances of death.

Another variety of partial disarticulation was observed in Feature 25 at DK10. The body of this individual, a mature male, was completely articulated, with two exceptions: The individual's head had been severed and placed at the left side of the body, and the right arm had also been severed and replaced in reverse anatomical position. This particular individual apparently died of a gunshot wound to the chest, as a spent lead ball was found within the rib cage. A consideration of artifact occurrence will further illuminate the significance of this alternative mortuary treatment.

A third basic type of differentiation in the funerary treatment was expressed through the use of at least two distinct burial areas (Figure 6.37). The age and sex composition of the two areas is very similar, although DK10 contains a greater number of interments. As other aspects of treatment differentiation tend to crosscut this spatial distinction, burial area location may be indicative of a horizontal social distinction. As was noted previously, although all the interments in these two areas probably were discovered during excavation, the existence of additional, undiscovered burial areas is highly likely.

TABLE 6.65

Big Village: Grave Dimensions by Sex

	Male average rank	Female average rank	U	Significance
Length	7.1 (8)	5.2 (4)	11.0	$p > .10$
Width	6.7 (8)	6.1 (4)	14.5	$p > .10$
Depth	8.3 (9)	6.1 (5)	15.5	$p > .10$

226   6. Mortuary Differentiation and Social Distinction

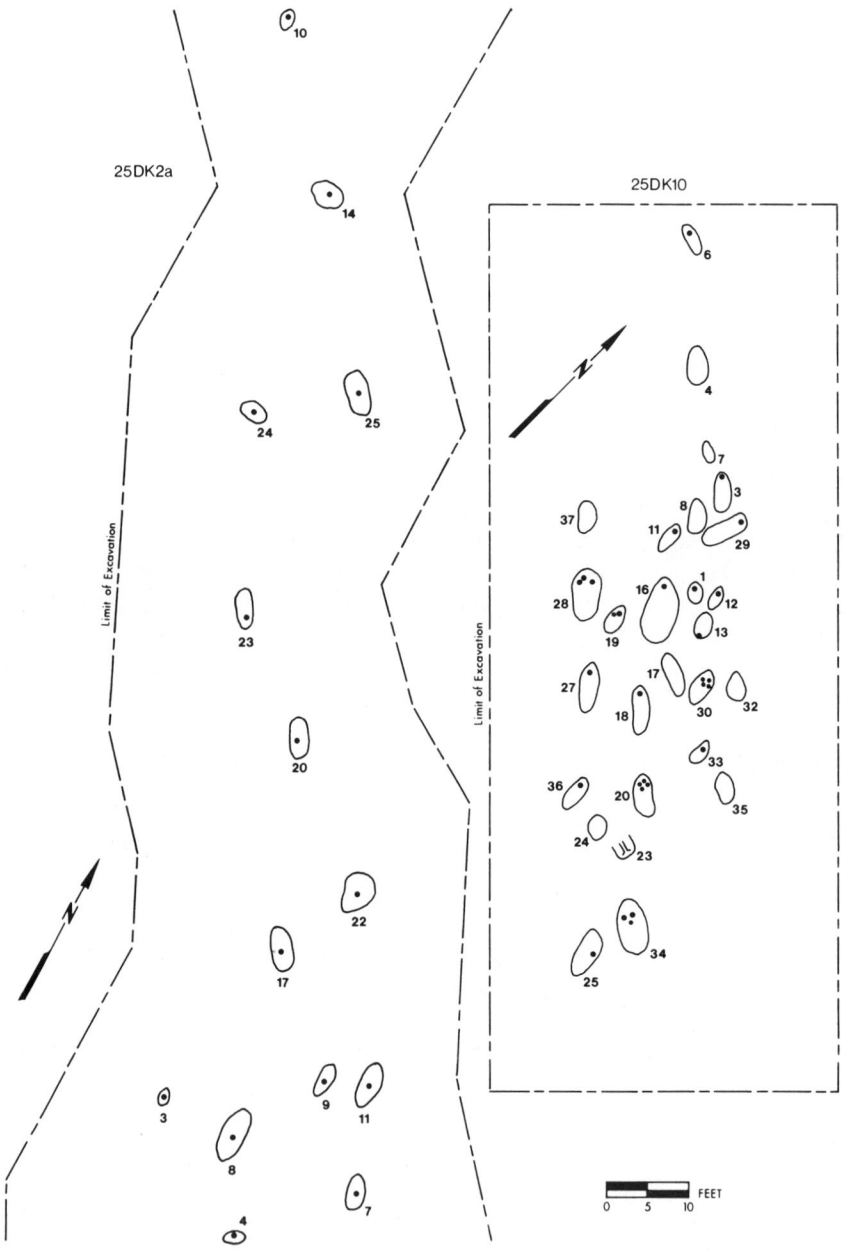

Figure 6.37 Plan of the Big Village site cemeteries.

Although the majority of individuals at Big Village were interred individually, in several instances a grave was found to contain more than a single individual (Table 6.63). Of these, eight contained the remains of two or more subadults, while six contained the remains of an adult with one or more subadults. In no case, however, were two adults found buried in the same grave. Furthermore, no apparent distinction was made regarding the sex of the adult in those cases where children were buried with adults. This pattern suggests an expedient alternative practice accorded to subadults. That adults were not buried together constitutes another distinction made in the mortuary ritual between adults and subadults.

Finally, burial coverings, either the log-and-pole type or a simple covering of bark matting, were found over a number of interments (Table 6.66). The limited distribution of these coverings, particularly at DK2, may signify their use as a form of grave elaboration, rather than as a normative aspect of the funerary treatment. A consideration of artifact occurrence will be necessary to test this possibility.

Taken together, treatment variables at Big Village served to differentiate a number of social distinctions, including at least two special status distinctions through alternative disposal programs; adults from subadults through grave size and likelihood of multiple burial; a possible horizontal distinction reflected in the location of burial; and a possible vertical dimension expressed through the use of a burial covering. These possibilities will be refined through a consideration of artifact usage in the Big Village mortuary ritual.

TABLE 6.66

Big Village: Burial Coverings[a]

Type of covering and burial area	Graves	Age	Sex
Log and pole			
25DK2	11	Adult	Male
	17	Mature	Male
25DK10	1B	Infant	—
	2	—	—
	7	Infant	—
	12	Infant	—
Bark			
25DK2	20+	Adult	Male
25DK10	9	Infant	—
	11	Child	—
	16	Adult	Male
	18	Mature	Male

[a] + = cremation, — = undetermined

TABLE 6.67

Big Village: Artifact Type Associations

Female
    Metal container

Male
    Bird beak
    Bird bone
    Gun parts/accessories
    Pin game cup
    Gorget
    Shell hair pipe
    Wampum bead
    Metal projectile point
    Large cast brass bell
    Smaller brass bell
    Thick wire coil
    Metal lace/braid
    Small silver brooch
    Stone sphere
    Stone pipe

Subadult
    —

Adult
    Glass bottle
    Bird beak
    Bird bone
    Gun parts/accessories
    Pin game cup
    Mussel shell
    Iron knife
    Small metal hardware
    Metal projectile point
    Metal container
    Finger ring
    Metal button
    Large cast brass bell
    Smaller brass bell
    Metal lace/braid
    Silver earring
    Small silver brooch
    Gunflint
    Sandstone shaft smoother
    Stone sphere
    Stone pipe
    Unretouched flake

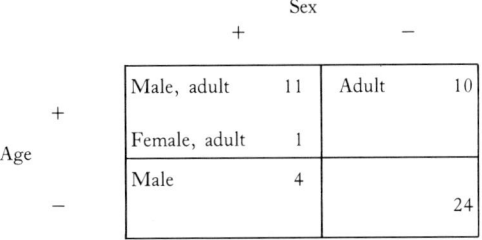

Figure 6.38 Age and sex constraints on artifact occurrence at the Big Village site.

Artifact Occurrence

A total of 50 types were found in association with the Big Village cemeteries: 18 of native manufacture and 32 of Euroamerican origin. Considerable structure was evident in the use of grave artifacts, with an overwhelming emphasis on adult- and male-associated goods (Table 6.67 and Figure 6.38). Over half of all types (17 of 32 trade types and 8 of 18 native types) exhibited significant age or sex association: 11 with adult males, and 1 with adult females; 10 with adults; and 4 with males regardless of age.

Similar structure was evident in the distribution of artifact classes (Tables 6.68 and 6.69). Male assemblages tended to have a greater number of sociotechnic objects than did female assemblages, while the grave assemblages of adults contained greater quantities of trade implements, native implements, native types overall, and all types, compared with those of subadults.

TABLE 6.68

Big Village: Artifact Class Associations by Sex

Artifact class	Average male rank ($N=8$)	Average female rank ($N=6$)	U	Probability
Trade goods				
Body ornaments	8.8	5.8	14.0	.1887
Clothing ornaments	9.0	5.5	12.0	.1035
Implements	7.3	7.8	22.5	.8414
All trade items	8.4	6.2	16.5	.3297
Native goods				
Ornaments	8.1	6.7	19.0	.4106
Implements	8.5	6.2	16.0	.2772
Sociotechnic	9.4	5.0	9.0	.0236
All native items	8.9	5.6	12.5	.1263

TABLE 6.69

Big Village: Artifact Class Associations by Age

Artifact class	Average adult rank ($N=14$)	Average subadult rank ($N=20$)	U	Probability
Trade goods				
Body ornaments	20.1	15.7	103.5	.1949
Clothing ornaments	20.4	15.5	99.5	.1325
Implements	22.9	13.7	64.5	.0019
All trade items	21.2	14.9	88.0	.0667
Native goods				
Ornaments	19.9	15.8	107.0	.0559
Implements	23.2	13.5	60.0	.0007
Sociotechnic	20.3	15.6	101.0	.0531
All native items	22.6	13.9	68.0	.0038

Principal Component Analysis

A total of 34 cases and 25 types were included in the Omaha sample for principal component analysis. Eight factors were extracted that jointly accounted for 78.7% of the total variance in the correlation matrix (Table 6.70). The main characteristics of these factors are summarized in Table 6.71.

The factors are of two basic types: those defining sets of primarily trade ornaments (Factors 2, 4, 5, 6, and 8), and those reflecting sex-linked implement sets (Factor 1 for males, and 3 for females). Factor 1 is of particular interest in that it combined standard male implements with two sociotechnic objects—bird beaks and bird bone. Factor 2 combined a series of types that, although not strictly limited to females, may well represent important female ornaments. Factor 4, within a primarily male context, discriminates between two modes of ornamentation: those varieties that are "strung" either as necklaces or as clothing ornamentation, and those ornaments that generally are worn on the body, such as bracelets, coils, and hair pipes. Factor 5 appears to represent a distinction between ordinary and elaborate ornamentation, while Factor 6 isolates lead artifacts, which occur most commonly with subadults, from other types more common to older individuals. The final factor, Factor 8, defines yet another ornament combination, linking metal bracelets with metal buttons. Factor 7 combines silver hair plates with small metal hardware. The hardware, in this case primarily nails, hinges, and locks, appears to be the remnants of wooden trunks.

Although these factors distinguish a number of age and sex categories that structure artifact occurrence, they do not offer any evidence for distinctions between native-made artifacts and trade goods in the funerary use of artifacts. The factors

TABLE 6.70

Big Village: Varimax Rotated Factor Matrix

	Factor 1	Factor 2	Factor 3	Factor 4	Factor 5	Factor 6	Factor 7	Factor 8
Glass bottle	−0.07460	0.21325	0.77253	0.15632	−0.22077	−0.22125	0.01707	0.12321
Glass trade beads	0.10508	−0.07036	0.16682	0.78143	0.13309	0.16320	0.03697	−0.03822
Animal teeth	0.64878	0.26905	0.17730	0.13647	−0.51950	−0.22132	0.26950	0.01535
Bird beak	0.80949	0.17759	−0.09867	−0.04510	0.30430	−0.03826	0.09248	0.13392
Gun parts/accessories	0.81576	−0.18032	−0.05280	0.14147	0.16833	−0.02744	−0.12518	0.24626
Gorget	0.86077	−0.13359	−0.01510	0.07649	−0.12813	−0.12035	0.07287	−0.13863
Shell hair pipe	−0.06783	0.42046	−0.36753	0.50678	0.36952	−0.00335	−0.21038	0.17892
Wampum bead	0.42874	0.25663	0.00522	0.62122	0.16213	−0.02388	0.10364	−0.24550
Metal bracelet	0.04856	0.21678	0.15099	−0.11617	0.06775	−0.04821	−0.05635	0.86795
Metal bead/bangle	0.09454	0.26641	0.34481	0.12375	0.60821	−0.10052	0.23663	0.01796
Iron knife	0.77047	−0.24560	0.07834	0.07309	0.02968	0.36870	0.28017	0.03622
Small metal hardware	0.40548	0.10179	0.48165	0.07295	0.10299	0.31114	0.50832	−0.11793
Metal container	0.10097	−0.07258	0.84675	−0.06274	0.18440	0.20322	0.07910	−0.01556
Finger ring	0.03344	0.84533	0.13066	−0.05944	0.03225	0.07119	0.08061	0.12501
Metal button	0.36021	−0.03310	−0.29745	0.17909	0.11698	0.17781	0.38710	0.58554
Smaller brass bell	0.35488	0.19381	−0.13008	0.20942	0.74466	−0.13002	0.01536	0.22276
Thick wire coil	−0.22953	−0.11581	0.17058	−0.54744	0.35071	0.31138	−0.23185	−0.29302
Thin wire coil	0.59323	0.14875	−0.00275	−0.44405	0.25647	0.16951	−0.23257	0.05414
Lead ring/coil	0.25818	0.32663	0.04685	0.08692	−0.46411	0.55448	0.05652	0.18866
Lead band	−0.13264	0.11504	0.00902	0.03470	−0.03933	0.89126	0.01382	−0.03857
Sheet silver bracelet	−0.04853	0.77814	−0.02520	0.00774	−0.06150	0.15245	0.12971	0.03790
Silver hair plate	0.07570	0.30664	0.11247	0.12294	−0.00247	0.02173	0.80914	0.06371
Silver earring	0.00900	0.86870	0.05265	0.24728	0.21819	0.01845	0.09959	0.07051
Gunflint	0.81618	0.20789	0.38186	0.01477	−0.09826	−0.05064	0.09894	0.02207
Unretouched flake	0.01446	0.55166	0.00938	−0.37399	0.10522	−0.26712	0.46025	−0.04649

TABLE 6.71

Big Village: Factor Summary[a]

Factor number	Loading pattern	Percentage variance	Diagnostic positive loadings	Diagnostic negative loadings
1	Group	22.7	Animal teeth Bird beak M+ Bird bone M+ Gorget M+ Iron knife + Thin wire coil Gunflint +	
2	Bipolar	14.3	Finger ring + Silver bracelet Silver earring + Unretouched flake +	Iron knife +
3	Bipolar	10.2	Glass bottle + Metal container F+	Shell hair pipe M Metal button +
4	Bipolar	8.1	Glass trade bead Shell hair pipe M Wampum bead M	Thick wire coil M Thin wire coil Unretouched flake +
5	Bipolar	7.1	Thick wire coil M Metal bead/bangle	Glass bottle + Animal teeth Lead ring/coil
6	Bipolar	6.9	Lead ring/coil Lead band	Glass bottle + Animal teeth Unretouched flake +
7	Bipolar	5.0	Small metal hardware + Silver hair plate	Shell hair pipe M Thick wire coil M Thin wire coil

[a] Constraints: +, adult only; −, subadult only; M, male only; F, female only.

also suggest the existence of symmetrical sets of male and female goods in the grave assemblages.

Hierarchical Fusion Cluster Analysis

The clustering of graves by factor scores provided further evidence for the highly structured use of artifacts in the Big Village funerary program. Cluster diagnostics for the six-cluster solution are presented in Table 6.72 and the dendrogram as Figure 6.39.

The clusters are arranged to present a rank ordering, with the most highly ranked cluster on the right of the dendrogram and the lower ranked on the left. Two mature

TABLE 6.72

Big Village: Hierarchical Fusion Cluster Diagnostics

Cluster number	Factor number	Mean origin	S.D.	Factor number	Mean origin	S.D.
1	1	−.2898	.3920	5	−.0621	.6761
	2	−.4124	.2042	6	−.3023	.6110
	3	.2102	.9837	7	−.1739	.5576
	4	.3820	.5623	8	−.5043	.6931
	Number of individuals	15				
	Number of males	1				
	Number of females	2				
	Number of adults	3				
	Number of subadults	12				
	Cluster members	DK2: 3,10,23; DK10: 1b,3,5,6,11,12,13,17b,19,22, 31,32				
2	1	−.2594	.2435	5	−.3941	.4358
	2	.4200	.8603	6	.4036	1.1500
	3	−.3991	.4572	7	−.4234	.8042
	4	−.9186	1.1879	8	.0668	.9166
	Number of individuals	10				
	Number of males	1				
	Number of females	2				
	Number of adults	3				
	Number of subadults	7				
	Cluster members	DK2: 4,24; DK10: 2,9,14,25,26,27,33,37				
3	1	.4409	0	5	−1.3184	0
	2	3.0337	0	6	−.6624	0
	3	3.0958	0	7	1.6586	0
	4	.2363	0	8	.0694	0
	Number of individuals	1				
	Number of females	1				
	Number of adults	1				
	Cluster member	DK2: 7				
4	1	−.1644	.5439	5	1.1819	1.0871
	2	.2570	1.5478	6	−.4684	.2231
	3	−.6004	1.5478	7	.5043	1.0984
	4	.5043	1.0984	8	1.2966	.7258
	Number of individuals	5				
	Number of males	4				
	Number of females	0				
	Number of adults	4				
	Number of subadults	1				
	Cluster members	DK2: 8,11,20; DK10: 1a,16				

(continued)

TABLE 6.72 *Continued*

Cluster number	Factor number	Mean origin	S.D.	Factor number	Mean origin	S.D.
5	1	.0066	0	5	−.1028	0
	2	−1.2748	0	6	3.3215	0
	3	.2122	0	7	3.3803	0
	4	.7903	0	8	.2037	0
	Number of individuals	1				
	Number of females	1				
	Number of adults	1				
	Cluster member	DK2: 14				
6	1	3.6567	.3561	5	.1924	3.1216
	2	−.5292	.3712	6	.0906	.2916
	3	.2661	1.4168	7	−.3592	.2117
	4	−.0479	.4039	8	.0702	2.0700
	Number of individuals	2				
	Number of males	2				
	Number of females	0				
	Number of adults	2				
	Number of subadults	0				
	Cluster members	DK2: 17; DK10: 18				

males, one from each burial area, loaded strongly on Factor 1, with its combination of expensive trade implements and sociotechnic objects (Cluster 6). Cluster 4 is also a male cluster, including four adult males and a single subadult. These assemblages contain quantities of clothing and body ornaments (Factors 5 and 8) and load negatively on the general factors associated with women (Factor 3) and infants (Factor 6). Clusters 3 and 5 are each composed of a single individual, both adult females. Although these grave assemblages are dissimilar in their particular composition, they are structurally equivalent, being the only instances of females with large quantities of grave goods. In addition, both contain certain artifacts (wampum beads) that normally were restricted to males. Clusters 1 and 2 represent grave assemblages that lack strong loadings on any factor or that load negatively on the more "expensive" varieties of trade goods. These two clusters contain nearly an even number of males and females, and the great majority of the subadults.

The distribution of cluster members in the two cemetery areas is presented in Figure 6.40. The members of each cluster are evenly dispersed between the two burial areas. The evenness of the distributions is well illustrated by the split occurrence of the two mature males of Cluster 6. The only exceptions to this pattern are the two solitary female clusters, which both occur at DK2.

The suggestion that this cluster result is indicative of a ranking of the population is supported by a comparison of the total variety of artifacts present in each grave (as opposed to the $\widetilde{25}$ frequently occurring types used in the principal component analysis). When artifact variety is plotted by cluster membership, the ordering of graves coincides closely with that observed in the dendrogram (Figure 6.41). The two mature males of Cluster 6 have the greatest number of types, the two ranked females (Clusters 3 and 5) and the males of Cluster 4 would hold an intermediate rank, and the rest of the population, occurring in Clusters 1 and 2, would occupy the lowest rank stratum. There may also be some internal gradation of individuals

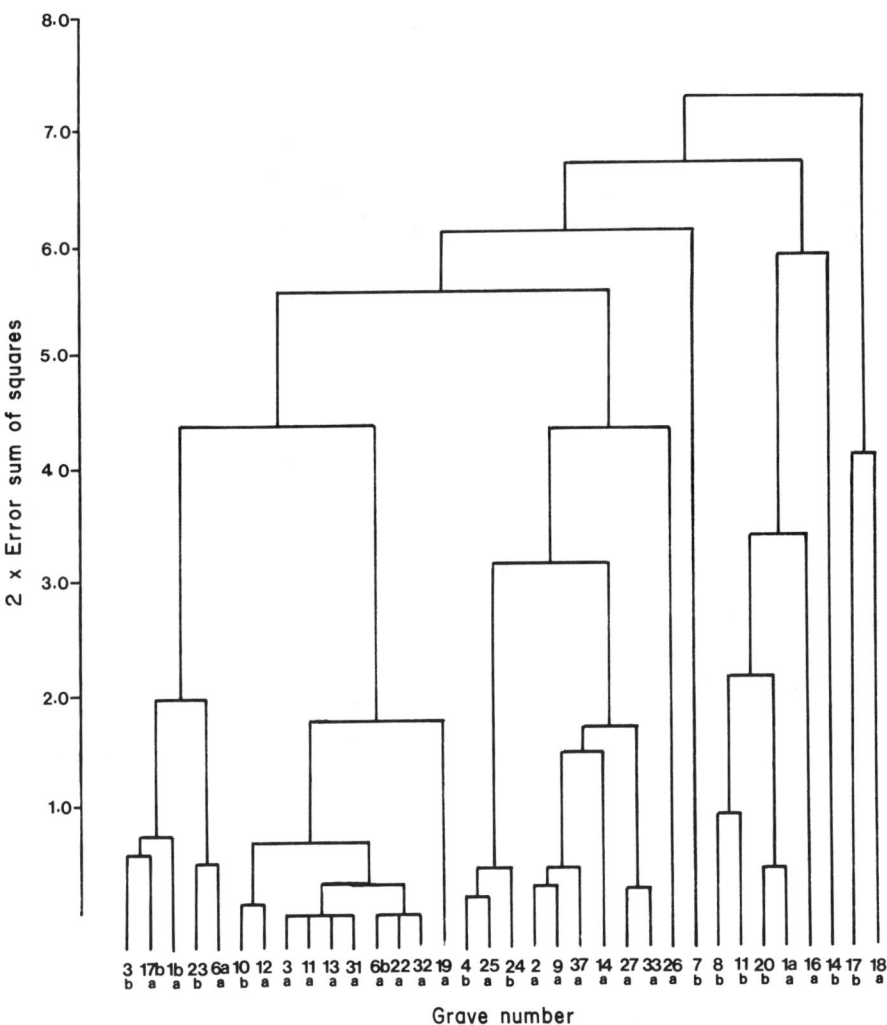

Figure 6.39 Dendrogram produced by the clustering of Big Village factor scores. Burial area is indicated for each case by a letter designation below the grave number: a, 25DK10; b, 25DK2.

236   6. Mortuary Differentiation and Social Distinction

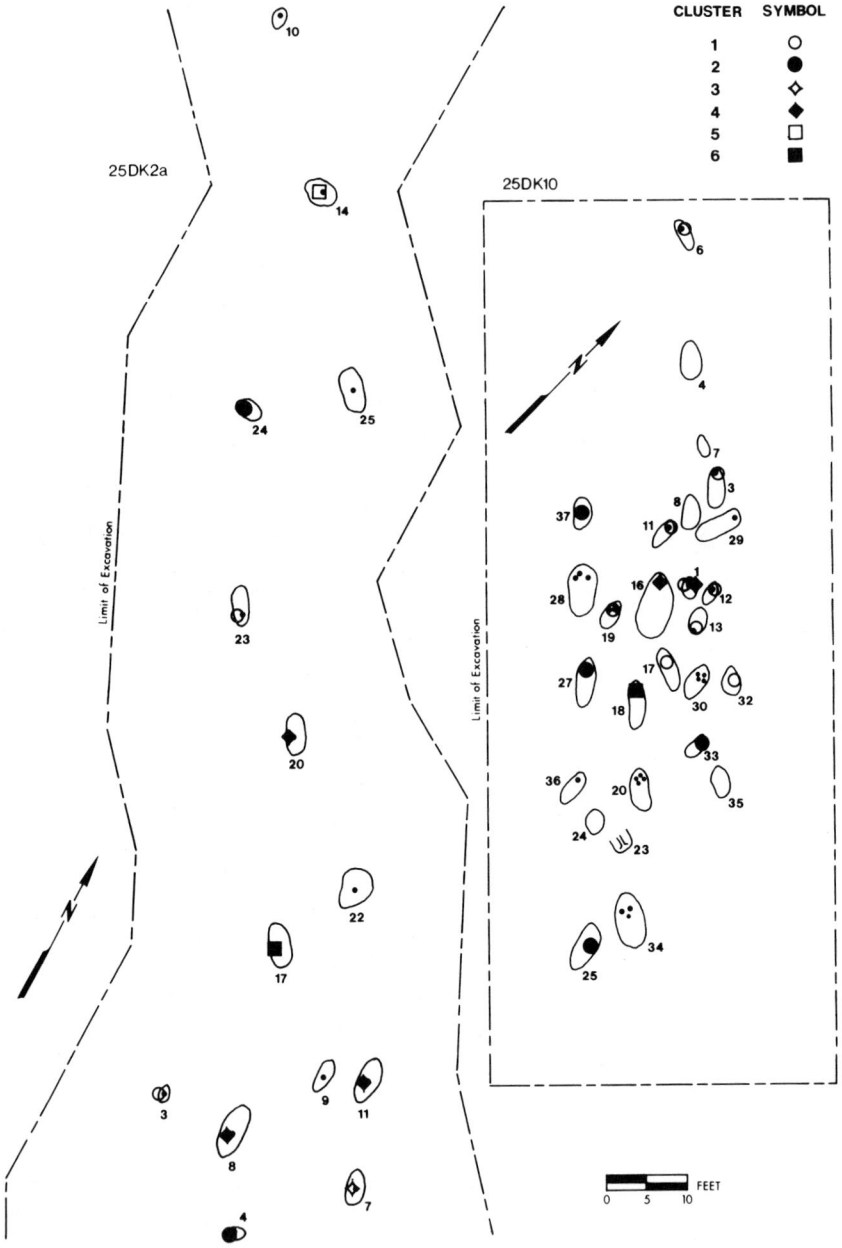

Figure 6.40 Distribution of hierarchical fusion clusters at the Big Village site cemeteries.

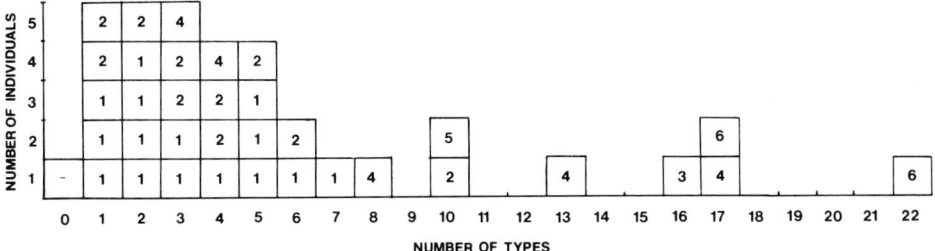

Figure 6.41 Comparison of artifact variety with hierarchical fusion cluster membership at Big Village.

within this lowest group, with members of Cluster 2 occupying a slightly higher level than those of Cluster 1.

These results suggest, not only that both males and females could hold positions of rank, but that two effectively parallel systems of ranking existed, one for each sex. Males could occupy one of three general levels, each of which was characterized by specific symbols and a stereotyped set of mortuary inclusions. Females could occupy one of only two distinct levels, and unlike males, such rank was not designated by specific symbols. Rather, rank among females was expressed through the inclusion of large, although unstructured, quantities of grave goods and through limited "rule breaking" (i.e., by the occurrence of types normally restricted to males). This lack of specific rank symbols for females may indicate the absence of a clearly institutionalized position for important females within the social system, or it might indicate that such rank or wealth was a characteristic that particular females acquired through affinal links rather than through specific ascription.

Monothetic Division Cluster Analysis

Monothetic divisive analysis was performed on all 35 cases in the Omaha sample. The major partitioning of the population was accomplished in three divisions, resulting in four terminal clusters. Table 6.73 presents the diagnostics for the four clusters, and Figure 6.42 plots the spatial distribution of the cluster members in the two burial areas. As the dendrogram (Figure 6.43) illustrates, the first division was made on the presence of wampum beads, a type normally limited in its occurrence to males without age restriction. The second division was made on the occurrence of bird beaks, a type restricted to adult males, and the final division was made on the presence of silver ear ornaments, an adult-associated type. Although the described analysis reflects only the first three divisions of the population, a total of eight divisions were completed. In no case, however, did the group lacking wampum beads (Cluster 2) subdivide.

The cluster results divided the mortuary population both on the basis of gender and on the quantity of grave offerings. Cluster 1 contains only adult males, whereas

TABLE 6.73

Big Village: Monothetic Division Cluster Diagnostics

	Cluster[a]			
	1	2	3	4
Glass bottle	0	1	1	1
Ceramic pot	0	0	0	0
Native glass pendant	0	0	0	0
Animal effigy	0	0	0	0
Glass trade beads	3	12	3	10
Bear claw	0	0	1	0
Animal teeth	1	0	1	1
Bird beak	3	0	0	0
Bird bone	1	0	1	0
Raptor talon	0	0	0	0
Small-mammal cranium	1	0	0	1
Rib shaft wrench	1	0	0	0
Squash knife	0	0	0	0
Scapula hoe	0	0	0	0
Quill flattener	0	0	0	0
Cancellous paint applicator	0	0	0	0
Awl	0	0	0	0
Metatarsal flesher	0	0	0	0
Elk horn scraper	0	0	0	0
Bone/antler implement	0	0	0	0
Gun parts/accessories	2	0	0	1
Pin game cup	1	0	1	0
Polished bone tube	0	0	0	0
Bone pendant	0	0	0	0
Curved rib ornament	0	0	0	0
Bone point	0	0	0	0
Mussel shell	0	0	2	0
Gorget	2	0	0	1
Shell hair pipe	1	1	2	3
Tubular shell bead	0	0	0	0
Wampum bead	3	0	3	10
Heavy shell bead	0	0	0	0
Rectangular shell bead	0	0	0	0
Shell runtee	0	0	0	0
Marine snail shell	0	0	0	0
Perforated shell pendant	0	0	0	0
Flat shell bead	0	0	0	0
Metal bracelet	2	9	2	1
Metal bead/bangle	2	3	2	1
Iron knife	2	0	0	1

TABLE 6.73 *Continued*

	Cluster[a]			
	1	2	3	4
Axe/wedge	1	0	0	0
Scissors	0	0	0	1
Strike-a-light	1	0	0	0
Metal eating implement	0	1	0	0
Small metal hardware	1	0	1	1
Horse gear	0	0	0	0
Small iron tool	0	0	0	0
Metal projectile point	1	0	1	0
Iron scraper	0	0	0	0
Iron digging implement	0	0	0	0
Metal container	1	4	1	3
Metal buckle	0	0	0	1
Finger ring	1	1	2	0
Metal button	2	1	0	2
Large cast brass bell	2	0	0	0
Smaller brass bell	2	0	1	1
Thick wire coil	1	4	0	1
Thin wire coil	3	3	0	1
Metal lace/braid	1	0	0	1
Copper crimp/clip	0	0	0	0
Sheet brass blade	0	0	0	0
Lead ring/coil	1	3	2	1
Lead band	0	3	1	1
Sheet silver bracelet	1	2	2	0
Silver cross	0	0	1	0
Silver hair plate	1	1	1	2
Silver earring	1	0	3	0
Small silver brooch	2	0	0	0
Gunflint	2	0	1	0
Bifacial spear point	0	1	0	0
Scoria abraider	0	0	0	0
Sandstone shaft smoother	1	1	0	0
Whetstone	0	1	0	0
Hammer stone	0	1	0	0
Stone sphere	1	0	0	1
Stone projectile point	0	0	0	0
Stone pipe	1	0	1	0
Petrified wood	0	0	0	0
Retouched flake	0	0	0	0
Unretouched flake	1	2	1	0
Stone knife	0	0	0	0
Plate chalcedony knife	0	0	0	0

(continued)

TABLE 6.73 *Continued*

	Cluster[a]			
	1	2	3	4
Side scraper	0	0	0	0
End scraper	1	0	0	0
Pipestone ornament	0	0	1	0
Gypsum	0	0	0	0

[a] Cluster composition:

Cluster		
1	Number of individuals	3
	Number of males	3
	Number of females	0
	Number of adults	3
	Number of subadults	0
	Cluster members	Dk2: 17; DK10: 16,18
2	Number of individuals	18
	Number of males	2
	Number of females	4
	Number of adults	6
	Number of subadults	11
	Cluster members	DK2: 3,4,20,23,24; DK10: 1a,1b,2,3,9,11,13, 14,25,27,31,33,37
3	Number of individuals	3
	Number of males	1
	Number of females	1
	Number of adults	2
	Number of subadults	1
	Cluster members	DK2: 7,8; DK10: 26
4	Number of individuals	10
	Number of males	2
	Number of females	1
	Number of adults	3
	Number of subadults	7
	Cluster members	DK2: 10,11,14; DK10: 5,6,12,17b,19,22,32

Cluster 2 is composed primarily of adult females and the majority of subadults. Cluster 3 is more difficult to characterize, containing two adults (one male and one female) and a single subadult. The occurrence of the female is perhaps the most significant, since it is one of only two females buried with wampum beads. The fourth cluster is composed of the other female with wampum beads, two adult males and the remaining seven subadults (of which two were disarticulated interments). The relationship between cluster membership and quantity of grave offerings is clearly illustrated in Figure 6.44. Clusters 1 and 3 have a markedly greater number of offerings, whereas Clusters 2 and 4 have distinctly fewer types on the average.

The spatial distribution of the four groups gives no indication of selection operating in cluster location. Cluster members are evenly proportioned between the two burial zones. Neither is there evidence for clustering within either cemetery area.

The Omaha 241

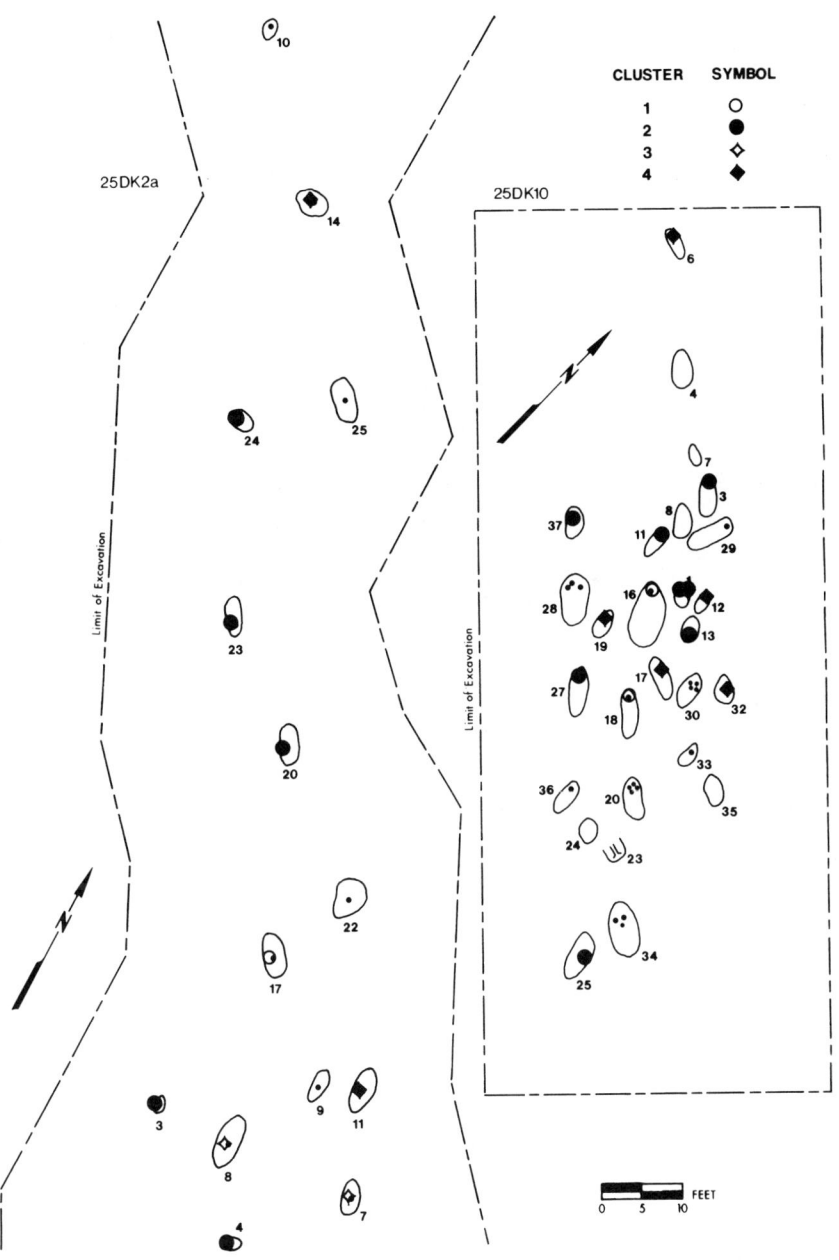

Figure 6.42 Distribution of monothetic division clusters at the Big Village site cemeteries.

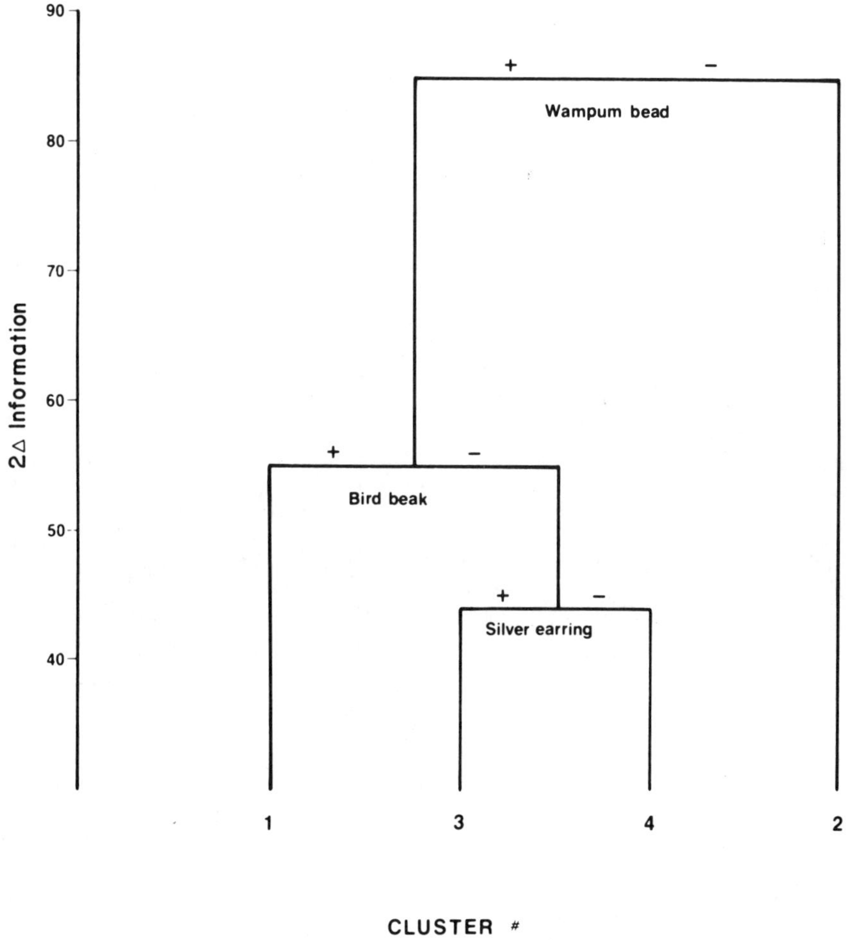

242   6. Mortuary Differentiation and Social Distinction

Figure 6.43 Dendrogram produced by monothetic divisive clustering at the Big Village grave assemblages.

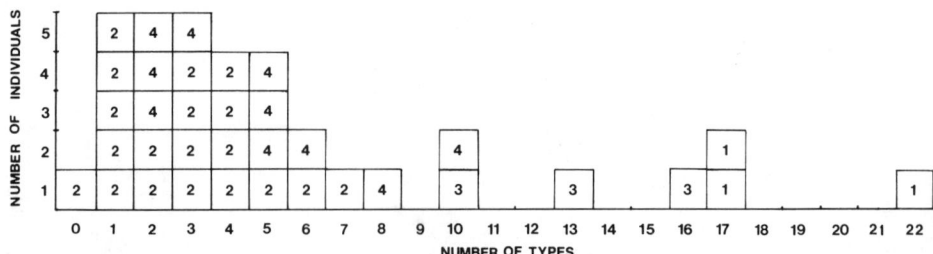

Figure 6.44 Comparison of artifact variety with monothetic divisive cluster membership at Big Village.

The monothetic division results, like those from hierarchical fusion cluster analysis, provide a rank ordering of the mortuary population. The males of Cluster 1 are directly comparable to the high-ranked male cluster in the preceding analysis (F16 at DK10 ranked in the highest cluster here, was the highest of the middle rank in the previous analysis). Cluster 3 contains another ranked male, along with the wealthier of the two ranked females and a subadult. The remaining clusters, however, reflect a different logic. Clusters 2 and 4 contrast not only rank or wealth standing but also gender. All but two of the females in the sample occur in Cluster 2, whereas (excluding ranked males) all but two of the males occur in Cluster 4. Furthermore, these exceptions were treated differently in other ways: both females have a male-restricted ornament (wampum beads), while, of the two males that occur in Cluster 2, one was cremated and the other decapitated. These results again emphasize the lack of a regular or institutionalized means for the expression of high rank among females. The females of high rank appear on the male side of the dendrogram and do not even occur in the same cluster. Overall, the monothetic divisive results might best be viewed as a simplification of the Omaha rank structure, which merges the distinctly separate ranking of males and females onto a single dimensional scale.

One further conclusion can be drawn from these results. Trade goods play a major role in the mortuary symbolism, both as qualitative markers and as indicators of wealth. Given this, the apparent rank ordering of burials also may be an indication of an individual's access to trade. The males of Cluster 1, in addition to their native implements and sociotechnic objects, have by far the greatest number and variety of trade goods (perhaps because of their direct access to the Euroamerican traders). The women and children of Cluster 2 apparently had the least direct access. This seems to suggest a close association between wealth and the Euroamerican trade.

Because of their highly structured use in the Omaha mortuary ritual, artifacts communicated a broad range of social information. Aside from the patterns of occurrence relating to an individual's age and sex, the most common use of grave offerings was as an indicator of each person's rank standing within the population. The nature of this ranking, however, was quite complex and will be considered further in the next section. Artifact usage in the funerary context also highlighted a basic asymmetry in the symbolic designation of male and female roles. The paucity of goods reflecting exclusively female activities and the lack of specific symbols marking rank among females would seem to suggest a male orientation to the social symbolism, at least in the funerary context, which may in turn be a product of the enhanced social importance of trade and warfare to the Omaha of the early nineteenth century.

Big Village Mortuary Differentiation

When mortuary distinctions expressed through treatment and artifact occurrence are considered, a very complex system of mortuary differentiation is apparent. The major elements of mortuary differentiation are presented in Table 6.74.

TABLE 6.74

Big Village: Mortuary Differentiation

Social distinction	Number	Sex	Age	Formal differentiation	Artifact differentiation	Comments
Vertical distinctions						
Achieved wealth						
Upper level	3	Male	Adult		Greatest artifact variety; expensive trade implements and ornaments	
Middle level	7	—	Adult		Quantity of trade ornaments and some implements	One subadult in this category.
Lower level	25	—	—		Few trade items, mainly clothing ornaments	
Elevated social position						
Chiefly office	3	Male	Adult	Burial covering(?)	Multiple sociotechnic objects; Upper wealth level	
Ranked females	2	Female	Adult		Wampum beads in burial assemblage; Middle wealth level	
Horizontal distinctions						
Corporate group (Lineage or clan)	20/60	—	—	Location of burial		
Adult/subadult	26/51	—	—	Grave size	Age-specific artifacts	
Male/female	15/14	—	—		Gender-specific artifacts	
Special status distinctions						
Circumstances of death						
War victim	2	Male	Young adult	Disarticulated burial	Lower wealth level	
?	1	Male	Adult	Cremation	Burial with trophy skulls	
?	1	Male	Adult	Decapitation		
Alternative subadult treatment		—	Subadult	Multiple interment		Probably represents an expedient treatment.

Vertical distinctions among the Omaha were the most complex because of the merging of the upper levels of the political and wealth hierarchy. Despite this, a dimension of achieved wealth was identified, along with a series of other elevated social positions.

Wealth, in terms of the type and quantity of grave offerings, divided the population into three distinct levels. The uppermost level was occupied solely by adult or mature males who possessed the greatest quantities of expensive trade implements and ornaments. The second level was composed of both males and females (along with a single subadult) who were buried with quantities of trade ornaments and some trade implements. The lowest wealth category included individuals with modest grave assemblages, composed primarily of small inexpensive clothing ornaments, such as glass beads. Both males and females, along with the majority of subadults, occurred in this category.

The second vertical dimension is consistent with the definition of a chiefly office. Only adult or mature males held this position. It was marked by the occurrence of many sociotechnic objects, particularly bird beaks, and by grave assemblages of the highest wealth level. In addition, the graves of all these individuals were covered by wood or bark coverings (although the actual meaning of burial coverings in the Omaha mortuary symbolism remains unclear). The importance of bird beaks in the denotation of this position is significant, as they were one important symbolic element in the Omaha calumet ceremony (O'Shea et al. 1982), stressing again the relationship between trade activities and rank among the Omaha.

The coincident distribution of native goods and sociotechnic objects with the greatest quantities of trade materials, as seen in these chiefly assemblages, seems to highlight a close correspondence between social standing and personal wealth. Yet, since personal wealth was apparently so dependent on participation in the Euroamerican trade, it must have placed serious and unequal constraints on the ability of various members of the population to acquire wealth. For this reason, personal wealth cannot be considered a purely achieved social distinction. At least among the males of the population, there was a close correspondence between an individual's social standing and his personal wealth, with the former perhaps tending to determine the latter. This assertion is supported by the fact that wealth, as measured in quantity of grave goods, was not distributed continuously across the population, but rather occurred in discrete levels.

The richness of the grave assemblages also expressed qualitative rank distinctions in the context of a female or subadult grave. Grave assemblages of one (and possibly two) subadults from the middle wealth level were observed. Since it is unlikely that the goods were accumulated by these individuals, their occurrence introduces a qualitative and ascriptive aspect to the status. It also seems to indicate that both wealth and social standing were influenced by ascribed as well as achieved elements.

A similar argument can be made for the ranking observed among females. The difference between the two ranked females and the rest of the female population is qualitative; they possessed a distinctly greater quantity of grave goods, and they possessed types that normally were limited in their occurrence to males. The absence of any specific symbolic markers associated with female rank is curious, however, and indeed, female rank was marked in much the same way as it was among subadults. The explanation for this pattern may well be found again in the relationship between participation in trade activities and rank. Neither females nor subadults were in a position to participate directly in the wealth acquisition process, and as a result, their social standing may have been acquired through kinship ties. In the case of subadults, this was certainly through the family, but for females, it may have come through either consanguinal or affinal ties. If this were the case, the two ranked females would presumably be sisters or wives of ranked males.

In all, we are left with a very complex set of overlapping vertical dimensions, with wealth among males as a primarily achieved distinction (although strongly linked with social standing) and wealth as a primarily ascribed or acquired marker of rank among females and subadults. The merging of symbols for rank and wealth observed at Big Village almost certainly obscures a finer level of symbolic detail, such as might express distinct ritual offices or other special prestige positions. The tendency for these markers to converge on the high-ranked males makes their separate significance indistinguishable from the symbols marking the high office.

Horizontal distinctions symbolized at the Big Village marked age and sex categories and corporate group membership. Males were differentiated from females on the basis of sex-specific artifacts. Adults were differentiated from subadults by grave size and depth, by age-specific artifact types, and by the greater likelihood that subadults would be included in multiple interments.

The use of distinct burial areas at Big Village seems to distinguish corporate group membership. This division appears to qualify as a true horizontal distinction, given the even distribution of age and sex categories between the two areas and the tendency of other social distinctions to crosscut this spatial boundary. No aspect of funerary treatment or artifact occurrence was significantly associated with one or the other burial area. In size and demographic structure, this division most probably is representative of distinct clans or lineages among the Omaha.

Although not statistically significant, the occurrence of both stone pipes and the two ranked females (but not the ranked subadult) at DK2a may be indicative of wealth and prerogative differences that existed between the two corporate groups. Without further samples for comparison, however, it is difficult to test this possibility. The limited distribution of pipes will be discussed further in the consideration of ethnographic observations on Omaha mortuary practices.

A great variety of special status distinctions were observed at the Big Village cemeteries. The disarticulated burial of two young adult males is likely indicative of the special circumstances of death—in this case, as victims of warfare. It seems most likely that the state of the corpse was the result of the well-known practice of dismembering war victims (see Chapter 5). If this were the case, these individuals represent Omaha war dead whose remains have been recovered for burial. These individuals had grave assemblages of the lowest rank level, primarily clothing ornamentation. The remaining two examples of alternative treatment, although clearly reflecting special status distinctions, cannot be adequately interpreted on the basis of present evidence. The cremation burial, along with its complement of trophy skulls and a red-painted horse skull may reflect a multistaged and time-consuming alternative treatment. Since considerable effort was expended in the burial, and since it was included within the community's cemetery area, it is unlikely that it represents the burial of a social deviant, although there is little evidence as to the actual nature of the distinction expressed.

A third special treatment, seen in Feature 25 from 25DK10, is similarly ambiguous. This individual appears to have died a violent death, with the corpse being selectively mutilated and dismembered. The individual was then interred with a large spear point. Although this represents a unique case within the Omaha sample, a similar pattern of treatment is known from the Larson site. This treatment, like the instance of cremation, cannot be further clarified.

A final category of special status distinction was the expedient treatment of subadult interment expressed as multiple burial. The frequency with which this occurred at Big Village suggests it to have been the norm for subadult burial, and as such, it would qualify as an aspect of adult–subadult differentiation. It is included as a special status distinction to maintain a consistency of description with the other sites analyzed.

When these mortuary distinctions are considered together, vertical differentiation was expressed almost solely through the composition of the burial assemblage, whereas horizontal differences and special status distinctions tended to be expressed through mortuary treatment. Only the primary demographic distinctions were expressed through channels of both treatment and assemblage composition.

Omaha Results

Archaeological Reconstructions

The results of archaeological analysis on the Big Village samples are in close agreement with the vertical features of Omaha social organization, although they fall short of characterizing the known variety of horizontal elements structuring the society. A comparison of those features recognized through archaeological analysis with the known principal elements of Omaha social organization is presented in Table 6.75.

Vertical social distinctions were recognized with considerable success, missing only ritual offices and special prestige categories. The merging of social rank and wealth hierarchies at the upper level and the connection of both with the Euroamerican trade is particularly interesting and is considered in the next chapter. This merging of distinctions at the upper end of the social scale may also be responsible for the invisibility of distinct ritual offices and prestige positions. The lack of specific symbols of rank for females is consistent with the ethnographic descriptions of male and female roles among the Omaha. That ranking among both

TABLE 6.75

Omaha: Comparison of Ethnographic and Archaeological Observations of Mortuary Differentiation

Type of differentiation	Source of observations		
	Ethnographic		Archaeological
	Society	Mortuary	Big Village
Vertical			
Chiefly office	+	+	+
Achieved wealth	+	+	+
Hereditary ascription	+	+	+
Ritual office	+	—	—
Special prestige position	+	—	—
Horizontal			
Moiety membership	+	—	—
Clan membership	+	+	+(?)
Patrilineal residence/descent	+	—	—
Society membership	+	+	—
Male/female	+	+	+
Adult/subadult	+	+	+
Special status			
Circumstance of death	+	+	+
Social deviant	+	+	—
Alternative subadult treatments	+	+	+
Other	+	—	+

females and subadults should be expressed in this qualitative form is also consistent with the strongly hierarchical character of Omaha social organization, marking kinship with a powerful male rather than rank or privilege in the individual's own right. In all, rank and wealth were so strongly interrelated in the Omaha mortuary ritual that any attempt to describe them separately is somewhat artificial.

Horizontal social distinctions were much more ambiguous in their archaeological expression. Beyond basic age and sex differences, only corporate group membership, suggested by the distinct burial areas, could be identified. Even here, the identification is somewhat speculative, in terms of the type of horizontal distinction actually represented. It further provides no demonstrable evidence for specifically patrilineal descent or residence.

A variety of special status distinctions were observed at the Big Village. While disarticulated burial probably reflected the circumstances of death (in this case war victims), cremation and decapitation cannot be satisfactorily interpreted given the present sample. The fact that both occurred in the community cemetery and in association with grave offerings does seem to suggest that these individuals were not social deviants. The alternative treatment for subadults probably represents a simple expedient in dealing with the remains of the young and may well correlate with a relatively high level of infant mortality at Big Village.

Although the overall agreement between known structural elements of the society and the archaeological reconstruction is good, the archaeological analysis was unable to detect the main horizontal features of Omaha society. As with the Pawnee, the size of the mortuary sample was small, and it is unlikely that a complete representation of the mortuary population was recovered for analysis. This sample problem poses great difficulty for the detection of horizontal social elements, since relative size and contrast sets are the only identifying features of most horizontal distinctions. If more burial areas had been discovered, for example, it might have been possible to determine whether these areas reflected lineage or clan groups, and perhaps also to determine the nature of interaction between these social units. The distribution of pipes in the cemetery areas (limited to DK2a) is, however, suggestive. Fletcher and LaFlesche (1911:147) note that pipe ownership was limited to the members of the Inkecabe clans.

Further consideration of the ethnographic documentation of Omaha mortuary treatment is presented in the next section.

Ethnographic Accounts of Omaha Mortuary Practices

The ethnographic accounts available for Omaha mortuary customs are unusually detailed because a member of the Omaha tribe was responsible for much of the ethnography. The account of horizontal differentiation documents one aspect of mortuary distinction that was not recognized by archaeological analysis: secret society membership. Ethnographic reports did not record differentiation due to residence or descent groups, nor did they document any differentiation associated with moiety membership. Accounts of vertical differentiation were equally detailed. Only two categories were not mentioned: special prestige positions and ritual offices, both of which were also invisible in archaeological analysis. The ethnographic accounts also provide examples of special status distinctions, including both treatment of deviants and treatments elicited as a result of unusual death circumstances, such as death by lightning (see Chapter 5). Although these classes of special status distinction are observed both ethnographically and archaeologically, the specific distinctions noted were different. This suggests that a much wider variety of special status distinctions was recognized in Omaha mortuary custom than was reflected in either the archaeological or ethnographic record. It is also interesting to note that archaeological analysis identified a range of special status distinctions that had not been documented in Omaha ethnography.

Overall, the results of archaeological and ethnographic analyses of Omaha mortuary differentiation are similar. Although ethnography in this case provides a more detailed view of horizontal social differentiation, neither data source provided a complete representation of the major structural elements.

Discussion

This chapter has assessed the reliability of social inferences based on the archaeological analysis of mortuary patterning. Each of the previous sections has described specific findings, and these results are now compared and the implications they have for archaeological mortuary analysis in general are considered.

The primary result of these tests is to demonstrate that accurate social reconstructions can be obtained from mortuary data. A wide variety of social categories were recognized through archaeological analysis, and in no case were social features identified in the mortuary sample that did not exist in the living society. Although the overall fit between the ethnographic and archaeological reconstructions was good, it was not uniformly so for all types of social differentiation. Vertical social distinctions were detected most successfully. Not only were positions of chiefly rank and achieved wealth recognized, but finer levels of special rank and prestige also were detected in several cases. More detailed analysis at sites such as Larson could no doubt reveal an even finer level of rank organization than has been presented here.

The detection of horizontal distinctions was less successful. Although simple age and sex differences were ascertained, large-scale horizontal distinctions were not found or could be identified only tentatively in the archaeological analysis. In no case was the society's system of descent or postmarital residence identified. Indeed, were it not for the frequent use of distinct burial areas as a marker for horizontal subdivisions, virtually no higher-order distinctions would have been recognized.

A number of special status distinctions also were identified. Some of these corresponded with practices known from ethnohistorical sources, whereas for others, no ethnographic precedent could be found. The relative completeness of these observations cannot, however, be assessed on the basis of present evidence. In all, these findings demonstrate that realistic social reconstructions can be obtained using funerary evidence. They suggest, however, that certain forms of social differentiation are more likely to be observed than others. To understand these results, it will be necessary to look in more detail at how each class of mortuary differentiation was recognized archaeologically and at the specific problems encountered during this process.

As was outlined in Chapter 3, the expected configuration of referent values for a vertical distinction include a skewed age or sex distribution, a hierarchical-type pyramid of frequency, and differential expenditure of energy in the treatment and/or in the goods placed with the deceased. In the present study, the detection of this type of attribute configuration was not difficult. One common feature of these data sets was that major differences in energy expended in the mortuary treatment or burial facility were observed only rarely. Instead, vertical distinctions were marked by the type and variety of goods interred with the deceased. Despite the relative success in the detection of vertical differentiation, several complications were encountered. These complications shed further light on the cultural and archaeological processes that affect the identification of vertical differentiation.

The ability to recognize special positions of enhanced prestige and ritual offices was dependent on the degree to which the upper levels of the society's rank and economic hierarchies were merged. In the present study, the extremes were represented at the Big Village and Larson sites. At Larson, the prestige and wealth hierarchies were relatively distinct, resulting in the recognition of numerous special prestige markers that had varying degrees of independence from the individual's wealth standing. This is contrasted with the situation at the Big Village, where the upper levels of rank and wealth were nearly completely merged. In this case it was not possible to isolate independent markers of prestige, even though such positions are known to have existed among the Omaha. The conclusion seems to be that the more positions of wealth and rank within a society are overlapped or merged, the less likely is it that the specialized prestige positions will be recognized in an archaeological study. Even if the markers themselves are plainly visible, it will not be possible to demonstrate their *independent* symbolic significance.

A second difficulty in the analysis of vertical distinctions related to the concept of "achieved wealth." A category of differentiation identified as achieved wealth was recognized in each of the six sites considered in this study. Yet in no instance did the demographic distribution of the respective wealth levels exactly match the pattern expected for a truly achieved status. Invariably, one or more infants or subadults were found with a grave assemblage that could not reflect their personal achievement. The extremes were seen at the Leavenworth site, where a large number of subadults were buried with upper-wealth-level assemblages, and at the Big Village, where a single subadult possessed an anomalously elaborate grave assemblage. Clearly, there frequently is a degree of blending between the achievement or wealth of an individual and that of the primary social unit to which he belongs, be it family, lineage, or clan. The degree to which this occurs no doubt varies from culture to culture and does not invalidate the overall achieved character of the distinction. In the Omaha case, the deliberately elaborate assemblage was used as a qualitative social marker. The richness of the assemblage implied not achieved wealth, but rather signified the qualitative uniqueness of this particular child (a similar symbolism was used to mark females of high rank).

This is an example of the use of "rule breaking" as a symbolic device. Although this use is precedented and logically consistent with Omaha mortuary symbolism, the same type of occurrence could arise as the result of solely idiosyncratic behavior. The Leavenworth pattern is characteristic of a situation with a high degree of status blending—that is, where the relative standing of the primary social unit (probably the extended family in this case) was expressed in the burial of all its members. This is not to say that individual achievement was not expressed—it clearly was—but that a base level of wealth, representing the social unit, was expressed regardless of this.

As a dimension of mortuary differentiation, it still reflects achieved wealth, but it reflects the achievement of the family or social unit as well as the achievement of the individual. It might well be argued that among adults, one views primarily individual achievement, whereas among subadults, one sees primarily the wealth of families.

Variation in the expression of achieved wealth, or any achieved-type status, may provide valuable insight into the overall organization of the society at large, but it must also caution that the real-life configuration of referent values or other mortuary symbols may not exactly coincide with the idealized models of such social dimensions. The Omaha example also highlights the potential problems that idiosyncratic variation in mortuary treatment can produce.

The detection of vertical differentiation was successful because it was expressed in forms that were readily visible to archaeological investigation. The complications that did arise tended to be problems of discrimination: of isolating unique, yet related, kinds of vertical differentiation. The success or failure of this discrimination in the various cases was influenced both by the limitations of archaeological detection and recognition and by specific social characteristics of the living societies that produced the cemeteries. Similar interactions were encountered in the analysis of horizontal and special status distinctions as well.

The search for horizontal differentiation employs an entirely different configuration of referent variables. Distinctions of this type are expected to exhibit a natural rather than a skewed demographic composition. They also should be marked through symbols or treatments that are of equal energy intensity. A particularly common means for signifying distinctions of this type is through spatial segregation. In practice, the recognition of horizontally differentiated units depends on the identification of mutually exclusive sets of symbols or treatments that isolate two or more equal-sized groups of individuals with normal demographic compositions. In the present study, the success of such identification was limited, even in instances where such social subdivisions were known to have been differentiated in the mortuary ritual. This lack of success can be related to difficulties in the identification of these contrastive sets of symbols and treatments.

The mortuary symbolism of the Omaha clan distinction provides a clear example of the potential problems encountered in the identification of horizontal social subdivisions. Clan membership of the deceased was symbolized in the following manner: "It will be recalled that the sign of the tabu was put on the dead in order that they might be recognized by their relatives, as on the feet of a dead member of the We'zhi^n shte gens, moccasins made from the skin of a male elk to whom before his death the animal was tabu" (Fletcher and LaFlesche 1911:589). Additional clan-level distinctions were expressed through hairstyle and designs painted on the face. Although these treatments are exactly the type of nonvaluable markers that theory predicts, they all have a very low potential for archaeological recovery. Although this suggests why analysis of this type did not clearly identify Omaha clans, it may also suggest factors that are likely to affect all archaeological investigations.

Since horizontal distinctions are not expected to have skewed demographic compositions or obvious differences in the value or effort expended in their symbolic designation, their detection is entirely dependent on the proper identification of the symbolic contrasts that exist between the subdivisions. This means that the archaeological detection of horizontal distinctions is particularly sensitive to any factor that influences the recovery or interpretation of the symbolic markers.

In the Omaha example, it is obvious that none of the markers were of a type that would normally be preserved for archaeological recovery. Yet, even if only a few of the clan symbols were perishable, the distinction might still be unrecognized, since the contrastive configuration of symbols would be incomplete and, in all probability, uninterpretable. The very requirement that such symbols or treatments be nonvaluable (in the sense of not elevating one subdivision above another) may mean that such symbols will more frequently be of types that will not preserve archaeologically. Symbolism reflected through the disposition of the body or by grave location offer greater hope for recovery, although in the present cases, body disposition was not employed in this manner.

Even if a horizontal marker is recovered, it must be correctly interpreted. Unlike the exotic and valuable tokens that denote positions of rank, the tokens that mark horizontal categories should be common and locally derived. Such tokens may be very difficult to isolate from the background of other grave inclusions. Even if a series of mutually exclusive artifact distributions are observed, it is still not certain that they have resulted from the marking of a horizontal social distinction, as opposed to some other random process. This was the problem encountered in the present analyses. In several instances, multiple interment areas were found, each with normal demographic parameters, that were tentatively identified as representing differentiated horizontal categories. Yet the confidence associated with these determinations was limited, since the distinctions lacked any other markers that paralleled the spatial division. In the absence of such redundant evidence, it is difficult to place great confidence in such a determination, even though the very nature of the symbols used to mark these distinctions makes it unlikely that a high level of redundancy will be observed.

The results of the present analyses do not suggest that horizontal differences are less likely to be given expression through a culture's mortuary practices. Rather, they suggest that it is the very nature of archaeological detection and recognition that limits the identification of such horizontal distinctions. It has been argued that the correct recognition of horizontal distinctions is more sensitive to the decay or misinterpretation of their symbolic markers, and that the very nature of the markers makes them less likely both to survive the process of archaeological deposition and to be recognized as significant symbolic markers even when recovered. In a real sense, the very factors that work to make vertical differentiation obvious tend to make horizontal differences ambiguous. This does not mean that major horizontal distinctions cannot be recovered from mortuary evidence, as indeed even the present cases illustrate that they can. These results rather argue that horizontal differences are less likely to be recognized, other things being equal. The failure to observe categories of horizontal differentiation in a given mortuary complex therefore does not necessarily indicate the absence of such features from the living society. These results do suggest, however, that the study of horizontal social subdivisions will, in most cases, be pursued most profitably in contexts other than funerary remains.

Special status distinctions have the least regular configuration of referent attributes, but are recognized by their low level of occurrence and effort expenditure and by their nonnormative character. In the analysis of the Plains cemeteries, a number of distinctions of this type were recognized. Several aspects of such statuses, however, limit their archaeological detection and interpretation. First, from ethnographic evidence it is obvious that certain kinds of special status distinctions cannot be recognized, since they involve mortuary disposal in a location other than the corporate cemetery. In some instances, these alternative treatments may be discovered during the course of other archaeological research, such as in the excavation of village areas. Other forms, such as treatments for social deviants, often either will not be found or, if discovered, may not be correctly associated with a local mortuary complex (see discussion in Chapter 3).

A second series of limitations in the identification of special status distinctions relates to their low incidence. One such limitation is the difficulty of distinguishing special status differentiation from wholly idiosyncratic behavior. Another is the stochastic effect that may cause a rarely occurring category of differentiation to be present or absent in cemeteries produced by the same community. Finally, even if a special status distinction is correctly identified, its meaning will often be indeterminable. The very uniqueness and abnormality of such statuses limit their interpretability. Thus, many of the differentiated special status distinctions recognized in the analysis of the Plains cemeteries could only be identified as probably relating to death circumstances. The ethnographic accounts of special status differentiation—particularly those of the Pawnee, which relate primarily to social deviants (see Chapter 5)—suggest that a strong idiosyncratic element is often involved in such treatments. If true, this would further obscure any culturally relevant interpretation of the mortuary treatment.

The present studies demonstrate that archaeological analysis frequently can identify special status differentiation within a mortuary population. At the same time, they suggest that it is unlikely that archaeological investigations can ever recover the complete set of special status distinctions actually employed by a society. It also appears that in many cases it will not be possible to determine the more precise meaning or significance of such statuses.

The contrast between ethnographic accounts of funerary treatment and the evidence for such treatment recovered from the archaeological record has also been considered. These results are of particular interest, since ethnographic data of this kind has played a major role in the development of archaeological mortuary theory (see Chapter 1).

The results of the present tests suggest that ethnographic accounts of funerary practice may often underrepresent the differential aspects of a culture's mortuary treatment, while describing in accurate terms the complex of normative treatments. When differential aspects of burial custom were described, they tended to focus on vertical (rank) distinctions (i.e., the elaborate treatment of important persons). Indeed, much of the documentation for special status differentiation was found, not in the formal ethnographies, but rather in folktales that recounted such treatments (see Chapter 5). Although these findings may not hold true for every ethnographic case, they argue for extreme caution in the use of massed ethnographic accounts of funerary custom as a source for new regularities in mortuary treatment.

This chapter has demonstrated that details of social organization can accurately be inferred through an analysis of mortuary differentiation. Reconstruction was most successful in the identification of rank differentiation, although horizontal and special status distinctions were also recognized. From this starting point, two further questions relating to mortuary variability and social reconstruction remain to be considered: What is the nature of temporal variation in funerary practices and its effect on social reconstruction? and, To what extent are ethnic boundaries distinguishable through funerary custom?

7
Temporal Variation in Mortuary Practices

Introduction

The previous chapter addressed the question of whether reliable social reconstructions can be obtained from an archaeological analysis of mortuary patterning. These results now form the basis for a consideration of temporal change and its effect on such archaeological reconstructions. This chapter first discusses the classes of change that may occur in a mortuary complex through time and explores the potential constraints or systematic aspects of such change. The Plains cemetery analyses from Chapter 6 are then employed as a source both for examples and, to a limited extent, for the investigation of the cause and explanation of change.

Variation in the organization and content of a society's funerary treatment program can be summarized in terms of two basic types of change: the manner in which a particular distinction is expressed through the funerary ritual, or the social positions that are marked or emphasized in the ritual.

Variation in the symbolic expression of social distinctions may arise as a result of a wide variety of factors. In general, however, such variation takes one of three basic forms: (1) the markers may change as a result of conscious design by the living; (2) they may vary due to alteration in the overall inventory of material culture; or (3) the markers may effectively change as a result of variation in the consistency with which the proscriptive and prescriptive conventions of funerary treatment are applied by the living.

Such change typically is the result of complex social, ideological, and environmental interactions that can be understood only in the context of the society as a whole and its social environment. Although change in mortuary symbolism of this kind offers considerable potential for the sociological study of past cultures, such studies require knowledge of the society at large and cannot be realistically evaluated using mortuary data alone.

Change in the array of social distinctions given symbolic recognition in the mortuary program would seem to be more directly indicative of fundamental alterations in both the funerary program and in the society. In instances where there is an increase in the number of recognized positions, archaeological inference is probably on its most secure ground. Change of this type is often associated with an increase in the structural complexity of the living society. Such alterations can, however, be produced by factors that have no bearing on social organization whatsoever. This potential was well illustrated in the analysis of the Larson site, where the gradual replacement of bead types gave the appearance of a superficially large number of social categories. Similarly, change in the tokens or treatments used to mark a given distinction might produce either an increase or a decrease in the apparent number of differentiated categories, depending on their relative archaeological visibility. Stochastic factors also may influence the apparent number of social categories symbolized, particularly in small samples. Since a number of differentiated social categories have a relatively low level of incidence (particularly special status distinctions), they may or may not be represented in a given sample. As such, even if no change occurs in the structure of mortuary differentiation practiced by a given society, the number of differentiated categories may vary between cemeteries.

Situations in which the number of distinctions appear to decrease through time are fraught with even greater ambiguity. Such change may be a consequence of decreasing social complexity. Alternatively, it could reflect a change in social emphasis, stressing other arenas for the display and legitimization of social standing, or a change in attitude toward the treatment of the dead or the ancestors. Since differentiation in death is consistent but not isomorphic with social differentiation in life, systems of mortuary treatment can be greatly simplified without any necessary change in the structure of the living society. In addition to these potentially confounding cultural factors, such observations also are vulnerable to the same range of archaeologically based distortions mentioned in connection with the recognition of increased differentiation. This does not mean that processes of simplification or collapse cannot be studied using mortuary evidence, only that such evidence must be used in conjunction with other classes of information relevant to social change.

This brief discussion of change in funerary practices has attempted to identify only the broad categories of change that might be recognized in an archaeological sequence. It has not addressed the questions of the likelihood or rate of change through time. In the following sections, the specific changes observed in the mortuary practices of the Plains Village groups are examined. Two trajectories are considered: change among the Arikara, spanning some 60 years between the abandonment of the Larson site around 1740 and the founding of the Leavenworth site in 1800, and change in Pawnee funerary practices over a period of some 70 years. The

Pawnee series is of particular interest because it includes three samples in sequence: Barcal (abandoned around 1750), Linwood (1777–1809), and Clarks (1820–1845). Each series is considered separately, and then they are compared and discussed in light of historical knowledge of the tribes during this time period.

It should be stressed that it is not possible in this chapter (and the next) to treat archaeological and ethnohistorical evidence as independent domains of information. Instead, such evidence is combined in a complementary fashion, with ethnohistory providing a background against which archaeological patterning or change can be understood. The degree to which such explanations can be generalized is limited, but the analysis of cause-and-effect relationships in these case studies may provide insight useful to the formulation of more general principles of change.

Pawnee Variation in Social Distinction and Symbolic Representation

The sequence of Pawnee cemeteries provides an ideal basis for the investigation of change in mortuary patterning, particularly for documenting the consistency and directionality of such variation. Although change is observed in virtually every aspect of Pawnee funerary custom, the overall impression gained from these sites is one of stability through time. This is all the more surprising given the small size of the three cemeteries analyzed. This section first describes changes in the social categories that were differentiated in the mortuary ritual and the means by which these categories were symbolized. This is followed by a consideration of material culture in Pawnee funerary practices.

No aspect of Pawnee mortuary custom was immune to change. At the most general level, variation was observed in the social categories represented in the funerary complex (Table 7.1). In most instances, this change was directional, representing the gradual phasing in (or out) of a given element of mortuary differentiation. In the Pawnee sequence, the most common pattern was for a new element of mortuary differentiation to be adopted through time. Examples of this pattern included the increased wealth differentiation of the population, the marking of a ritual office independent of personal wealth, special funerary treatment for individuals whose remains were not recovered for burial, and the expedient treatment of subadults. This pattern was reversed in the marking of social society membership, which, although present in the earliest site, was not distinguished at the later sites.

One additional example of change was not directional. The marking of corporate group membership was distinguished at both the youngest and oldest site, but was absent at Linwood. Although this nontrending pattern may accurately reflect a short-term shift in Pawnee mortuary differentiation, such a change might also be an

TABLE 7.1

Pawnee: Social Categories Represented in the Funerary Complex

Social categories	Barcal	Linwood	Clarks
Vertical distinctions			
Chiefly office	+	+	+
		(male, adult)	(male, adult)
Achieved wealth	Two levels	Three levels	Three levels
Hereditary ascription	—	+	+
Ritual office			
(a)	—	Male	—
(b)	—	—	Adult
Horizontal distinctions			
Corporate group	+	—	+
Society membership	+	—	—
Male/female	?	+	+
Adult/subadult	+	+	+
Special status distinctions			
Circumstances of death			
(a) Location or time of death	+	+	+
(b) Remains not recovered	—	+	+
Alternative subadult treatments	—	—	+

artifact of archaeological analysis. The apparent absence of corporate groups at Linwood is a good case in point. At both Barcal and Clarks, such units were distinguished by the occurrence of discrete spatial groupings of burials. At Linwood, similar discrete burial areas were observed. The areas, however, correlated strongly with a dimension of wealth. These observations allow two alternative explanations: (1) corporate group membership was not differentiated in the Linwood funerary treatment; or (2) corporate groups were marked, but by treatments not recognized in the archaeological analysis. This second alternative includes the possibility that wealth and corporate group membership became closely associated, with the result that the more visible vertical dimension (see discussion in Chapter 6) masked the horizontal component. If the first possibility is correct, it would suggest that corporate group membership was being deemphasized in Pawnee society but that such a trend was short lived. It would still be necessary to explain the nontrending shift in the symbolic use of separate burial areas. If the latter alternative is correct, the shift in mortuary symbolism or the connection between corporate group membership and wealth would require further explanation.

The symbolic designation of social categories remained relatively constant throughout the Pawnee sequence. The variation that was observed tended to follow the basic temporal themes already discussed (Table 7.2).

The major normative aspects of funerary treatment remained constant throughout

TABLE 7.2

Pawnee: Social Category Designation

Social categories	Barcal	Linwood	Clarks
Normative treatment	Flexed posture Wood covering Westward orientation	Flexed posture	Flexed posture Wood covering Northward orientation
Vertical distinctions			
Wealth	Artifact variety Implements versus ornaments	Artifact variety Expensive trade goods Some spatial segregation	Artifact variety Expensive trade goods
Chiefly rank	Pipe ownership Upper wealth level Mussel shell society member	Pipe ownership Upper wealth level Extended posture Spatial segregation	Pipe ownership Upper wealth level
Ritual office		Pipe ownership	Bird beak ownership
Horizontal distinctions			
Corporate group	Grave location		Grave location
Society membership	Mussel shell		
Adult/subadult	Grave size and depth Age-specific types	Grave size Age-specific types	Grave size Age-specific types
Male/female	?	Sex-specific types Grave orientation	Sex-specific types
Special status distinctions			
Circumstances of death	Disarticulated burial Skull-only burial Nonnormative orientation	Disarticulated burial	Disarticulated burial Nonnormative orientation
Remains not recovered		Symbolic grave	Symbolic grave
Alternative subadult treatment			Extended burial posture

the Pawnee sequence and included an emphasis on primary, single inhumation; use of a flexed burial posture; and disarticulated interment as an alternative burial program. Yet, variation was observed in other aspects of normative treatment. The use of a consistent pattern of grave orientation was not maintained at the three sites. At Barcal and Clarks the graves were uniformly oriented, although in different directions (Barcal toward the west, Clarks toward the north), whereas at Linwood there was the suggestion of a sex-specific orientation of graves (males toward the northwest, females toward the southeast).

A second possible change involved the use of wood burial coverings. These small funerary structures appeared to have been part of the normative treatment at both Barcal and Clarks. In contrast, their less-frequent occurrence and their tendency to occur with wealthy grave assemblages suggests that burial coverings may have functioned as a form of mortuary elaboration at the Linwood site.

These results indicate that, although normative treatment was relatively stable, aspects could and did vary, even over short periods of time. A similar pattern of change was observed in the marking of differential social categories.

Only a low level of variation was observed in the symbols used to mark major categories of social differentiation. Wealth was expressed through the variety and value of goods interred with the dead. Not only did the wealthier individuals have the greatest variety of grave goods, but their assemblages also tended to be composed of expensive objects and often lacked more commonly occurring artifact types. This tendency is well illustrated in the consistent dichotomy between ornaments and implements, particularly among trade goods. At Linwood there also was evidence for the spatial segregation of wealthier individuals, a feature not observed elsewhere.

Chiefly rank, likewise, was expressed through a common symbolism at all these sites: burial with a stone pipe and a grave assemblage characteristic of the uppermost wealth category. Beyond this, additional elaboration varied from site to site. At Barcal, chiefs were also members of a social society that was symbolized by the occurrence of a mussel shell, and at Linwood, chiefs were interred in an extended burial posture.

Additional rank offices were observed at Clarks and Linwood, although their structure and symbolic markers were distinct. At Linwood, the position was marked by burial with a stone pipe, but without the wealth or special burial posture associated with chiefly rank. At Clarks, the position was distinguished by burial with a bird beak, a type that was mutually exclusive in distribution with stone pipes. The dual importance of bird beaks and pipes to the calumet ceremony (cf. O'Shea *et al.* 1982) may suggest, nonetheless, some correspondence between these two social positions and their respective markers.

Of the shared horizontal social statuses, symbolic markers were again very stable. Corporate group membership was distinguished by burial in distinct areas, as was previously discussed. Age distinctions were marked by the use of age-associated artifact types and by grave size. Gender was symbolized by sex-specific artifact types. The apparent use of grave orientation as a gender marker was unique to the Linwood site.

The marking of special status distinctions remained constant throughout the Pawnee sequence, in the use of both disarticulation and symbolic burial. The changes in detail that do occur are consistent with the gradual internal development of this basic set of treatments.

Overall, the Pawnee series exhibited relative stability in the manner in which major social subdivisions were expressed in the mortuary ritual. The shifts that were observed tended to be elaborations that were added to a core symbolic representation that persisted throughout the Pawnee sequence.

Although patterns of mortuary symbolism remained relatively constant in the Pawnee series, considerable variation can be observed in the detail of artifact usage at the three sites. A closer examination of this variation is warranted, since it is this detailed level of artifact occurrence and distribution that often forms the starting point for an analysis of mortuary patterning.

From the perspective of social reconstruction, the least-meaningful trend in artifact occurrence is variation that can be attributed to the introduction of new types into the material culture inventory. Even though the typology employed in the study was designed to lessen temporal influences, it is clear that a series of new types were progressively incorporated into Pawnee material culture, while other types, predominantly but not exclusively native made, were falling into disuse. However, the view obtained from these mortuary contexts tends to exaggerate this process, as can be seen from Table 7.3. More than half of the types that appear unique to any one of

TABLE 7.3

Pawnee: Comparison of Type Occurrence[a]

Type	Barcal	Linwood	Clarks
Glass bottle	O	X	X
Ceramic pot	X	X	X
Glass trade beads	X	X	X
Bear claw	O	X	—
Animal teeth	O	X	—
Bird beak	—	—	X
Bird bone	O	X	X
Raptor talon	—	X	X
Small mammal cranium	O	X	O
Rib shaft wrench	X	X	O
Squash knife	O	X	O
Quill flattener	—	X	—
Cancellous paint applicator	X	O	O
Awl	X	X	X
Metatarsal flesher	O	O	X
Elk horn scraper	X	—	X
Gun parts/accessories	X	X	X
Polished bone tube	O	X	—
Mussell shell	X	X	X
Gorget	—	X	X
Tubular shell bead	O	X	X
Wampum bead	—	—	X
Perforated shell pendant	—	X	—

TABLE 7.3 *Continued*

Type	Barcal	Linwood	Clarks
Metal bracelet	O	X	X
Metal bead/bangle	X	X	X
Iron knife	X	X	X
Axe/wedge	O	X	X
Scissors	—	X	X
Strike-a-light	X	X	X
Metal eating implement	—	X	X
Small metal hardware	O	X	X
Horse gear	—	X	X
Small iron tools	O	X	X
Metal projectile point	X	X	X
Iron scraper	O	—	X
Iron digging implement	O	X	X
Metal container	X	X	X
Metal buckle	—	X	X
Finger ring	X	X	X
Metal button	—	X	X
Large cast brass bell	—	X	X
Smaller brass bell	X	X	X
Thick wire coil	X	—	—
Thin wire coil	O	X	—
Metal lace/braid	—	—	X
Sheet brass blade	O	X	—
Lead ring/coil	—	X	X
Lead band	X	X	—
Sheet silver bracelet	—	X	—
Silver cross	—	X	X
Silver hair plate	—	O	X
Silver earring	—	X	X
Small silver brooch	—	X	—
Gunflint	O	X	X
Scoria abraider	X	O	—
Sandstone shaft smoother	X	X	X
Whetstone	O	X	X
Stone sphere	O	O	X
Stone projectile point	X	X	X
Stone pipe	X	X	X
Petrified wood	O	X	—
Retouched flake	X	X	X
Unretouched flake	O	X	X
Stone knife	O	X	—
Plate chalcedony knife	—	—	X
Side scraper	X	X	X
End scraper	X	X	O
Pipestone ornament	X	O	X
Gypsum	—	X	—
Total	48	62	54

a X, present in cemetery; O, present in village, but not in cemetery; —, not found.

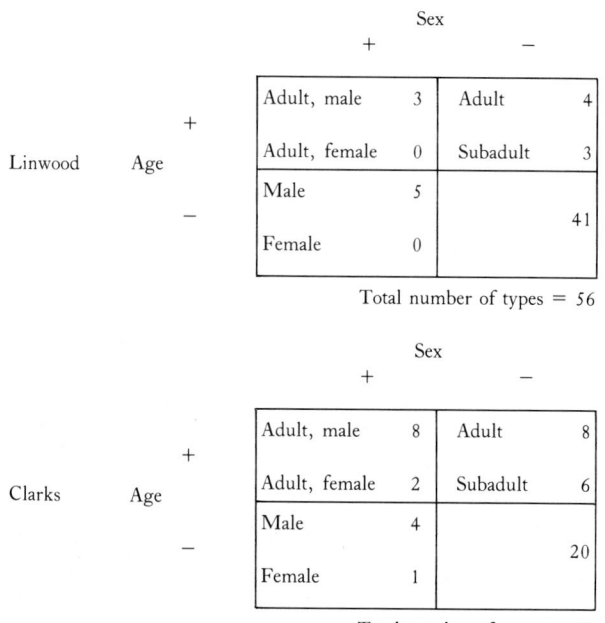

Figure 7.1 Age and sex constraints on Pawnee artifact occurrence.

the three cemeteries turn out to be shared when settlement as well as cemetery finds are considered. This effect is well illustrated by the distribution of metatarsal fleshers. Although this is a native-made type, among the cemeteries it was found only at Clarks, the latest site in the sequence. Yet, this type occurs in the village refuse at both Barcal and Linwood, as well as in prehistoric sites on the Plains (cf. Lehmer 1971:86). This again emphasizes the nonrandom character of mortuary deposits. The factor(s) controlling the appearance of this type (and no doubt others as well) was not availability in the material culture inventory, but rather the perceived meaning and use of the object by the living society.

Variation also was apparent in the structure of artifact occurrence relative to age and sex. Figure 7.1 contrasts the overall number of age- and sex-specific constraints on artifact distribution at the Linwood and Clarks sites (such comparison is limited for the Barcal site). The trend seems to be one of increased structure in the use of artifacts relative to age and sex through time, specifically: (1) a greater emphasis on female roles and (2) a greater emphasis on age-based differentiation. Specific discontinuities in type constraint between the three sites are presented in Table 7.4. Although there is certainly a stochastic element influencing this comparison, due to the small sample sizes involved, this table clearly illustrates the underlying consistency in the association of artifact types with particular age or sex categories and at the same time highlights the increasingly stereotyped use of artifacts within the

TABLE 7.4

Pawnee: Comparison of Artifact Type Associations

Type	Barcal	Linwood	Clarks
Glass trade beads	Unconstrained	Male	Subadult
Bird beak			Adult
Awl			Female, adult
Metatarsal flesher			Female
Gun parts/accessories	Unconstrained	Unconstrained	Male, adult
Mussel shell	Unconstrained	Unconstrained	Adult
Tubular shell bead		Male	Male
Metal bracelet		Unconstrained	Male
Metal bead/bangle		Male	Adult
Iron knife	Adult	Adult	Adult
Axe/wedge			Adult
Strike-a-light		Unconstrained	Male
Metal eating implement		Unconstrained	Subadult
Small metal hardware		Male, adult	Unconstrained
Small iron tools			Male, adult
Metal projectile point		Subadult	Male, adult
Iron scraper			Female, adult
Iron digging implement		Unconstrained	Subadult
Metal buckle		Male, adult	Adult
Finger ring		Male	Subadult
Metal button		Subadult	Unconstrained
Large cast brass bell			Subadult
Smaller brass bell		Adult	Unconstrained
Thick wire coil	Adult		
Metal lace/braid			Male
Sheet brass blade		Adult	
Lead ring		Subadult	Subadult
Gunflint		Adult	Adult
Sandstone shaft smoother	Adult	Unconstrained	Male, adult
Whetstone		Male, adult	Male, adult
Stone projectile point		Unconstrained	Male, adult
Stone pipe	Adult	Male	Male, adult
Retouched flake	Adult	Unconstrained	Unconstrained
Side scraper			Adult
End scraper	Adult	Unconstrained	
Pipestone ornament			Male, adult
Total number of constrained types	6	15	29

Pawnee mortuary complex as time progressed. In only five instances do artifacts at Clarks lose a characteristic association that was observed in an earlier site (Table 7.4). In each of these instances, the weakening of association seems to be a result either of the type's obsolescence, as in the case of retouched flakes or sheet brass blades, or of its becoming exceedingly common, as with metal buttons, small bells, and small metal hardware.

These results suggest that, although the major categories of mortuary differentiation remained constant among the Pawnee, the use of material culture within the mortuary ritual was changing.

To evaluate the higher-order organization of artifact usage within the Pawnee series, two aspects of the principal component analyses will be compared: (1) the similarity of the specific components produced by the analyses; and (2) the multivariate organization of types within each cemetery. The first will be assessed using the coefficient of congruence (see Chapter 4) to numerically compare the derived components, while the second will be evaluated by comparing the falloff curve of "explained" variance for each site.

The coefficient of congruence starts with the set of variables common to the two analyses and determines the cosine of the angle formed by the two factors (Rummel 1970:461). The value of the coefficient varies from $+1.0$ to -1.0 and can be interpreted in the same manner as a correlation coefficient r. Because only a subset of the variables employed in either analysis is compared, there is the potential for spurious similarity in these comparisons, particularly in the later components, which are characterized by significant loadings on only one or two variables. For this reason, the mathematical comparison of factors will be limited to the first four, which comprise the bulk of the variance represented in the principal component solution and which also include substantial weightings on a greater number of variables (see the specific analysis sections of Chapter 6 for the exact makeup of the compared factors).

Table 7.5 presents factor congruence between the Linwood and Barcal site analy-

TABLE 7.5

Pawnee: Factor Congruence, Barcal and Linwood[a]

Linwood	Barcal			
	Factor 1	Factor 2	Factor 3	Factor 4
Factor 1	.00021	−.22621	−.53282	−.30199
Factor 2	.01565	.54937	.42617	.06697
Factor 3	.01680	.51108	.12149	−.22276
Factor 4	.48120	−.00801	−.17777	−.34661

[a] Number of shared variables = 7.

TABLE 7.6

Pawnee: Factor Congruence, Barcal and Clarks[a]

	Barcal			
Clarks	Factor 1	Factor 2	Factor 3	Factor 4
Factor 1	.26189	.30743	−.30737	−.37565
Factor 2	.80761	.20549	−.18258	.10904
Factor 3	.02022	.64063	−.25387	−.13697
Factor 4	.21618	.52155	−.38560	−.25244

[a]Number of shared variables = 8.

ses. These calculations are based on 7 shared types from the original 12 at Barcal and 27 from the Linwood analysis. The pattern of factor congruences indicates an underlying similarity in the structure of artifact type covariation between the two sites, but with greater differentiation in the pattern of occurrence of trade items at the later, Linwood site.

Although there is greater specificity in the pattern of covariation of trade materials, there is still a relatively high degree of equivalency in the derived factors. Barcal Factor 1 corresponds with the adult male-associated Factor 4 at Linwood. Barcal Factor 3 appears to correspond with the other adult male-associated factor at Linwood, Factor 1. The two remaining Barcal factors have less clear-cut counterparts. Barcal Factor 2 contrasts native goods with trade items. No direct equivalent to this theme was present in the Linwood analysis, although high congruence values were observed with both Factors 2 and 3. Similarly, the weaponry complex distinguished in Barcal Factor 4 has no direct counterpart. Its highest congruence values are with the two adult male Linwood Factors, 1 and 4, yet neither is particularly strong. This tendency for factors to have high values split between several comparable factors stresses the greater degree of differentiation in the use and co-occurrence of artifacts, particularly trade materials, at the later site.

A similar pattern is observed when the factor congruence values for Barcal and Clarks are considered (Table 7.6). These coefficients were generated on the basis of 8 shared types out of an original 12 at Barcal and 27 at Clarks. Again, we see a high level of congruence between the adult-associated Factor 2 at Clarks and Barcal Factor 1. Beyond this point, however, no one-to-one correspondence between the factors is observed. Yet, the moderately high levels of congruence do suggest similar patterns of artifact combination at the two sites.

A more detailed view of multivariate change is provided by the comparison of factor results from the Linwood and Clarks analyses. This comparison was based on 22 shared types from an original 27 at both Linwood and Clarks (Table 7.7). A divergence in the factor results again is apparent. A high level of congruence is observed between the first component at each site, which both have strong adult male associations. Linwood Factor 4, which similarly is associated with adult males, also has its highest congruence value with Clarks Factor 1. The second strong correspondence is between the adult-female-associated Factor 4 at Clarks and Factor 3 at Linwood. However, no equivalent for the adult-associated Clarks Factor 2 is found among the four Linwood factors. Indeed, two factors that might superficially be expected to coincide, Linwood Factor 3 and Clarks Factor 2, actually exhibit a weak negative congruence value. The lack of correspondence is of particular interest, since this factor expresses age-specific differences in artifact association, a type of differentiation that is weakly expressed at the Linwood site. A similar shift in emphasis is evident in the congruence values for Clarks Factor 3. This factor is associated with adult male status at Clarks, yet it shares affinity at a moderate level with all three adult male or simply male-associated factors at Linwood. These results seem to indicate that, although a similar organization of artifacts by age and sex did exist at Linwood and Clarks, considerable variation between the sites did occur in the manner in which these various types were regularly combined. Much of the difference between the two analyses can seemingly be attributed to the increasing emphasis on age-based distinctions in artifact occurrence at the later site.

As in the case of basic age and sex association, the small sample sizes involved in the principal component analyses must be responsible for a degree of the divergence between the three factor results. Nevertheless, the variation is consistent with the patterns of change already observed, both in mortuary symbolism and artifact distribution; that is, the distribution of grave artifacts in the mortuary context becomes more stereotyped through time, with an increased specification of the age and sex associations of the material culture, particularly trade materials. This does not mean, however, that the use of artifacts within the mortuary context was necessarily more organized in the later sites than in the earlier ones (as is shown below). It

TABLE 7.7

Pawnee: Factor Congruence, Linwood and Clarks[a]

Linwood	Clarks			
	Factor 1	Factor 2	Factor 3	Factor 4
Factor 1	.58951	.32047	.43991	−.04336
Factor 2	.20076	.02422	.40663	−.01800
Factor 3	.26969	−.12770	.05224	.46500
Factor 4	.49712	.24120	.30785	−.20823

[a] Number of shared variables = 22.

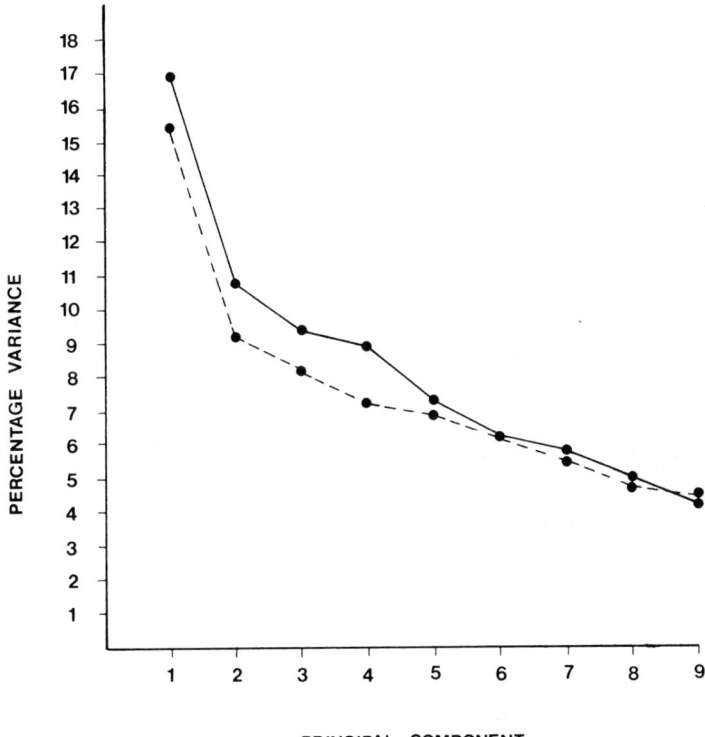

Figure 7.2 Comparison of variance falloff for the Linwood and Clarks site principal component analyses. Solid line, Linwood; dashed line, Clarks.

rather suggests that the focus of mortuary treatment was shifting, as were the particular goods associated with each social component.

The overall organization of artifact occurrence can be compared via the falloff in explained variance derived from the principal component analyses. Given the marked difference in the number of variables employed, only the falloff curves from Linwood and Clarks will be compared in this manner.

The falloff trend is very similar for both sites, with 11 factors from Linwood accounting for 82.6% of the total variance, and 9 factors at Clarks accounting for 67.8% of the variance (at the level of 11 factors, 74.9% of the Clarks variance was accounted for). Figure 7.2 compares the falloff in explained variance for the first nine components from the two sites. The similarity in slope and trend suggests that, in spite of changes in the detail of artifact use, the occurrence of artifacts in mortuary activities was organized at a similar level. A different pattern of falloff will be seen when the curves from the two Arikara sites are compared.

Arikara Variation in Social Distinction and Symbolic Representation

As with the Pawnee sites just discussed, a number of changes were observed in the detail of Arikara funerary activities through time. The larger size of the Arikara cemeteries increases the confidence with which such variation can be viewed, although the use of only two sites precludes a more detailed study of directional change.

The comparison of social categories differentiated at the two sites (Table 7.8) reveals a moderate level of stability through time. No radical shift is observed in the social categories given symbolic recognition. The differences that do emerge relate to the level of social detail expressed through the mortuary symbolism. Both sites, for example, shared a distinct chiefly position and a similar structure of acquired wealth. Yet, while only a single category of special prestige was recognized at Leavenworth, the earlier Larson site provided evidence for at least four additional ranked positions.

Horizontal differentiation was minimal at the two sites, with the exception of a form of corporate group membership marked at the later Leavenworth site. This is

TABLE 7.8

Arikara: Social Categories Represented in the Funerary Complex

Social categories	Larson	Leavenworth
Vertical distinctions		
Chiefly office	+	+
	(male, adult)	(male, adult)
Wealth	Two levels	Two levels
Hereditary ascription	+	+
Ritual office		
(a)	Male, adult	
(b)	Male	
Special prestige position		
(a)	Male, adult	
(b)	Male	
(c)		Adult
Horizontal distinctions		
Band membership	—	+
Male/female	+	+
Adult/subadult	+	+
Special status distinctions		
Circumstance of death	+	+
Alternative subadult treatments	+	+
Surrogate warrior	+	—

the sole instance in which a category of differentiation was recognized at the later site but not the earlier one.

Both sites provided evidence for several special status distinctions, most probably relating to the circumstance of an individual's death. The other special status recognized, provisionally termed *surrogate warrior*, was unique to the Larson site, although a similar occurrence was recorded at the Big Village of the Omaha (Chapter 6).

Overall, the predominant trend in the Arikara mortuary sequence was a gradual loss of differentiated categories through time. The categories that disappear are not major positions, such as chiefly rank or personal wealth, but rather are the smaller-scale distinctions. The exception to this trend is the marking of corporate group membership at Leavenworth, in which a relatively major category of differentiation was added to the mortuary complex. An explanation for this trend reversal is offered in the following section.

Significant changes were observed in the manner in which distinctions were differentiated in the two Arikara samples. A comparison of symbolic markers is presented in Table 7.9. The greatest variation is observed in the composition of the normative funerary treatments and in the representation of vertical social categories.

Although both sites shared a core of normative treatments, including single inhumation, a flexed burial posture, and the use of wood burial coverings, other differences were apparent. Larson exhibited consistent grave orientation (toward the northwest), which was not found at Leavenworth. It is useful to note that at the yet earlier protohistoric Sully site (39SL4) (Bass *et al.* 1971:152) a similar consistent pattern of grave orientation was observed, suggesting a qualitative shift away from the traditional pattern of grave orientation at Leavenworth. Burial in a common cemetery was also limited to the earlier site. Both of these features may be related to the marking of corporate group membership at Leavenworth.

Among the vertical distinctions, wealth was expressed in a similar fashion at both sites, by the type and variety of artifacts interred with the dead, although the significance of such wealth indicators was somewhat different. At Larson, wealth was predominantly an achieved status, whereas at Leavenworth it served more as an indicator of the economic standing of the individual's familial group. The symbolic designation of chiefly rank was quite different at the two sites. At Larson, chiefly rank was distinguished by burial in the central portion of the cemetery and by the presence of an arrow maker's kit and other sociotechnic objects in a grave assemblage characteristic of the upper wealth stratum. At Leavenworth, by contrast, burial with a stone pipe and an upper wealth level assemblage were the sole markers of chiefly rank.

The pattern of change suggested by this shift in mortuary symbolism is repeated in other vertical categories. At Larson, at least two special prestige positions were in evidence, whereas Leavenworth appeared to have had only one such category. These all were structurally similar, in that one or more special tokens were included in a

TABLE 7.9

Arikara: Social Category Designation

Social categories	Larson	Leavenworth
Normative treatment	Flexed posture	Flexed posture
	Wood covering	Wood covering
	Northwest orientation	
	Burial in village cemetery	
Vertical distinctions		
Wealth	Artifact variety	Artifact variety
Chiefly rank	Arrowmaker's kit	Pipe ownership
	Sociotechnic object	Upper wealth level
	Burial in central portion of cemetery	
	Upper wealth level	
Ritual office	Stone pipe ownership	
	Bird beak ownership	
Special prestige positions	Carved catlinite ornament	Spear point
	Upper wealth level	Bird beak
	Curved rib ornament	Upper wealth level
	Upper wealth level	
Horizontal distinctions		
Corporate group		Grave location
Adult/subadult	Grave size	Grave size
	Age-specific types	Age-specific types
Male/female	Sex-specific types	Sex-specific types
Special status distinctions		
Circumstances of death	Multiple interment	Multiple interment
	Nonnormative extended postures	Nonnormative extended postures
	Nonnormative orientation	Decapitation (?)
Special adversary/surrogate	Decapitation	
	Nonnormative posture	
	Large spear point(s)	

small number of grave assemblages from the uppermost wealth level. However, there was no correspondence in the specific tokens used—carved catlinite or curved rib ornaments at Larson, spear points and bird beaks at Leavenworth. No rank positions of the type associated with ritual office were found at Leavenworth, so no direct comparison of symbolism is possible. Yet, all the tokens that were used to mark special vertical distinctions at Leavenworth were also used at Larson, although with an apparently different meaning. Burial with a stone pipe, a sign of chiefly authority at Leavenworth, was the exclusive marker for a non-wealth-tied ritual office at Larson. Similarly, bird beaks, which marked the other ritual office at Larson, were a designator for the Leavenworth special prestige position. A similar kind of transformation is observed in the use of stone spear points as burial symbols, which shifted from an indicator of a special status distinction (see below) to an element used to mark elevated prestige at Leavenworth.

The symbolic definition of horizontal distinctions remained unchanged through time. Grave size and age-specific artifact types marked age statuses, while another set of limited distribution artifacts differentiated individuals by sex. The only other horizontal dimension recognized, corporate group membership, was not distinguished in the Larson funerary complex.

A comparison of special status differentiation reveals considerable similarity between the two sites. The occasional use of multiple burial and nonnormative burial postures was common to both. The use of grave orientation as a differential treatment was not possible at Leavenworth, since no consistent pattern of grave orientation was followed. Nor was the surrogate warrior distinction found at the Leavenworth site. It is interesting, nonetheless, that all the treatments and symbols used to mark this distinction at Larson occur in the Leavenworth mortuary complex, although not in combination and with different meanings.

Taken together, the main trends in Arikara mortuary symbolism seem to be (1) a restructuring of the use (and meaning) of certain critical symbols, and (2) the de-emphasis of a broad range of other social markers. Those objects that continue to serve as important symbols, such as stone pipes and bird beaks, tend to become more closely associated with high economic standing. This pattern of change parallels the decreasing number of social categories being differentiated in the mortuary ritual itself.

The trend toward less detail and organization in the Arikara funerary complex through time is seen most clearly in the use of artifacts within the grave assemblages. In terms of the artifact types that could occur in a grave, very little difference is observed between the two sites (Table 7.10) if one excludes the range of trade items that simply were not available for use at the time of the Larson village occupation. Yet, although the basic inventories were similar, the structure of their occurrence was very different.

A comparison of artifact occurrence relative to age and sex highlights this difference. Figure 7.3 contrasts the overall number of age- or sex-associated artifact types at the two sites. Two trends are suggested by this comparison: (1) the degree of organization, at least relative to age and sex, decreases through time; and (2) the emphasis on female activities increases (although modestly) through time. The first of these trends is further clarified when the actual changes in specific type association are considered. Table 7.11 lists those types that exhibit some form of constraint in their distribution at one or both of the sites. It should be noted that this table excludes types that occur too infrequently to permit a comparison of their distribution at either one of the sites. The tendency for material culture to be highly

TABLE 7.10

Arikara: Comparison of Type Occurrence[a]

Type	Larson	Leavenworth
Glass bottle	—	X
Ceramic pot	X	X
Native glass pendant	X	X
Ceramic effigy figure	—	X
Glass trade beads	X	X
Bear claw	X	X
Animal teeth	X	X
Bird beak	X	X
Bird bone	X	X
Raptor talon	—	X
Small mammal cranium	X	X
Rib shaft wrench	X	X
Squash knife	X	X
Scapula hoe	X	X
Quill flattener	X	X
Cancellous paint applicator	—	X
Awl	X	X
Metatarsal flesher	—	X
Elk horn scraper	—	—
Bone/antler implement	X	X
Gun parts/accessories	X	X
Pin game cup	—	—
Polished bone tube	X	X
Bone pendant	X	X
Curved rib ornament	X	—
Bone point	X	—
Mussel shell	X	X
Gorget	—	X
Hair pipe	—	X
Tubular shell bead	X	X
Wampum bead	X	—
Heavy shell bead	X	—
Rectangular shell bead	X	—
Shell runtee	X	—
Marine snail shell	X	X
Perforated shell pendant	X	X
Flat shell bead	X	—
Metal bracelet	X	X
Metal bead/bangle	X	X
Iron knife	X	X
Axe/wedge	O	O
Scissors	—	X
Strike-a-light	—	—

TABLE 7.10 *Continued*

Type	Larson	Leavenworth
Metal eating implement	—	X
Small metal hardware	—	X
Horse gear	—	X
Small iron tools	—	X
Metal projectile point	X	X
Iron scraper	—	O
Iron digging implement	—	O
Metal container	X	X
Metal buckle	—	X
Finger ring	—	X
Metal button	—	X
Large cast brass bell	—	O
Smaller brass bell	—	X
Thick wire coil	—	X
Thin wire coil	X	X
Metal lace/braid	X	X
Copper crimp/clip	X	—
Sheet brass blade	X	X
Lead ring/coil	—	X
Lead band	—	—
Sheet silver bracelet	—	—
Silver cross	—	—
Silver hair plate	—	X
Silver earring	—	O
Small silver brooch	—	—
Gunflint	X	X
Stone spear point	X	X
Scoria abraider	X	X
Sandstone shaft smoother	X	X
Whetstone	X	—
Hammer stone	X	O
Stone sphere	—	X
Stone projectile point	X	X
Stone pipe	X	X
Petrified wood	X	X
Retouched flake	X	X
Unretouched flake	X	X
Stone knife	X	X
Plate chalcedony knife	X	—
Side scraper	X	X
End scraper	X	X
Pipestone ornament	X	X
Gypsum	X	X
Total	55	69

[a] All artifacts recovered from the two cemeteries are included in this listing, including those in graves that were excluded from analysis. X, present in cemetery; O, present in village but not in cemetery; —, not found at site.

structured in its mortuary use at Larson and for much of this structure to be lost at the later, Leavenworth site is clear. This trend runs parallel to the diminishing importance of a number of social symbols already observed in the Arikara sequence. Most of the types that do exhibit some association by age or sex in their occurrence at Leavenworth are trade goods. During the span of time between the Larson and Leavenworth sites, there is a weakening of the structured use of artifacts within the funerary complex and a partial replacement of native goods by trade materials as significant grave inclusions. The observation of increased emphasis on female roles is also of interest, as it parallels a similar trend among the Pawnee during this same time period (see section above on Pawnee variation in social distinction). This pattern of change in artifact association and usage belies the major impact of trade materials on Arikara culture and the perceptual shift that appears to have accompanied these goods. These themes are repeated in the larger-ordered multivariate distribution of artifacts in the mortuary complex.

The principal component analysis of the Larson site extracted 11 components, which accounted for 65.1% of the variance present in the correlation matrix, while 9 components, account for 63.9% of the variance, were extracted for Leavenworth (71.7% would be accounted for by 11 components). Despite the large sample sizes, the relatively small number of shared types used in the two analyses ($N = 10$) makes the comparison of component results somewhat difficult and subject to spurious

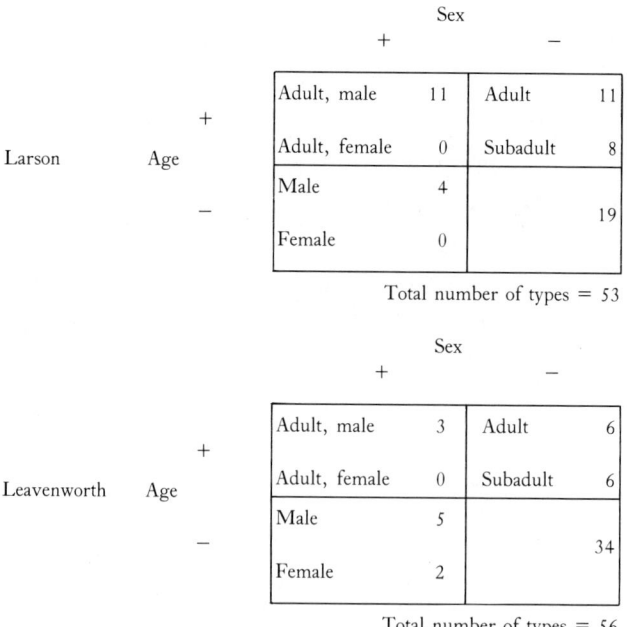

Figure 7.3 Age and sex constraints on Arikara artifact occurrence.

TABLE 7.11

Arikara: Comparison of Artifact Type Associations

Type	Larson	Leavenworth
Ceramic pot	Subadult	Subadult
Native glass pendant	Male	Male
Glass trade beads	Subadult	Unconstrained
Animal teeth	Subadult	Female
Bird beak	Adult, male	Unconstrained
Small mammal cranium	Male	Unconstrained
Rib shaft wrench	Adult, male	Unconstrained
Quill flattener	Adult	Unconstrained
Polished bone tube	Male	Male
Gun parts/accessories	Subadult	Unconstrained
Mussel shell	Adult	Unconstrained
Perforated shell pendant	Adult, male	Unconstrained
Metal bracelet	Subadult	Unconstrained
Metal bead/bangle	Unconstrained	Subadult
Metal container	Adult	Unconstrained
Stone spear point	Adult, male	Adult
Scoria abraider	Adult	Adult
Sandstone shaft smoother	Adult	Unconstrained
Stone projectile point	Adult, male	Unconstrained
Stone pipe	Unconstrained	Male
Petrified wood	Adult	Adult
Unretouched flake	Adult	Unconstrained
Stone knife	Adult	Unconstrained
End scraper	Adult, male	Adult, male
Total number of constrained types	34	22

variation. Nonetheless, coefficients of congruence were calculated for the first four factors from the two sites. These are presented in Table 7.12.

The congruence values line up much as would be expected. Larson Factor 2, an adult male factor reflecting an implement set used in arrow manufacture, corresponded very closely with Leavenworth Factor 3, also an adult male factor, characterized by iron knives and other hardware. Larson Factor 3, another adult male tool kit composed of stone tools and bird beaks, corresponded with Factor 4 at Leavenworth, a factor composed of bird beaks and animal bone ornaments. Factor 4 at Larson, an adult-associated combination of side scrapers and scoria abraiders, exhibited a strong, although negative, congruence value for Leavenworth Factor 2 (marine snail shell beads, smaller brass bell, and metal container).

The one obvious nonmatch was Larson Factor 1. This factor combined most of the trade articles found in the Larson assemblages, emphasizing that such goods

TABLE 7.12

Arikara: Factor Congruence[a]

Larson	Leavenworth			
	Factor 1	Factor 2	Factor 3	Factor 4
Factor 1	.26668	−.15868	.08756	.13032
Factor 2	.18843	.56265	.91319	.09652
Factor 3	.32527	.13672	.14458	.66188
Factor 4	−.08031	−.61427	.12463	.13931

[a]Number of shared variables = 10.

were still a novelty and had not yet been fully integrated into the social fabric of Arikara culture. Trade goods at Leavenworth, in contrast, were more common and were fully incorporated into the material culture. As such, no single factor characterizing trade materials was produced—thus, the weak congruence values associated with Larson Factor 1. Weak congruence values for Leavenworth Factor 1 also are revealing. This factor combines most available weaponry, primarily of trade origin, with several sociotechnic objects—bird beaks and small mammal crania. The low congruence values would certainly be expected, given the nonintegrated character of trade materials at Larson, as already mentioned. The linkage of these implements of prestige and wealth (i.e., weaponry) with such items as bird beaks also accentuates the role shift experienced by this particular social symbol, which changed from the marker of an independent ritual position to a wealth-tied prestige position.

The most surprising result from this series of comparisons probably is that there is as much agreement between the factor results as there is, given the underlying changes in symbolism and artifact use that were occurring. Yet, it is of interest that it was the first factor from both analyses (i.e., the factor that accounted for the greatest percentage of the original variance) that lacked any clear counterpart in these paired analyses.

The apparent similarity of factor results is in contrast to the falloff curves for explained variance produced by the two analyses. These two curves are compared in Figure 7.4. The Larson analysis, despite its greater number of variables, exhibits a much steeper falloff, indicative of a greater degree of overall organization in the use of artifacts within the mortuary complex. The Leavenworth curve, which levels off after only the first factor, is suggestive of a much less organized pattern of artifact occurrence and covariation. Such a difference fits with what is by now a familiar pattern of change within the Arikara mortuary complex through time, or at least is a complement to it. Whereas the comparison of mortuary differentiation at the two sites suggested that the number of social categories and of specific symbols decreased through time, these results show that the consistency or regularity with which material objects were used in the mortuary complex simultaneously decreased.

Causal Factors

The preceding sections have summarized the patterns of change observed in the Pawnee and Arikara sequences. Attention now shifts toward an evaluation of their causes (in a historical sense). In particular, it is of interest to determine whether the changes observed in mortuary treatment can be systematically linked with alterations occurring in the society at large.

The historic period was a time of substantial change for all Amerindian groups, and it is not surprising, therefore, that a number of likely causes for the variation observed in the Pawnee and Arikara examples can be found in the ethnohistorical literature. Yet, it is significant that much of the variation observed in the mortuary treatment can be related to a small number of crucial alterations in Plains Village culture.

One such major change was depopulation, resulting from a series of devastating epidemic outbreaks. A major consequence of depopulation was the conflation of

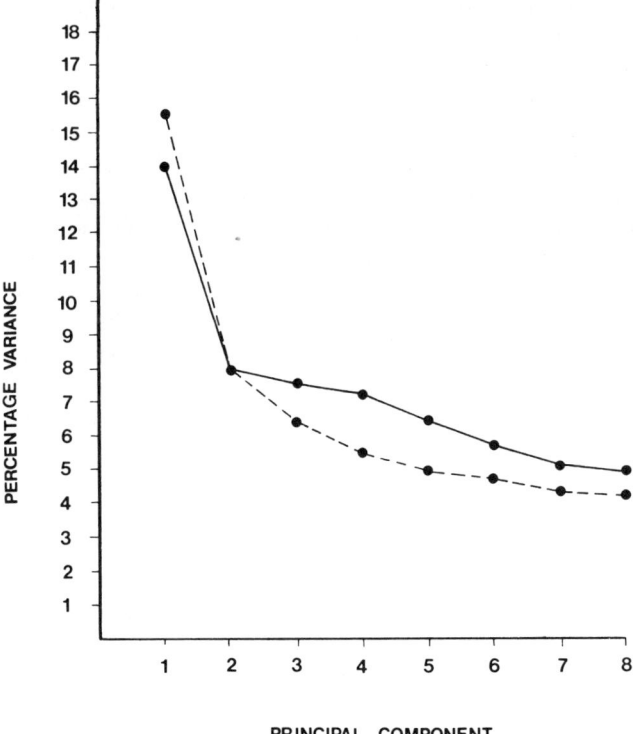

Figure 7.4 Comparison of variance falloff for the Larson and Leavenworth site principal component analyses. Dashed line, Larson; solid line, Leavenworth.

previously autonomous communities into composite villages. It is well documented, ethnohistorically, that village merger occurred among both the Arikara and the Pawnee. The 10–12 Arikara villages known in the late 1700s were reformed into three closely located villages by 1804 (Lewis and Clark 1893:162) (two of which were the double Leavenworth villages used in this study, Denig 1961:42n), whereas the 12 Skidi and 10 South Band villages of the Pawnee noted by Delisle in 1718 (Tucker 1942) were reduced to 1 Skidi and 2 South Band villages by 1806 (Pike 1966).

It should be stressed that these earlier villages were autonomous. They possessed unique village bundles and rituals, as well as their own chiefs and systems of leadership and authority (cf. Parks 1979b). Despite tribal-level affinities between these communities, merger must have produced considerable friction and ambiguity, as previously autonomous rank and ritual systems collided in the composite villages. Denig provides an example of just such ambiguity among the nineteenth-century Arikara: "There is no wise ruler at this time at the head of the nation. Several men of equal standing, or rather no standing, pretend to govern. . . . Indeed, no man can show how or in what way he is superior to his fellows" (1961:61). Similar comments on internal strife among the Pawnee are numerous in the ethnohistorical literature (see Kracht 1982). Disharmony in these composite villages was sufficiently severe, on occasion, to cause the village to fission, at least temporarily (O'Shea 1979).

Several of the observed changes in mortuary symbolism may be indicative of adaptations to merged villages. In both the Arikara and Pawnee examples, a shift from single to multiple burial areas was observed. One explanation is that despite village merger, autonomous social units continued to maintain discrete burial locations. Larson and Barcal would then represent cemeteries associated with premerger communities, whereas the rest would have been associated with composite villages. This certainly is the case with the Leavenworth village and with the two later Pawnee villages. Additional support for this interpretation can be found in later Pawnee history. After 1857, the four Pawnee bands (each of which had coalesced from autonomous villages 70 years earlier) moved to a single site near Genoa, Nebraska. At this village, each of the bands maintained a separate cemetery area (Wedel 1936:29).

These results suggest that the spatially separated burial areas represent an effort to maintain the identity of formerly autonomous communities. Among the 1857 Pawnee, village identification seems to have given way to band solidarity as the significant relationship marked in the mortuary symbolism. Among the Omaha (the third instance where distinct burial areas were used), this same treatment was employed in the symbolic designation of clan membership.

A number of other changes may also be attributable to village merger. The reduction of the number of smaller-scale social distinctions in Arikara mortuary symbolism through time seems to reflect an attempt to form a new unambiguous system of social statuses. The use of a limited number of symbols and the selection of specific objects of widespread value and importance, such as stone pipes or expensive European trade materials, would represent logical steps in such a reorganization. The accumulation of trade materials, in particular, seems to have been an adaptive response to the lack of a coherent system of social ordering in the period immediately following depopulation and village merger.

The structural changes associated with the fur trade may be responsible for other observed shifts in mortuary behavior. One trend that was observed in both the Arikara and Pawnee mortuary sequences was a gradual increase in the emphasis on female activities through time. Although the symbolic representation of female activities never equaled that of males, the increasing importance of female roles observed in the mortuary treatment may well be linked to the increased importance of agricultural production, particularly maize (commodities owned by women), in the trade with Euro-Americans.

As a result females gradually developed their own access channels to trade materials, which were largely independent of males or trade chiefs. In circumstances in which the accumulation of trade goods was a significant indicator of social standing, as among the Arikara, the traditional horticultural activities of women must have come to hold increasing significance within the community, particularly as fur-bearing animals became more difficult to obtain.

This increased social standing seems to correspond with the concurrent elaboration of female-associated goods in the mortuary symbolism. It is interesting to note, however, that the tools that came to reflect female roles were not, as might be expected, agricultural implements, but rather tended to be processing and manufacturing tools. The increased economic status of females is well illustrated by the wealth distribution observed at Leavenworth and by the wealthy females at the Omaha Big Village.

The present cases illustrate a shift from an asymmetrical emphasis on male activities and wealth to one that recognizes (although still unequally) male and female roles. The earlier emphasis on male activities may itself be a product of Euroamerican contact and trade. During protohistoric times, only males were in a position to participate in long-distance exchange. Therefore, the early distribution of European trade materials would presumably have been controlled by males. Since these items, particularly iron tools and firearms, were rapidly perceived as valuable and strategic resources, their possession and accumulation was no doubt a source of influence and prestige. Only when traders began visiting and living among the Plains Villagers did females have direct access to trade goods, and it is at this point that female roles began to acquire greater symbolic resolution in the funerary rites.

These examples serve to illustrate how social change may be expressed through specific alterations in mortuary symbolism. A more processual view of the complex relationship between mortuary variability and social change can be obtained by considering the divergent trajectories followed by the Pawnee and the Arikara during the early historic period.

Ironically, neither historical nor ethnographic accounts of the Plains Village tribes are sufficiently detailed to provide more than a very general outline of specific social change during this period. Despite the late date of these sites, archaeological evidence provides the only real means for documenting the detailed level of social change that took place among the Pawnee and Arikara. It is only with the combination of existing ethnohistorical documentation and the archaeological evidence of alterations in the pattern of mortuary differentiation that a plausible picture of Arikara and Pawnee social change emerges.

Despite similarities in language, culture, and subsistence practices, the Pawnee and the Arikara exhibited fundamentally different responses to the stresses of the nineteenth century. Both groups experienced depopulation, village merger, and the reorientation of their economic systems as a result of contact. The Grand Pawnee response was to intensify their existing level of social differentiation. The Arikara, by contrast, appear to have simplified their system of social differentiation. The extent of these alterations was not extreme, yet the opposite direction of the responses is clear, particularly in their effects on mortuary symbolism. The Arikara decreased the number of distinct status positions recognized in the funerary complex and similarly limited the range of items that carried qualitative symbolic meaning. At the same time, the Arikara adopted a simplified system of vertical ranking. The Pawnee, on the other hand, retained their pre-existing social symbols and made certain rank positions even more exclusive, increasing the wealth differentiation within the population and giving greater importance to age-based distinctions.

Both adaptations represent logical responses to stress of the kind experienced by these groups in the nineteenth century. The question that remains is why two so ethnically similar groups adopted such radically different solutions?

Suffice it to say, the satisfactory answer to this question is well beyond the scope of the present study. Yet, certain possibilities can be suggested. The critical historical factor may be the rate at which change occurred. The Arikara, with their villages placed in the center of the trade routes to the Upper Missouri, were ideally located to function as middlemen in the fur trade, a role they readily and jealously adopted (Thwaites 1904:127–128, Vol. 8). As a result, the rate of change, economic and social, was rapid. The Pawnee villages, located to the west on the Platte River, were not on an intensive trade route, and although they were visited with increasing frequency during the eighteenth and nineteenth centuries, the amount of interaction probably did not equal that of the Arikara until the late 1830s. It appears that the Pawnee, by virtue of their relative isolation, were given more time to adjust to the altered social environment of the Plains. Their response was to intensify their existing societal organization. This adaptation was so successful that despite starvation, intense warfare, Presbyterian missionaries, and ultimately relocation to a reservation in Oklahoma, the social organization of the tribe remained intact and functional. Change was much more rapid among the Arikara, such that simplification was the only feasible alternative. As an alternative, it appears to have been less effective than the Pawnee solution. In any event, it was insufficient to cope with the increasingly hostile environment of the Middle Missouri region. The Arikara continued to suffer from raiding by hostile Sioux (and the U.S. Army), and by 1862 were forced by necessity to join with the epidemic devastated Mandan and Hidatsa at Like-a-fishhook village (Smith 1974:10–11).

From the perspective of the archaeological study of change in funerary behavior, the importance of these divergent developmental sequences is that such fine-grained social changes were indeed reflected in each society's mortuary symbolism, and that these expressions were of a type that could be detected and potentially understood through archaeological analysis. In a sense, it argues for a reversal of one of the traditional uses of mortuary data. It was argued in Chapter 2 that funerary remains are of little value for defining chronological sequences. These results suggest, however, that in situations where close chronological control is available, mortuary remains can be used to monitor social change in very fine detail.

Conclusions

The most obvious conclusion that emerges from this consideration of temporal change and funerary practices is that a society's practices for the disposal of the dead may vary, sometimes considerably, even over short periods of time. In none of the present cases did more than about 60 years elapse between any of the sites, a time period that in most prehistoric investigations can only rarely be distinguished. Yet, significant change was observed, even in cemeteries produced by a single ethnic subdivision.

Not only is such instability possible, but based on the present cases, no class of mortuary treatment is immune from change. Both normative elements of treatment and major categories of differentiation exhibited temporal instability. In the present cases, such normative treatments as grave orientations, use of grave coverings, and the structure of the cemetery itself varied in use or meaning even in the sites of a single ethnic group. Likewise, major categories of differentiation varied. Among the Arikara, change was observed in the number and nature of rank and prestige positions, in corporate group membership, and even in the special status distinctions recognized. Similarly among the Pawnee, the nature of wealth differentiation, corporate group membership, ranked prestige positions, and special status distinctions all varied through time. At a finer level, instability was observed both in the symbols used by a society as status markers as well as in the level of consensus governing the usage of artifacts within the mortuary context.

A second observation is that variation within a mortuary complex need not be trending or consistent through time. That is, change may be episodic and short term. This was best illustrated in the use of multiple burial areas by the Pawnee, in which grave clusters apparently were first used to mark corporate units and then employed to designate primarily rank relations and then reverted to marking corporate groups. A similar series of shifts was observed in Pawnee grave orientation. Although the causal factors for such changes have not been considered here, the critical archaeological observation is that change can be abrupt, even over short periods of time.

Finally, these cases demonstrate the potentially confounding effects that can result from change in the material culture inventory. This was shown (most clearly) in the analysis of the Larson site, in which apparently parallel categories of mortuary differentiation, resulting from the replacement of certain native-made bead types by equivalent European glass beads, were observed. Had this process not been identified, the assessment of mortuary differentiation would have grossly overestimated the complexity represented at the site. Indeed, if such changes were more subtle or complex, they might have become too difficult to control effectively in an archaeological study. This is most likely to be a concern when dealing with periods of flux and change, or in border–boundary situations. It might also be added that such changes in material culture inventory can have other, unexpected consequences. One such effect, which will be discussed in more detail in the next chapter, is that changes of this type may create a false appearance of cultural integration or homogeneity within a region that is subject to the influx of an array of valuable nonlocal goods. The use of similar mortuary symbols to mark an equivalent position of high status does not necessarily imply cultural or ethnic similarity between the groups responsible for the observed cemeteries. The parallel importance of stone pipes and expensive trade items for chiefly individuals—be they Pawnee, Omaha, or Arikara—should clearly establish this premise.

One encouraging aspect of these results is that variation through time is not random, but rather it is patterned by changing conditions or perceptions within the living society. The examples summarized in this section provide clear evidence that changes in the society at large induced related changes in the mortuary symbolism of each culture. These changes were not uniform among the different ethnic groups, but all were consistent with the structural alterations that were occurring in each society. The demonstration that such a relationship does indeed hold for archaeological cases has two valuable implications for future archaeological research. First, changes in funerary behavior are integrally related to the overall configuration of the living society, and as such, there is the potential to explain change in mortuary patterning within the context of the total configuration of the past society. Second, in cases where fine-grained chronological control exists, funerary remains can provide a very sensitive indicator of organizational and consensual change within prehistoric societies.

These observations, although based on only a very limited set of cases, hopefully add to the universe of the archaeologically possible and serve to inform the archaeologist of basic kinds of relationships that can *not* be assumed to constrain mortuary variability. A priori, the archaeologist can make no assumption concerning either the temporal stability or instability of a culture's mortuary activities, nor can it be assumed that any specific aspect of such treatment will be more or less stable. It can be assumed, however, that changes in the funerary complex will be related to other changes in the society as a whole.

8

Ethnic Differentiation in Mortuary Practices

Introduction

The use of funerary patterning to distinguish group or ethnic boundaries is the final aspect of mortuary variability considered in this study. The focus of the chapter is limited to archaeological patterning. The possible uses of human biological analysis for the assessment of group affinity are not considered here.

Although similarity in funerary treatment has long been employed in archaeology as a basis for inferring cultural affinity, the justification for such inference has rarely been considered. It has been argued throughout this study that funerary behavior is patterned by and dependent on the overall adaptive posture of the living society, and as such, the specific form or content of funerary treatment exhibited by a given group may result from any of a number of factors, of which cultural affinity is but one. What remains unclear is whether there exists any necessary systematic linkage between mortuary patterning and cultural affinity that might permit archaeological discrimination between groups.

At least two general factors would seem to limit such a usage. The first is the nature of group boundaries themselves. We know, for example, that social units may or may not emphasize boundaries, depending on a variety of social and economic factors (Hodder 1979). We also know that differing kinds and levels of social units may each mark their own boundaries, ranging from transcultural ideological movements to individual strata within a single social hierarchy. Both these characteristics of cultural boundaries would introduce ambiguity into the interpretation of specific mortuary patterning.

The second factor relates to the character of mortuary symbolism itself. Wobst (1977:328) has stressed the systematic relationship that must exist between a symbol and its intended receiving audience. Simply put, a symbol must be both visible and interpretable to the relevant audience if it is to successfully transmit information.

Although this may be a truism in the abstract, its practical implications in the realm of mortuary symbolism are rarely considered. Who observes an individual's funerary treatment? Is it reasonable to suppose that the placing of a particular artifact in the grave or the direction in which the body is oriented will communicate an individual's cultural association to the next tribe up the river?

That cemeteries do function, on occasion, as territorial markers is hardly surprising, since they tend to be well-marked features of the landscape, a characteristic that may be accentuated by their location on prominences or by the construction of monuments. Such features are public and highly visible symbols that are readily seen and recognized. Elements of funerary ritual, on the other hand, are typically short lived, and although usually accessible to most members of the community, such ritual would be much less effective as a marker beyond the limits of the community. The effectiveness of such symbols could, of course, be enhanced if visitors were brought in to witness the burial rite or if the funerary treatment itself entailed particularly elaborate or gaudy public elements, as with the Feast of the Dead among the Huron (Quimby 1966) or the great funeral pyre and funerary games of the ancient Greeks (cf. the funeral of Patroclos, Homer 1938).

The present sample of Plains cemeteries can offer some insight into the question of cultural affinity and its relationship to mortuary variability. The sample is crosscut by two different levels of cultural affinity, first by the three ethnic groups represented—the Pawnee, Omaha, and Arikara—and also by two language families—the Northern Caddoans (Pawnee and Arikara) and the speakers of Dhegihan Sioux (Omaha). In the brief tests that follow, an attempt is made to assess the degree to which such ethnic or cultural divisions constrain or structure archaeologically observable mortuary variability.

Tests

To investigate the relationship between ethnic group affiliation and mortuary patterning, three classes of evidence will be evaluated: normative funerary treatment, primary categories of mortuary differentiation, and the use of material culture in the funerary ritual. The comparison of material culture is limited because of the nature of the typology employed, and only examines the structure of artifact usage. Each of these classes of mortuary data is compared between known ethnic groups and between individual sites. In this way intercultural variability can be compared with variability between the sites of a single ethnic group.

As an aid to these comparisons, a simple measure of similarity is calculated for each pair of sites. The coefficient used is the simple matching coefficient (Sokal and

TABLE 8.1

Normative Funerary Treatments

	Barcal	Pawnee Linwood	Clarks	Arikara Larson	Arikara Leavenworth	Omaha Big Village
Posture	Flexed	Flexed	Flexed	Flexed	Flexed	Extended
Orientation	West	Males: northwest Females: southeast	North	Northwest	No regular orientation	Northwest
Burial areas	Single	Multiple (3)	Multiple (5)	Single	Multiple (5)	Multiple (2)
Burial structures as normative element	Yes	No	Yes	Yes	Yes	No
Frequency of multiple interment	Low (0)	Low (2%)	Low (0)	Low	Moderate (15%)	Moderate (34%)

TABLE 8.2

Similarity in Normative Funerary Treatments[a]

	Pawnee			Arikara		Omaha
	Barcal	Linwood	Clarks	Larson	Leavenworth	Big Village
Barcal		2	3	4	2	0
Linwood	.4		3	2	2	1
Clarks	.6	.6		3	3	1
Larson	.8	.4	.6		2	1
Leavenworth	.4	.4	.6	.4		2
Big Village	.0	.2	.2	.2	.4	

[a] Lower half of matrix presents simple matching coefficient of similarity; upper half presents number of positive matches.

Sneath 1963:133), which ranges in value from 0 to 1.0. The use of this coefficient allows the degree of similarity between sites or sets of sites to be conveniently expressed in numerical form.

A summary of Pawnee, Omaha, and Arikara normative funerary treatment is presented in Table 8.1. The comparisons between ethnic groups and sites according to these normative features are summarized in Tables 8.2–8.4. Several observations can be made from these comparisons. First, although the Omaha site is clearly separated from the Caddoan sites, normative practices were insufficient to reliably distinguish Pawnee from Arikara sites. On the average, Pawnee sites were only marginally more similar to each other than they were to the sites of other groups (within group similarity .53, between group .40), whereas the two Arikara sites were more similar to sites of other groups than they were to each other (.40 compared with .48). The cause of these results is clear from Table 8.4. Among the individual Pawnee and Arikara sites, there were as many mismatches as matches in terms of ethnic affiliation. Indeed, the strongest factor influencing this comparison seems to be the date of site use, with earlier sites being more similar to earlier sites regardless of tribal affiliation, and later sites being more similar to later sites.

TABLE 8.3

Comparison of Normative Funerary Treatments by Ethnic Group

	Average similarity	
	Within group	Between groups
Pawnee	.53	.40
Arikara	.40	.48
Omaha	—	.20

8. Ethnic Differentiation in Mortuary Practices

TABLE 8.4

Comparison of Normative Funerary Treatments by Site

Site	Most similar site	Same ethnic division
Barcal	Larson (.8)	−
Linwood	Clarks (.6)	+
Clarks	Linwood (.6)[a]	+/−
Larson	Barcal (.8)	−
Leavenworth	Clarks (.6)	−
Big Village	Leavenworth (.4)	

[a] Both Arikara sites, Larson and Leavenworth, exhibited the same similarity value with the Clarks site, as did the Pawnee Linwood site.

Beyond this simple numerical comparison, the one striking and consistent distinction between the sites is the pattern of flexed versus extended burial posture that separates the Omaha Big Village site from the Caddoan-affiliated Pawnee and Arikara sites. Indeed, burial posture is one attribute of normative treatment that is both consistent and temporally stable.

The second comparison involves the most general categories of mortuary differentiation observed at each site. These are summarized in Table 8.5. The categories generalize the specific findings of Chapter 6. From this table it is clear, first of all, that the six sites are really more similar than different, at least in the structure of

TABLE 8.5

Categories of Mortuary Differentiation

	Pawnee			Arikara		Omaha
Differential category	Barcal	Linwood	Clarks	Larson	Leavenworth	Big Village
Chiefly office	+	+	+	+	+	+
Wealth structure	2 level	3 level	3 level	2 level	2 level	3 level
Ritual office	−	+	+	+	+	−
Corporate group	+	−	+	−	+	+
Society membership	+	−	−	−	−	−
Adult/subadult	+	+	+	+	+	+
Male/female	?	+	+	+	+	+
Circumstance of death	+	+	+	+	+	+
War captive	−	−	−	+	−	+?
Expediant treatment	−	−	+	+	+	+
Remains not recovered for burial	−	+	+	−	−	−

TABLE 8.6

Similarity in Mortuary Differentiation[a]

Site	Pawnee			Arikara		Omaha
	Barcal	Linwood	Clarks	Larson	Leavenworth	Big Village
Barcal		5	5	5	7	6
Linwood	.50		9	7	7	6
Clarks	.50	.82		7	9	8
Larson	.50	.64	.64		9	8
Leavenworth	.70	.64	.82	.82		8
Big Village	.60	.55	.73	.73	.73	

[a] Lower half of matrix presents simple matching coefficient of similarity; upper half presents number of positive matches.

mortuary differentiation. As in the previous comparison, the degree of similarity between each site was calculated, and the results are presented in Tables 8.6–8.8.

With mortuary differentiation, as with normative treatments, the Omaha site tended to be distinct whereas those of the Pawnee and Arikara exhibited a degree of mixing. In this particular comparison, the Arikara sites clustered together, while those of the Pawnee were slightly more similar to non-Pawnee sites, on average, than to other Pawnee sites. The same temporal effects, noted earlier, were also seen, particularly among the later sites in the sequence, Big Village, Leavenworth, and Clarks.

As mortuary differentiation is closely tied to the organization of the living society, it is not surprising that it is a poor discriminator between these three ethnic groups—particularly between the Pawnee and Arikara, which shared very similar forms of societal organization. What may be of more interest is the fact that all three cultures provide such a consistent view of social differentiation. Even though they are similarly organized, there is, in theory, nothing to prevent a much simpler representation of this structure from being expressed in their mortuary rituals. This

TABLE 8.7

Comparison of Differential Funerary Treatments by Ethnic Group

	Average similarity	
	Within group	Between groups
Pawnee	.61	.65
Arikara	.82	.68
Omaha	—	.67

TABLE 8.8

Comparison of Differential Funerary Treatments by Site

Site	Most similar site	Same ethnic division
Barcal	Leavenworth (.70)	−
Linwood	Clarks (.82)	+
Clarks	Linwood (.82)[a]	+/−
Larson	Leavenworth (.82)	+
Leavenworth	Larson (.82)[b]	+/−
Big Village	Clarks (.73)[c]	

[a] Leavenworth site exhibited the same similarity value with Clarks.
[b] Clarks site exhibited the same similarity value with Leavenworth.
[c] Larson site exhibited the same similarity value with Big Village.

may, indeed, suggest the operation of hereto unspecified systematic factors that affect the amount of differentiation that cultures will express through their mortuary treatment.

Finally, the use of artifacts in the mortuary ritual was considered. Since the types employed in this study tended to obscure minor or stylistic differences between sites and assemblages, direct comparison of material culture as a means of distinguishing ethnic affinity could not be carried out. Instead, the basic structure of artifact usage in the mortuary treatment, as reflected in the regular association of artifact types with specific age or sex categories, was analyzed. The comparisons first focus on gender-based associations and then examine age-based associations.

Table 8.9 lists those artifact types that are significantly associated with males in at least one site, and Table 8.10 presents a similar listing of female-associated types. It is obvious from both tables that the degree of overlap in gender-associated artifact types is low among the five sites. This is most extreme in the case of female-associated types, where no overlap between sites is observed. The situation is more complex for the male-associated artifacts, and for this reason a numerical comparison will again be employed. However, because of the large number of potential types relative to the actual number of constrained types at any given site, similarity will be measured using Jaccard's coefficient of similarity (Sokal and Sneath 1963:133), a measure that disregards negative matches. Table 8.11 presents the number of positive matches in the upper half of the matrix and the measure of similarity between sites in the lower half. These results are further summarized in Tables 8.12 and 8.13.

Two observations can be drawn from these tables:

1. The overall level of similarity is low—that is, none of the sites exhibit patterns of male artifact association that are similar in detail.

TABLE 8.9

Male-Associated Artifact Types

Type	Linwood	Clarks	Larson	Leavenworth	Big Village
Native glass pendant	—	—	Male	Male	—
Glass trade beads	Male	—	—	—	—
Bird beak	—	—	Male, adult	—	Male, adult
Bird bone	—	—	—	—	Male, adult
Small mammal cranium	—	—	Male	—	—
Rib shaft wrench	—	—	Male, adult	—	—
Gun parts/accessories	—	Male, adult	—	—	Male, adult
Pin game cup	—	—	—	—	Male, adult
Polished bone tube	—	—	Male	Male	—
Curved rib ornament	—	—	Male, adult	—	—
Bone point	—	—	Male, adult	—	—
Gorget	—	—	—	—	Male
Shell hair pipe	—	—	—	—	Male
Tubular shell bead	Male	Male	—	—	—
Wampum bead	—	—	—	—	Male
Perforated shell pendant	—	—	Male, adult	—	—
Metal bracelet	—	Male	—	—	—
Metal bead/bangle	Male	—	—	—	—
Iron knife	—	—	—	Male	—
Scissors	—	—	—	Male	—
Strike-a-light	—	Male	—	—	—
Small metal hardware	Male, adult	—	—	Male, adult	—
Small iron tools	—	Male, adult	—	—	—
Metal projectile point	—	Male, adult	—	—	Male, adult
Metal buckle	Male, adult	—	—	—	—
Finger ring	Male	—	—	—	—
Large cast brass bell	—	—	—	—	Male, adult
Smaller brass bell	—	—	—	—	Male, adult
Thick wire coil	—	—	—	—	Male
Metal lace/braid	—	Male	—	Male, adult	Male, adult
Small silver brooch	—	—	—	—	Male, adult
Stone spear point	—	—	Male, adult	—	—
Sandstone shaft smoother	—	Male, adult	—	—	—
Whetstone	Male, adult	Male, adult	—	—	—
Stone sphere	—	—	—	—	Male, adult
Stone projectile point	—	Male, adult	Male, adult	—	—
Stone pipe	Male	Male, adult	—	Male	Male, adult
Retouched flake	—	—	Male, adult	—	—
Plate chalcedony knife	—	—	Male, adult	—	—
End scraper	—	—	Male, adult	Male, adult	—
Pipestone ornament	—	Male, adult	—	—	—
Gypsum	—	—	Male, adult	—	—

TABLE 8.10

Female-Associated Artifact Types

Type	Linwood	Clarks	Larson	Leavenworth	Big Village
Animal teeth	—	—	—	Female	—
Awl	—	Female, adult	—	—	—
Metatarsal flesher	—	Female	—	—	—
Horse gear	—	—	—	Female	—
Iron scraper	—	Female, adult	—	—	—
Metal container	—	—	—	—	Female, adult

TABLE 8.11

Male-Associated Artifact Type Comparison[a]

Site	Linwood	Clarks	Larson	Leavenworth	Big Village
Linwood	8	3	0	2	1
Clarks	.15	12	1	2	4
Larson	0	.04	14	3	2
Leavenworth	.12	.10	.09	8	2
Big Village	.04	.15	.03	.09	15

[a] Total male-associated types in principal diagonal. Similarity values calculated using Jaccard's coefficient.

TABLE 8.12

Similarity in Male-Associated Artifact Types by Ethnic Group

	Average similarity	
	Within group	Between groups
Pawnee	.15	.08
Arikara	.09	.06
Omaha	—	.08

TABLE 8.13

Similarity in Male-Associated Artifact Types by Site

Site	Most similar site	Same ethnic division
Linwood	Clarks	+
Clarks	Linwood[a]	+/−
Larson	Leavenworth	+
Leavenworth	Linwood	−
Big Village	Clarks	

[a] Big Village exhibited the same similarity value with Clarks.

2. The sites of both the Pawnee and Arikara do tend to be slightly more similar to sites of the same ethnic division than to sites produced by other groups.

This latter observation suggests that ethnic affinity is at least weakly expressed through the pattern of male-associated artifact types. The sensitivity of these values to even small-scale sampling error and the complete lack of overlap among female-related types serve, however, to weaken the potential diagnostic value of this finding.

Comparison of age-associated artifact usage was carried out next. Table 8.14 summarizes the variation in adult-associated artifact types, whereas Table 8.15 compares artifacts associated with subadults.

It is apparent that the absolute number of types exhibiting a significant association with adults varied widely over the samples, from 6 at the Barcal site to 22 at the Larson and Big Village sites. The assessment of site similarities (Tables 8.16–8.18)

TABLE 8.14

Adult-Associated Artifact Types

Type	Barcal	Linwood	Clarks	Larson	Leavenworth	Big Village
Glass bottle						+
Bird beak			+	+	+	+
Bird bone						+
Raptor talon					+	
Rib shaft wrench				+		
Quill flattener				+		
Awl			+			
Bone/antler implement				+		
Gun parts/accessories			+			+
Pin game cup						+
Curved rib ornament				+		
Bone point				+		
Mussel shell			+	+		+
Perforated shell pendant				+		
Metal bead/bangle			+			
Iron knife	+	+	+			+
Axe/wedge			+			
Small metal hardware		+			+	+
Small iron tools			+			
Metal projectile point			+			+
Iron scraper			+			
Metal container				+		+
Metal buckle		+	+			
Finger ring					+	+

(*continued*)

TABLE 8.14 *Continued*

Type	Barcal	Linwood	Clarks	Larson	Leavenworth	Big Village
Metal button						+
Large cast brass bell						+
Smaller brass bell		+				+
Thick wire coil	+					
Metal lace/braid					+	+
Sheet brass blade		+				
Silver earring						+
Small silver brooch						+
Gunflint		+	+			+
Stone spear point				+	+	
Scoria abrader				+	+	
Sandstone shaft smoother	+		+	+		+
Whetstone		+	+			
Hammer stone				+		
Stone sphere					+	+
Stone projectile point			+	+		
Stone pipe	+		+			+
Petrified wood				+	+	
Retouched flake	+			+		
Unretouched flake				+		+
Stone knife				+		
Plate chalcedony knife				+		
Side scraper			+	+		
End scraper	+			+	+	
Pipestone ornament			+			
Gypsum				+		

provides results similar to those seen with male-associated artifacts. The average values for sites from the same ethnic group are higher than values between sites from differing groups, such that similarity in the pattern of adult-associated artifacts does tend to coincide with ethnic affiliation. It is worth noting, however, that the Omaha site exhibited a higher average similarity value with the Pawnee sites than the three Pawnee sites did among themselves. Because of these high similarity values, the Big Village site would almost certainly be misclassified on this basis. It is also interesting to note the strong temporal effect expressed in these similarity values, particularly among the later sites in the sequence.

The comparison of subadult-associated artifacts among the six sites (Tables 8.19–8.21) provides results that are much more ambiguous in their expression of ethnic affinity. For both the Pawnee and the Arikara, the levels of within-group similarity are actually lower than the between-group values. Indeed, every site considered either was most similar to a site belonging to a different ethnic group or was ambiguous, with tied similarity values. Interestingly, no types were signifi-

TABLE 8.15

Subadult-Associated Artifact Types

Type	Linwood	Clarks	Larson	Leavenworth
Glass bottle				+
Ceramic pot			+	+
Glass trade beads		+	+	
Animal teeth			+	
Gun parts/accessories			+	
Heavy shell bead			+	
Rectangular shell bead			+	
Flat shell bead			+	
Metal bracelet			+	
Metal bead/bangle				+
Metal eating implement		+		+
Small iron tools				+
Metal projectile point	+			
Iron digging implement		+		
Finger ring		+		
Metal button	+			
Large cast brass bell		+		
Lead ring/coil	+	+		+

cantly associated with subadults at either the Big Village or Barcal sites. If these sites had been included in the comparison, the divergence between subadult artifact association and ethnic division would have been even more pronounced.

Similar ambiguities arise when considering the more specific symbolic function of particular artifacts (e.g., the uniformity in the symbolic usage of stone pipes and bird beaks) or when comparing the results of multivariate analysis (see Chapter 7). Any group-specific pattern of artifact usage tends to be obscured both by the set of

TABLE 8.16

Adult-Associated Artifact Types Comparison[a]

	Barcal	Linwood	Clarks	Larson	Leavenworth	Big Village
Barcal	6	1	3	3	1	3
Linwood	.08	7	4	0	1	4
Clarks	.12	.16	18	2	1	8
Larson	.11	0	.05	22	5	5
Leavenworth	.06	.06	.04	.16	10	5
Big Village	.11	.14	.20	.11	.16	22

[a] Total adult associated types in principal diagonal. Similarity values calculated using Jaccard's coefficient.

TABLE 8.17

Similarity in Adult-Associated Artifact Types by Ethnic Group

	Average similarity	
	Within group	Between groups
Pawnee	.12	.09
Arikara	.16	.07
Omaha	—	.14

TABLE 8.18

Similarity in Adult-Associated Artifact Types by Site

Site	Most similar site	Same ethnic division
Barcal	Clarks	+
Linwood	Clarks	+
Clarks	Big Village	−
Larson	Leavenworth	+
Leavenworth	Larson[a]	+/−
Big Village	Clarks	

[a] Big Village exhibited the same similarity value with the Leavenworth site.

TABLE 8.19

Subadult-Associated Artifact Types Comparison[a]

Site	Linwood	Clarks	Larson	Leavenworth
Linwood	3	1	0	1
Clarks	.11	6	1	2
Larson	0	.07	8	1
Leavenworth	.11	.17	.07	6

[a] Total subadult associated types in principal diagonal. Similarity values calculated using Jaccard's coefficient.

TABLE 8.20

Similarity in Subadult-Associated Artifact Types by Ethnic Group

	Average similarity	
	Within group	Between groups
Pawnee	.11	.12
Arikara	.07	.12

TABLE 8.21

Similarity in Subadult-Associated Artifact Types by Site

Site	Most similar site	Same ethnic division
Linwood	Clarks[a]	+/−
Clarks	Leavenworth	−
Larson	Leavenworth[b]	+/−
Leavenworth	Clarks	−

[a] Leavenworth exhibited the same similarity value with the Linwood site.
[b] Clarks exhibited the same similarity value with the Larson site.

artifacts that have a consistent function in all sites as well as by the relatively high level of variation in the specific associations of other types at each site. These two divergent aspects of mortuary patterning render artifact usage an unreliable indicator of ethnic affiliation, at least in the present samples.

Results

Two results emerge from this brief consideration of ethnic boundaries and mortuary practices. Most important, it was demonstrated that ethnic distinctions could not reliably be distinguished in these samples. It also was shown, however, that the Omaha site tended to stand alone in the comparisons, particularly in the comparison of normative treatment attributes. This raises the possibility that differences in normative treatment may yet be useful as a measure of cultural affinity.

The discrimination of Omaha, Pawnee, and Arikara cemeteries was hindered by two related factors. First, distinctions between groups were overshadowed by the broadly shared social forms and material culture elements that were basic to the Plains Village lifeway. In terms of their social and economic adaptations, the Omaha, Pawnee, and Arikara were more similar than different. This was further accentuated by the typology used in the study, which tended to de-emphasize minor stylistic differences in the material culture. The second factor that operated to mask ethnic differences was the rapid rate of culture change. The comparisons demonstrated that contemporary sites produced by differing groups were often more similar than the sites produced by a single group over time. Considering the small intervals of time separating these sites (at least by archaeological standards), this conclusion cannot be seen as encouraging for archaeological reconstructions of this kind.

It might be argued that the present sample of sites does not allow a reasonable test for ethnic differentiation to be carried out since all three groups were very similar in their basic life-style and economic organization, and all three were subject to stress.

There is no question that this particular sample has limitations, but if ethnic differentiation were an important factor in the mortuary symbolism, one might actually expect it to be most clearly emphasized among adjacent groups living in the same environment. In the case of groups living in differing environments and with different economies, differences might well be attributable to distinctive social and economic structures rather than to the intentional symbolic designation of cultural identity. A similar problem may affect the apparent operation of normative funerary treatments as an indicator of cultural affinity in the present sample.

Although normative treatment attributes (particularly burial posture) did serve to differentiate larger-scale cultural units (the Dhegiha from the northern Caddoans), it is not clear that it resulted from any intentional effort to symbolize cultural affinity, nor can it be assumed that these traits actually functioned to communicate such information. The Pawnee and the Arikara both acknowledged a close relationship and a recent common origin (see Chapter 5). But the similarities need not represent any intentional effort to symbolize this relatedness. The similarities may simply be the result of the continuation through time of once common (now shared) customs and ideology pertaining to the treatment of the dead.

On the one hand, whether or not the distinction was intentional is irrelevant since the cultural boundary or affinity was expressed regardless. On the other hand, if the similarities did arise solely as historical accident, it suggests that there is no necessary systematic relationship between broad, normative-type similarities in mortuary custom and (shared) cultural affinity or ideology.

The nature of such similarity is further complicated by the fact that more than one type of culture process may produce an identical pattern of mortuary behavior. In the present case, certain normative treatments did serve to denote cultural and linguistic affinity. Yet, completely differing processes may produce similar patterns. An entirely new complex of funerary customs accompanied the Christianization of Europe (cf. Rahtz and Watts 1980), which crosscut both ethnic and national boundaries. In this instance, shared ideology, and not cultural affinity, was responsible for many of the broad similarities that were observed in burial custom.

How, then, do we account for, or explain, the common occurrences of flexed burial during the Early Bronze Age (cf. Primas 1977), or of cremation cemeteries in the Late Bronze Age (cf. Gimbutas 1965)? The answer is, at least a priori, that we can say very little unless data from nonmortuary contexts can also be brought to bear. The fact that radically differing kinds of social processes can produce similar regional patterns of mortuary treatment must argue for extreme caution when such patterns are interpreted, particularly in the case of so-called cemetery cultures, where, either as an artifact of preservation or of professional interest, only the burials of a past culture have been examined.

Although mortuary analysis, on its own, is very limited in its ability to ascertain the mechanisms producing similarities in normative mortuary practices, the frequency with which such broad similarities occur in the archaeological record suggests that such mechanisms should be given a high research priority, particularly as archaeologists move to address problems of regional interaction and boundary formation in the past.

This chapter has considered the ability of archaeological analysis to discriminate ethnic groupings in funerary remains. The results of this brief investigation suggest that such distinctions have relatively low visibility and tend to be overshadowed in the mortuary treatment by the overall form and character of the society. In the present study, as much variation was observed between sites of the same ethnic group as between those of differing groups. Although this is not to say that ethnic distinctions are not symbolized in mortuary ritual, or that archaeological analysis is incapable of recognizing such differentiation in all cases, such distinctions cannot be assumed, a priori, to significantly structure the archaeologically observable mortuary domain.

While ethnic distinctions were not clearly recognized, a broader level of cultural and linguistic affinity was observed in aspects of the normative funerary treatments. Although this result is encouraging for the future use of mortuary evidence for the study of broad cultural boundaries in the past, the fact that cultural forces other than group boundaries, such as ideological movements, can produce similar patterns argues that indications of cultural similarity should best be sought through the combined use of differing classes of archaeological evidence, rather than relying on funerary remains alone.

9
Concluding Remarks

This study has treated funerary remains as a distinct category of archaeological phenomenon and has delimited some of the more basic systematic factors that pattern mortuary variability. The results of these investigations suggest that there are systematic effects produced when ethnographically observed regularities are cast into an archaeological context. The observation that vertical distinctions are more likely to be recognized than horizontal differentiation is a good example. The limited nature of the present investigation, however, has precluded the exploration of many other aspects of mortuary variability, particularly those relating variation in funerary behavior with differing levels of social complexity. It is not clear, for example, to what extent the results of the present study can be generalized for societies organized at a greater or lesser level of complexity. Indeed, it seems highly plausible that regularities in funerary behavior may be found that are limited or specific to particular levels of sociocultural integration. The identification of regularities of this kind, and their correlates, would represent a major refinement in the archaeological analysis of mortuary variability and, I suspect, would go a long way toward resolving the ambiguity that often surrounds the interpretation of funerary patterning.

This study also has formulated an approach through which new regularities and correlates of mortuary variability might be identified and assessed. Since it will not always be possible to obtain matched ethnographic and archaeological data, this approach, which allows ethnographic patterns to be modeled in terms of their expected archaeological representation, may provide an important tool for future archaeological research. Conversely, by transforming archaeologically observed mortuary patterning into a structural description of social differentiation, it may finally be possible to identify varieties of societal organization that are wholly undocumented in the ethnographic record.

Although this study has stressed the importance of funerary remains as a distinct class of archaeological phenomenon, it hopefully has also emphasized the necessary interdependence of mortuary analysis on convergent lines of archaeological, human biological, and environmental research. Likewise, I hope it has highlighted the potential contribution that mortuary analysis can make to other aspects of archaeological research. This is particularly true in the realm of material culture studies. What could be more useful to an analyst considering the differential distribution of artifacts on a site or between structures than knowing the age, gender, and prestige associations that the culture attached to the various artifacts? Indeed, the simple contrast between artifacts that occur on settlements as opposed to those that are found only in mortuary contexts may provide valuable insight into the perceived use, value, and replaceability of various items. This type of cross-fertilization between differing lines of archaeological research will increasingly be necessary as archaeology attempts to confront the more complex issues of culture process in the past.

The present study has outlined a formal approach that allows the archaeologist to interpret a broad range of mortuary variability and to use these observations to reconstruct in detail elements of the social organization of past societies. I am confident that as such research continues and as both stratified and nonstratified comparative cases become available, mortuary analysis will be able to play an even greater role in our understanding of past societies.

Appendix

Artifact Associations

Since the majority of the sites analyzed in the case study are unpublished, artifact occurrence data for each site are presented in full for independent evaluation. Information on grave location and treatment variables can be obtained from the maps and tables included in the text.

The format of the data is as follows. The first column in the table of artifact occurrence data indicates the grave number as recorded in field documentation or published sources; the second and third columns present the age and sex of the individual, using the following key:

Column 1: grave number
Column 2: sex (1 = male, 2 = female, 0 = undetermined)
Column 3: age (1 = 0–2 years, 2 = 3–12, 3 = 13–17, 4 = 18–30, 5 = 31–40, 6 = 41–50+, 8 = undifferentiated child, 9 = undifferentiated adult)

The artifacts associated with each grave are then specified via the sequence codes that follow. The artifact occurrence data may be used directly in this form, or they may be converted into a full incidence matrix.

Artifact Sequence Code

Var04	Glass bottle	Var47	Metal eating implement
Var05	Ceramic pot	Var48	Small metal hardware
Var06	Native glass pendant	Var49	Horse gear
Var07	Animal effigy	Var50	Small iron tool
Var08	Glass trade beads	Var51	Metal projectile point
Var09	Bear claw	Var52	Iron scraper
Var10	Animal teeth	Var53	Iron digging implement
Var11	Bird beak	Var54	Metal container
Var12	Bird bone	Var55	Metal buckle
Var13	Raptor talon	Var56	Finger ring
Var14	Small mammal cranium	Var57	Metal button
Var15	Rib shaft wrench	Var58	Large cast brass bell
Var16	Squash knife	Var59	Smaller brass bell
Var17	Scapula hoe	Var60	Thick wire coil
Var18	Quill flattener	Var61	Thin wire coil
Var19	Cancellous paint applicator	Var62	Metal lace/braid
Var20	Awl	Var63	Copper crimp/clip
Var21	Metatarsal flesher	Var64	Sheet brass blade
Var22	Elk horn scraper	Var65	Lead ring/coil
Var23	Bone/antler implement	Var66	Lead band
Var24	Gun parts/accessories	Var67	Sheet silver bracelet
Var25	Pin game cup	Var68	Silver cross
Var26	Polished bone tube	Var69	Silver hair plate
Var27	Bone pendant	Var70	Silver earring
Var28	Curved rib ornament	Var71	Small silver brooch
Var29	Bone point	Var72	Gunflint
Var30	Mussel shell	Var73	Bifacial spear point
Var31	Gorget	Var74	Scoria abrader
Var32	Shell hair pipe	Var75	Sandstone shaft smoother
Var33	Tubular shell bead	Var76	Whetstone
Var34	Wampum bead	Var77	Hammer stone
Var35	Heavy shell bead	Var78	Stone sphere
Var36	Rectangular shell bead	Var79	Stone projectile point
Var37	Shell runtee	Var80	Stone pipe
Var38	Marine snail shell	Var81	Petrified wood
Var39	Perforated shell pendant	Var82	Retouched flake
Var40	Flat shell bead	Var83	Unretouched flake
Var41	Metal bracelet	Var84	Stone knife
Var42	Metal bead/bangle	Var85	Plate chalcedony knife
Var43	Iron knife	Var86	Side scraper
Var44	Axe/wedge	Var87	End scraper
Var45	Scissors	Var88	Pipestone ornament
Var46	Strike-a-light	Var89	Gypsum

Appendix

Artifact Occurrence

Site	Grave number	Sex	Age	Artifact
Barcal (25BU4)	1	0	3	8 30
	2	2	4	22 43 82
	3	0	8	8
	4	0	8	
	5	0	8	8
	6	0	3	
	7	2	4	56
	8	0	4	20 24 30 74 75
	9	0	0	8 19 24
	10	0	9	30 60 80
	11	0	9	8 60 79
	12	1	9	30 46 51 80 82 86 87
	13	0	8	30
	14	0	8	30
	15	0	5	30 43
	16	0	4	
	17	0	4	30 87
	18	0	9	
	19	0	4	8 15 54 75
	20	0	8	30
	21	0	0	5 8
	22	0	8	66
	23	0	0	5 8 30 54 60 75 82
	24	0	2	30
	25	0	9	42 66
	26	0	9	
	27	1	5	43
	28	0	2	
	29	0	0	
	30	0	4	59
	31	0	8	
	32	0	0	8 60
	33	0	0	88
	34	0	0	30
Linwood (25BU1)	1	1	9	33
	2	0	0	8 9 12 24 42 45 48 49 50 57 58 59 65 83 89
	3	0	1	8
	4	0	1	
	5	0	2	24 33 41 54 59 65
	6	0	2	4 30 42 54 76
	7	0	1	4 8 39 42 54
	8	1	6	8 14 31 42 54 59 64 76 80
	9a	0	1	8 26 30 56 57
	10	0	0	70
	11	0	0	41 42 70

Site	Grave number	Sex	Age	Artifact
	12	0	2	57 65 75
	13	0	2	8
	14	0	1	4
	15	0	8	
	16	0	1	
	17	0	0	8 24 33 47 48 55 57 70 71
	18	0	8	
	19	0	0	14 33 43 54 57
	20	1	5	8 33
	21	2	4	5
	22	0	2	8 15 16 18 42 51 75 80 84
	23	0	0	
	24	0	2	42 51 80
	25	1	5	8 12 33 43 48 49 54 55 75
	26	0	2	8 13 24 33 65 66 70 80
	27	0	0	20
	28	0	0	
	29	0	0	8 9 24 33 45 46 49 54 61 70 72 76
	30	0	0	14 30 54 55 75 76
	31	0	1	33 54
	32	0	0	8 10 41 59 61 65
	34	0	2	8 33 54
	35	1	4	4 8 24 41 42 48 55 56 72 76 80 81
	36	0	2	8 54 67 79
	37	1	5	24 43 46 51 54 72 76 79 82 83 84 86 87
	38	0	1	65
	39	2	4	
	40	2	4	4 30 53 54
	41	0	0	4 8 30 44 47 53 54
	42	2	9	
	43	0	1	41 65
	44	0	9	
	45	0	9	
	46	0	1	8 31 47 54
	47	1	5	4 8 30 33 56 59 68
	48	2	4	8
	50	0	0	
	51	2	5	8 59
	52	0	0	41
	Cache Burial B	0	4	8 24 43 55 64 72 76 79 82 83 84 87
Clarks (25PK1)				
Burial Hill 1	1	1	9	8 11 43 50 57 75 79 86
	2	1	6	42 46 54 72 76 79 80 83 88

(continued)

Appendix

Site	Grave number	Sex	Age	Artifact
Burial Hill 4	1	1	5	8 30 34
	2	1	4	8 46 51 75
	4	0	1	8 41 57
	5	0	9	21 54 56 86
	6	0	8	8 31 33 41 54 58
	7	0	1	
	8	0	0	
	9	2	4	
	10	2	4	4 20 21 30 43 44 52 54
	12	0	0	8 70 72
	13	0	0	59
	14	0	8	8 54 57 62 65 70
	15a	0	0	24 30 41 43 48 50 54 68 76 80
	15b	0	9	
	16	0	8	8 33 41
	17	1	5	11 12 30 42 59 62 70
	18	0	9	5 8 22
	19	0	3	8 24 33 47 70
	20	0	8	8
	21	0	8	8 47 53 59 69
	22	0	9	8 43 51
	23	1	9	
	24	2	4	65 72 86
	25	0	8	8 65
	26	2	4	
	27	0	9	8 24 42 48 54 57 72 76 79
	28	0	0	
	30	0	8	4 8 24 30 43 45 46 48 54 59 79 82
	32	0	0	8
Burial Hill 5	1	0	1	8 30 52 65
	2	0	8	8 65
	3	0	1	8 13 30 65
	4a	0	1	4 8 47 48
	4b	0	1	
	5	0	2	8 54 56
	6	0	1	56 65
	7	2	4	8 11 21 30 52 54 57 59 65
	8	0	1	
	9	0	2	22 30 54 76
	10	1	9	11 24 41 43 49 50 57 62 72 75 76 80 82 88
	11	1	4	8 65
	12	0	2	59 65
	13	0	2	8
	14	0	9	8 22 24 30 33 42 43 51 52 54 55 56 76 82 85 86
	15	0	2	8 33 49

Artifact Associations 309

Site	Grave number	Sex	Age	Artifact
	16	1	6	30 33 43 44 51 54 75 76
	17	0	8	8 33 54 57 59 65 82 86
	18	1	5	24 30 43 48 76
	19	0	1	47
	21	0	1	
	22	0	1	8 41 47 53 54 56 57 65
	BP3	0	8	8 43 58
Burial Hill 6	1	1	6	33 41 43 55
	2	0	8	4 8 33 42 51 56 58 65
	3	0	0	48 51
	4	0	2	20 22 53 65
	BP3	1	4	43 54 80
Burial Hill 7	1	0	0	8 33 48 56
	2	0	8	65
	3	0	9	78
	4a	0	8	8 33 43 47 54 56 57
	4b	0	1	4 8 33 54 56
	5	0	1	54 56 65
Larson (39WW2)				
Feature 101	2	0	2	8
	11	0	1	33 35 42
	12b	2	5	8
	15	0	1	38
	17b	0	1	8 14
	19	0	2	38
	22b	0	1	5 24
	27c	1	6	33 35 42
	29e	0	2	35
	32d	2	4	82
	32e	0	2	35
	33b	2	5	30 35
	33e	1	5	12
	35a	0	1	82
	38c	0	2	35 81
	40a	0	1	79
Feature 103	1	0	2	16 82
Feature 201	2d	1	4	82
	3a	2	5	12
	3f	2	5	74 82
	6a	1	5	16
	8c	1	6	18 27 38 42 84
	8d	1	4	38
	10a	0	1	38
	10b	0	1	5 38
	11a	0	1	82

(*continued*)

Appendix

Site	Grave number	Sex	Age	Artifact
	11d	0	1	38
	14c	0	1	10
	19d	2	4	38
	27a	1	4	74 82 83
	27d	0	1	81
	29	0	2	5 8 18 20 24 26 30 39 41 42 51 63 64 73 81 84 87
	30c	0	1	40 42
	30e	0	2	38
	30g	0	2	12 27 39 42
	31	0	2	8
	32c	1	5	11 78 81 82 83 86
	34b	2	4	8 48
	35c	2	4	38
	38b	2	4	38
	40	0	1	38
	44	0	1	17
	46	0	2	35
	47e	0	2	35
	49	0	1	38
	50	0	3	8 11 17 41 48 87
	52a	0	1	38
	52b	1	3	15
	53	0	2	8 33 40
	54a	1	4	28 86
	54b	1	4	8 37
	55f	2	5	8 63
	55g	1	4	11 73 78
	55i	1	4	14 18 73 78
	58	0	3	8 35
	61a	0	1	8 38 82
	62	0	1	8
	63a	0	2	35
	63c	1	6	42 61 74 81 85 87 88
	64c	0	2	35 38 39
	65	0	3	8 41 82
	68a	1	5	15 74
	69b	1	6	39 42
	69c	1	5	8 38
	71a	0	1	5 36
	75a	1	5	26 28 54 81 84 86
	78	0	1	8 38
	80b	0	2	35
	81	0	1	5 10
	82a	0	2	35 81 82 83
	84a	1	5	8 73 82

Site	Grave number	Sex	Age	Artifact
	84c	2	6	42 83
	85	1	5	14 26 42 82 85
	88	0	2	8 41 42 63
	91	0	2	42 87
	93d	2	4	5 38
	94a	1	5	9 15 18 38 54 75 78 80 81 82 84 86
	94b	1	4	38
	95	1	9	81
	96	0	1	38
	97g	1	5	11 17
	99	0	1	8 38 40
	100	0	2	42
	101a	0	1	8
	101b	2	5	8 18 42 54 64 81 85
	102g	0	2	11 12
	104	0	2	8
	106	0	1	8 82
	107	0	1	8
	109a	0	2	8 33
	110a	0	1	8 33 40
	110b	0	1	8 33 40
	113c	0	2	8 36
	116a	0	1	8 33 40
	117	2	4	8 82
	119	0	2	8 38
	122b	2	4	8 42
	124a	0	1	8
	124b	1	4	81 82 86
	125	0	1	14 86
	126a	0	2	8 14
	127b	1	5	6 11 81 86
	128	1	5	39
	130c	0	5	28
	131	0	2	16
	132	2	4	18
	133c	1	4	8 40
	134	0	2	35 82
	136a	0	2	8 81 82 86
	142	2	4	8 82
	145d	1	5	39
	146b	1	4	38 78
Feature 301	2f	0	4	12 72 75 76 78 81 82 83 86 88
	3h	1	5	8 11 15 23 30 33 38 41 51 64 73 74 78 81 82 83 84 85 86 87 88
	4	0	1	33 38

(*continued*)

Site	Grave number	Sex	Age	Artifact
	5	0	3	8 37
	7	0	9	8 14 16 20 42 51 79 84
	8b	0	1	8
	8c	0	1	8
	9b	0	1	8 33 35 36
	11	1	4	79
	13	0	1	8 37
	14	0	3	8 36 42 51 64 87
	15	0	2	8 62
	16	2	6	18
	19b	0	3	8 14
	19c	0	3	8 35
	20	1	9	8 38
	21	0	9	35 82
	22a	1	5	8 29 40 42
	29c	1	4	11 28 38 39 78
	31	0	2	8 42 63
	32	0	2	8 42 54
	33c	2	4	11 82
	38c	0	2	6 82
	39c	0	1	10 38
	40	0	2	8
	41a	0	9	8 15 20 30 35
	42	0	9	8 12 15 33 39 74 75 76 78 80 81 82 84 85 88
	43a	0	9	8 80
	45	0	1	5 8 37 38 40 82
	47	2	9	35
	49b	0	9	18
	50b	2	9	8 33 51
	50e	1	9	5 8 78
	50f	0	3	8 33 35
	50g	1	9	29 73
	50h	0	9	73
	55b	0	1	5
	55c	0	1	8
	58e	0	1	38
	58f	2	9	75 82
	59c	0	2	38
	60a	0	1	8
	60b	2	9	23
	60c	1	9	15 23 39 51 54 63 75 78 81 82 84 86 87 88
	61	0	2	8 35 41
	62a	0	1	16
	62b	1	9	6 73
	65	0	2	18 20 35 41 42 87
	66	2	9	8 34 37 42 74 81 82 85

Artifact Associations 313

Site	Grave number	Sex	Age	Artifact
	67b	0	1	8 33
	68a	0	2	8 37 40 64 82 86
	70	0	3	8 87
	72a	0	1	81
	78	2	9	18
Leavenworth (39CO9)				
Area A, F101	1a	1	4	8
	3b	1	4	42 77
	6	0	2	38 78
	7	1	6	8
	9	2	3	8 41 42
	11	0	2	8 41 56
	12	2	4	8
	14	0	2	6 8
	15	1	6	6 8 9 13 24 26 51
	17	0	2	8 42 54
	18a	1	5	7 42
	19	0	1	41 42
	24	1	4	8 42
	25	0	2	4 6
	26	2	4	42 54 56
	28	0	2	8 9
	30	1	6	8
	31a	2	5	19 56
	32	0	1	6 8
	34	0	1	8 19 24 39 75
	35	2	6	8 11 13 14 24 49 51 72 74 78 80 83
	36	0	3	8
	38c	0	2	8 9 11 57
	38d	0	1	8
	40	0	1	24 26 72 78
	41	0	1	42
	42	2	4	8
	45	0	2	8 47
	46	0	2	8 57
	47	0	1	8 33 39
	48a	2	4	8 18
	51	0	1	8 42
	54a	2	6	7 8 10 38 54 57 75 78
	55	0	1	8
	56	0	1	8 57
	57	0	1	8
	58	0	1	8
	59	0	1	7 18 24 42 51
	60	0	1	8 9 26

(continued)

314 Appendix

Site	Grave number	Sex	Age	Artifact
	61	0	2	5 8 41
	63	0	1	8 31 32 59
	64	0	2	8
	65	1	5	8 24 43 48 54 60 72 74 80 82 86
	66	0	1	6 8 57
	67	0	1	8
	68	1	5	8 38
	69	2	4	6 8 10
	73	2	5	42
Area A, F201	1	2	4	8 15
	3	0	1	6 8 51
	4	2	5	8 39 42
	5a	2	4	8 49 51
	5b	0	3	6 8 14 19 24 30 41 42 57 72
	7b	0	2	8
	8	0	1	8
	10	1	5	8
	11	0	3	8 24
	12	0	1	8 56
	13	2	4	8 21 57
	15	1	4	8 48 56
Area B,C, F102	1	0	3	8 38
	3d	1	4	6 8 12 30 41
	4	2	4	8
	12a	1	5	41 48 56
	16	2	3	8 38 41 54 59
	17	1	4	6 8 9 32
	18d	1	4	6 8 12 18 38 45 54 56 59
	20	0	1	6 8 10 59
	22	1	5	8 56 72 84
	24a	0	1	8 42
	24b	0	1	6 8
	25	1	5	8 13 72
	27	0	1	8 9 10 11 12 13 24 51 72
	28	0	2	8 60 65
	31	0	2	8 57 75
	33	0	2	8 32 42 54 75
	36b	1	6	8 43 48 62 79
	42	1	6	8 9 11 14 20 24 41 54 59 73 78 87
	43	1	6	26 48 57
	46	1	5	8
	49	0	1	8 9 10 31
	51	0	1	6 8 10 41 42 55 83
	52	0	1	8 42
	53a	0	2	8
	54	0	1	8 42
	55	1	4	9

Artifact Associations

Site	Grave number	Sex	Age	Artifact
Area B,C, F202	1	0	2	8 10
	3	1	5	6 8 13
	4	0	1	4 6 8 9 14 15 24 32 43 45 48 49 50 51 54 72 75 79 80 83
	5a	0	1	8 9
	5b	0	1	8 42
	5c	0	2	8 12 23 47
	6	0	5	11 14 48 74 78
	7	0	2	12 13 19
	8a	2	3	8 10 82
	9	0	1	8 14
	10a	0	2	6 8 38 57
	10b	2	3	8 41 42
	12	1	5	8 10 24 57 59 62 86
	13	1	5	42 51
	14	0	9	8 57
	17a	0	1	8 48
	17b	0	1	8
	17c	2	5	8 9 11 12 13 24 31 41 48 54 55 73
Area D, F103	2	0	1	8 9 24 65
	5	0	1	24 42 54 61 78
Area D, F203	1	1	5	8 24 43 45 48 54 56 78 79 80 83
	2	0	9	8 24
	4	0	9	6 8
	6	0	8	6 8 43 51 54
	7	0	1	8
	8	0	4	8 24 41
	9	1	5	8 24
	11	0	1	8
	15	0	1	43 48 50
	17a	0	1	8 57
	17b	0	9	6 8 54 56
	18	0	2	8 54
	20	0	4	8 19 43 77
	21	0	9	41
	23	1	4	72
	25	0	1	5
	26	0	5	8
	27	0	6	8 48 51
	28	0	9	8 54
	30	0	1	6 8 42
	31	0	1	8
	32	0	9	8 60
Area E, F120	1	0	1	11
	5	0	2	9 41 57
Area E, F220	4b	0	1	8 38 42 65

(*continued*)

Appendix

Site	Grave number	Sex	Age	Artifact
Big Village (25DK2,10)				
DK2	3	0	1	8 42 54
	4	2	4	83
	7	2	4	4 8 10 30 34 41 42 48 54 56 65 67 69 70 72 83
	8	1	6	8 9 12 25 30 32 34 41 42 51 59 70 80
	10	0	3	8 32 34 42 55
	11	1	4	8 24 32 34 41 57 59 62
	14	2	4	8 34 43 45 48 54 57 65 66 69
	17	1	6	8 11 12 15 24 31 34 42 43 44 48 51 54 58 59 60 61 62 72 75 78 80
	20	1	4	8 41 57
	23	2	4	4 8 41 54
	24	0	2	67
	25	0	8	
DK10	1a	2	0	2 8 41 42 69
	1b	0	2	8 41 42 47 54 60 66
	2	0	8	8 41 66 67 76
	3	2	4	8 75
	5	1	6	4 8 34 54 78
	6	0	8	8 34
	9	0	1	8 32 41 65
	11	0	8	8
	12	0	1	8 32 34
	13	0	2	8
	14	0	2	8 60 61 65 66 77
	16	1	4	8 11 32 34 41 42 56 57 58 59 61 67 69 70 71 83
	17b	0	1	8 34 54 60 61
	18	1	6	8 10 11 14 24 25 31 34 41 43 46 57 61 65 71 72 87
	19	0	2	8 10 14 31 34 69
	22	0	1	8 34
	25	1	6	60 73 83
	26	0	2	8 32 34 56 65 66 67 68 70 88
	27	2	4	41 54 56 61
	31	0	0	8
	32	0	1	8 34
	33	0	1	41 60 61
	34	0	1	41 65

References

Abel, A. H.
 1939   *Tabeau's Narrative of Loisel's Expedition to the Upper Missouri.* Norman: University of Oklahoma Press.

Acsádi, Gy., and J. Nemeskéri
 1970   *History of Human Life Span and Mortality.* Budapest: Akadémiai Kiadó.

Allen, W., and J. Richardson
 1971   The reconstruction of kinship from archaeological data: The concepts, methods, and the feasibility. *American Antiquity* 36:41–45.

Allis, S.
 1887   Forty years among the Indians and on the eastern borders of Nebraska. *Transactions and Reports of the Nebraska State Historical Society* Vol. II: 133–166.

Angel, J. L.
 1954   Human biology: Health and history in Greece from first settlement until now. *Yearbook of the American Philosophical Society* 98:168–174.
 1969   The bases of paleodemography. *American Journal of Physical Anthropology* 30:427–437.

Asch, D.
 1976   The Middle Woodland Population of the Lower Illinois Valley: A Study in Paleodemographic Methods. *Northwestern University Archaeological Program, Scientific Papers* 1.

Bartos, S., Jr.
 1939   The Ryan site, 25DK2A. Manuscript on file, Department of Anthropology, University of Nebraska.

Bass, W. M., E. R. Evans, and R. L. Jantz
 1971   The Leavenworth site cemetery: Archaeology and physical anthropology. *University of Kansas Publications in Anthropology* 2.

Bass, W. M., and M. D. Rucker
 1976   Preliminary investigation of artifact association in an Arikara cemetery (Larson site), Walworth County, South Dakota. *National Geographic Society Research Reports, 1968 projects*, pp. 33–48.

Bell, R., E. Jelks, and W. W. Newcomb
 1974   *Wichita indians.* New York: Garland Publishing Inc.

Bendann, E.
 1969   *Death customs: An analytical study of burial rites.* London: Dawson of Pall Mall.

Binford, L. R.
- 1962 Archaeology as anthropology. *American Antiquity* 28:217–225.
- 1963a An Analysis of cremations from three Michigan sites. *Wisconsin Archaeologist* 44:98–110.
- 1963b "Red Ochre" caches from the Michigan area: A possible case of cultural drift. *Southwestern Journal of Anthropology* 19:89–108.
- 1964 Archaeological Investigations on Wassam Ridge. *Southern Illinois University Museum Archaeological Salvage Report* 17.
- 1968 Archaeological perspectives. In *New perspectives in archaeology*, edited by L. R. Binford and S. R. Binford. Chicago: Aldine Publishing Co. Pp. 5–32.
- 1972 *An archaeological perspective.* New York: Seminar Press.
- 1977 General introduction. In *For theory building in archaeology*, edited by L. R. Binford. New York: Academic Press. Pp. 1–10.

Binford, L. R., and J. B. Bertram
- 1977 Bone frequencies and attritional processes. In *For theory building in archaeology*, edited by L. R. Binford. New York: Academic Press. Pp. 77–156.

Binford, S. R.
- 1968 A structural comparison of disposal of the dead in the Mousterian and the Upper Paleolithic. *Southwestern Journal of Anthropology* 24:139–154.

Blau, P.
- 1970 A formal theory of differentiation in organizations. *American Sociological Review* 35:201–218.

Brackenridge, H. M.
- 1962 *Views of Louisiana together with a journal of a voyage up the Missouri River in 1811.* Chicago: Quadrangle Books, Inc.

Bradbury, J.
- 1904 Travels in the interior of America, 1809–1811. In *Early western travels*, Vol. 5, edited by R. G. Thwaites. Cleveland: Arthur H. Clark Co.

Braun, D.
- 1977 Middle Woodland–early Late Woodland social change in the prehistoric central midwestern U.S. Ph.D. dissertation, University of Michigan. Ann Arbor: University Microfilms.
- 1979 Illinois Hopewell burial practices and social organization: A reexamination of the Klunk–Gibson mound group. In *Hopewell archaeology, The Chillicothe Conference*, edited by D. Brose and N. Greber. Kent, Ohio: Kent State University Press. Pp. 66–79.
- 1981 A critique of some recent North American mortuary studies. *American Antiquity* 46:398–415.

Brothwell, D. R.
- 1965 *Digging up bones.* London: British Museum.

Brown, J. A.
- 1971a The dimensions of status in the burials at Spiro. In Approaches to the social dimensions of mortuary practices, edited by J. A. Brown. *Memoirs of the Society for American Archaeology* 25:92–112.
- 1971b Introduction. In Approaches to the social dimensions of mortuary practices, edited by J. A. Brown. *Memoirs of the Society for American Archaeology* 25:1–5.
- 1979 Charnel houses and mortuary crypts: Disposal of the dead in the Middle Woodland period. In *Hopewell archaeology, The Chillicothe Conference*, edited by D. Brose and N. Greber. Kent, Ohio: Kent State University Press. Pp. 211–219.
- 1981 The search for rank in prehistoric burials. In R. Chapman, I. Kinnes, and K. Randsborg (eds.), *The Archaeology of Death*, New York: Cambridge University Press. Pp. 25–38.

Buikstra, J.
- 1976 Hopewell in the Lower Illinois Valley: A regional approach to the study of human

biological variability and prehistoric behavior. *Northwestern University Archaeological Program Scientific Papers* 2.

1977 Biocultural dimensions in archaeological study: A regional perspective. In *Biocultural adaptations in prehistoric America*, edited by R. Blakely. *Southern Anthropological Society Proceedings* 11:67–84.

Burling, R.
1964 Cognition and componential analysis: God's truth or hocus-pocus? *American Anthropologist* 66:20–27.

Bushnell, D. I.
1927 Burials of the Algonquian, Siouan and Caddoan Tribes west of the Mississippi. *Bureau of American Ethnology Bulletin* 83, Washington, D.C.

Carleton, J. H.
1943 *The prairie logbooks, dragoon campaigns to the Pawnee villages in 1844*, edited by L. Pelzer. Chicago: The Caxton Club.

Carlson, G. F., and T. L. Steinacher
1976 Nebraska Highway Archaeological and Historical Salvage Investigations 1969–1973. Manuscript on file, Nebraska State Historical Society, Lincoln.

Catlin, G.
1876 *Illustrations of the manner, customs and condition of the North American Indians*. Edinburgh: John Grant.

Ceram, C. W.
1953 *Gods, Graves and Scholars*. New York: Alfred A. Knopf.

Chagnon, N.
1968 *Yanomamö: The fierce people*. New York: Holt, Rinehart and Winston.

Champe, J. L.
1939 Unpublished field documentation.
1940 Field records. Manuscript on file, Department of Anthropology, Univeristy of Nebraska, Lincoln.
1946 Ash Hollow Cave: A study of stratigraphic sequence in the Central Great Plains. *University of Nebraska Studies*, n.s. 1.

Champe, J. L., and F. Fenenga
1974 *Notes on the Pawnee*. New York: Garland Publishing.

Chapman, R.
1977 Burial Practices: An area of mutual interest. In Archaeology and anthropology, areas of mutual interest, edited by M. Spriggs. *British Archaeological Reports, Supplementary Series* 19:19–33.
1981 The emergence of formal disposal areas and the 'problem' of megalithic tombs in prehistoric Europe. In *The archaeology of death*, edited by R. Chapman, I. Kinnes, and K. Randsborg. New York: Cambridge University Press. Pp. 71–82.

Chorley, R., and P. Haggett (Editors)
1967 *Models in geography*. London: Methuen.

Christenson, A. L., and D. W. Reed
1977 Numerical taxonomy, r-mode factor analysis and archaeological classification. *American Antiquity* 42:163–179.

Clark, J. G. D.
1965 *Archaeology and society: Reconstructing the prehistoric past*. New York: Barnes and Noble.

Clarke, D. L.
1972a Models and paradigms in contemporary archaeology. In *Models in archaeology*, edited by D. L. Clarke. London: Methuen. Pp. 1–60.
1972b A provisional model of an Iron Age society and its settlement system. In *Models in archaeology*, edited by D. L. Clarke. London: Methuen. Pp. 801–870.

1973 Archaeology: The loss of innocence. *Antiquity* 47:6–18.
1977 Spatial information in archaeology. In *Spatial archaeology*, edited by D. L. Clarke. London: Academic Press. Pp. 1–32.

Coale, A. J., and P. Demeny
1966 *Regional model life tables and stable populations.* Princeton, N.J.: Princeton University Press.

Cook, D. C.
1981 Mortality, age-structure and status in the interpretation of stress indicators in prehistoric skeletons: A dental example from the Lower Illinois Valley. In R. Chapman, I. Kinnes, and K. Randsborg (eds.), *The Archaeology of Death*, New York: Cambridge University Press. Pp. 133–144.

Cowgill, G. L.
1968 Archaeological applications of factor, cluster and proximity analysis. *American Antiquity* 33:367–375.
1977 Review of Doran and Hodson: Mathematics and computers in archaeology. *American Antiquity* 42:126–129.

Cumming, R. B.
1940 Unpublished field notes on file, Nebraska State Historical Society, Lincoln.

Curtis, E. S.
1970 *The North American Indian*, Vol. 5. London: Johnson Reprint Company.

Czaplicka, M.
1914 *Aboriginal Siberia, A study in social anthropology*. Oxford: Clarendon Press.

Deetz, J.
1965 *Dynamics of stylistic change in Arikara ceramics*. Urbana: University of Illinois Press.

Denig, E. T.
1961 *Five Indian tribes of the Upper Missouri*, edited by J. C. Ewers. Norman: University of Oklahoma Press.

Doran, J.
1972 Computer models as tools for archaeological hypothesis formation. In *Models in archaeology*, edited by D. L. Clarke. London: Methuen. Pp. 425–452.

Dorsey, G.
1904a *Traditions of the Skidi Pawnee*. New York: The American Folklore Society.
1904b Traditions of the Arikara. *Carnegie Institution of Washington Publication* 17.
1906 The Pawnee, mythology (Part I). *Carnegie Institution of Washington Publication* 59.

Dorsey, J. O.
1884 Omaha sociology. **Bureau of American Ethnology Annual Reports** 3:205–370.
1886 Migrations of Siouan tribes. *American Naturalist* 20:210–222.
1890 Omaha clothing and personal ornaments. *American Anthropologist* 3:71–78.
1896 Omaha dwellings, furniture, and implements. *Bureau of American Ethnology, Annual Reports* 13:263–288.

Dumond, D. E.
1977 Science in archaeology: The saints go marching in. *American Antiquity* 42:330–349.

Dunbar, J. B.
1880 The Pawnee Indians, their history and ethnology. *Magazine of American History* 4:241–281.

Eggan, F.
1955 Social anthropology: Methods and results. In *Social anthropology of the North American tribes*, edited by F. Eggan. Chicago: University of Chicago Press. Pp. 485–551.

Everitt, B.
1974 *Cluster analysis*. London: Heinemann Educational Books, Ltd.

Ewers, J. C.
  1954 The Indian trade of the Upper Missouri before Lewis and Clark: An interpretation. *Bulletin of the Missouri Historical Society* 10:429–446.

Farkas, Gy.
  1970 Supposition of genetic connections of Bronze-Age finds on the basis of blood-groupings. *Acta Biologica Szeged* 16:149–154.

Fletcher, A.
  1908 The Arikara. In Handbook of American Indians North of Mexico, edited by F. W. Hodge. *Bureau of American Ethnology Bulletin* 30(1):83–86.

Fletcher, A., and F. La Flesche
  1911 The Omaha tribe. *Bureau of American Ethnology Annual Reports* (1906) 27:17–654.

Fried, M.
  1967 *The evolution of political society, an essay in political anthropology*. New York: Random House.

Gilmore, M. R.
  1927 Notes on Arikara tribal organization. *Indian Notes* 4:332–350.
  1928 The making of a new head chief by the Arikara. *Indian Notes* 5:411–418.

Gimbutas, M.
  1965 *Bronze Age cultures in Central and Eastern Europe*. The Hague: Mouton and Co.

Girić, M.
  1971 *Mokrin, The Early Bronze Age Necropolis*. Beograd: *Dissertationes et Monografiae XI*.

Glob, P. V.
  1974 *The mound people*. London: Faber.

Goldstein, L.
  1976 Spatial structure and social organization: Regional manifestations of Mississippian society. Ph.D. dissertation, Northwestern University. Ann Arbor: University Microfilms.

Goodenough, W. H.
  1965 Rethinking 'status' and 'role': Toward a general model of the cultural organization of social relationships. In *The relevance of models for social anthropology*, edited by M. Banton. London: Tavistock. Pp. 1–24.

Goody, J. R.
  1962 *Death, property and the ancestors*. Stanford, Calif.: Stanford University Press.

Gordon, C., and J. Buikstra
  1981 Soil pH, bone preservation, and sampling bias at mortuary sites. *American Antiquity* 46:566–570.

Grange, R. T., Jr.
  1968 Pawnee and Lower Loup pottery. *Nebraska State Historical Society Publications in Anthropology* 3.

Greber, N.
  1976 Within Ohio Hopewell: Analysis of burial patterns from several classic sites. Ph.D. dissertation, Case Western University. Ann Arbor: University Microfilms.
  1979 Variations in social structure of Ohio Hopewell peoples. *Midcontinental Journal of Archaeology* 4:35–78.

Grinnell, G. B.
  1889 *Pawnee hero stories and folk tales*. New York: Forest and Stream Publishing Co.
  1891 Marriage among the Pawnee. *American Anthropologist* 4:275–281.
  1923 *The Cheyenne Indians*, Vol. 2. Lincoln: University of Nebraska Press.

Gruber, J. W.
  1971 Death in a late prehistoric village in Pennsylvania. *American Antiquity* 36:64–76.

Gunnerson, D. A.
 n.d. The Stanton site. Unpublished manuscript.
Hammel, E. A. (Editor)
 1965 Formal semantic analysis. *American Anthropologist* 67, part 2.
Harary, F.
 1959 Status and contrastatus. *Sociometry* 22:23–43.
Harman, H. H.
 1976 *Modern factor analysis.* Chicago: The University of Chicago Press.
Harvey, A.
 1971 Challenge and response: Environment and Northwest Iowa Oneota. Ph.D. dissertation, University of Wisconsin. Ann Arbor: University Microfilms.
Hatch, J. W.
 1976 Status in death: Principles of ranking in Dallas culture mortuary remains. Ph.D. dissertation, Pennsylvania State University. Ann Arbor: University Microfilms.
Hays, W.
 1973 *Statistics for the social sciences.* New York: Holt, Rinehart and Winston, Inc.
Hertz, R.
 1960 *Death and the right hand,* translated by R. Needham and C. Needham. Glencoe, Ill.: Free Press.
Hill, J. A.
 1970 Broken K. Pueblo: Prehistoric social organization in the American southwest. *University of Arizona Anthropological Papers* 18.
Hodder, I.
 1979 Economic and social stress and material culture patterning. *American Antiquity* 44:446–454.
Hodder, I., and C. Orton
 1976 *Spatial analysis in archaeology.* New York: Cambridge University Press.
Hodson, F. R.
 1977 Quantifying Hallstatt: Some initial results. *American Antiquity* 42:394–412.
Holder, P.
 1970 *The hoe and the horse on the plains.* Lincoln: University of Nebraska Press.
Hole, B. L.
 1980 Sampling in archaeology: A critique. *Annual Review of Anthropology* 9:217–234.
Homer
 1938 *The illiad,* edited by W. H. D. Rouse. New York: Mentor Books.
Howard, J. H.
 1974 The Arikara buffalo society medicine bundle. *Plains Anthropologist* 19:214–271.
Howe, G. M.
 1972 *Man, environment and disease in Britain.* London: Penguin Books.
Hughes, J.
 1968 Prehistory of the Caddoan speaking tribes. Ph.D. dissertation, Columbia University. Ann Arbor: University Microfilms.
Hyde, G. E.
 1974 *The Pawnee Indians.* Norman: University of Oklahoma Press.
Hymes, Dell
 1964 Direction in (ethno-) linguistic theory. In A. K. Romney and R. Goodwin D'Andrade (eds.), *Transcultural Studies in Cognition,* Special Publication, *American Anthropologist* 66(3.2):6–56.
James, E.
 1823 *Account of the S. H. Long Expedition, 1819–1820.* London: E. James.

Jantz, R.
   1973   Microevolutionary change in Arikara crania: A multivariate analysis. *American Journal of Physical Anthropology* 38:15–26.

Jardine, N., and R. Sibson
   1971   *Mathematical taxonomy.* London: John Wiley and Sons, Ltd.

Kendall, D. G.
   1971   Seriation from abundance matrices. In *Mathematics in the archaeological and historical sciences*, edited by F. R. Hodson, D. G. Kendall, and P. Tautu. Edinburgh: Edinburgh University Press. Pp. 215–252.

King, L.
   1969   The Medea Creek cemetery (Lan-243): An investigation of social organization from mortuary practices. *Archaeological Survey Annual Report* 11:23–68.

Kracht, B. R.
   1982   The effects of disease and warfare on Pawnee social organization, 1830–1859: An ethnohistorical approach. Unpublished master's thesis, Department of Anthropology, University of Nebraska.

Krause, R. A.
   1972   The Leavenworth site: Archaeology of an historic Arikara community. *University of Kansas Publications in Anthropology* 3.

Kristiansen, K.
   1979   Consumption of wealth in Bronze Age Denmark: A study of the dynamics of economic processes in tribal societies. In *New Directions in Scandinavian Archaeology* 1:158–190, edited by K. Kristiansen and C. Paludan-Müller. Copenhagen: Museum of Denmark.

Kroeber, A. L.
   1927   Disposal of the dead. *American Anthropologist* 29:308–315.

La Flesche, F.
   1889   Death and funeral customs among the Omahas. *Journal of American Folklore* 2:3–11.

Lane, R., and A. Sublett
   1972   Osteology of social organization: Residence patterns. *American Antiquity* 37:186–200.

Leach, E.
   1977   A view from the bridge. In Archaeology and anthropology: Areas of mutual interest, edited by M. Spriggs. *British Archaeological Reports Supplementary Series* 19:161–176.

Lehmer, D. J.
   1971   Introduction to Middle Missouri archaeology. *National Park Service Anthropological Papers* 1.

Lehmer, D. J., and D. T. Jones
   1968   Arikara archaeology: The Bad River phase. *Publications in Salvage Archaeology* 7. Smithsonian Institution, River Basin Surveys, Lincoln.

Lengyel, I.
   1972   Laboratory analysis of the human bone finds from the Early Bronze Age cemetery of Mokrin. In *Mokrin: The Early Bronze Age Necropolis*, Vol. 2, edited by N. Tasić. Beograd: *Dissertationes et Monografiae XII*. Pp. 75–90.

Lesser, A.
   1930   Levirate and fraternal polyandry among the Pawnees. *Man* 30:98–101.

Lévi-Strauss, C.
   1963   *Structural anthropology.* New York: Basic Books.

Lewis M., and W. Clark
   1893   *History of the expedition under the command of Lewis and Clark*, edited by E. Coues. New York: Dover Press.

Linton, R.
    1936   *The study of man.* New York: Appleton-Century Company, Inc.

Longacre, W. A.
    1970   Archaeology as anthropology: A case study. *University of Arizona Anthropological Papers* 17.

Lowie, R. H.
    1916   Societies of the Arikara Indians. *Anthropological Papers of the Museum of Natural History* 11:647–678.
    1954   Indians of the Plains. *American Museum of Natural History Anthropological Handbook* 1.

Mainfort, R. C., Jr.
    1979   Indian Social Dynamics in the Period of European Contact. *Publications of the Museum, Michigan State University Anthropological Series* Vol. 1(4).

Malinowski, B.
    1955   Magic, science and religion. Reprinted in *Magic, science and religion and other essays.* Garden City, N.Y.: Doubleday. Pp. 10–87.

Miles, D.
    1965   Socio-economic aspects of secondary burial. *Oceania* 35:161–174.

Miller, J. G.
    1965   Living systems: Basic concepts. *Behavioral Science* 10:193–237.

Morgan, D. L.
    1953   *Jedediah Smith and the opening of the West.* Lincoln: University of Nebraska Press.

Morgan, L. H.
    1959   *The Indian journals,* edited by L. A. White. Ann Arbor: The Univeristy of Michigan Press.

Murdock, G. P.
    1949   *Social structure.* New York: Macmillan.

Murie, J. R.
    1916   Pawnee Indian societies. *American Museum of Natural History Anthropological Papers* 11:543–644.

Murray, C. A.
    1900   *Travels in North America during the years 1834, 1835, and 1836.* London: William Blackwood and Sons.

Nie, N. H., C. Hull, J. Jenkins, K. Steinbrenner, and D. Bent
    1975   *Statistical package for the social sciences.* New York: McGraw-Hill Co.

Oehler, B. C., and D. Z. Smith
    1914   *Description of a journey and visit to the Pawnee Indians.* Moravian Church Miscellany (1851–1852).

Ordway, J.
    1916   Sergeant Ordway's journal, edited by M. Quaife. *Wisconsin Historical Society Collections* 22.

Orser, C.
    1980   Toward a partial understanding of complexity in Arikara mortuary practice. *Plains Anthropologist* 25:113–120.

O'Shea, J. M.
    1979   Models for the emergence of ethnic groupings on the Central Plains. Paper presented at the 37th Plains Conference, Kansas City.
    1981   Social configurations and the archaeological study of mortuary practices: A case study. In *The archaeology of death,* edited by R. Chapman, I. Kinnes, and K. Randsborg. New York: Cambridge University Press. Pp. 39–52.

O'Shea, J. M., and J. Ludwickson
  n.d.   Tonwontonga, The Big Village on Omaha Creek: A study in historic Omaha archaeology and ethnohistory. Manuscript in preparation.
O'Shea, J. M., G. Schrimper, and J. Ludwickson
  1982   Ivory-billed woodpeckers at the Big Village of the Omaha. *Plains Anthropologist* 27:245–248.
Owsley, D. W.
  1975   A demographic analysis of skeletons from the Larson site (39WW2), Walworth County, South Dakota. Unpublished master's thesis, University of Tennessee.
Parks, D.
  1979a   Bands and villages of the Arikara and Pawnee. *Nebraska History* 60:214–239.
  1979b   The northern Caddoan languages: Their sub-grouping and time depths. *Nebraska History* 60:197–213.
Peebles, C.
  1971   Moundville and surrounding sites: Some structural considerations of mortuary practices. In Approaches to the social dimensions of mortuary practices, edited by J. A. Brown. *Memoirs of the Society for American Archaeology* 25:69–91.
  1972   Monothetic divisive analysis of the Moundville burials: An initial report. *Newsletter of Computer Archaeology* 8:1–13.
Peebles, C., and S. Kus
  1977   Some archaeological correlates of ranked societies. *American Antiquity* 42:421–448.
Perry, W. J.
  1914   The orientation of the dead in Indonesia. *Journal of the Anthropological Institute of Great Britain and Ireland* 44:281–294.
Petersen, W.
  1975   A demographer's view of prehistoric demography. *Current Anthropology* 16:227–245.
Pike, Z. M.
  1966   *The Journals of Zebulon Montgomery Pike*, D. Jackson (ed.). Norman: University of Oklahoma Press.
Primas, M.
  1977   Untersuchungen zu den Bestattungssitten der ausgehenden Kupfer und frühen Bronzezeit. *Bericht der Römisch-Germanischen Kommission* 58:1–160.
Quimby, G. L.
  1966   *Indian culture and European trade goods*. Madison: University of Wisconsin Press.
Rahtz, P. A., and L. Watts (Editors)
  1980   Anglo-Saxon cemeteries. *British Archaeological Reports* 82.
Randsborg, K.
  1973   Wealth and social structure as reflected in Bronze Age burials—a quantitative approach. In *The explanation of culture change: Models in prehistory*, edited by A. C. Renfrew. London: Gerald Duckworth and Co., Ltd. Pp. 559–564.
  1974   Social stratification in Early Bronze Age Denmark: A study in the regulation of cultural systems. *Prehistorische Zeitschrift* 49.
Rathje, W.
  1973   Models for mobile Maya: A variety of constraints. In *The explanation of culture change: Models in prehistory*, edited by A. C. Renfrew. London: Gerald Duckworth and Co., Ltd. Pp. 731–760.
Reed, D. W., and A. L. Christenson
  1978   Comments on "Cluster analysis and archaeological classification." *American Antiquity* 43:505–506.

Renfrew, A. C.
- 1973 Monuments, mobilization and social organization in Neolithic Wessex. In *The explanation of culture change: Models in prehistory*, edited by A. C. Renfrew. London: Gerald Duckworth and Co., Ltd. Pp. 529–538.
- 1977 Alternative models for exchange and spatial distribution. In *Exchange systems in prehistory*, edited by T. Earle and J. Ericson. New York: Academic Press. Pp. 71–90.

Rivers, W. H. R.
- 1914 *The History of Melanesian Society*. London: Cambridge University Press.

Rothschild, N. A.
- 1979 Mortuary behavior and social organization at Indian Knoll and Dickson Mounds. *American Antiquity* 44:658–675.

Rouse, I.
- 1948 The Carib. In *The handbook of South American Indians*, Vol. 4, edited by J. Steward. Washington, D.C.: Bureau of American Ethnology. Pp. 547–566.

Rowe, J. H.
- 1962 Worsaae's law and the use of grave lots for archaeological dating. *American Antiquity* 28:129–137.

Rummel, R. J.
- 1970 *Applied factor analysis*. Evanston, Ill.: Northwestern University Press.

Saxe, A.
- 1970 Social dimensions of mortuary practices. Ph.D. dissertation, University of Michigan. Ann Arbor: University Microfilms.
- 1971 Social dimensions of mortuary practices in a Mesolithic populations from Wadi Halfa, Sudan. In Approaches to the social dimensions of mortuary practices, edited by J. A. Brown. *Memoirs of the Society for American Archaeology* 25:39–57.

Schiffer, M.
- 1976 *Behavioral archaeology*. New York: Academic Press.

Schneider, D. M.
- 1965 American kin terms and terms for kinsmen: A critique of Goodenough's componential analysis of Yankee kinship terminology. In Formal Semantic Analysis, edited by E. A. Hammel. *American Anthropologist* 67:288–308.

Sears, W. H.
- 1961 The study of social and religious systems in North American archaeology. *Current Anthropology* 2:223–246.

Service, E.
- 1962 *Primitive social organization, an evolutionary perspective*. New York: Random House.

Shakespeare, W.
- 1948 *Shakespeare: Major plays and the sonnets*, edited by G. B. Harrison. New York: Harcourt, Brace and Co.

Shannon, C. E. and W. Weaver
- 1949 *The Mathematical Theory of Communication*. Urbana: University of Illinois Press.

Shennan, S. E.
- 1975 The social organization at Branč. *Antiquity* 49:279–287.

Shennan, S. J.
- 1977 Bell beakers and their context in Central Europe: A new approach. Unpublished Ph.D. dissertation, University of Cambridge.

Siegel, S.
- 1956 *Nonparametric statistics for the behavioral sciences*. Tokyo: McGraw-Hill.

Skinner, M.
  1972   The Seafort burial site (FcPr100), Rocky Mountain House (1835–1861): Life and death during the fur trade. *Western Canadian Journal of Anthropology* 3:126–145.
Smith, G. H.
  1974   *Omaha Indians.* New York: Garland Publishing, Inc.
Sneath, P., and R. Sokal
  1973   *Numerical taxonomy.* San Francisco: W. H. Freeman and Co.
Sokal, R., and P. Sneath
  1963   *Principles of numerical taxonomy.* San Francisco: W. H. Freeman and Co.
South, S.
  1977   *Method and theory in historical archaeology.* New York: Academic Press.
Speth, J. D., and G. A. Johnson
  1976   Problems in the use of correlation for the investigation of tool kits and activity areas. In *Culture change and continuity*, edited by C. E. Cleland. New York: Academic Press. Pp. 35–58.
Sprague, R.
  1968   A suggested terminology and classification for burial description. *American Antiquity* 33:479–485.
Stickel, E. G.
  1968   Status differentiation at the Rincon site. *Archaeological Survey Annual Report* 10:209–261.
Strong, W. D.
  1935   An introduction to Nebraska archaeology. *Smithsonian Miscellaneous Collections* 93.
Sullivan, A.
  1978   Inference and evidence in archaeology: A discussion of the conceptual problems. In *Advances in archaeological methods and theory* I, edited by M. Schiffer. New York: Academic Press. Pp. 183–222.
Tainter, J.
  1973   The social correlates of mortuary patterning at Kaloko, North Koua, Hawaii. *Archaeology and Physical Anthropology of Oceania* 8:1–11.
  1975a The archaeological study of social change: Woodland systems in West-Central Illinois. Unpublished Ph.D. dissertation, Northwestern University. Ann Arbor: University Microfilms.
  1975b Social inference and mortuary practices: An experiment in numerical classification. *World Archaeology* 7:1–15.
  1976   Spatial organization and social patterning in the Kaloko cemetery, North Koua, Hawaii. *Archaeology and Physical Anthropology in Oceania* 11:91–105.
  1977   Modeling change in prehistoric social systems. In *For theory building in archaeology*, edited by L. Binford. New York: Academic Press. Pp. 327–351.
Tainter, J., and R. Cordy
  1977   An archaeological analysis of social ranking and residence groups in prehistoric Hawaii. *World Archaeology* 9:94–112.
Taylor, W.
  1969   *A Study of Archaeology.* Carbondale: Southern Illinois University Press.
Thomas, D., and J. Beaton
  1968   The Trancas Canyon cemetery site (4-LA17-197); an analysis of mortuary customs. *Archaeological Survey Annual Report* 10:162–174.
Thwaites, R. G. (Editor)
  1904   *Early western travels, 1784–1897*, 8 volumes. Cleveland: Arthur H. Clark Co.
  1906   *Travels in the interior of North America by Maximilian, Prince of Weid.* Cleveland: Arthur H. Clark Co.

Tucker, S. J.
: 1942 Indian villages of the Illinois country. *Illinois State Museum Scientific Papers* 2, Part 1 (atlas).

Ubelaker, D.
: 1974 Reconstruction of demographic profiles from ossuary skeletal samples: A case study from the Tidewater Potomac. *Smithsonian Contributions to Anthropology* 18.

Ubelaker, D., and P. Willey
: 1978 Complexity in Arikara mortuary practice. *Plains Anthropologist* 23:69–74.

Ucko, P.
: 1969 Ethnography and archaeological interpretation of funerary remains. *World Archaeology* 1:262–280.

van de Velde, P.
: 1979 The social anthropology of a Neolithic cemetery in the Netherlands. *Current Anthropology* 20:37–58.

Voorrips, A.
: 1982 Mambrino's helmet: A framework for structuring archaeological data. In *Essays on archaeological typology*, edited by R. Whallon and J. A. Brown. Evanston, Ill.: Center for American Archaeology Press. Pp. 93–126.

Watson, R. A.
: 1973 Limitations on archaeological typologies and on models of social systems. In *The explanation of culture change: Models in prehistory*, edited by A. C. Renfrew. London: Gerald Duckworth and Ço., Ltd. Pp. 209–213.

Wedel, Mildred
: 1981 The Ioway, Oto, and Omaha Indians in 1700. *Journal of the Iowa Archaeological Society* 28:1–14.

Wedel, W. R.
: 1936 An introduction to Pawnee archaeology. *Bureau of American Ethnology Bulletin* 112.
: 1938 The direct historical approach in Pawnee archaeology. *Smithsonian Miscellaneous Collections* 97.
: 1955 Archaeological materials from the vicinity of Mobridge, South Dakota. *Bureau of American Ethnology Bulletin* 157.
: 1961 *Prehistoric man on the Great Plains.* Norman: University of Oklahoma Press.
: 1979 Some reflections on Plains Caddoan origins. *Nebraska History* 60:272–293.

Weltfish, G.
: 1965 *The lost universe.* New York: Basic Books.

Whallon, R.
: 1973 Spatial analysis of occupation floors. I; Applications of dimensional analysis of variance. *American Antiquity* 38:266–278.

Willey, G. R.
: 1966 An introduction to American archaeology, Vol. 1. Englewood Cliffs, N.J.: Prentice-Hall.

Wishart, D.
: 1975 *Clustan 1C, user's manual.* London: University College.

Wishart, D. J.
: 1979 The dispossession of the Pawnee. *Annals of the Association of American Geographers* 69:382–401.

Wobst, H. M.
: 1977 Stylistic behavior and information exchange. In For the director: Essays in honor of James B. Griffin, edited by C. Cleland. *Anthropological Papers of the Museum of Anthropology, University of Michigan* 61:317–342.

Wood, W. R.
- 1955 Historical and archaeological evidence for Arikara visits to the Central Plains. *Plains Anthropologist* 4:27–39.
- 1974 Northern plains village cultures: Internal stability and external relationships. *Journal of Anthropological Research* 30.

Wood, W. R., and D. L. Johnson
- 1978 A survey of disturbance processes in archaeological site formation. In *Advances in archaeological methods and theory*, Vol. 1, edited by M. Schiffer. New York: Academic Press. Pp. 315–383.

Zimmerman, L., T. Emerson, P. Willey, M. Swegle, J. Gregg, P. Gregg, E. White, C. Smith, T. Haberman, and M. P. Bumsted
- 1980 The Crow Creek site (39BF11) massacre: A preliminary report. Report to the U.S. Army Corps of Engineers, Omaha District.

Index

A

Achieved wealth, *see also* Vertical social differentiation
 ambiguity in definition, 217, 251–252
Acsádi, Gy., 3, 34, 40
Ad hoc assumption, 3, 13, 39
Affinity, 41
Allis, S., 72–74
Anaehoomalu, 17
Angel, L., 3, 34, 40
Archaeological formation process, 15, 23–28, 49
Arikara
 archaeological reconstruction, 218–220
  differentiation of ethnic groups, 288–300
  ethnographic accounts, comparisons with, 220–221
  horizontal social distinctions, 219
  limitations, 220
  special status distinctions, 219–220
  temporal variation, 270–283
  vertical social distinctions, 219
 ethnohistory, 79–80
 kinship, 80
 mortuary practices, 81–82
 sites, 51, 58–59
 social ranking, 80–81
 village agglomeration, consequences of, 280–281
Arrow-maker's kit, 180, 190
Asch, D., 3
Ashanti, 10

B

Barcal site
 archaeological analysis
  artifact occurrence, 93–103
  burial covering, 90–91
  disarticulated burial, 90–91
  formal treatment, 87–93
  hierarchical fusion cluster analysis, 96–100
  monothetic division cluster analysis, 100–105
  mortuary differentiation, 103–108
  normative treatment program, 90
  principal component analysis, 94–96
 band affiliation, 56–57
 dating of, 56, 59–60
 description, 56–57
 plan, 92
Bartos, S., 57
Bass, W., 58–59, 195, 198, 271
Beaker network, 3
Beaton, J., 2
Bell, E., 57, 62
Bendan, E., 33–34
Bertram, J., 23
Big Elk, 79
Big Village site, *see also* Tonwontonga
 archaeological analysis
  artifact occurrence, 229–243
  burial covering, 227
  disarticulated burial, 221–225, 246–247
  female ranking, 237, 243, 245–246, 281
  formal treatment, 221–229

hierarchical fusion cluster analysis,
    232–237
monothetic division cluster analysis,
    237–243
mortuary differentiation, 243–249
normative treatment program, 221
principal component analysis, 230–232
dating of, 57–60
description, 57–58
plan, 226
Binford, L., 3–8, 13–16, 23, 29–30, 33,
    35–36, 39, 45–46, 61–62
hypotheses, 5–7
Binford, S., 33
Blackbird, 77
Black Buffalo, 79
Blau, P., 4, 16, 20
Blood group, 40
Blood Run site, 52, 78
Bontoc Igorot, 10
Boundaries
    ethnic, 14
    nature of, 286
    visibility in funerary remains, 301
Bowers, A., 58
Brackenridge, H., 59, 80
Bradbury, J., 58–59, 79
Braun, D., 2, 17–18, 45, 48
Bronze Age
    cemeteries and tumuli, 26
    Early, 300
    economic systems, 2–3
    Late, 300
Brothwell, D., 3
Brown, J. A., 2, 8–9, 11, 13, 19, 21, 26, 31,
    46, 48
Buikstra, J., 3, 25, 40
Burial covering, *see also* individual sites, 53
Bushnell, D., 78–79

C

Caldwell, J., 59
Calumet, 151, 245, 261
Cannibalism, 34
Carleton, J., 74
Carib, 34
Carlson, G., 55
Catlin, G., 59, 77–78
Cemetery, as territorial marker, 13, 287
Chambered tombs, 25, 37
Champe, J., 55–58, 72

Chapman, R., 2
Charnel house, 37
Chaui, *see* Grand Pawnee
Cheyenne, 36
Choctaw, 8
Chorley, R., 43
Christenson, A., 68
Circumstance of death
    mortuary treatment, effect on, 36
Clark, J. G., 25
Clark, W., 55, 59, 280
Clarke, D. L., 24, 27, 31, 33, 41
Clarks Site
    archaeological analysis
        artifact occurrence, 140–152
        burial covering, 139
        disarticulated burial, 138–139
        formal treatment, 132–140
        hierarchical fusion cluster analysis,
            145–150
        monothetic division cluster analysis,
            148–155
        mortuary differentiation, 152–158
        normative treatment program, 132
        principal component analysis, 140–146
    dating of, 56, 59–60
    description, 56
    grave destruction at, 56
    plan, 137
Clustan, 1-C, 68
Cluster analysis, 68–69; *see also* individual sites
    interpretation of results, 69
    monothetic division, 68
    Ward's method, 68
Coale, A., 34
Coefficient
    congruence of, 67–68, 266–268,
        276–278
    phi, 66
    similarity
        Jaccard, 29, 292
        Gower, 29
        simple matching, 287
Componential analysis, 10
Constraint, determination of, 65–66
Control, experimental, 28–29, 31, 50, 86
Cook, D., 3
Cordy, R., 17–18
Corpse treatment, variability in, 39–40
Correlate, archaeological, 8, 44–46, 48–49
Cowgill, G., 66, 68

Cross cultural regularity, 4, 12–13, 17
  role in mortuary theory, 20–21
Crow Creek site, 34
Culture change
  expressed through mortuary patterning, 281–282
  historic period, 60, 83, 220, 299
Cumming, R., 56
Cumulative record, mortuary remains as, 13–14, 35
Curtis, E., 80–81
Czaplicka, M., 33

D

Deetz, J., 1, 80, 83
Delaware, 60
Delisle, G., 75, 280
Demeny, P., 34
Demographic analysis, 3, 34
Denig, E., 80, 280
Depopulation, among Plains tribes, 279, 282
Depositional pathway, 24–27, 41
Deritualization of mortuary symbols, 216
Diachronic variation, 2, 14, 30; *see also* Temporal change
Diet, 40
Directional inference, 12–13, 18, 29–30, 36, 45
Disintegration of Plains Village lifeway, 70, 282
Dog burial, 57
Doran, J., 2
Dorsey, G., 73–75, 82
Dorsey, J., 57, 62, 75–76
Drift, in mortuary behavior, 30, 35
Dunbar, J., 73

E

Eggan, F., 83
Ethnic differentiation in mortuary practices, 288–301
  artifact usage, 292–299
    age related, 295–299
    gender related, 292–295
  normative treatment program, 288–290, 300
  social categories differentiated, 290–292
Energy expenditure, 4, 15–19, 45, 47, 250
  measurement of, 18–19
  unbiased indicator of rank differentiation, 17–18
Environmental evidence, inclusion of, 39, 41, 83

Epidemic, Plains, 60, 279
Ethnographic accounts of funerary practices, *see also* Arikara, Omaha, Pawnee
  limitations of, 9, 21, 86, 161, 254–255
Evans, E., 59, 195, 198, 271
Explanation, 44–49

F

Factor, *see also* Principal component analysis
  loading pattern, 66–67
  scores, 68–69
Farkas, Gy., 3, 40
Feast of the dead, 287
Fenenga, F., 57, 72
Fisher Exact Test, 6
Fletcher, A., 62, 76–79, 81, 83, 252
Formal analysis of mortuary remains, 8–9, 11, 29, 31, 39, 48, 303
Fort Clark, North Dakota, 81
Fur trade, changes associated with, 281–282

G

Galley Pond Mound, 3–4, 46–47
Genoa village, 280
Gilmore, M., 80–81, 107
Gimbutas, M., 300
Goldstein, L., 12–13, 18, 20, 42–45
Goodenough, W., 4, 10–11
Goody, J., 42
Gordon, C., 25
Grand Pawnee, 54–56, 72; *see also* Pawnee
Grange, R., 54–56, 71–72
Grave furnishing, variability in, 39–40
Grave plundering, 26
Great Oasis phase, 57–58
Greber, N., 2
Greeks, ancient, 287
Grinnell, G., 36, 72–73
Gruber, J., 2

H

Haggett, P., 43
Hamlet, Prince of Denmark, 25
Harvey, A., 52, 78
Hatch, J., 2
Hawaiian chiefdom, 15–17
Heirloom, 37
Hertz, R., 42
Hidatsa, 80, 283
Hill, J., 1
Hodder, I., 43, 286

334 Index

Hodson, F., 2
Hoffman, J., 58
Holder, P., 59, 70, 72, 80
Homer, 287
Hopewell, 25, 48
Horizontal social differentiation, 15–16, 19, 46–47, 49, 64
  definition, 16
  detection of, 53, 250, 252–254
Howard, J., 81
Hughes, J., 73–74, 82
Human Relations Area Files, 5, 21
Huron, 287
Hyde, G., 74, 80, 82–83

I

Idiosyncratic variation, 35–36, 49, 218
Information
  analysis, 68
  measure of, 10, 17
Intervening variable, 11, 29
Isomorphism, 5

J

James, E., 73, 77–78
Jantz, R., 40, 58–59, 195, 198, 271
Jardine, N., 68
Johnson, C., 58
Johnson, D., 25
Johnson, G., 66, 68
Jones, D., 62

K

Kamchadal, 33
Kansas, University of, 58–59
Kapauku, 10
Kendall, D., 2
Key diagram, 8–10
King, L., 2
Kitkahahki, 72; *see also* Pawnee
Kracht, B., 280
Krause, R., 59
Kristiansen, K., 2
Kroeber, A., 30
Kus, S., 2, 13–15, 18–19, 45–48

L

La Flesche, F., 62, 76–79, 83, 252
Lane, R., 3, 40

Larson site
  archaeological analysis
    artifact occurrence, 167–187
    burial covering, 165
    disarticulated burial, 167
    formal treatment, 163–167
    hierarchical fusion cluster analysis, 170–182
    monothetic division cluster analysis, 182–188
    mortuary differentiation, 187–194
    normative treatment program, 163
    principal component analysis, 169–172
    sociotechnic objects, 186
    surrogate warrior distinction, 180, 191–194, 271, 273
    temporal change in bead availability, 181–182, 257, 284
  dating of, 58–60
  description, 58–59
  plan, 162
Leach, E., 3
Leavenworth, Colonel H., 59–60
Leavenworth site
  archaeological analysis
    artifact occurrence, 199–216
    burial covering, 196
    disarticulated burial, 196–198
    formal treatment, 194–199
    hierarchical fusion cluster analysis, 203–209
    monothetic division cluster analysis, 209–216
    mortuary differentiation, 216–218
    normative treatment program, 194
    principal component analysis, 200–203
  cases excluded from analysis, 59
  dating of, 59–60
  description, 216–218
  plan, 192–193
Lehmer, D., 58, 62
Lengyel, I., 3, 40
Lesser, A., 72
Le Sueur, J., 75
Level of sociocultural integration, 302
Lévi-Strauss, C., 42
Lewis, M., 55, 59, 280
Like-a-fishhook village, 283
Linton, R., 42
Linwood site
  archaeological analysis
    artifact occurrence, 115–129

burial covering, 112, 131
disarticulated burial, 108
formal treatment, 108–115
  hierarchical fusion cluster analysis, 119–123
  monothetic division cluster analysis, 123–129
  mortuary differentiation, 129–132
  normative treatment program, 108
  principal component analysis, 116–119
dating of, 55, 59–60
description, 54–56
grave destruction, 56
plan, 113
Local symbol, 14
Locational variability, 39–41
Longacre, W., 1
Loup River phase, 72
Lower Loup phase, 54, 56, 72
Lowie, R., 72

M

Mainfort, R., 2
Malinowski, B., 33
Mandan, 80, 283
Material culture
  change, effects of, 284
  among Plains tribes, 70, 262–264, 299
Maximillian, Prince of Wied, 59, 81
Miles, D., 33
Mississippian period, 3, 8, 26
Model
  categories of social differentiation, 41–48, 64
  Chinese box, 41
  controlling, 33
  exchange systems, 43
  Plains social differentiation, 84–85
Mokrin, Yugoslavia, 26
Morgan, L. H., 73, 76–77, 81–82
Mortuary analysis
  demographic, 3
  diachronic, 2
  site systems, 2–3
  social reconstruction, 2
Mortuary facility, variability in, 39–40
Mortuary symbolism, nature of, 107, 286–287
Mortuary variation, archaeological categories of
  corpse treatment, 39–40
  environmental, 39, 41
  grave furnishing, 39–40
  locational, 39–41

mortuary receptacle, 39–40
osteological, 39–40
Moundville site, 13–14, 18–20, 47–48
Mousterian period, 33
Multiple interment, 53
Multistaged burial program, 26, 33, 37
Murie, J., 72
Murray, C., 73
Mutilation of war dead, 82, 225, 246–247

N

Natchez–Taensa, 8
Nebraska Archaeological Survey, 55, 57
Nebraska State Historical Society, 55–56
Nebraska, University of, 59
Negative evidence, 13, 28–30
Nemeskéri, J., 3, 34, 40
New archaeology, 1–2

O

Oehler, B., 55
Omaha
  archaeological reconstruction
    differentiation of ethnic groups, 288–300
    ethnographic accounts, comparison with, 249
    horizontal social distinctions, 248
    limitations, 249
    special status distinctions, 248–249
    vertical social distinctions, 247–248
  clan designation in funerary treatment, 252–253
  ethnohistory, 75
  kinship, 76
  mortuary practices, 77–79
  sites, 52, 57–58
  social ranking, 76–77
Onpontonga, see Big Elk
Ordway, Sgt. J., 79
Organization, 15, 26–27
  measure of, 17
  relative, 17; see also Redundancy
Orser, C., 167
Orton, C., 43
Over, W., 59
Owsley, D., 58–59, 167

P

Paper chief, 77

Papuans, 34
Parks, D., 72, 79–80, 82, 280
Pathology, skeletal, 40
Patroclos, funeral of, 287
Pattern, 25
 and process, 300
 recognition, 29–31, 64
Pawnee
 archaeological reconstruction
  differentiation of ethnic groups, 288–300
  ethnographic accounts, comparison with, 161
  horizontal social distinctions, 159
  limitations, 160
  special stuatus distinctions, 159–160
  temporal variation, 258–269, 279–283
  vertical social distinctions, 158–159
 ethnohistory, 71–72
 four bands of, 72
 kinship, 72
 mortuary practices, 73–75
 sites, 51, 54–57
 social ranking, 72–73
 village amalgamation, consequences of, 280–281
Peebles, C., 2, 13–15, 18–19, 21, 45, 47–48, 65
Personal identity, 11
Petersen, W., 34
Pike, Z., 55, 280
Pitahawirata, 72; see also Pawnee
Plaque pit, 34
Plains Village tradition, 70, 279
Ponca, 78
Postcontact Coalescent tradition, 58
Postdepositional process, 8, 24–27, 34, 37
 cultural, 25–26
 natural, 25
 in Plains samples, 52, 54
Primas, M., 300
Principal component analysis, 66; see also Factor
Principle of mortuary variability, 33–38
Procedure for social analysis of funerary remains, 48–49, 64–69
Pyramid, Egyptian, 26
Pyramid of rank, 15, 45, 47, 250

Q

Quimby, G., 62, 287

R

Rahtz, P., 300
Random effect, 31
Randsborg, K., 2
Rank differentiation in mortuary practices, 14–15, 17–19, 47–48
Recovery, in Plains study, 52–54
Redundancy, 19, 29; see also Organization
 measure of, 17
Reed, D., 68
Referent of mortuary variability, 41–44, 252
 defined, 41
 expected patterns for Plains study, 64
Renfrew, A. C., 2, 43
River Basin Survey, Smithsonian Institution, 58
Rothschild, N., 2
Rowe, J., 37
Rucker, M., 58–59
Rule breaking, as a symbolic device, 251

S

Sample completeness, 9, 14, 27, 34
 considerations for Plains tests, 52–54
 effects on detection of horizontal distinctions, 253
Sarmatian, 26
Saxe, A., 2, 7, 9–15, 20, 30, 36, 48
 hypotheses, 7, 10–12, 30
Say, T., 77–79
Schiffer, M., 24, 44
Shannon–Weaver information statistic, 17
Shennan, S. E., 2
Shennan, S. J., 3
Sibson, R., 68
Sioux, 74, 82–83, 283
Site description
 Barcal, 56–57
 Clarks, 56
 Larson, 58–59
 Leavenworth, 59
 Linwood, 54–56
 Ryan, 57
 25DK10, 58
Site selection criteria, 51
Skeletal Remains, analysis of, 34–35, 39–40
 Plains study in, 54
Skidi, 57, 72–73, 80, 82, 280; see also Pawnee
 account of mortuary treatment, 73
Skinner, M., 2
Smith, D., 55

Smith, G. H., 57, 75, 77, 283
Smithsonian Institution, 59
Sneath, P., 287, 292
Social
  analysis of mortuary patterning, 48–49
  identity, 10–11, 15–16
  persona, 4, 8, 10
  reconstruction, 2
Sociotechnic artifact, 14
  in Plains study, 62–63, 186
Sokal, R., 287, 292
South Dakota, University of, 59
South, S., 46
Special status differentiation, 49, 64
  detection of, 250, 254
Speth, J., 66, 68
Spiro Mound, 8–9, 11, 26
Sprague, R., 39
Spurious
  correlation, 66, 68
  structure, 26–27, 30
Stanton site, 52
Statistical methodology, 31, 39, 65–69
Statistical Package for the Social Sciences, 66
Steinacher, T., 55
Stickel, G., 2
Stirling, M. W., 59
Strong, W. D., 55, 59, 72
Structural complexity, 16
Structure, defined, 15
Sublett, A., 3, 40
Subordinate dimension, 15, 47
Sullivan, A., 25
Sully site, 271
Superordinate dimension, 15, 47
Supralocal symbol, 14

T

Tabeau, P., 80, 82
Tainter, J., 2, 7, 15–21, 45, 68
Tatankasapa, *see* Black Buffalo
Taylor, W., 28, 41
Technomic artifact, 14
Temporal change, *see also* Diachronic variation
  altered material culture inventory, effect of, 161, 284
  causal factors for, 279–283
  ethnic discrimination, effect on, 299
  in artifact usage, 262–269, 273–278
  in social categories, 30, 258–259, 270–271

  in symbolic expression, 30, 259–262, 271–273
Theory
  analytic, 31
  depositional and postdepositional, 24–26
  middle range, 33
  of mortuary differentiation, 9, 14–15, 20, 32, 37
  retrieval, 31
Thomas, D., 2
Tonwontonga, 57; *see also* Big Village site
Tribal interaction, 82–83
Trophy skull, 221, 247
Typology
  artifact categories, 62–63
  artifact function, 62–63
  basis of, 61–62
  eighty-six element, 61–62
  limitations of, 262, 287, 299
  validity of, 60–61

U

Ubelaker, D., 3, 41, 167, 198
Ucko, P., 27, 35
Unmodified artifact, 53
Upper Republican phase, 72, 83

V

van der Velde, P., 2
Varimax rotation, 66
Vertical social differentiation, 15–16, 19, 49, 64
  defined, 16
  detection of, 15, 250–252
Village amalgamation
  Arikara, 280–283
  Pawnee, 72, 74, 280–283
Voorrips, A., 61

W

Watson, R., 61
Watts, L., 300
Wazingacabe, *see* Blackbird
Wedel, M., 78
Wedel, W., 54–56, 59, 62, 70, 72, 74, 280
Weltfish, G., 72–73
Whallon, R., 43
Willey, G., 70
Willey, P., 41, 167, 198
Wishart, D. J., 71

Wobst, H. M., 286
Woodland period, 15, 17, 57
Wood, W. R., 25, 82
Worsaae, J., 24, 37

Worsaae's Law, 37–38

Y

Yanomamö, 34

STUDIES IN ARCHAEOLOGY

Consulting Editor: Stuart Struever

Department of Anthropology
Northwestern University
Evanston, Illinois

Charles R. McGimsey III. **Public Archeology**

Lewis R. Binford. **An Archaeological Perspective**

Joseph W. Michels. **Dating Methods in Archaeology**

C. Garth Sampson. **The Stone Age Archaeology of Southern Africa**

Fred T. Plog. **The Study of Prehistoric Change**

Patty Jo Watson (Ed.). **Archaeology of the Mammoth Cave Area**

George C. Frison (Ed.). **The Casper Site: A Hell Gap Bison Kill on the High Plains**

W. Raymond Wood and R. Bruce McMillan (Eds.). **Prehistoric Man and His Environments: A Case Study in the Ozark Highland**

Kent V. Flannery (Ed.). **The Early Mesoamerican Village**

Charles E. Cleland (Ed.). **Cultural Change and Continuity: Essays in Honor of James Bennett Griffin**

Michael B. Schiffer. **Behavioral Archeology**

Fred Wendorf and Romuald Schild. **Prehistory of the Nile Valley**

Michael A. Jochim. **Hunter-Gatherer Subsistence and Settlement: A Predictive Model**

Stanley South. **Method and Theory in Historical Archeology**

Timothy K. Earle and Jonathon E. Ericson (Eds.). **Exchange System in Prehistory**

Stanley South (Ed.). **Research Strategies in Historical Archeology**

John E. Yellen. **Archaeological Approaches to the Present: Models for Reconstructing the Past**

Lewis R. Binford (Ed.). **For Theory Building in Archaeology: Essays on Faunal Remains, Aquatic Resources, Spatial Analysis, and Systemic Modeling**

James N. Hill and Joel Gunn (Eds.). **The Individual in Prehistory: Studies of Variability in Style in Prehistoric Technologies**

Michael B. Schiffer and George J. Gumerman (Eds.). **Conservation Archaeology: A Guide for Cultural Resource Management Studies**

Thomas F. King, Patricia Parker Hickman, and Gary Berg. **Anthropology in Historic Preservation: Caring for Culture's Clutter**

Richard E. Blanton. **Monte Albán: Settlement Patterns at the Ancient Zapotec Capital**

R. E. Taylor and Clement W. Meighan. **Chronologies in New World Archaeology**

Bruce D. Smith. **Prehistoric Patterns of Human Behavior: A Case Study in the Mississippi Valley**

Barbara L. Stark and Barbara Voorhies (Eds.). **Prehistoric Coastal Adaptations: The Economy and Ecology of Maritime Middle America**

Charles L. Redman, Mary Jane Berman, Edward V. Curtin, William T. Langhorne, Nina M. Versaggi, and Jeffery C. Wanser (Eds.). **Social Archaeology: Beyond Subsistence and Dating**

Bruce D. Smith (Ed.). **Mississippian Settlement Patterns**

Lewis R. Binford. **Nunamiut Ethnoarchaeology**

J. Barto Arnold III and Robert Weddle. **The Nautical Archeology of Padre Island: The Spanish Shipwrecks of 1554**

Sarunas Milisauskas. **European Prehistory**

Brian Hayden (Ed.). **Lithic Use-Wear Analysis**

William T. Sanders, Jeffrey R. Parsons, and Robert S. Santley. **The Basin of Mexico: Ecological Processes in the Evolution of a Civilization**

David L. Clarke. **Analytical Archaeologist: Collected Papers of David L. Clarke. Edited and Introduced by His Colleagues**

Arthur E. Spiess. **Reindeer and Caribou Hunters: An Archaeological Study**

Elizabeth S. Wing and Antoinette B. Brown. **Paleonutrition: Method and Theory in Prehistoric Foodways**

John W. Rick. **Prehistoric Hunters of the High Andes**

Timothy K. Earle and Andrew L. Christenson (Eds.). **Modeling Change in Prehistoric Economics**

Thomas F. Lynch (Ed.). **Guitarrero Cave: Early Man in the Andes**

Fred Wendorf and Romuald Schild. **Prehistory of the Eastern Sahara**

Henri Laville, Jean-Philippe Rigaud, and James Sackett. **Rock Shelters of the Perigord: Stratigraphy and Archaeological Succession**

Duane C. Anderson and Holmes A. Semken, Jr. (Eds.). **The Cherokee Excavations: Holocene Ecology and Human Adaptations in Northwestern Iowa**

Anna Curtenius Roosevelt. **Parmana: Prehistoric Maize and Manioc Subsistence along the Amazon and Orinoco**

Fekri A. Hassan. **Demographic Archaeology**

G. Barker. **Landscape and Society: Prehistoric Central Italy**

Lewis R. Binford. **Bones: Ancient Men and Modern Myths**

Richard A. Gould and Michael B. Schiffer (Eds.). **Modern Material Culture: The Archaeology of Us**

Muriel Porter Weaver. **The Aztecs, Maya, and Their Predecessors: Archaeology of Mesoamerica, 2nd edition**

Arthur S. Keene. **Prehistoric Foraging in a Temperate Forest: A Linear Programming Model**

Ross H. Cordy. **A Study of Prehistoric Social Change: The Development of Complex Societies in the Hawaiian Islands**

C. Melvin Aikens and Takayasu Higuchi. **Prehistory of Japan**

Kent V. Flannery (Ed.). **Maya Subsistence: Studies in Memory of Dennis E. Puleston**

Dean R. Snow (Ed.). **Foundations of Northeast Archaeology**

Charles S. Spencer. **The Cuicatlán Cañada and Monte Albán: A Study of Primary State Formation**

Steadman Upham. **Polities and Power: An Economic and Political History of the Western Pueblo**

Carol Kramer. **Village Ethnoarchaeology: Rural Iran in Archaeological Perspective**

Michael J. O'Brien, Robert E. Warren, and Dennis E. Lewarch (Eds.). **The Cannon Reservoir Human Ecology Project: An Archaeological Study of Cultural Adaptations in the Southern Prairie Peninsula**

Jonathon E. Ericson and Timothy K. Earle (Eds.). **Contexts for Prehistoric Exchange**

Merrilee H. Salmon. **Philosophy and Archaeology**

Vincas P. Steponaitis. **Ceramics, Chronology, and Community Patterns: An Archaeological Study at Moundville**

George C. Frison and Dennis J. Stanford. **The Agate Basin Site: A Record of the Paleoindian Occupation of the Northwestern High Plains**

James A. Moore and Arthur S. Keene (Eds.). **Archaeological Hammers and Theories**

Lewis R. Binford. **Working at Archaeology**

William J. Folan, Ellen R. Kintz, and Laraine A. Fletcher. **Coba: A Classic Maya Metropolis**

David A. Freidel and Jeremy A. Sabloff. **Cozumel: Late Maya Settlement Patterns**

John M. O'Shea. **Mortuary Variability: An Archaeological Investigation**

Lewis R. Binford. **Faunal Remains From Klasies River Mouth** *in preparation*

Robert I. Gilbert, Jr. and James H. Mielke (Eds.). **The Analysis of Prehistoric Diets**

John Hyslop. **The Inka Road System**

Christopher Carr (Ed.). **The Analysis of Archaeological Data Structures**